African American Sites in Florida

African American Sites in Florida

Kevin M. McCarthy

Pineapple Press, Inc.
Sarasota, Florida

Inquiries should be addressed to:

Pineapple Press, Inc.
P.O. Box 3889
Sarasota, Florida 34230

www.pineapplepress.com

Library of Congress Cataloging-in-Publication Data

McCarthy, Kevin (Kevin M.)
  African American sites in Florida / Kevin M. McCarthy. -- 1st ed.
      p. cm.
  Includes bibliographical references and index.
  ISBN 978-1-56164-385-1 (hardback : alk. paper)
  1. African Americans--Florida--History. 2. Historic sites--Florida. 3. Florida--History, Local. I. Title.
  E185.93.F5M378 2007
  975.9'00496073--dc22

                                                        2006035194

First Edition
10 9 8 7 6 5 4 3 2 1

Design by Shé Heaton
Printed in the United States of America

Contents

1. Alachua County
2. Baker County
3. Bay County
4. Bradford County
5. Brevard County
6. Broward County
7. Calhoun County
8. Charlotte County
9. Citrus County
10. Clay County
11. Collier County
12. Columbia County
13. DeSoto County
14. Dixie County
15. Duval County
16. Escambia County
17. Flagler County
18. Franklin County
19. Gadsden County
20. Gilchrist County
21. Glades County
22. Gulf County
23. Hamilton County
24. Hardee County
25. Hendry County
26. Hernando County
27. Highlands County
28. Hillsborough County
29. Holmes County
30. Indian River County
31. Jackson County
32. Jefferson County
33. Lafayette County
34. Lake County
35. Lee County
36. Leon County
37. Levy County
38. Liberty County
39. Madison County
40. Manatee County
41. Marion County
42. Martin County
43. Miami-Dade County
44. Monroe County
45. Nassau County
46. Okaloosa County
47. Okeechobee County
48. Orange County
49. Osceola County
50. Palm Beach County
51. Pasco County
52. Pinellas County
53. Polk County
54. Putnam County
55. St. Johns County
56. St. Lucie County
57. Santa Rosa County
58. Sarasota County
59. Seminole County
60. Sumter County
61. Suwannee County
62. Taylor County
63. Union County
64. Volusia County
65. Wakulla County
66. Walton County
67. Washington County

Introduction

In 1990, the Florida Legislature established a Study Commission on African American History in Florida. Two years later that Commission published a booklet called *Florida Black Heritage Trail*, which was later updated in 1994. The Trail consists of several hundred sites of significance to African Americans. When Dr. Maxine Jones of Florida State University and I co-authored *African Americans in Florida* (1993), we included the 141 sites of the first edition of the Trail.

This book includes those 141 sites plus the places added in the second edition plus several dozen other sites that I have discovered as I traveled around the state, interviewed scholars, studied archives and public records, and read dozens of history books about Florida. All sixty-seven Florida counties are included in this survey, some with far more examples than others. This is not meant to be a complete record of all those places that are of importance in the African American history of Florida. Rather, it is a start, a document that can and must be added to as we learn more about that history.

Because many people, including myself, like to be able to see/touch/experience places associated with history, whether it be a house or school or church or some such tangible structure, this book is meant to provide that for the African American sites of this state. Florida has a poor track record in preserving historic sites, either because new arrivals to the state are not interested in their new home's history, or because the constant demand of some nine hundred new residents each day has led to the development of much of the prime areas, or because its younger residents see no benefit in preserving "old buildings."

This record is not complete nor can it ever be complete. The author therefore welcomes additions, emendations, and suggestions as to further sites that should be mentioned in subsequent editions of the book.

Finally, a personal note on why I, a white Yankee, undertook this study. I've lived in Florida for thirty-eight years and it's now "my state." When each of my four children would come from school, whether fourth grade or eighth grade or the university, I would invariably ask them what they had learned about the history of African Americans in this state. They would tell me about Martin Luther King Jr. or Jesse Jackson or the *Amistad* slave ship or a slave cemetery unearthed in New York City. "Yes," I said, "but what about Florida African Americans?" "Not much" or "very little" they would admit. This book, then, is an attempt to remedy that situation in whatever way it can.

Among the people I wish to thank are the following: Ellen J. Babb, Steve Benn, James Bradley, Canter Brown Jr., Eliza Brown, Sharon Coon, Areca Cotton, Johnny Eubanks, Roz Foster, Daisy M. Fulton, Tom Hambright, Leland Hawes, Eugene Hunter, Cliff Jackson, Cheryl Jennings, Maude Johnson, Murray Laurie, Len Lempel, Lonnie Matthews, Pete McCabe, Joel McEachin, David Nolan, Ernestine Ray, Sandra Rooks, Jim Stephens, and James Washington. I particularly want to thank the members of the Florida Commissioner of Education's African American History Task Force, especially its chair, Dr. Bernadette Kelley. I dedicate this book to Dr. Kelley and the other members of that task force.

1.

Alachua County

Alachua County, a name that meant "jug" in the Seminole-Creek language and referred to a chasm in the earth, was established in 1824, three years after the United States acquired Florida from Spain. The area had been the scene of Native American settlements for hundreds, maybe thousands, of years. During the colonial period, the Spanish had missions and large cattle ranches in the area, and William Bartram visited during the British occupation of Florida in the late 1700s.

The county had a population of 217,955 in the 2000 census, 42,065 (19.3%) of whom were African Americans.

Archer

Among the county personages recognized in The Great Floridians 2000 program, which recognized distinguished individuals, was **Mahulda Gussie Brown Carrier** (1894–1948), who was born in Archer. After teaching school in Levy County, she moved to nearby Rosewood in 1915, where she taught until 1923, the year of the Rosewood Massacre. During that tragedy, she helped women and children escape by train. The evacuation train stopped in Archer where her sister, **Theresa Brown Robinson**, sheltered her. After the massacre, Mahulda Carrier returned to college to complete her degree and became the first African American female principal in Florida. Her Great Floridian plaque is located at the former Seaboard Airline Railroad Depot (now the **ARCHER HISTORICAL SOCIETY**), Magnolia Avenue and Main Street, Archer.

Bland

About seven miles north of Alachua on S.R. 241 is the town of Bland, where descendants of pioneer African American families still live and work. One of those early families was that of **Lillie** and

Augustus "Gus" Day, both of whom are buried with other African Americans in **DAMASCUS CEMETERY** on S.R. 236. The church where they worshipped, Damascus Church—which was built around 1900, but no longer exists—merged with **NEW HOPE BAPTIST CHURCH** in 1966. A monument there commemorates the original Damascus Church.

Cross Creek

Many African Americans such as **Idella Parker** and the **Mickens** family lived in small tenant houses such as the one standing in the orange grove at the **MARJORIE KINNAN RAWLINGS HISTORIC STATE PARK** (MKRHSP) in Cross Creek. Rawlings, the author of *The Yearling*, came to Cross Creek in 1928 and wrote with wit and affection of those who helped tend her house and grove and garden while she wrote. The MKRHSP interprets the literary legacy of Rawlings and the lives of those who were part of her world in Cross Creek. The Tenant House was moved to the site in 2000, replacing the original one that had been demolished. The simply furnished wood structure gives visitors to the park a reminder of the importance of workers and laborers in Cross Creek and other parts of rural Florida. For information about tours and for directions, visit www.marjoriekinnanrawlings.org or call (352) 466-3672.

Several miles away from the Rawlings House is the **COLEMAN CHURCH CEMETERY**, a black cemetery that has about a dozen gravestones, none more recent than the 1970s. It is just one of hundreds of poorly documented cemeteries that need to be surveyed and described in detail before weather and time will obliterate the gravestones.

Directions to cemetery: At Grove Park, a wildlife management area .8 miles west of Highway 325 on Highway 346, drive about 1.5 miles north on a dirt road until you reach two white posts, near which is a sign to the cemetery.

The Coleman Church Cemetery is a black cemetery with about a dozen gravestones.

Another black cemetery in the vicinity is **HAYNES MEMORIAL CEMETERY**, which is east of Highway 325 on Memorial Lane, just north of Cross Creek. It has several dozen gravesites, some of which are covered by underbrush, but local residents have begun taking good care of the cemetery.

Gainesville

After the United States acquired Florida from the Spanish in 1821, many white settlers moved into the area and began farming the land, despite resistance from the Seminoles, who had been there for decades before. In 1824, the Florida Legislature established Alachua County, which extended from the Georgia border to Charlotte Harbor in the southwest. The formation of more counties from this large area eventually reduced the county to an inland district with Gainesville its county seat. The town was named after General Edmund P. Gaines, a commander in the Seminole Indian Wars.

The 1860 census indicated that 46 blacks (21% of the total population) and 223 whites lived in Gainesville. By 1870, the 765 blacks outnumbered the 679 whites in the city limits, partly because many of the black soldiers stationed there during the Civil War, such as the all-black 3rd Regiment, remained after the war, to be joined by newly freed slaves looking for good opportunities to make a living. They migrated to two areas in the city: Pleasant Street and Seminary Street.

Pleasant Street, the area bordered today by NW 1st Street, NW 8th Avenue, NW 6th Street, and NW 1st Avenue, became the religious, educational, and social center of the black community. The **PLEASANT STREET HISTORIC DISTRICT** had some 255 historic buildings, including churches, schools, and homes. The skilled blacksmiths, carpenters, tailors, and teamsters found much work in the area and settled down with their families.

MT. PLEASANT UNITED METHODIST CHURCH, which used to be called Mt. Pleasant AME Church, became the religious center for many blacks. With its first building dedicated in 1867, the church at 630 NW 2nd Street is the oldest black congregation in Gainesville. Three years after a fire destroyed the structure in 1903, the congregation built the present red-brick Romanesque-Revival style building.

Another important early black church was the **FRIENDSHIP BAPTIST CHURCH** at 426 NW 2nd Street. The first church, built in 1888, was destroyed by fire in 1911. The congregation then built the present Romanesque Gothic Revival structure with its rusticated concrete block and beautiful stained-glass windows.

One of Gainesville's earliest and most impor-

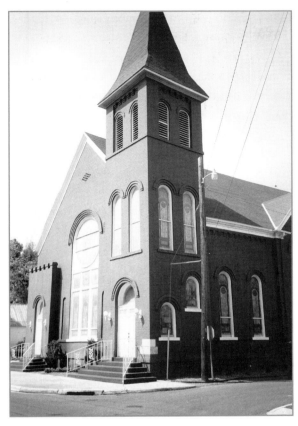

Mt. Pleasant United Methodist Church is the oldest black congregation in Gainesville.

tant educational institutions, and one of the first state-funded grade schools for blacks in the nation, was the **UNION ACADEMY**, which the Freedman's Bureau established around 1867 on the southwest corner of NW 1st Street and NW 6th Avenue. This was the city's first public school for blacks, offering grades one through ten, with at least 179 students enrolled. The first teachers were white missionaries from New England, but by the next decade, black teachers were teaching all the grades. By 1898 the school had five hundred students and was responsible for training many local teachers. The last principal was **A. Quinn Jones**, who served from 1921 until the Union Academy closed in 1925, at which time Professor Jones moved with his students to a new red-brick school in the 1000 block of NW 7th Avenue, called Lincoln High School. This building, renamed the **A. QUINN JONES CENTER**, is now a school for students with spe-

cial needs. It was located two blocks north of Seminary Street (NW 5th Avenue today) where many of the black businesses and social clubs were concentrated. Among the stores were Cato's Sundry Store for snacks at 737 NW 5th Avenue, Walter's Blue Room for dancing at 912 NW 5th Avenue, Plummer's Barber Shop at 743 NW 5th Avenue, and the Lyric Theater for movies at 820 NW 5th Avenue.

A recreation center, named for civic activist **Rosa Williams**, stands on the former site of the Union Academy in the Pleasant Street Historic district. A colorful mural of the old wood-frame school can be seen on a wall inside this building.

During the 1930s, 1940s and early 1950s, Lincoln High School held its proms and football victory dances on the second floor of Wabash Hall, located at 918 NW 5th Avenue. On the ground floor, sisters **Fannie Glover** and **Elzora Gill** and their husbands operated the Glover and Gill Grocery. The 1932 sign can still be seen on the façade of the two-story brick building, a landmark in Gainesville's Fifth Avenue neighborhood.

THE OLD COTTON CLUB is located in Gainesville's Springhill neighborhood at 837 SE 7th Avenue. The large wood-frame building was first constructed in 1940–41 at Camp Blanding in Starke, Florida. At the end of World War II, the Perryman family purchased the surplus post exchange and moved it to Gainesville, converting it into a movie theater for African American patrons. A few years later it became The Cotton Club, where performers such as **BB King** and **James Brown** were featured during the days when black musicians toured a circuit of live venues. In the 1950s, it was renamed The Blue Note Club, where patrons danced to jukebox music.

The **JOSIAH WALLS HISTORICAL MARKER** on W. University Avenue between West 1st and 2nd Streets honors the first black U.S. Congressman from Florida. **Josiah Walls** (1842–1905) was born in Virginia and later served as a soldier in the Civil War on the Union side. After the war he moved to Jacksonville, then to Archer, Florida, where he worked as a lumberman and taught school. Local voters recognized his skill as a public speaker and elected him to Florida's House of Representatives in 1868 and then the state Senate.

In 1870, he was elected to the U.S. Congress, where he served until 1876. For several years he was Florida's only Congressman in the House of Representatives and would be the last black representing the state until 1992.

In 1873, he bought a newspaper in Gainesville, *The New Era*, the first Florida newspaper owned by a black, and in that paper he promised that "the wants and interests of the people of color will receive special attention." The paper lasted until the following year, but in the mid-1880s Walls joined **Matthew M. Lewey** in publishing *The Farmers' Journal.* That same Mr. Lewey established *The Gainesville Sentinel* in 1887, changed its name to *The Florida Sentinel* when he moved to Pensacola in 1894 (see Chapter Sixteen). Finally, Josiah Walls served as mayor of Gainesville before eventually returning to farming; he had a large farm on Paynes Prairie and was in charge of the farm at the State College in Tallahassee when he died in 1905. Walls, who was buried in the Negro Cemetery in Tallahassee, was the last black to represent Florida in the U.S. House of Representatives until the November 1992 election sent **Corrine Brown**, **Alcee Hastings**, and **Carrie Meek** to Washington.

FIRST MORNING STAR BAPTIST CHURCH at 115 NW 55th Street was established in 1890 by members of the Rutledge community, which was founded after the Civil War on land given to former slaves by the Freedman's Bureau. Later, parishioners moved the church from its original site off 23rd Avenue to its present site.

Directions to church: go south on NW 54th Terrace off W. Newberry Road, then right on NW 4th Place, then left at the first turn. The church is down the street on the left.

On land deeded to the elders of the church in 1900 stands the **SHADY GROVE PRIMITIVE BAPTIST CHURCH**, one of the oldest congregations in Gainesville. The present church at 804 SW 5th Street was built in the Porters' neighborhood in the 1930s of coquina block to replace the original wood-frame church. During the Civil Rights era,

the local NAACP committee sometimes met at Shady Grove to plan school integration strategies. Porters' Quarters, as it is still called, dates back to the late nineteenth century when a Canadian physician, Dr. Watson Porter, platted the addition and sold land exclusively to African American families, encouraging them to plant and cultivate gardens to become self-sufficient

World War II brought an influx of black soldiers stationed at Camp Blanding, 25 miles north of Gainesville. On weekends the soldiers would come into town for a day or two of entertainment. After the war many of those soldiers settled in the area. A school that opened up in east Gainesville right before World War II was **WILLIAMS ELEMENTARY**, named after **Joseph Williams**, a civic-minded black who had asked for the school; in its first year it had 150 students and eventually reached six hundred students. In 1970, the local schools were integrated with relatively few disturbances. The city elected another black man, **Neil Butler**, to be mayor in 1974, and he helped pass an ordinance that prohibited discriminatory practices on the basis of race, religion, creed, gender, marital status, or physical handicap.

Joseph Williams Elementary School was named for an African American who had petitioned for the facility.

The University of Florida (UF), established in 1905 for white male students, was finally integrated in 1958. Recently, UF named a law school program designed to provide legal assistance to poor people "The Virgil Darnell Hawkins Civil League Clinic" in honor of a man the school had denied admission to in 1949. **Virgil Hawkins**, who was born in Okahumpka, Florida, in 1906, graduated from a Jacksonville high school and attended Lincoln University in Pennsylvania. By selling insurance and teaching school, he saved enough money by the time he was 42 to attend law school, but the University of Florida Law School denied him admission. At that time Florida law would not allow black and white students to attend school together.

The Board of Control, which ran the universities, decided to open a new law school at Florida Agricultural and Mechanical College for Negroes (later Florida A&M University) in Tallahassee in order not to have the races mix at the white law schools, but Hawkins asked the Florida Supreme Court for permission to attend the UF Law School. When the Florida Supreme Court denied his request, he took his case to the U.S. Supreme Court, which in 1956 ordered the UF Law School to admit him. The university still refused, arguing that violence would result if he were admitted to the school.

In 1958, a federal district court judge ordered UF to admit qualified blacks to its graduate schools, but that time UF would not admit Hawkins on the grounds, according to the school, that he did not meet their admission standards. Other blacks were able to enter the school's graduate programs, but not Hawkins, the man who had begun the litigation process in the first place. He then entered the New England School of Law in Boston, Massachusetts, and graduated in 1964, but Florida officials would not permit him to take the Florida Bar Exam, which all lawyers had to pass to be able to practice law in Florida, because he had not attended an accredited law school. In 1976, the Florida Supreme Court allowed him to become a lawyer without taking the bar exam. At age 70, Hawkins finally became a lawyer and opened his office in Leesburg. He died in 1988 after spending a lifetime fighting the racial practices of the state's educational system. Today, the Florida university system has a Virgil D. Hawkins Scholarship for minority students in law school. (For a photograph of a monument to Virgil Hawkins, see Chapter Thirty-four.)

In 2000, the population of Gainesville, which does not include the students at Santa Fe Community College or the University of Florida, was 95,447; the number of African Americans was 22,181 or 23% of the total.

Outside Gainesville

HAILE PLANTATION HOUSE eight miles west of Gainesville off S.R. 24 was the homestead of the Thomas Haile family, who moved to Alachua County from South Carolina in the early 1850s. Eventually Haile owned sixty-six slaves and had fifteen children. While the Hailes lived in the two-story plantation house with six rooms on the first floor and two more upstairs, the slaves lived in eighteen slave cabins. The homestead, built by skilled slave carpenters, still stands, but the slave cabins have not survived. After the Civil War, some of the freed slaves continued to work the cotton fields, but crop failures in 1868 forced Haile into bankruptcy. The property remained in the family, but the Hailes moved into Gainesville and only used the old homestead for social occasions, until it finally fell into ruin. The house has been restored and is open for tours. Officials call it the Historic Haile Homestead to distinguish it from the nearby development, Haile Plantation. (Open Sundays, 12 P.M.–4 P.M. and on special occasions. Phone (352) 372-2633)

The **LIBERTY HILL SCHOOL**, a weathered one-room school building at 7600 NW 23rd Avenue, next to the Liberty Hill United Methodist Church, holds an important place in the history of African American education in Alachua County, dating back to 1869, when the county board of public instruction first listed Liberty Hill as a school for rural black children.

The Liberty Hill School stands just outside the city limits of Gainesville.

The first teacher, **George Smith**, earned $22 a month for a three-month term. He taught fourteen boys and fifteen girls, and their parents helped supplement his meager salary with food and wood to heat the school.

The board of trustees and the parents of the children attending provided and maintained the schoolhouse and its furnishings. In 1892, the school board built a new schoolhouse, the one visitors can see today on the site, at a cost of $450. It provided the first six years of schooling for generations of African American children from Alachua County. Many of the students who graduated from Liberty Hill School continued their education at the Union Academy and later at Lincoln High School. Around 1952, the little school closed, and the students were bused into Gainesville. The schoolhouse is listed on the National Register of Historic Places.

Hawthorne

One of the most important African Americans in the history of Hawthorne was **Chester Shell**, a man who did much for the education of Afri-can American children in his community. Born in Orange Springs, Florida, in 1892, he grew up in rural north Florida and became so skilled in hunting and fishing that, besides working as a porter for the Seaboard Railroad, he became a much-sought-after hunting and fishing guide for Northern visitors. Many of them were wealthy white people from Connecticut, New York, New Jersey, and Massachusetts, who stayed in Moore's Hotel in Hawthorne.

Mr. Shell was concerned that Hawthorne's African American children could go to school for only two to three months each year in the first part of the twentieth century. They had no school building and had to attend classes in private homes, in churches, and in an old Masonic hall owned by the black community. In 1926, when he went to the Alachua County School Board and requested a school for the children, officials told him that, if he raised half of the necessary money, they would match the funds and build a school. He then went north by train, called on the many wealthy clients he had had on hunting and fishing trips around Hawthorne, and raised the money, which the black community in Hawthorne supplemented by fund-raising activities. The community raised $10,000, and the school was built, but it housed only kindergarten through the eighth grade, after which the black students had to be bused to Gainesville's Lincoln High School.

When a high school for Hawthorne's black students was finally built in 1955, officials named it Shell High School to honor Chester Shell. After the court-ordered desegregation of the early 1970s, it became **CHESTER SHELL ELEMENTARY SCHOOL**, located at 21633 SE 65th Avenue in Hawthorne.

Mr. Shell, who was very active in his church and was president of the Alachua County Voters League, died in 1967 and is buried in the Hawthorne Cemetery. A plaque honoring him is at Shell Elementary School in Hawthorne.

Chester Shell Elementary School honors an African American who did much for the education of children in Hawthorne.

The **HAWTHORNE HISTORICAL MUSEUM AND CULTURAL CENTER** at 7225 SE 221st Street used to house the New Hope Methodist Church, which was established in 1907, one of the town's oldest black congregations. In 1997, workers carefully moved the building four blocks to its present location, refurbished it, and filled it with artifacts, for example, forceps used by the town's first doctor, a quilt showing photographs of the town's oldest homes, and a menu from the popular Fried Chicken Factory Restaurant. (Open Wednesday and Friday, 10 A.M.–2 P.M., and Saturday and Sunday, 1–4 P.M. Phone: (352) 481-4491)

The **HAWTHORNE CEMETERY** on S.R. 20 east of Hawthorne has well-tended burial plots of African Americans at the rear of the white cemetery. Among the interred are soldiers from World War I, World War II, the Korean Conflict, and the Vietnam War.

In the 2000 census, Hawthorne had 680 African Americans or 48% of the total population of the city.

Jonesville

PLEASANT PLAIN UNITED METHODIST CHURCH at 1910 NW 166th Street in Jonesville, near Newberry, has a cemetery behind it that has three legible headstones that tell a terrible story. The headstones are for the gravesites of the Rev. **J. J. Baskins**, **James Dennis**, and **Andrew McHenry**, who were three of six—four men and two women—African Americans lynched in 1916, who came to be known as the Newberry Six.

Of all the Southern states Florida had the highest lynching rate, and thirty-six percent of those hangings took place in what is called the Old Plantation Belt, which stretched from the Panhandle to the central part of Florida. Between the 1880s and the 1940s, more than two hundred lynchings occurred in the state. The two counties that led the state in lynchings were Marion County with twenty-one and Alachua County with twenty confirmed, although the actual total was probably much higher than that in each county.

From time to time, the U.S. Congress has attempted to pass anti-lynching legislation in the U.S. Senate, but some legislators have been able to filibuster or block such legislation. Lynching is defined by the NAACP as "any murder that was/is conducted extra-legally or beyond the rule of the court, under the pretense of upholding justice."

Waldo

The town of Waldo, which was incorporated in 1907 and honors in its name Dr. Benjamin Waldo, attracted a number of African Americans who wanted to work and raise their families there. For example, **Henry Hill** went to Waldo from North Carolina in the early 1920s; he married **Josie Mitchell** in 1926. Their descendants are still involved in the historic preservation of the town. Mr. Hill, a member of Philadelphia Baptist Church and a 33-degree Mason, was one of the first African American firemen in Waldo and also worked on the railroad. He donated some of his land for the Masonic Lodge. That building at 14858 NE 139th Street now belongs to the Concerned Citizens of Waldo, who are using it as the **MUSEUM FOR THE PRESERVATION OF BLACK HISTORY**. For more information call (352) 378-1329.

Mr. Hill is buried in a cemetery just north of Waldo on U.S. 301. Among the gravestones of African Americans are several of servicemen in the different wars, including one serviceman from the colored infantry.

2.
Baker County

Baker County, located between Duval and Columbia Counties in north central Florida, was named in 1861 for Judge James McNair Baker (1822–1892), one of the state's two Confederate States' Congress Senators at Richmond and a former judge of the Fourth Judicial District, which Baker County was a part of at that time. Most of the settlers before the Civil War were hunters and farmers, but after the war the turpentine and logging industries became important. The money-making crops were cotton, then corn, and finally tobacco. The first "tax assessor" determined that there were 112 sane white males between the ages of 21 and 50, as well as 212 slaves, all of whom were assessed fifty cents each per year as taxes.

The population of Baker County in 2000 was 22,259, of whom 3,094 (13.9%) were African Americans. It is a rural county with 38 persons per square mile, compared to the state-wide average of 296.

Olustee

To the east of Lake City on U.S. 90 is **OLUSTEE BATTLEFIELD,** the site of the most important land battle of the Civil War in Florida. Around 5,500 Union troops coming from Jacksonville in February 1864 met a similar size Confederate force at a place called Ocean Pond in what came to be known as the Battle of Olustee. Serving on the Union side were black soldiers in units like the 8th U.S. Colored, the 1st North Carolina, and the 54th Massachusetts. The latter unit had Sergeant **William H. Carney**, who later became the first black to win the prestigious Medal of Honor for his bravery at the Battle of Fort Wagner, South Carolina.

The blacks fighting for the Union side at Olustee faced a terrible situation. If they were wounded during the battle and left behind on the battlefield, Southern soldiers might injure them further, send them to infamous prisons like the one at Andersonville, Georgia, or kill them. The

Black soldiers in the Union army fought at the Battle of Olustee. *Florida State Archives* battle raged on for hours and saw the wounding and death of many soldiers on both sides. In the end the Confederates claimed victory as the Union troops retreated to Jacksonville.

The doctor who served with one of the black units, the 8th U.S. Colored Troops, later praised the great courage of those soldiers:

> Here they stood for two hours and a half, under one of the most terrible fires I ever witnessed; and here, on the field of Olustee, was decided whether the colored man had the courage to stand without shelter, and risk the dangers of the battlefield; and when I tell you that they stood with a fire in front, on their flank, and in their rear, for two hours and a half, without flinching, and when I tell you the number of dead and wounded, I have no doubt as to the verdict of every man who has gratitude for the defenders of his country, white or black.

Directions: Olustee Battlefield is located 2.5 miles east of Olustee on U.S. 90, 15 miles east of Lake City. The battlefield is open daily 9 A.M.–5 P.M.; the museum is open Thursday–Monday 9 A.M.–5 P.M. A nominal donation is expected of visitors. Phone: (386) 758-0400. Each February around the anniversary of the battle men dressed in the military uniforms of both sides show visitors how the battle was fought.

Visitors to the battlefield in February can witness the re-enactment of the battle. *Florida State Archives*

3.
Bay County

Bay County in the Florida Panhandle takes its name from its position on St. Andrews Bay. The Florida Legislature established the county in 1913 as the state's forty-ninth county. In the 2000 census it had 15,711 African Americans, almost 11% of the total county population of 148,217.

Panama City

As in so many Florida sites, the first settlers there were the Indians, eventually succeeded by the English, who came after the Revolutionary War. Development began in the 1830s and increased after the Civil War, as more and more people discovered the beaches and fishing grounds and isolation of the area. The Panama City area, which had only 987 people in 1830, attracted more and more residents in the nineteenth century; the place took its name from the fact that it lies on a direct line between Chicago and Panama City in the Canal Zone. The 2000 census indicated that the city had 7,813 blacks (22%) out of a total population of 36,417.

The Bay Country of Northwest Florida by Marlene Womack mentions that the black community of Panama City, Shinetown, had several different names, such as East End because it was the eastern-most section of development in the greater St. Andrews area. The main industry in the small community was a sawmill. The community took its name from a man whose nickname "Shine" probably came from his practice of making and selling rum.

The children of the community attended classes in homes and churches until 1928, when the first official school opened in Shinetown. However, it operated for only four months each year and had only grades one, two, and three. Parents who wanted their children to attend school beyond that had to pay for the extra months. The parents also had to buy all the books, papers, and pencils used at the school.

In 1944, the Shinetown Post Office, which was also known as Rosenwald, opened, but lasted only until 1949, when service was transferred to Panama City. Today the old Shinetown community is known as Glenwood.

REDWOOD CEMETERY, which is in the Old Orchard section of Panama City on Redwood Avenue and Seventh Street, began in 1916, when W. J. Lee sold over two acres of land for the Colored Peoples' Cemetery of Millville. This cemetery across the street from the Potter Temple Holiness Church has many blacks buried there, including one of the most famous of them, **Narcisco "Hawk" Massalina**. He is buried in an unmarked grave next to that of his grandson, **Andrew Cooper**.

Hawk Massalina was born a free-Spanish black near Massalina Bayou in 1840. His father was a Spanish trader who spelled his name **José Masslieno**. When a fierce hurricane destroyed much of the area in 1856, José offered to sell his family and himself into slavery, but fortunately all of the planters who received the offer turned it down. In 1863, Hawk joined the Union forces and served as a gun cleaner on the U.S. bark *Roebuck* and then the *Restless*. After the Civil War, he worked as a fisherman, boat builder, and tour guide, but had to leave his land when the U.S. government bought it and built Tyndall Field. Hawk died in 1948 at the age of 107.

One other cemetery for African Americans was the Black Cemetery, which is north of Oakland Cemetery and near the southwest corner of Balboa Avenue and 15th Street in Panama City. Over one hundred blacks were interred in that cemetery, which later included convicts who died at the six-acre convict camp that the state built in 1934 just south of the cemetery. In the 1960s, when a controversy arose over the valuable land there, about thirty of the identifiable graves were moved to Lynn Haven Community Cemetery. Some city maps still indicate the location of the Black Cemetery in its original place.

Panama City was the home of **ROSENWALD JUNIOR COLLEGE**, which began in 1958 as one of twelve black junior colleges in Florida. Its first president was **Calvin Washington**, who was also principal of nearby Rosenwald High School. Its first-year enrollment of 35 total students, including those in the vocational program, was so much lower than the 125 expected that the junior college had to meet in a wing of the black school, but little by little it added students until it had 177 students in the 1964–1965 school year, before merging with Gulf Coast Junior (later Community) College in 1966. Mr. Washington was given a job in the school board office. The enrollment figures, which included college-parallel courses and vocational courses, for Rosenwald Junior College were as follows:

        1958–59: 35 students
        1959–60: 65 students
        1960–61: 96 students
        1961–62: 84 students
        1962–63: 147 students
        1963–64: 151 students
        1964–65: 177 students
        1965–66: 143 students

In 1994, almost three decades after the black junior college merged with the white school, officials at Gulf Coast Community College dedicated the Rosenwald Junior College Center on its main campus.

Lynn Haven

Lynn Haven to the north of Panama City is unusual in that, although situated in a former Confederate state, it actually has a monument to the Union soldier. Its founder, W. H. Lynn, established the town and also St. Cloud in Osceola County, Florida, as a settlement for Union veterans of the Civil War. Later, veterans of the Spanish-American War joined the Union veterans. In 1920, workers built at Lynn Haven a war memorial, complete with a soldier wearing a Union uniform.

Lynn Haven has a monument to the Union soldier.
Florida State Archives

4.
Bradford County

Bradford County in north central Florida was first named New River County when it was established in 1858. Three years later, the name was changed to Bradford to honor Captain Richard Bradford, the first Florida officer killed in the Civil War.

Bradford County had a population of 26,088 in the 2000 census, 5,426 (20.8%) of whom were African Americans.

Starke

In 1913, three members of the African American community, the Rev. **James W. Robinson, A. O. Jenkins**, and **R. M. Ellerson**, spearheaded efforts to acquire a school for blacks in the county. The result was what came to be known as RJE (for the three men) HIGH SCHOOL.

Robinson, the first black insurance agent in Starke and—along with R. M. Ellerson—the first black funeral director in the area, supervised the project. Jenkins, the long-time principal of the black school in Starke, became the spokesman for the project and its builder. Ellerson, a partner with Robinson as an undertaker, served as the treasurer. All three men raised money for the school, and the local citizens volunteered to build it, which they did in just 58 days. The two-story frame building, which the Starke Recreation Department uses today, opened in 1914 on Pine and Florida Streets and operated for black students until 1945, when local leaders, realizing the community was outgrowing the school, asked the school board for a new building, but funds were nonexistent for such a facility.

The community, including the students at RJE High School, took up collections and, in July 1945, bought land on Pine and Jenkins Streets, where the school board built a school three years later. After serving the community well until de-segregation closed the black schools in the 1970s, the building became part of the Head Start Program. When fire, possibly deliberately set by arsonists, severely damaged the building in 1977, the school board decided to tear it down.

At that point, concerned citizens rallied under the leadership of the Rev. **Levy Lennon, Theresa Holliday**, and **Elizabeth Walker** to establish the Concerned Citizens of Bradford County and rehabilitated the structure.

Among the leaders of the African American community in Starke in the twentieth century were several that should be mentioned. **R. M. Ellerson** and Rev. **Robinson** were the first black funeral directors in the area; Ellerson was also the owner of a popular soda fountain at Oak and Brownlee Streets and a grocery store on Brownlee. **"Fess" Jenkins** was the son of a Georgia slave and a man who taught many subjects to the children of Bradford County; and **Eddie Thompkins** was the principal of the second RJE School in the 1940s.

Directions: The former RJE High School on Pine Street is off S.R. 16 to the east of Starke. Go north on Pine several blocks to the former school, which is on the right at 1080 Pine Street.

SPARKMAN CEMETERY in southern Bradford County is like many throughout the state in

The former RJE High School is now a recreational center in Starke.

This small headstone with an "S" on it indicates that a slave was buried there in Sparkman Cemetery.

that it has a grave stone that probably belongs to that of a slave. The dozen headstones name the people buried there, but one half-buried headstone in a distant part of the small cemetery has simply "S. 8" on it, probably indicating a slave. Small groups of historians are documenting the cemeteries throughout Florida, both the large ones and the small ones, even the private ones. And while we may never know who "S. 8" was, just knowing of the presence of such graves may help historians and genealogists help identify the final resting places of families from long ago.

Directions to the cemetery: Go south on C.R. 225, which turns south off C.R. 18, 7.5 miles east of Brooker and .2 miles west of Graham. Go .8 miles south on C.R. 225, and the private, fenced, unmarked cemetery is on the left just before the Santa Fe River and the start of Alachua County. The grave of "S. 8" is in the northeast corner of the cemetery away from the other headstones.

5.
Brevard County

Brevard County, established in 1844, commemorates Theodore Washington Brevard (1804–1877), a North Carolinian who came to Florida in 1847 and served as state comptroller (1853–1861). The original name of the county was St. Lucie, but that was changed to Brevard in 1855.

Brevard County had a population of 476,230 in the 2000 census, 40,003 (8.4%) of whom were African Americans.

Cocoa

Native Americans, especially those from the Ais tribe, settled here first, to be followed by the Spanish, pirates, and hardy explorers who pushed down from Georgia and the Carolinas in the nineteenth century. High temperatures, mosquitoes, hurricanes, and angry Indians did much to discourage permanent settlement, but, as time passed, the pluses of living there attracted more people.

Newly freed slaves were some of the first non-Indians to settle in the area. According to historian Glenn Rabac, a group of freedmen moved to the Cocoa Beach area after the Civil War and claimed all of the land south of the cape between the Atlantic Ocean and the Banana River. An 1885 hurricane flooded out the homesteaders and discouraged others from living near the ocean, but people still headed here by boat and train.

A local black woman may have been responsible for the name of Cocoa. According to Allen Morris's *Florida Place Names*, when some local citizens were trying to decide on a name for the settlement, a black woman saw the label on a box of Baker's Cocoa and suggested that they name the place Cocoa. In any case fishermen founded the town long ago; officials incorporated the town of Cocoa in 1895.

In the nineteenth and early twentieth centuries blacks came to the area to work on the railroad, in the orchard fields, and in the homes of wealthy summer residents. By the mid-1920s blacks made up almost one-third of the town's population, but in those days of segregation they usually lived west of Florida Avenue and south of Willard Street. The focus point was Magnolia Street, which has since been renamed Stone Street to honor **Richard E. Stone**, a prominent black mortician who helped improve the area during his long stay there. Stone Street is east of U.S. 1, south of King Street, and north of Poinsett Drive. Blacks had a thriving, self-sufficient community with their own businesses, including grocery stores, a post office, pharmacy, and restaurant.

Because the only school open to them was an elementary school, those who wanted to attend high school had to move to another city. In the 1930s officials began busing children to a black high school in Melbourne, a practice which lasted until desegregation in the 1950s began to give them access to schools in Cocoa. The 2000 census indicated that the city had 5,298 African

This funeral home was the first one for African Americans in the county.

Americans (32%) out of a total population of 16,412.

The **RICHARD E. STONE HISTORIC DISTRICT** from 121 to 304 Stone Street honors a man who did much to help his fellow blacks of Cocoa. The district, which is east of U.S. 1, west of Hughlett Avenue, and south of King Street (S.R. 520), is an area that blacks have lived in for most of the last hundred years, even when they worked in white areas of the town or at the Florida East Coast Railway and the East Coast Lumber Company. Cocoa's early black community was settled along the Indian River in the mid-1800s, but gradually moved west to where it is today.

Richard Stone (1902–1985), the son of the owner of Melbourne's first grocery store and stable, established Brevard County's first black funeral home and first black professional baseball team, the Cocoa Black Indians. He also helped establish Cocoa's first civic organization, Liberty League, Inc., which today is known as the Cocoa-Rockledge Civic League, and the city's first recreational center. On the national scene, in 1935 he invented and patented a directional signal light for automobiles, but was unable to mass-produce

the lights and did not see a profit from his invention. In his professional medical practice, he patented the trocar, a surgical instrument used in the process of embalming.

The **STONE FUNERAL HOME** at 516 King Street (S.R. 520) was established in 1923 to serve the whole county. By the 1930s, two brothers, Richard and **Albert Stone**, had established the Stone Brothers Funeral Homes, with branches in Cocoa, Fort Pierce, and Melbourne.

Among the important sites in the district other than the Malissa Moore Home and Mount Moriah AME Church, both of which will be described below, are the **GRACE EDWARDS HOME** (121 Stone Street) that one of the town's first black families built; the **GREATER ST. PAUL BAPTIST CHURCH** (213 Stone Street), whose one-hundred-year-old foyer windows came from the original church on that site; the **JOHN HENRY HALL ESTATE** (221 Stone Street), one of the first grocery stores in the area; the **JOHNSON HOME** (225 Stone Street); **THE DR. B.C. SCURRY HOME** (231 Stone Street), where Cocoa's first black doctor lived; and the **BROWN HOME** (241 Stone Street), where the town's first shoe shiner lived.

The **MALISSA MOORE HOME**, today a private residence at 215 Stone Street, was home to one of the area's most prominent residents, **Malissa Moore**. The house, which was first located near the Indian River in 1890, was moved to its present location to become a rooming house and restaurant, for a while the only one in Cocoa and supposedly a favorite eating place for railroad builder Henry Flagler. Having moved to the area in 1884, Malissa Moore decided to build a church similar to the ones she had attended in Atlanta and in her hometown, Monroe, Georgia. Through many Saturday night social gatherings, where she often served her famous fish sandwiches and collected donations of 50 and 75 cents, Mrs. Moore raised enough money in two years to buy land for the church on Florida Avenue and hired a Titusville carpenter to build it (see next entry).

MOUNT MORIAH AFRICAN METHODIST EPISCOPAL (AME) CHURCH at 304 Stone Street (formerly Magnolia Street) has a long history of service to the community. Enough blacks lived in Cocoa by 1886 for one of the area's prominent citizens, Malissa Moore, to think about establishing this church, the first African American church in Cocoa. When the original building on Florida Avenue burned down around 1922, Mrs. Moore once again raised money through her well-attended Saturday-night socials to buy land for a new building on Magnolia Street. Workers put up a new building at the present site, using bricks for the Gothic structure that were manufactured on the site with sand donated by the generous Richard Stone. The local African American Preservation League has worked hard to preserve the Mount Moriah Church.

The **HARRY T. MOORE CENTER**, a single-story building at 307 Blake Avenue two blocks south of King Street, is today a child-care facility and community center. Cocoa's first black school used to be on this site. It may be the only original African American high school still standing in the county. The school, which was built in 1924 as Cocoa Junior High School, remained until 1947, when it was renamed Monroe High School in honor of **Jessie Ruth Monroe**, a pioneer teacher and principal of Cocoa Junior High School. When Monroe High School moved to a new facility on S. Avocado Avenue in 1954, the old schoolhouse was renamed the Harry T. Moore Center in honor of the civil rights activist who was killed by a bomb in 1951. (See the section on Mims in Chapter Five for more details.)

The **HILLTOP CEMETERY** on U.S. 1, which is .2 miles north of S.R. 520 and on the west side of the highway, has a plaque on the concrete pillar at the entrance identifying the site. This African American cemetery was established in the 1880s, and its oldest grave-stone is dated 1889. Tropical Storm Gabrielle revealed 58 previously unknown graves. Before that discovery in 2001, only 417 graves were known.

Hilltop Cemetery in Cocoa dates back to the 1880s.

In 2004, **Michael C. Blake**, an eighth grade teacher at Clearlake Middle School, became the first African American mayor of Cocoa since the city incorporated in 1895. A lifelong resident of Cocoa, he attended Cocoa High School and South Carolina State University before becoming a teacher in Brevard County and serving on Cocoa's City Council (1998–2000).

Melbourne

By the time the railroad arrived in 1893, this Brevard County town on the Indian River, which was named after Melbourne, Australia, was already developed due to steamboat activity. Three of the first men to arrive before then were blacks: **Balaam Allen**, **Wright Brothers**, and **Peter Wright**. According to *The Melbourne Bicentennial Book* (p. 39), they were freedmen "who after the Civil War had been reluctant to leave their former owner. But their master, unable to support them, sailed with them beyond the last southern outpost and staked out for each of them what he considered was about 160 acres for a homestead. There he left them to shift for themselves." Today BROTHERS PARK at the corner of Church Street and Race Street in south Melbourne honors **Wright Brothers**.

One of those men, **Peter Wright**, became the largest landholder in the area as well as a trader and boatman. As the first postal carrier in the area, he brought the mail twice a week from Titusville (then Sand Point) to Melbourne on his boat, *Mist*, while his brother, **Dick Wright**, brought the mail from New Smyrna to Titusville via the Mosquito Lagoon and the Haulover Canal on his boat, *Nelly*. Peter's first homestead was at the top of the River Bluff at the north end of Front Street. When he sold that place in 1878, he and his wife, **Leah**, built a larger homestead on the south side of Crane Creek, where the Roy Couch house now stands. By 1885, he sold his interests in the Melbourne area and moved to Rockledge to become a fruit grower. He died in 1925 and is buried in Cocoa.

Mary Silas Brothers, who helped her husband, **Wright**, grow citrus on the 7.5 acres of land they lived on near Crane Creek, gave birth in 1882 to **William Rufus Brothers**, the first black child born in Melbourne. William attended school at the little red school house, the first school in Melbourne, in Tarheel on what is now S. Riverview Drive. That school dates back to 1883, when **John Goode** established it in the Tarheel section of Crane Creek (Melbourne). The

school segregated the students, with nine white students attending in the morning that first year and six black students attending in the afternoon. **Maude Good** and **May Valentine** were the first teachers there. The schoolhouse, originally located on Riverview Drive in the Tarheel section south of the creek, now stands on the campus of the Florida Institute of Technology at 150 W. University Boulevard in Melbourne. A brochure entitled *The Founders' Trail*, which is available at the school, describes an interpretive walking tour of the campus.

Then in 1909 workers built a one-room school for black youngsters on the corner of Line and Lipscomb streets, where the Church of God in Christ now stands. The school had two rows of seats with two students sitting in a seat. About sixteen students attended school there.

When that school became too small, workers built the Melbourne Vocational School in the area where Brothers Park is located today. Black students attended that school until it burned in 1953, at which point they attended school in a building at the old Naval Base at Melbourne Airport, until the present Stone School was built in 1958. Officials considered calling the new school Hopkins since the area had been called Hopkins when the Union Cypress Sawmill was there. Because a Mr. Stone donated the land for the new school and was a leader in the community, officials named the school after him. The first graduating class from Stone School took place in 1955. Today Stone Junior High School is at 1101 E. University Boulevard.

William Rufus Brothers, the first black child born in Melbourne, later married **Estelle Stone**, and they had three children, including **John Brothers** (1907–1981). William's mother, Mary Brothers, was one of several black women, including **Lydia Duncan**, **Anneda Harris**, and **Estella Jackson**, who became midwives at a time when the area had few doctors. Other blacks opened up successful businesses, including Stone Funeral

Home and Tucker Plumbing.

In the home of Wright and Mary Brothers, local residents like **Carrie** and **Robert Lipscomb** and Balaam Allen and his wife established the AL-LEN CHAPEL AME CHURCH in the late nineteenth century and built the first structure on the northern end of Lipscomb Street in 1885. In 1964, they built a new church at 2416 S. Lipscomb Street. The church bell, which members acquired in 1928 and which is in the new building, is made of solid brass and weighs about 1,000 pounds.

CARVER JUNIOR COLLEGE, which was established in 1959, was one of twelve black junior colleges in Florida. Its first president was Mr. **James R. Greene**, who also served as principal of Monroe High School. The school was about ten miles from Cape Canaveral, fifteen miles from the Kennedy Space Center, and twelve miles from Patrick Air Force Base. It merged with Brevard Junior College in 1964 after an NAACP official complained to the U.S. Commission on Civil Rights that the school had cost the taxpayers $100,000 a year for three years, had been using high school teachers and facilities, and had graduated poorly educated black students.

The enrollment figures, which included college-parallel courses and vocational courses, for Carver Junior College were as follows:

1960–61: 168 students
1961–62: 263 students
1962–63: 143 students

In the 1990s, officials at Brevard Community College named a new administrative facility the George Washington Carver Administration Center after the black junior college and placed a portrait of President Greene there.

Early black settlers of the pioneer Brothers, Ford, and Stone families established the LINE STREET CEMETERY in south Melbourne that over a period of eighty years after its establishment became forgotten and overrun with weeds, trees, and garbage, until it was restored in 1980 by Boy

Scout Troop 730. The scouts cleaned up the cemetery and the five tombstones found there, including those of **Alice Chambers**, **Franklin Johnson**, Carrie E. Lipscomb, **John H. Whitfield**, and the cryptic Wm. W. W. (probably referring to **William W. Whitfield**).

A Boy Scout troop has cleaned up Line Street Cemetery.

An early black church of the community was MACEDONIA BAPTIST CHURCH. Because the Florida East Coast Railway had not reached Melbourne by 1891, the church's pastor, Rev. **Parson Miller**, had to transport the lumber for the first sanctuary by boat from Titusville. Twelve members of the congregation, including **J. E. Austell**, built the first church building on E. Brothers Avenue. Between 1970 and 1975 the congregation built a new sanctuary on Lipscomb Street. Among the distinguished pastors of the church one name stands out: Rev. **James Massey**, who served a term of twenty years.

By 1900 only about two hundred people lived in Melbourne, but the land boom of the 1920s brought many new settlers to the area, and the development of the National Aeronautics and Space Administration (NASA) facility at Cape Canaveral brought in thousands more. Among those who worked hard to desegregate the schools in the area in the 1950s and 1960s was **Harry Lawrence**, the one-time president of the South Brevard Civic League; the HARRY LAWRENCE PARK at the juncture of New Haven and Strawbridge Avenues in

Melbourne honors him.

Brevard County had many demonstrations in the 1960s as local blacks sought an end to segregation. Interracial advisory committees met to make the move to integration as painless as possible, despite the efforts by the Ku Klux Klan to harass the blacks. Black leaders in Melbourne included **John Brothers**, descendant of one of the first settlers there; **U. F. Gibbs**, the principal of the all-black Stone High School; and **Henry Jackson**, the president of the local NAACP. As a result of many discussions, one-fourth of local restaurant owners agreed to integrate their facilities, and the Melbourne Country Club was desegregated.

The integration of Brevard schools took place in 1964. Soon after that, **Ted Nichols**, a Stone High School teacher, won a two-year term on the Melbourne City Commission, the first black elected to public office in the county. The 1980s saw further progress. For example, local Melbourne officials made a decision in the 1980s to change the name of Lynching Tree Drive to Legendary Lane; according to local legend, a black man who had been involved in trying to free a cow tangled in a rope in 1926 was accused of accosting several children playing nearby. He was arrested and taken to an oak tree where he was hanged. The name of Lynching Tree Drive had perpetuated a sad chapter in the city's history and had offended enough people to have it changed.

The 2000 census indicated that the city had 6,658 African Americans (9%) out of a total population of 71,382.

Merritt Island

The **MOUNT OLIVE COURTENAY COMMUNITY CEMETERY**, which was originally known as the White Lily Cemetery, was located on the grounds near the **BETHEL AFRICAN AMERICAN EPISCOPAL CHURCH**, one of the first black churches on the island. The cemetery, which is still used, has grave stones dating back to 1919, including the final resting place of early black pioneers, for example the Rev. **Fred Gillins** and **Joseph McDonald**, both of whom were born on Merritt Island in the late 1800s. When the Bethel AME Church burned in 1958, the **MOUNT OLIVE AME CHURCH** at 1212 N. Tropical Trail began managing the property.

The first black doctor to deliver white babies on Merritt Island, the first black to have a racially mixed medical practice in the county, and the only black physician in Brevard County for more than twenty years was **Henry R. Jerkins III**, who was born in Lake City and raised in Perry and Daytona Beach. He earned degrees from Edward Waters College, Morehouse College, the University of Wisconsin, and Howard University Medical School; studied at Cambridge University in England; and taught at Tuskegee, Dillard, and North Carolina A&T. He died in 2001 at age 94.

Mims

This small town, which in 2000 had a population of 9,412, of whom 1,194 (13%) were black, was the scene of a double murder in 1951 that has still not been solved. On Christmas night of that year, **Harry** and **Harriette Moore** retired for the night after spending the holiday with relatives, celebrating their twenty-fifth wedding anniversary with their twenty-four-year-old daughter and Harry's mother. Soon after Harry and Harriette got ready for bed at around 10:15 that fateful night, a huge explosion ripped open the house, destroying the bedroom and killing one of this state's most effective civil rights activists. His wife died nine days later from injuries suffered in the blast. To this day investigators have never been able to solve that crime, the nation's first assassination of a civil rights leader, although FBI agents suspected it was the work of the Orange County Ku Klux Klan. Moore would be the first of several assassinations that later included **Medgar Evers** in Mississippi and **Martin Luther King Jr.** in Tennessee.

The forty-six-year-old Moore had spent his adult life fighting for civil rights. In 1941, he became president of the Florida National Association for the Advancement of Colored People (NAACP). In 1947, after twenty years working in the Brevard County school system he lost his job as a junior high school principal because of his civil rights activism, but continued organizing blacks around the state, concentrating on three areas: trying to have a new trial for two blacks sentenced to death for raping a white woman in Lake County, obtaining equal pay for the state's black public school teachers; and registering more than one hundred thousand black voters as the executive secretary of the Progressive Voters League. He was succeeding in all three areas and was therefore considered a threat by the segregationists of the state.

The house where the explosion took place was in an isolated orange grove about one mile south of Mims about one hundred yards from the Dixie Highway. Harry and Harriette were buried from St. James Missionary Baptist Church, which is at 2396 Harry T. Moore Avenue (formerly Palmetto Avenue); this avenue is behind the water tower, which says, "Welcome to Mims, The Friendly Town," and about 1/4 mile east of U.S. 1 across the railroad tracks.

The gravesite of Harry and Harriette is in **LAGRANGE CEMETERY** on Old Dixie Highway south of Mims. A plaque at the cemetery, which was once known as the LaGrange Colored Cemetery, describes the African American community in the

A sign marks the site of the house where the Moores were killed.

area. The gravesite of the Moores is about eighteen yards behind and to the left of the second plaque. The graves of other early African Americans from the community are in the same part of the cemetery.

Directions to the cemetery: Go south of S.R. 46 on U.S. 1 for 1.9 miles (or 2.5 miles north of S.R. 406 in Titusville), then west at the light for Old Dixie Highway, then north at the LaGrange Baptist Church; the old church and cemetery are on the east at a historic plaque).

The LaGrange Baptist Church, established in 1869 as the first Protestant church on Florida's east coast between New Smyrna and Key West, had segregated services for whites and blacks. The building also served as a schoolhouse and civic meeting house.

The site of the house where the bombing took place is now part of the **HARRY T. & HARRIETTE V. MOORE CULTURAL COMPLEX** at 2180 Freedom Avenue in Mims. That site may also eventually

The gravesite of the Moores is in LaGrange Cemetery.

have an original school that African Americans used on Merritt Island from 1890 on. The cultural complex, which has Moore family artifacts and historical documents, offers lectures, cultural programs, and conferences

Directions to the Moore Cultural Complex in Mims: Turn west off U.S. 1 at Parker Street, which is .4 miles south of S.R. 46; go .1 mile west on Parker Street, then left on Freedom Avenue and .2 miles to the end of the road. If you are traveling north, go about 2.5 miles north of Titusville, then 1.4 miles north of Dairy Road to Parker Street and follow the above directions. Open Monday–Friday, 9 A.M.–7 P.M.; Saturday, 12 P.M.–4 P.M. Phone: (321) 264-6595.

The 2000 census indicated that the town had 1,004 African Americans (11%) out of a total population of 9,147.

Titusville

This area began attracting white settlers when, in 1843, a captain in the Second Seminole Indian War, Douglas Dummett, received a permit to settle on Merritt Island. He began growing citrus and did so well that many more settlers arrived to take advantage of the good soil and climate. In 1845, Florida entered the Union as a slave state and continued depending on slaves to grow the many crops that its white plantation owners grew rich on. In 1867, Colonel Henry Titus arrived in the area and soon built the first hotel in the town he founded: Titusville. The next year saw the arrival of the first black settler, **Joe Warren.** By 1880, the census listed 13 blacks. In 1882, workers built the town's first jail at a cost of $500; a black resident, **Andrew J. Gibson,** was the first jailer and cooked the prisoners' meals in his own kitchen. Gibson was also a barber, restaurant owner, and supervisor of the only public road in Brevard County. In 1885, the Jacksonville, Tampa, and Key West Railroad reached Titusville and brought in many more settlers.

Harry T. Moore (see Mims, p. 20) is com-

memorated by a small bust outside the **HARRY T. MOORE SOCIAL SERVICE CENTER** at 725 DeLeon Street in Titusville.

Directions to the center: Go west on South Street (S.R. 405) from U.S. 1, then .3 miles to DeLeon Street; turn east at the light and go .3 miles to the center on the left.

Titusville has a bust of Harry T. Moore.

One African American who worked in Titusville as a carpenter for the Flagler organization in the second half of the nineteenth century was **Dana A. Dorsey,** who saw more opportunities south of there. He built a raft in 1892 or 1893 and sailed alone to Biscayne Bay, where he built many houses in what came to be known as "Colored Town," rented them out, and became Miami's first black millionaire (see Chapter Forty-three).

6.
Broward County

The first inhabitants of the area were Native Americans, who lived there for some four thousand years. In the nineteenth century, the coming of white and black settlers was hastened by the building of Henry Flagler's Florida East Coast Railway, beginning in 1896. In 1915, the Florida Legislature formed Broward County from parts of Dade and Palm Beach Counties and named it for *Napoleon Bonaparte Broward,* who as Florida governor (1905–1909) was greatly responsible for draining the Everglades. While governor, he demanded more humane treatment for prisoners, but did not try to stop the convict-lease system that punished so many people, especially blacks, nor did he try to improve working conditions in turpentine camps, where so many of the abused workers were blacks (see Chapter Fourteen). Governor Broward also believed that the state's blacks, who made up as much as forty percent of the population when Broward was in office, should be shipped off to a distant place like Africa and therefore kept away from whites.

Broward County, which had a population of only thirty-six thousand in 1950, increased dramatically to 1,623,018 in the 2000 census, 332,719 (20.5%) of whom were African Americans. This county has the second-highest number of African Americans among all sixty-seven Florida counties.

Fort Lauderdale

Among the first settlers to that part of Florida when the Spanish controlled it in the eighteenth century were slaves escaping from northern plantations. Some of those slaves joined the Seminole Indians battling both white settlers and bounty hunters looking for escaped slaves; other slaves went to the Bahamas to escape the harsh conditions in this country. In the early nineteenth century black slaves working for Count Odet Philippe built the first salt-making operation on the area's beaches.

In the Reconstruction period after the American Civil War, politicians had established Black Codes that attempted to keep the former slaves in a new type of bondage. The Codes did not allow blacks to own knives, guns, or other weapons, allowed the police to arrest blacks and sentence them to forced labor, and gave the state the right to execute any black who raped a white woman or who encouraged others to rebellion. The Codes also provided for separate schools for black children. Black men were to pay a dollar tax for the schools, and the children were required to pay tuition, all of which was supposed to cost the state nothing.

Broward County developed as more and more people moved to south Florida and as Henry Flagler's railroad opened up the area for settlement and cultivation. As Flagler pushed construction of his Florida East Coast Railway south to Miami and the Florida Keys, he hired many black workers, and, when they finished extending the railroad to Key West, many of them settled in south Florida and became sharecroppers. Even if they did not own their own fields, many owned their own residential lots. Among the blacks who moved there in the late 1880s and early 1890s were the descendants of freed or runaway slaves, immigrants from the Bahamas, and farmers and craftsmen seeking more opportunities.

In 1907, African Americans in Fort Lauderdale acquired their first permanent school when white pioneer Tom M. Bryan donated a one-room, frame building on the west side of NW 3rd Avenue. When workers tore down the building to build an ice plant, black children who wanted an education had to go to private homes or to the Knights of Pythias Hall at NW 4th Street and NW 4th Avenue. Black children were still expected to work in the fields picking crops after school and during the winter harvest, a practice that shortened their school year by a month or two.

Fort Lauderdale was incorporated in 1911, four years before Broward County split from Dade County. The increased shipping and better highways attracted more and more visitors and settlers to south Florida in the early part of the twentieth century. The first school census of the county showed that in 1915 Fort Lauderdale had 421 white students and 75 black students.

When blacks moved to Fort Lauderdale, they usually settled in the northwestern section, called "colored town," which was north of Broward Boulevard and west of the railroad tracks. As more and more blacks settled in the county, they began demanding schools for their children in the belief that education would allow them to earn a good living and take them out of poverty.

As black parents continued to press for a black school, the Broward County School Board finally agreed in 1923 to open a "colored school" in Fort Lauderdale on land sold at a modest cost by Frank and Ivy Cromartie Stranahan, two leading white citizens of the city. The school was to be in Tuskegee Park, a black subdivision. When the school opened in 1924, Joseph Ely became its first principal and renamed it to honor James Hardy Dillard, a white man who had done much to foster good relations between the races in the South.

In 1927, the city government helped reinforce segregation by restricting black homes to the northwest quadrant and not allowing blacks to travel to other parts of the city after certain hours. Many blacks worked in tourism, construction, and agriculture, but employers often needed more workers than were readily available. One way that local officials got workers around harvest time in the years of segregation was to arrest blacks on vagrancy charges and "allow" them to pay off the $35 fine by working in the fields.

During the Great Depression of the 1930s, **Lincoln Brown** and **J. W. Mickens** succeeded Ely as principals of Dillard. Because the school was still not a full high school, students had to leave Broward County and go elsewhere to complete their education—for example black schools in West Palm Beach and Miami. When **Clarence C. Walker** (1880–1942) became principal of Dillard in 1937, he worked to extend the school's curriculum from eight grades to twelve. The first senior high school commencement for blacks in Fort Lauderdale took place in 1938. His efforts to expand the school term for black children to nine months did not come to fruition until soon after he died in 1942.

When a new Dillard Elementary School and a new Dillard High School were opened at 2365 NW 11th Street just west of Old Dillard High School between 1952 and 1954, the old 1924 building remained open as an elementary school and was eventually named the Clarence C. Walker Elementary School. In 1974, the old building became an administrative annex for the Division of Instruction. The Broward County Black Historical Society eventually succeeded in restoring **OLD DILLARD HIGH SCHOOL** at 1009 NW 4th Street as a black museum and cultural center. Local officials began integrating the schools in 1961 without incident, and by 1970 were able to integrate all the schools of Broward County, thanks in great part to the efforts of **George Allen**, the first black to receive a law degree from the University of Florida.

Today, the **OLD DILLARD MUSEUM** has artifacts and displays dealing with the African American history of Broward County. Phone: (954) 765-6952. It also has a plaque there honoring **Estelle Rouse Pinkett** (1892–1961), an educator at Old Dillard School from the 1930s to the 1950s. Mrs. Pinkett, who taught fifth and sixth grades there from 1932 until 1959, encouraged students to attend college. While many African Americans struggled to finish grade school, Mrs. Pinkett sent the majority of her students to Bethune-Cookman College and Florida A&M University. In her community, during World War II, she founded the first African American United Service Organization (USO). She also established the "Teachers for Tomorrow" program, an initiative to train students to become teachers. She taught Sunday school and served as a church officer at Mt. Olive Baptist Church.

The Old Dillard High School is now a museum.

Another so-called Great Floridian honored at the museum is **Margaret Blake Roach** (1910–1999). Born in Summerville, Georgia, and raised in Chattanooga, Tennessee, and Atlanta, Georgia, she earned a bachelor's degree in English and Social Science from Clark Atlanta University's Laboratory High School and served as an administrator in Broward County schools for more than twenty years. She was instrumental in helping the Women in Distress Shelter and the United Way; was founding president of the Broward Urban League; and was the first woman and African American on the Broward Community College Board of Trustees, a charter member of the Florida Council on Human Relationships, a founding member of the local National Conference of Christians and Jews, and the first president of Fort Lauderdale LINKS, a national intercultural, civic and social organization. She also served on the Council of Elders for the Old Dillard Museum, won the *Sun-Sentinel* award for community service in Broward County in 1991, and was inducted into the Broward County Women's Hall of Fame in 1993.

The **DR. JAMES F. SISTRUNK BOULEVARD HISTORICAL MARKER** in the 1400 block of NW 6th Street honors a man who delivered 5,000+ babies during his many years serving the local black community. Born in Midway, Florida, and educated in Ocala and in Meharry Medical College in Nashville, Tennessee, **James F. Sistrunk** (1891–1966) went to Fort Lauderdale in 1921 and served as the first black medical doctor in the city and the only one for almost sixteen years. When Dr. **Von Delaney Mizell**, the city's second black physician, arrived in 1938, he and Dr. Sistrunk established Provident Hospital at 1409 NW 6th Street. The city commemorates Dr. Sistrunk, who served as Chief of Staff of Provident Hospital, in the name of Sistrunk Boulevard and in the name of the bridge over the North Fork of the New River on NW 6th Street.

The city honors his fellow doctor in the **VON D. MIZELL LIBRARY** at 1408 Sistrunk Boulevard, which serves the community on the same site as the old Provident Hospital and also has a plaque honoring Dr. Mizell as part of the Great Floridians 2000 program. It notes that he challenged the medical establishment, staged sit-ins and protests, and started the first NAACP chapter in south Florida. In 1942, he participated in a boycott of Fort Lauderdale's "Colored School" to end the practice of a split school year that allowed children to work in the fields during the winter. A federal court ordered the local school board to stop the practice, which also allowed the school to become accredited. He successfully sued the Broward County Medical Association for admittance. He died in 1973 after a long and distinguished career in Broward County.

In 1927, city officials declared that public beaches in the city were off limits to blacks. In searching for another beach, local blacks found the Ocean Mile that developer Arthur Galt of Chicago had bought in 1913. Galt, a Chicago lawyer and the son of the law partner of Hugh Taylor Birch, had tried to sell 8,000 acres of nearby land to a development company, but the Depression and real estate bust ended that scheme. The blacks used the Ocean Mile, which many called the "black beach" and which they reached by driving across a wooden swing bridge on Oakland Park Boulevard, until Galt eventually sold his land after World War II for $19,000,000, the largest private land transaction up to that time in the history of this country. When builders began constructing a new development, one that would culminate in today's many high-rise condominiums on Ocean Mile worth millions of dollars, the blacks had to move to another beach south of the Port Everglades Inlet.

In 1956, after blacks marched on the county courthouse to demand a beach of their own, the county bought beachfront land where John U. Lloyd State Park is today. Because no road linked the mainland to the beach, blacks had to use a ferry, an inconvenience and expense that angered

many of them. On July 4, 1961, they marched to the white beaches near Las Olas Boulevard and staged a wade-in. Dr. Von D. Mizell later recalled: "I was scared that day. I had to walk through a little corridor there with a human wall on both sides. It was tense, and one little spark could have started a riot. I had to look straight ahead, and I was not at ease at all." The police arrested several black leaders, but the city commission finally agreed to build a road to the black beach.

But local black leaders demanded more; they wanted an end to the segregated beaches. **Eula Johnson**, a widowed mother of three who had become president of the Broward NAACP in 1958, led seven carloads of young people to the white beaches in late July 1961. The Ku Klux Klan destroyed her car and threatened more violence, but the FBI protected the demonstrators. The Fort Lauderdale police tried to convince her to call off wade-ins on the grounds that her actions would keep away tourists, but she prevailed. Officials took Mrs. Johnson to court, but a federal judge ruled that blacks had the right to swim at the public beaches.

That history and the story of African Americans in south Florida is told today in the **AFRICAN-AMERICAN RESEARCH LIBRARY AND CULTURAL CENTER** at Sistrunk Boulevard and NW 27th Avenue. It has over 75,000 books, documents, and artifacts, a community cultural center, a 300-seat auditorium, meeting rooms, and a viewing/listening center. Among its collections are the papers of W.E.B. DuBois, the Langston Hughes Collection, the Bethune-Cookman College Collection, the Alex Haley Collection, and the papers of Carter G. Woodson. Phone: (954) 357-7514. For more about the African American who helped establish the cultural center, **Samuel Morrison**, see Chapter Fifty-three.

Integration began to take effect throughout the state, including Broward County, in the mid-1960s. In 1966, a local teacher, **Boisy Waters**, became the first black elected to a Broward County

The library and cultural center has displays about the history of African Americans in Broward County.

office, and eight years later **Kathleen Wright** became the first county-wide black official. The next year **Sylvia Poitier** became the first black mayor of nearby Deerfield Beach and eventually chairperson of the Broward County Commission. Another local official, **Alcee Hastings**, became the first black federal judge appointed from south Florida and eventually won a seat in the U.S. Congress.

In 2000, Fort Lauderdale had a population of 152,397, of whom 44,010 (29%) were African Americans. Among places of importance in this area are the CARROLL VINNETTE REPERTORY COMPANY at 503 SE 6th Street, which offers black-oriented productions, and the AFRICAN AMERICAN CARIBBEAN CULTURAL CENTER at 1601 S. Andrews Avenue with its permanent black arts exhibits. The "African American History Wall" in the Sistrunk Entryway Park shows the history of blacks in the area. Finally, the Museum of Art at 1 E. Las Olas Boulevard in downtown Fort Lauderdale has an African Collection worth noting, and the city also has an annual Black Film Festival.

Pompano Beach

WESTVIEW COMMUNITY CEMETERY is an African American Cemetery at 428 NW 6th Avenue in Pompano Beach. Among the people buried there is **Esther Rolle** (1920–1998), who was born in Pompano Beach, the tenth child of eighteen born to Caribbean farming immigrants. She played the feisty maid in the hit 1970s TV sitcom "Maude" and the strong-willed mother who kept her family together in the spin-off series "Good Times."

The Westview Community Cemetery is where actress Esther Rolle is buried.

7.

Calhoun County

Calhoun County in northwest Florida is bordered by Bay, Jackson, Liberty, and Gulf Counties. The Florida Legislature established Calhoun County from a portion of Escambia County in 1838 and named it for South Carolina Senator John C. Calhoun, an outspoken advocate of the doctrine of states' rights.

The county had a population of 13,017 in the 2000 census, 2,057 (15.8%) of whom were African Americans. That number of blacks was the eighth lowest of all Florida counties.

Blountstown

The **MAYHAW SCHOOL COMMUNITY HISTORICAL PROJECT** on River Street consists of old tenant houses dating back to the 1930s. Local organizers of the project hope to revitalize the area and establish a park, after-school facility, assembly room, and archive center.

Directions: Go north on S.R. 20 .3 miles from the intersection of S.R. 71 and S.R. 20, then right on River Street .7 miles to the corner of Ward and River Streets. The old buildings are behind a fence near a church.

Old tenant houses from the Mayhaw School Community Historical Project are all that remain of a black community.

8.

Charlotte County

Charlotte County in southwest Florida was established in 1921 and named for the nearby body of water, Charlotte Harbor, which supposedly was named for the Calusa tribe of Native Americans that used to live there. Spanish surveyors may have anglicized the name "Calos" on early maps and changed it to honor their queen: Charlotte Sophia, wife of King George III.

Charlotte County had a population of 141,627 in the 2000 census, 6,232 (4.4%) of whom were African Americans.

Cleveland

Cleveland, whose name honors President Grover Cleveland because he was inaugurated in 1885, the year before the naming of the site, is a small town in Charlotte County. It is on U.S. 17 along the Peace River and east-northeast of Punta Gorda, the county seat. Although the 1990 census showed no blacks among the population of 2,922 and the 2000 census showed only thirteen, Cleveland does have two sites of significance to blacks, both places relating to **George Brown**, a black carpenter who went there in 1890 to work for the DeSoto Phosphate Mining Company at Hull on the Peace River.

The phosphate industry, which attracted him, required labor-intensive work by strong men who could stand the long hours in the hot sun. The phosphate companies paid black workers a dollar a day to do the hard labor of working in the mines. Some of the phosphate companies leased black convicts for the difficult work and treated them badly until the Florida Legislature finally outlawed the leasing of convicts.

In 1897, George Brown bought a small Punta Gorda boat-repair business from another black, **Peter W. Miller**, and moved it to Cleveland. Around 1916, Brown bought eight acres to construct the **CLEVELAND STEAM MARINE WAYS**, now at 5400 Riverside Drive, to build and repair luxury yachts. His crew handled boats as long as eighty feet and built large pleasure boats, sail or power, for wealthy clients, many of whom wintered in Charlotte Harbor. Today a mobile home park uses the machine shop as a community hall, which visitors can tour.

Directions: To reach the community hall, turn west off U.S. 17 onto Cleveland Avenue in the middle of the town, then right on Riverside Drive when the avenue dead-ends; the structure is a green building on Georgia Drive in the mobile home park.

After his first wife died and later his young daughter from tuberculosis, Brown married a young woman and built her a large, two-story house on Riverside Drive (Old Highway 17). The **GEORGE BROWN HOME**, now private, is at 27430 Cleveland Avenue. One of the large rooms in the house had Brown's extensive library. He also had one of the first automobiles, player pianos, and radios in the area. The Browns had no children, but took in several black children who needed a

George Brown and his wife are buried in the Lt. Carl A. Bailey Memorial Cemetery in Cleveland, Florida.

home and also opened up their home to children, both black and white, to see and hear the piano and radio.

Brown was an "equal opportunity employer," hiring whites and blacks and paying equal wages for equal skills. He also bought and sold property throughout the county, especially in the county seat, Punta Gorda. In 1921, he donated land for the all-black Masonic Tuscan Lodge 92 in Punta Gorda at the southwest corner of Marion and Nesbit Streets. In 1924, he sold prime land in downtown Punta Gorda for the county courthouse.

When he finally died in 1951 at age 83, he left behind a legacy of charitable giving and fair treatment for all. He is buried in the LT. CARL BAILEY MEMORIAL CEMETERY in what used to be the black cemetery of Cleveland. At this gravesite workers put up a double tombstone with his birth and death dates and the birth date of his wife; her death date would be filled in when she died. But when she did die sixteen years later, no money remained for the carving of the date, and so that part is still blank on the marker.

The cemetery is named for one of the first black fighter pilots of World War II, a man who survived the war but was later killed in a 1957 automobile accident. The Punta Gorda Colored Investment Company originally platted the cemetery, but the county later took it over.

The cemetery is off Riverside Drive, toward the river to the west of the town; the gravesites are well-marked in the central part of the cemetery.

Punta Gorda

This town on the south side of the Peace River traces its beginnings back to 1883, when Colonel Isaac Trabue arrived from Kentucky and made plans to establish a settlement, called Trabue. Albert Gilchrist, a white civil engineer and important land speculator from Punta Gorda who served as governor of Florida from 1909 until 1913, hired black foremen and surveyors to help the Florida Southern Railway reach Punta Gorda in 1886, after which several of the blacks settled in the town. Seven of the first fifteen men to settle there were African American, and four of them helped incorporate the town. Local townspeople voted to change the name to Punta Gorda, meaning "wide point," and it later became the county seat of Charlotte County, although the town grew very slowly in comparison to Tampa to the north.

The Seventh Day Adventist Church established the first school for African Americans in 1895 on the corner of Cochran and Charlotte Streets and run by a **Mrs. Giles**. Parents raised enough money to buy land for a public school and established the Public Colored School, a two-room frame building on E. Marion and Cooper Streets in 1902.

By 1900, thirty-four percent of the African American community, including three women, owned their own homes. Seventy percent could read, and sixty percent could write. Several became businessmen, including four merchants and a barber. Others became ministers, fishermen, and at least one teacher.

In 1903, when Albert Gilchrist was elected state representative, he appointed the first black man, **Dan T. Smith**, a man he had once hired as a surveyor, to the DeSoto County Board of Education. When Smith went to an educators' conference in New Orleans to recruit a black teacher, he persuaded **Benjamin J. Baker**, a thirty-one-year-old man with twelve years' experience in Live Oak, Florida, to come to Punta Gorda. Baker, the son of Suwannee County slaves, became the first principal-teacher for the county's first black school. When the number of students needed to have the county pay for a teacher was two short, Dan Smith and another man, **Alex Stephens**, enrolled in the school.

Baker was a quiet man known for his strict discipline and high moral standards. Twice widowed, he never had children of his own, but was much loved by the students and parents associated with his school. In order not to show any favoritism for either of the two black churches in town, St. Mark Baptist and Bethel African Methodist Episcopal, he attended one on one Sunday and the other one on the next Sunday.

When enrollment outgrew the two-room school, a four-room school was built at the southeast corner of Mary and Showalter Streets (now the playground of the Cooper Street Recreation Center) to serve black students; people began referring to it as "Baker's Academy" in honor of the beloved principal. Three other black teachers taught grades one–eight, while the older children were bused to Dunbar High School in Fort Myers (see Chapter Thirty-five) until integration took effect in Charlotte County in 1964.

In 1940, after forty-nine years in education in Live Oak and Punta Gorda, Baker retired, becoming the first person to benefit from the 1939 Teachers' Retirement Act. He died two years later and was buried in Live Oak, Florida, the town he was born in just seven years after the Civil War. Soon after he died, a large school for black children was built near his Punta Gorda home and named for him. Today **BAKER ELEMENTARY SCHOOL** at 311 E. Charlotte Avenue is used in the Head Start and pre-school development classes. Baker's Academy was eventually torn down to make room for the Cooper Street Recreation Center. The Baker Academy Alumni Association meets twice a year to keep alive the memory of Charlotte County's first black educator.

Another black from Punta Gorda, **Charles P. Bailey**, became a fighter pilot with the all-black 99th Fighter Squadron and won the Distinguished Flying Cross after flying 133 combat missions over Europe and shooting down three enemy airplanes. He later moved to DeLand, Florida, to establish the Charles P. Bailey Funeral Home.

One of the great black leaders of the Reconstruction period in Florida, **Robert Meacham** (1835–1902), served as postmaster in Punta Gorda and helped establish the African Methodist Episcopal Church in the state, as well as Florida's public education system.

BETHEL AFRICAN METHODIST EPISCOPAL CHURCH at 260 E. Olympia Avenue at Wood Street began as to a thatched-roof hut constructed there in 1885 by **Dan Smith**, a local African

American religious leader. Colonel (later Governor) Albert Gilchrist and several local white families attended the first service there. The congregation built the first permanent sanctuary, a wooden-frame building, on the site in 1897, but Hurricane Donna destroyed it in 1960. Members then replaced that building with a concrete-block facility. Smith also organized ST. MARK PROGRESSIVE BAPTIST CHURCH in the late 1890s. By 1920, African Americans had five churches in Punta Gorda.

The BLANCHARD HOUSE at 623 Fitzhugh Street was a 1925 house belonging to Joseph Blanchard, a steamboat pilot, and Minnie, his mail-order bride. Mrs. Bernice Russell, historian of the African American community, bought the house in the late 1980s and moved it to 406 Martin Luther King Jr. Boulevard, where today,

the building, called the BERNICE A. RUSSELL CENTER, houses the MUSEUM OF AFRICAN AMERICAN HISTORY AND CULTURE. Tours by appointment. Phone: (941) 639-2914.

NEW OPERATION COOPER STREET at 650 Mary Street in the East Punta Gorda Historical District was built after activists in the 1960s pressed for a building where the black community could meet. Workers renovated the building in 2001. Phone: (941) 639-3034

ST. MARY PRIMITIVE BAPTIST CHURCH at 605 Mary Street traces its history back to 1901, when Reverend Austin bought land for the church. St. Mary's, rebuilt there in 1968, has provided the community services for over one hundred years.

Although Punta Gorda had a population of only 1,883 by 1930, in 2000 the town had 10,878 residents, of whom 651 (6%) were black.

The Blanchard House has exhibits about African Americans in the community.

9.

Citrus County

Citrus County, located on "Florida's Nature Coast," is seventy miles north of Tampa and sixty miles northwest of Orlando, along the Gulf of Mexico. The Florida Legislature established the county in 1887 and named it after Florida's main agricultural product. Like much of Florida before statehood in 1845, the area received an influx of residents after Congress passed the Armed Occupation Act of 1842. That act gave 160 acres to any man who built a house, cultivated five acres of the land, lived there for at least five years, and kept a gun and ammunition handy in case the Native Americans caused any trouble. Once the Native Americans were pushed south into the Everglades or removed to Indian Territory in the West and after Florida attained statehood, more and more white people moved into what became Citrus County.

Citrus County had a population of 118,085 in the 2000 census, 2,834 (2.4%) of whom were African Americans. That percentage (2.4%) was the second-lowest among Florida counties, barely above the 2.1% of Pasco County.

Floral City

Before and after Spanish explorer Hernando de Soto passed through the area in 1539 on his way to the Mississippi River, Indian tribes established villages in the vicinity. In the nineteenth century white settlers began moving in. Floral City was settled in 1883 and two years later had a population of three hundred, twice that of Miami in south Florida. The many flowers and crops there gave Floral City its name. In 2000, Floral City had a population of 2,698, of whom just 28 (1%) were blacks.

Although the hard freeze of 1894–95 ended the citrus industry in the area, the discovery of phosphate near Floral City brought in hundreds of new residents, including many African Americans. One historian estimated that ninety-six percent of the ten thousand or more local residents in the late 1890s were African American. When the onset of World War I ended the shipment of phosphate to European markets, many people left to seek work elsewhere, but a good number remained to raise their families and engage in other work, for example in sawmills and turpentine stills.

One of the churches they established was the **PLEASANT HILL BAPTIST CHURCH** at 8200 E. Magnolia Street, the oldest religious building of the black community in Floral City and one of three black churches in town; the other two are **MOUNT CARMEL FREE METHODIST CHURCH** and **GRACE TEMPLE CHURCH OF THE LIVING GOD** (see below). The wood-frame, folk-styled Pleasant Hill Baptist Church with a gable roof and steeple on top was built between 1895 and 1910; the congregation added asbestos siding and modern screen windows more recently. E. Magnolia Street is west of U.S. 41 below E. Orange Avenue and above E. Walnut Lane toward the south end of town.

The Pleasant Hill Baptist Church is the oldest religious building of the black community in Floral City.

ST. LUKE BAPTIST CHURCH on Old Floral City Road dates back to around 1904. In 1958, it became the **GRACE TEMPLE CHURCH OF THE LIVING GOD**. A masonry/brick building replaced the original structure in the 1960s. In 2001, the congregation built a new building there and made the former church building into a meeting hall.

About one-half mile south of E. Magnolia Street is **FRASIER CEMETERY** on the southwest corner of E. Tower Trail and S. Great Oak Drive east of U.S. 41. The cemetery took its name from **H. C. Frasier**, who donated the land in 1908 so that he could bury his son in the area. One grave there was of **Arthur Norton**, who, when he died in 1986 at age 109, was the oldest known resident of Citrus County. Like many other blacks, Norton had moved to the area around the turn of the twentieth century to work in the phosphate mines. The graves, which are scattered over a wide area, have gravestones of family members as well as of former residents. Some markers have no name attached to them; others have faded wooden crosses or marble headstones. The earliest graves date back to the early 1900s. In 1966, the owners of the cemetery donated it to the county, which then named it the Floral City Community Cemetery.

A short distance further south is another black cemetery—**WILLIAMS CEMETERY**, a small, privately owned cemetery with about a dozen headstones that memorialize members of five families: the Lindseys, Mobleys, Spicers, Vickers, and Williams.

Inverness

Inverness, the county seat of Citrus County, was named by a Scotch settler after the Scottish city of Inverness because of the similarities of topography, namely lakes and the highlands nearby. Voters approved the transfer of the county seat from Mannsfield to Inverness in 1891, but not without much fist fighting and many arguments. The county did well in the citrus boom before the 1894–95 freeze, but suffered much damage in that freeze and others. The 2000 population of the Florida town was 6,789, of whom just 353 (5.2%) were black, but the town has an important place related to the black history of the area.

That place, in the northeast section of **OAK RIDGE CEMETERY**, was where blacks used to bury their dead. Unofficially called Pine Ridge Cemetery, the site is at the south edge of Oak Ridge Cemetery, which is several blocks due south of Citrus Memorial Hospital; to reach Pine Ridge, turn east at the end of S. Line Avenue and proceed to the top of the small hill, where you can see dozens of small, white columns marking the sites where black families in the area buried their dead for over fifty years.

In 1988, when the county learned that it owned the 1.8 acre black cemetery, workers cleaned up the neglected site and used ground-penetrating radar to locate unmarked graves. The workers placed column markers on those sites and cleaned the metal markers that showed the name of the deceased, as well as the name of the funeral home that arranged for the burial. The East Dampier Street Funeral Home, owned and managed by Mr. **Eli White**, had arranged many of the burials. Mr. White, who ran the funeral home for forty-three years, carefully maintained the black cemetery until he was no longer able to. One can still read the headstones or markers of over one hundred of those buried there. At least twenty-three servicemen from all branches of the U.S. Armed Forces are buried there.

Finally, an island off the coast of Citrus County that was popular with African Americans had the name of Negro Island. When local officials realized how offensive the name might be to African Americans, they changed it to Horseshoe Island.

10.

Clay County

Clay County, established in 1858 along the northern part of the St. Johns River and named after U.S. Secretary of State Henry Clay of Kentucky, includes unincorporated Middleburg and four municipalities: Orange Park near Jacksonville, Green Cove Springs (the county seat), Penney Farms, and Keystone Heights.

Clay County had a population of 140,814 in the 2000 census, 9,435 (6.7%) of whom were African Americans.

The location of much of Clay County along the St. Johns River was a mixed blessing during the Civil War. Historian Daniel Schafer points out that runaway slaves who could reach the river could flag down Union boats and sail away to freedom, in many cases to return to fight for the Union. One slave owner, Samuel Fairbanks, thought that Clay County was far enough away from Jacksonville as to be safe from the federal troops, but two of those slaves stole a boat and rowed back to Jacksonville. When city officials, many of them slave owners themselves, caught the two escapees, they put them in jail. A few days later, however, the slaves escaped from jail and found refuge with Union vessels at Mayport.

Green Cove Springs

This town earned the title of "The Parlor City" in the 1880s because the residents kept it so neat and clean. Situated on the beautiful St. Johns River and boasting of a sulfur spring used for therapeutic bathing, it attracted many tourists, especially after town boosters claimed that they had "no mosquitoes, flies, gnats, sand flies to annoy and make one's life miserable." The town still boasts of its beauty and relaxed life style and keeps attracting new residents seeking a less-frenzied pace of life.

One of the state's best sculptors, a woman who is barely known in Florida, was **Augusta Savage** (1900–1962). Born in Green Cove Springs to **Cornelia** and **Edward Fells**, she was the seventh of fourteen children. Her fundamentalist preacher-father disapproved of Augusta's habit of making figures out of the clay she found in the neighborhood, but she was determined to develop the talent she had and maybe win her father over. She eventually moved to West Palm Beach, where a potter gave her some clay; she molded it into a statue of the Virgin Mary that won a prize and the approval of her father. In 1921, she went to New York City and eventually became a member of the Harlem Renaissance, a literary movement that produced works by and about blacks and included other Floridians like composer/poet **James Weldon Johnson** (see Chapter Fifteen), his musician brother **Rosamond**, civil rights leader **A. Philip Randolph** (see Chapter Forty-four), and writer **Zora Neale Hurston** (see Chapters Forty-eight and Fifty-six).

Augusta won a scholarship to the Cooper's Union Woman's Art School and began a formal study of sculpture. She also won a scholarship to study in France, but was then turned down by the awards committee when they found she was black. She eventually won a Julius Rosenwald Fellowship to study in Paris for two years and there perfected her craft. Among her famous sculptures were "The Head of Dr. DuBois," "Lift Every Voice and Sing," and "Gamin." She opened an art school to teach others, helped organize the Harlem Artist Guild, and directed the Harlem Community Art Center.

Green Cove Springs does not yet have any memorial to Augusta Savage, but each spring has an Augusta Savage Festival. She gave her family plot of land at 1107 Middleburg Avenue to the county in the 1940s to build a school on it, the Dunbar School, which honored black poet/novelist **Paul Lawrence Dunbar**. After desegregation, the students there went to Clay High School. The former Dunbar School is now being used as the Clay Association for the Retarded.

Clay High School, which is about two miles west of Green Cove Springs on S.R. 16, is where Coach **Ron Riddle** spent thirty-seven years of his career coaching athletic teams and inspiring his students to succeed in life. When Coach Ron began teaching there in 1966, he became the first African American to teach in a Clay County school. At his retirement in 2003, officials announced that the annual region-wide track meet would henceforth be known as the Ron Riddle Invitational.

Green Cove Springs had 1,312 African Americans in the 2000 census, and that represented 24% of the total population of the town.

Fleming Island

One local African American needs to be mentioned here. **Louise "Lulu" Cecelia Fleming** (1862–1899) was born to slave parents on Fleming Island in 1862, shortly before her father was captured and taken away by the Union Army. Lulu grew up on Hibernia Plantation before its white owners had to flee with her. She was baptized at Bethel Baptist Institutional Church in Jacksonville at age 14, trained to become a teacher, taught in St. Augustine, attended Shaw University in North Carolina and graduated as class valedictorian. In 1886, she became the first African American woman appointed to be a foreign missionary and was assigned to Zaire, Africa. After serving there, she returned to America and attended medical school and became the first African American at The Women's Medical College at Philadelphia, from which she graduated in 1895 and returned to Africa to work. She served there only four years before contracting African sleeping sickness and dying back in Philadelphia.

Middleburg

The last survivor of pioneer African Americans who homesteaded in Middleburg was **Grant Forman**, who had gone to the area with his family at an early age. As an adult, he farmed over 160 acres of land there, but had to leave the area when local whites rose up and drove out their black neighbors. Mr. Forman entrusted his land to the care of a local white man and mailed back his property taxes each year from his new home in South Carolina. There at the age of sixty, he met and married a widow, **Estell Johnson**, in 1919. He eventually lost half his land due to unpaid back taxes, but returned to Middleburg in 1936 to take over his remaining land. He sold much of that land to

This small monument near Forman's former home honors him in an area where his descendants still live.

This former one-room schoolhouse is now a museum about African Americans.

others, both black and white, and lived with his family on what remained until he died in 1951. A street name and small monument near his former home off S.R. 21 honor him in an area where his descendants still live.

The **HILL TOP BLACK HERITAGE EDUCATION CENTER/MUSEUM** in Hunter-Douglas Park about .3 miles down Longmire Avenue from the Forman monument has a one-room schoolhouse, built in 1903 to serve the needs of local African American children. Today, it houses artifacts, newspaper articles, and photographs that document the history and heritage of Clay County African Americans.

In 1995, **Maude Jackson**, who attended the schoolhouse before desegregation and who is now the director of the Hill Top Heritage Development Inc., converted the schoolhouse into the center/museum. (For information about visiting the school call (904) 282-4168.)

Middleburg had 334 African Americans in the 2000 census, a figure which represented just 3% of the total population of the city.

Orange Park

The 2002 edition of the *Florida Black Heritage Trail* listed two places in Orange Park that are on the Trail: the Joseph Green House at 531 McIntosh Avenue and the Orange Park Negro Elementary School at 440 McIntosh Avenue.

The first place is no longer there, or at least at that address. The second place now has the Putnam-Clay-Flagler Economic Opportunity Council, Inc. Finished in 1938, the school is one of the few remaining buildings from the 1930s. The City of Orange Park now owns the building.

The former Orange Park Negro Elementary School.

11.
Collier County

The Florida Legislature established Collier County in 1923 and named it after Barron Collier, a leading developer of southwest Florida.

Collier County had a population of 251,377 in the 2000 census, 11,312 (4.5%) of whom were African Americans.

Everglades City

According to Charlton Tebeau's history of the region, in 1927 local African Americans opened their own church, which Barron Collier built for them in Port DuPont, the industrial center of the Baron Collier interests in the county. In attendance at the opening service, which local dignitaries Barron Collier, F. Irwin Holmes, and D. Graham Copeland also attended, was the pastor, Reverend **D. A. Hamilton**, who announced that he would open a school that fall for African American children. The DuPont School for Negro Children, which opened on October 4, 1927, was run by the local Port DuPont Church, which was Methodist or Baptist depending on the affiliation of the visiting pastor. The school at Everglades City began with only grades one through four, but eventually went through the eighth grade. Those who wanted to attend high school had to go to Immokalee, where they attended Bethune High School. Workers at Port DuPont repaired the huge machines that Barron Collier was using to cross the Everglades with the Tamiami Trail in the 1920s.

Likewise, Carver School at Naples went only through the eighth grade. After that, those who wanted to go to high school were taken to Fort Myers, where they attended Dunbar High School.

Naples

One early black church was **MACEDONIA MISSIONARY BAPTIST CHURCH**, now located at 1006 3rd Avenue North in Naples. In the 1920s, blacks met in a building near 13th Avenue South and 3rd Street. When the hurricane of 1926 blew down that building, local residents bought the lumber from the congregation and moved it to some land on Church Street in East Naples that was given to the Church of God by Billy Weeks. That was one of the first churches—if not the first—built in the Naples area.

The congregation that sold the lumber used a small building for worship on what was called the Ditch Bank, the first black section of Naples. When workers cut a canal ("the Ditch") to connect Naples Bay to the Gulf of Mexico, they piled up the excavated dirt on the banks, which came to be known as the Ditch Bank. Mr. Crayton built small houses on the Ditch Bank, and blacks lived there until Mr. J. C. McDonald Sr. built the Quarters (see below).

In 1929, some of the blacks there organized the Macedonia Baptist Church, which remained at the Ditch Bank until the 1950s, when developers convinced the people there to move to the area on 3rd Avenue North, where the church is today.

In 1949, white Fort Myers contractor **J. C.**

The Macedonia Missionary Baptist Church dates back to the 1920s.

McDonald Sr. built the QUARTERS for African Americans. The houses on that 4.9 acres of land, located between 10th Street and Goodlette Road and nearly encircled by the Atlantic Coast Line Railroad tracks and bisected by 1st Avenue North, were built at the instigation of city officials in order to provide adequate housing for African Americans, housing that would keep them close to their jobs and shopping. That development lasted until the early 1980s, when the city evicted the residents and razed the houses, which had deteriorated badly over the previous three decades.

One of the early black pioneers was **Annie Mae Perry**, who was born in Monticello, Florida. Her father had graduated from Tallahassee College, but Annie Mae had to overcome many obstacles to obtain even an eighth-grade education, an achievement that made her even more determined to see that her own children went on to high school. In 1947, she arrived in Copeland in Collier County with her husband and became the only licensed midwife in the county for twenty-five years. She delivered 514 babies (white, black, and Hispanic), earned the title "Mother Perry," and sent her five children to high schools elsewhere because Collier County had no high schools for blacks: two children went to Fort Myers, two to West Palm Beach, and one to Alabama.

Naples had 975 African Americans in the 2000 census, a figure which represented just 5% of the total population (20,976) of the city.

12.

Columbia County

The Florida Legislature established Columbia County in 1832 and named it for a poetical nickname of the United States, which derived from Christopher Columbus.

Columbia County had a population of 56,513 in the 2000 census, 9,607 (17.0%) of whom were African Americans.

Lake City

This city, which had a population of 9,980 in the 2000 census, of whom 3,739 (38%) were black, has two sites of importance to blacks.

NIBLACK ELEMENTARY SCHOOL at 837 NE Broadway Avenue was built in 1954 in order to consolidate elementary schools that served African American students in Columbia County. The school honors in its name Mrs. **Minnie Jones Niblack**, who worked to build, consolidate, and improve local schools and also served that particular school as teacher and principal, and later as county supervisor. The school is still operating today.

RICHARDSON HIGH SCHOOL on E. North Street (renamed Coach Anders Way for the former football coach) was built in 1957 as a school for African Americans. The Richardson High School (RHS) Wolves captured the 1967–68 State Basketball Championship, but the high school closed in the early 1970s when integration took place. Although the main structure has been torn down, part of the school that served as the gym and the cafeteria still exists. The basketball court, still painted in the green and orange team colors, is in excellent shape, and the trophy case in the lobby proudly displays awards won by RHS teams. The playing fields and gym are now part of the **RICHARDSON COMMUNITY CENTER**, located at 255 Coach Anders Way. The commu-

The Minnie J. Niblack Elementary Choir from Lake City singing at the 1957 Florida Folk Festival in White Springs. *Florida State Archives*

nity center has a commemorative plaque for the school.

A plaque there also honors **McKinley Jeffers** (1896–1973), one of the people honored as a Great Floridian in 2000. Born in Roxboro, North Carolina, and a graduate of North Carolina A & T State University, he was recruited in 1939 by the University of Florida (UF), where he worked as a faculty member for twenty-five years; UF did not have any black faculty on its main campus in Gainesville, but some worked as extension agents throughout the state. He was a county extension agent for the black farmers of Columbia County; trained staff to teach proper methods for farming, canning, health and sanitation; and served as recruiting representative for the U.S. Navy, a member of the Lake City Chamber of Commerce, liaison for the State Welfare Board, and Chairman of the American Red Cross Drive. He was awarded a Congressional Medal for his work with draftees, a certificate for meritorious service from the American Red Cross, a certificate of appreciation in 1944 from President Franklin D. Roosevelt, and a certificate for outstanding service to the state and nation from President Harry S. Truman.

A notable graduate of Richardson High School was **Alfonso (Al) Lofton** (1945–1984), who graduated in 1963 as salutatorian before joining the U.S. Marines and serving in the Vietnam War. In 1968, after an honorable discharge from the Marines, he was hired by the Department of Corrections before joining the Florida Highway Patrol in 1970 and becoming the state's first black state trooper. Two years after his retirement in 1982, after a distinguished career in which he won many commendations, he died of multiple sclerosis.

The stately Gothic architectural style and stained glass windows distinguish the **TRINITY UNITED METHODIST CHURCH** at 248 Martin Luther King Street as a historic landmark in Lake City. The African American congregation first organized in 1863 as the Gethsemane Methodist Episcopal Church, but the church standing today was built in 1927.

The entrance to a segregated railroad depot in Lake City. *Florida State Archives*

One might-have-been in Lake City was the establishment of the state's first higher-educational institution for African Americans. Florida trustees of the African Methodist Episcopal Church (AME) wanted to establish such an institution after the Civil War. At their 1870 conference in Tallahassee, they decided to establish such a school and then bought ten acres in Lake City for $3,000. The new school, **BROWN THEOLOGICAL INSTITUTE**, was to provide general education opportunities, as well as train new teachers and ministers.

The state legislature officially chartered the school in 1872, and workers began building it the next year. Its name was changed to Brown University in 1874. But the embezzlement of $3,000 in construction funds and the loss of $20,000 in bond and script in a house fire led to the cessation of construction. Because of a mechanics' lien filed by unpaid carpenters, officials sold the building and land in a public auction. A high school in Palatka attempted to replace the school, but the effort failed. The AME Church would eventually establish a high school in Jacksonville in 1884 (see Chapter Fifteen).

13.

DeSoto County

The Florida Legislature established DeSoto County in 1916 and named it for Hernando de Soto, the Spanish explorer who traveled through Florida in 1539. The county had a population of 32,209 in the 2000 census, 4,091 (12.7%) of whom were African Americans.

Arcadia

Fifty miles southeast of Sarasota is Arcadia, a small inland town that used to be cowboy country complete with range wars and cattle rustling. It still has an annual rodeo that attracts participants from near and far, and it was the only Florida town profiled in Norman Crampton's book *The 100 Best Small Towns in America.* Some have speculated that the name of the town goes back to Arcadia, Greece, and symbolizes peace and serenity, but it actually comes from the first name of the daughter of an early settler.

The town was incorporated in 1887 and became the county seat of DeSoto County. Around 1900 it had its own Chautauqua, a series of concerts and lectures held in a large amphitheater, but time and the lack of good jobs have forced many young people to leave town after graduating from high school. The population of the town according to the 2000 census was 6,604, of whom 1,855 (28%) were black.

Blacks moved to the area in the nineteenth century to work in the turpentine operations, in the phosphate mines, and on the building of the Florida East-West Coast Railroad between Arcadia and Bradenton. Racial problems broke out from time to time and lynchings occurred. For example, in 1892, according to historian Canter Brown Jr., angry whites lynched a black man who

had supposedly killed an official of the Arcadia Phosphate Company.

As recently as 1968, writer Richard Nellius could write that the town's 1,800 blacks lived in segregated slums in the southwest part of town called "The Quarters." And while the schools were integrated, the downtown restaurants and lunch counters were not. The bus station café tried to justify such segregation with a sign that read: "This is a privately owned business. It is not based on municipal, county, state or federal property. It is not a public utility, school, church or polling place. We receive no grants or subsidies from any city, county, state or federal funds. We reserve the right to seat our patrons or deny service to anyone."

A series of nationwide race riots in 1967 led to the establishment in Arcadia of an interracial group to combat inflammatory rumors, and the sheriff appointed fifty-five black auxiliary policemen who served without pay to ensure peace in the Quarters, all of which have helped to secure good relations between the races.

Of significance to blacks is Arcadia's **HICKSON FUNERAL HOME**, the town's first black funeral home, located at 142 S. Orange Avenue, three blocks west of U.S. 17 in the downtown area. The funeral home was established in 1924 as the Arcadia Funeral Home and was owned by

Mrs. **Minnie L. Brown** (1884–1975), the step-grandmother of **Eugene Hickson Sr.**, the present owner. It may be the oldest continuously operated funeral home in DeSoto County. Eugene Hickson Sr. bought the business from Minnie Brown in 1960 and changed its name to Hickson Funeral Home.

In 1971, Hickson became the first black elected to the position of city councilman. He later served for four years as vice mayor and then in 1979 became mayor of Arcadia. When asked to pass on his philosophy to the next generation, Mayor Hickson had words for all: "There is still a racial gap to be closed today. Our goal should be for everyone, no matter what race, to close that gap. And the only way to catch up is to run faster. We are not that dumb that we cannot learn if we study and yet we are not that smart that we can learn without studying."

Arcadia's black history became front-page news in many newspapers around the country when seven children were poisoned to death in October 1967. Local authorities arrested the children's father, **James Richardson**, and charged him with the crime, partly because he had taken out a large insurance policy on the children short-ly before they died. He was sentenced to die in the electric chair, but had that sentence commuted to twenty-five years in prison after the U.S. Supreme Court disallowed Florida's death-penalty law.

Washington, D.C., attorney Mark Lane, who wrote *Arcadia,* which is about the killing of the children, was convinced that James Richardson was innocent and wrote in very derogatory terms of Arcadia in the 1960s. In 1989, after spending twenty-one years in prison, Richardson was freed when a prosecutor appointed by the governor ruled that the prosecution had obtained his conviction by perjury and the suppression of evidence. Visitors to Arcadia occasionally visit the graves of the seven murdered children in the very back of OAK RIDGE CEMETERY, which is north of the downtown area and west of U.S. 17.

Directions to the gravesite: Go in the main entrance of the cemetery, go .3 miles straight back along the dirt road, and turn right over the little dirt bridge; the graves are on the left at the very back of the rows and near the edge of the cemetery.

For more about another African American from Arcadia see **Charles Stebbins Jr.** in Chapter Fifty.

The gravestones of the Richardson children in Oak Ridge Cemetery.

14.

Dixie County

The Florida Legislature established Dixie County in 1921 and named it after the old name of the South. The county had a population of 13,827 in the 2000 census, 1,244 (9.0%) of whom were African Americans.

Dixie County, one of the smallest counties in Florida in population (fifty-eighth out of sixty-seven counties), has two main population centers: Cross City and Old Town. For decades, the African Americans of the county worked in the turpentine industry. A 1936 report, for example, indicated that three hundred African Americans worked in the turpentine camp of Aycock and Lindsey northwest of Cross City; those workers were part of a community of 1,500 African Americans in the area. Dixie County led the southeastern United States in the production of lumber and naval stores for ten years (1928–1938), but the failure to replant and replenish the natural resources eventually led to the demise of the industry.

Author **Zora Neale Hurston** wrote an essay about the workers in a turpentine camp near Cross City. The work was tedious and hot and did not pay very well, but it provided enough income for the workers to raise their families there.

When some of the poor counties in Florida in the nineteenth century, like Dixie, did not want to pay wages to such workers, they relied on the infamous convict-lease system. The system began in 1877, after the Civil War, as a way that the nearly bankrupt Southern states could avoid maintaining prisons and as a way that white men, who had regained control of state government after Reconstruction, could return their black

neighbors to a kind of servitude just as bad as slavery had been.

States like Florida passed vagrancy laws, which allowed arbitrary arrest and conviction of those who could not produce the proper identification or seemed unable to pay bills or fines. Even those who were moving from one town to another or who walked off a job in search of better job opportunities were liable to be picked up and prosecuted. John C. Powell, a convict camp captain in one of those places, wrote in *The American Siberia or Fourteen Years Experience in a Southern Convict Camp* that "In the early days it was possible to send a negro to prison on almost any pretext, but difficult to get a white man there, unless he committed some very heinous crime." In the late 1870s and early 1880s over ninety percent of the prisoners were black. Such prisoners were subject to intense abuse and torture, all of which local officials usually ignored, content to profit monetarily from such a system.

In the turpentine camps the workers/prisoners worked from dawn to dusk as each man was required to attach sap collectors to a certain number of trees a day, usually between sixty and ninety, all the while being manacled to prevent their escape into the woods. At night, the guards would chain the prisoners to their beds. There were seldom if ever doctors on the scene and prisoners who collapsed at work were given only the barest medical assistance. The camp guards punished the prisoners for even the slightest offense, flogging the "guilty" ones or putting them into lightless, unventilated sweatboxes. Florida continued to rely on the convict-lease system until 1923, when public officials finally reacted to public outrage when a white boy from North Dakota died at a lumber camp in Dixie County after being flogged to death by a whipping boss.

After Florida legislators abolished that system, they built a new prison at Raiford and created work farms throughout the counties. The legislature outlawed floggings, but continued to allow the sweatboxes. Officials in the different counties came up with new methods of persecuting prisoners and demeaning them. For example, as Stetson Kennedy wrote in his *Palmetto Country*, "Until 1939 the county and city 'Blue Jay' prison farms at Jacksonville employed a novel method of plowing. Trios of Negro women prisoners were harnessed to the plows, which were also guided by Negro women." It would take much more time for the criminal justice system in Florida to begin to treat its prisoners in humane ways.

Cross City

Behind the Dixie County High School at 16077 SE 19 Highway is the **PRINCE B. OLIVER SR. VOCATIONAL SCHOOL**, formerly the Dixie County Vocational School. The name honors **Prince Benjamin Oliver Sr.,** an African American who spent almost fifty years as an educator in the county. Having grown up in Jacksonville, Florida, and been educated at Florida Normal College in St. Augustine, he began teaching in 1933 at a segregated school in rural Hines northwest of Cross City. In 1956, he worked at Oliver Junior-Senior High School, a school behind the current Dixie County High School and named in his honor. The school also served as an elementary school before being closed in 1968. In the 1970s, the building at the Oliver School was used for vocational classes.

When the Oliver School closed again, Prince Oliver became an assistant principal at Anderson Elementary School in Cross City, where he worked until he retired in 1979.

Gathering sap from turpentine pines was hard work. *Florida State Archives*

15.
Duval County

Florida's fourth county was established in 1822 and named for William Pope Duval, the first territorial governor of Florida. The county had a population of 778,879 in the 2000 census, 216,528 (27.8%) of whom were African Americans. The county had the third-highest number of African Americans among all sixty-seven Florida counties.

Jacksonville

When the Timucuan Indians lived in this area on the St. Johns River, they called the site "wacca pilatka," which means "place where cows cross." After the United States gained control of Florida in 1821, the name of the town, which had been Cow Ford under the British, became Jacksonville to honor Andrew Jackson, the governor of the territories of East and West Florida and later the seventh president of the United States.

The 1860 census showed that of the city's 2,118 inhabitants 908 were slaves and only eighty-seven were free blacks. Slave labor, in fact, was used to build the city's hotels, railroad, and port facilities.

By the end of the nineteenth century some blacks were operating small businesses and owned property, but most were laborers, barbers, laundresses, or servants; in 1894, sixty-two percent of the city's black workers were unskilled laborers. A poll tax and confusing ballot system meant to confuse illiterates had virtually disenfranchised them. Many blacks saw education as a way to good jobs and stressed that to their children to such an extent that by 1900 seventy-three percent of the city's blacks were literate.

In 1968, at a time when the inner-city blacks of Jacksonville had become numerous and powerful enough to take control of the city, officials consolidated most of Duval County, which effectively became the City of Jacksonville. Author Herbert Hiller argued in his *Highway A1A* that the move disenfranchised the city's blacks because the whole county, including white, conservative areas, voted in municipal elections and therefore kept control of the city.

Duval County is the home to several important educational institutions open to African Americans from an early date. Because formal education—that is, education conducted in schools and colleges—was open to very few blacks before the Civil War, the emancipation of the slaves led to, among other changes, an emphasis on education as a way to get out of poverty and to begin a life cycle that would better the living conditions of themselves and their descendants. Throughout the South, education has enabled blacks to obtain economic security, personal respect, and racial progress.

In 1865, at the end of the Civil War, the federal government established the Bureau of Refugees, Freedmen, and Abandoned Lands, at first to take care of the general welfare of African Americans, but then to establish schools for blacks and poor whites. For the next five years, it sent teachers from the North into Southern cities and cooperated with missionary and religious organizations to set up schools. Newly freed slaves saw those schools as a great opportunity to better their lot, despite the attacks by the Ku Klux Klan, who found schools an easy target for their hatred.

Black colleges in the South, which were often little more than secondary schools, received sporadic funding from state or federal forces and usually had to rely on the generosity of religious congregations and the students themselves.

Among the institutions of importance to blacks in Jacksonville is EDWARD WATERS COLLEGE at 1715 Kings Road. This four-year, liberal arts college associated with the African Methodist Episcopal (AME) Church is the oldest independent institution of higher education for blacks in Florida and the oldest institution of higher education in Jacksonville. The college resulted from the efforts by the African Methodist Episcopal Church (AME) during Reconstruction to provide educational opportunities for Florida's African Americans. It was the first of four higher education institutions established in Florida in the second half of the nineteenth century for the purpose of providing educational opportunities for African Americans, while at the same time training teachers and ministers. (The other institutions were Bethune-Cookman College in Daytona Beach, 1872; Florida A&M University in Tallahassee, 1883; and Florida Memorial College in Miami, 1892.)

Midwives attending a meeting at Edward Waters College in Jacksonville. *Florida State Archives*

Edward Waters College dates its history to 1866, when AME missionary **Charles Pearce** arrived in Jacksonville. In 1867, the AME Church had its first annual conference in Jacksonville, followed by a second conference in 1868. (See Chapter Twelve for information on the attempt to establish the college's predecessor in Lake City, Florida.)

After aborted attempts to establish the school in Lake City and Palatka, the AME church in 1884 decided to establish a single high school in Jacksonville for blacks. The new facility, called Florida Scientific and Divinity High School, was housed in a building leased to the church by members of

This is what rural schools for African Americans in Duval County looked like in the nineteenth century. *Florida State Archives*

Mount Zion AME Church. Officials then bought the school for $10,000 in 1889 and had its first graduating class (five students) two years later. In that same year (1891) the name of the school was changed to Edward Waters College in honor of Reverend **Edward Waters**, the third bishop of the African Methodist Episcopal Church. The 1901 Jacksonville fire burned down the school building on E. Beaver Street, but officials rebuilt the campus in 1904 on the present Kings Road property.

Four years later, officials built the first building, Salter Hall, named for Bishop **B. F. Salter**, the leader of the conference at that time. Salter Hall housed women's dormitories, classrooms, and a dining hall. Fire destroyed that building in 1936.

The oldest building on the twenty-acre campus is Centennial Hall, which dates back to 1916, is on the National Register of Historic Places, and commemorates in its name the one hundredth anniversary of the AME Church. The contractor for that building, which became the college library in 1980, was **Richard Lewis Brown** (1854–1948), the city's first-known black architect. Born into poverty in South Carolina before the Civil War, he moved with his family to Florida, where he worked as a farmer, carpenter, and minister. He bought several acres of land in east Jacksonville, including the site of what became the RICHARD L. BROWN ELEMENTARY SCHOOL at 1535 Milnor Street. He served two terms (1881–84) in the Florida House of Representatives and worked for the Duval County School Board in the construction and repair of schools.

Among the many distinguished graduates of Edward Waters College was **A. Philip Randolph**, founder of the Brotherhood of Sleeping Car Porters and an important figure in the Civil Rights movement (see Chapter Fifty-four for more about him). Today some 670 students attend the college. Phone for the college: (904) 355-3030.

The BISHOP HENRY Y. TOOKES RESIDENCE at 1001 W. 8th Street is the former home of Bishop **Henry Tookes**, who served the Florida District of the AME Church and for whom the house was built in 1939. He helped Edward Waters College earn accreditation and paid off its $52,000 bonded indebtedness. The ALPHA KAPPA ALPHA SORORITY HOUSE, which now occupies the residence, has helped preserve the building.

The B.F. LEE THEOLOGICAL SEMINARY BUILDING at Edward Waters College, 1658 Kings Road, is a three-story Tudor Revival–style building built in 1925–1927 to house the college's Theological Department. The department's first graduating class (1914) included **Henry Tookes**, who later became bishop. Today the building has the Milne Auditorium and administrative and business offices for the college.

Among the churches that played an important role in the life of African Americans in Duval County are several that need to be mentioned here. The BETHEL BAPTIST INSTITUTIONAL CHURCH at 1058 Hogan Street dates back to 1904, from which time this Neo-classical Revival-style building has served the community well. The congregation, which included two slaves belonging to the Rev. J. Jaudon, was first organized in 1838 and is therefore the first organized Baptist church in Jacksonville. Within two years the congregation built on the northeast corner of Duval and Newnan streets Jacksonville's first church building and called it Bethel Baptist Church. They later sold the property to the Presbyterians and constructed a new building in West LaVilla. During the Civil War the church was used as a hospital. In the early years of the church, the congregation included both white and black members, but right after the Civil War the congregation split along racial lines with the black members keeping the original name.

In 1868, the black members of the church received $400 for their interest in the church property and left to build a new church with the Bethel Baptist name. After the 1901 fire destroyed that building, members of the congregation built an impressive structure that still dominates the lo-

Jacksonville, Fla.   Bethel Baptist Institutional Church

An early postcard showing what Bethel Baptist Institutional Church looked like. *Florida State Archives*

cal scene. Today the church's main bell tower and two small towers anchor the rectangular building, which is on the National Register of Historic Places. From 1892 until 1907, the pastor of the church, which was located in the 1890s at the northwest corner of Main Street and W. Union Street, was Rev. **J. Milton Waldron**, who also helped organize the very important Afro-American Life Insurance Company in 1901 (see page 52) and is honored today by Waldron Street in American Beach (see Chapter Forty-five).

The church is part of the James Weldon Johnson Heritage Tour because Johnson's brother, Rosamond, besides giving private music lessons and teaching music at the Florida Baptist Academy, served as choirmaster and organist for Bethel Baptist Institutional Church.

MOUNT OLIVE AME CHURCH at 841 Franklin Street has a history dating back to 1887, when workers built the first wooden sanctuary of the church on that site. Builder **Richard L. Brown**,

the city's first black architect (see page 49 for Centennial Hall), drew up plans for a new building in the early 1920s and workers finished the present structure in 1922. The brown mortar used throughout the structure, a large portico at the entrance, and the three huge columns at the front all add a distinctive flavor to the colorful building.

MOUNT ZION AME CHURCH at 201 E. Beaver Street traces its history back to 1866, when a group of freed slaves, who had organized themselves into the Society for Religious Worship, formed the church. They built a small structure there for worship services, replaced it in 1870 with a large wooden building, and replaced that one twenty years later with a larger brick structure that could seat 1,500. The Jacksonville fire of 1901 destroyed the building, but the congregation soon built the present one.

The **MASONIC TEMPLE BUILDING** at 410 Broad Street is also on the National Register of

Historic Places. The Most Worshipful Union Grand Lodge of the Most Ancient and Honorable Fraternity of Free and Accepted Masons of Florida and Jurisdiction, Inc., founded in 1870, has been the Masonic organization for blacks in Florida. The group decided to construct this building in the early part of the twentieth century as a meeting place for blacks and as a site for offices and stores. After ten years of fund-raising, they built the tall, red-brick structure in 1912 at the northwest corner of Broad and Duval Streets; the 1926 *Negro Blue Book* called it "one of the finest buildings owned by Negroes in the world." It has served as the headquarters of the Masons of the State of Florida Grand East, and the first black bank in Jacksonville, the Anderson Bank, also occupied one level. Over the years many black businesses used the building, including black dentists, physicians, insurance agents, and others.

Another site on the James Weldon Johnson Heritage Tour is the *FLORIDA TIMES UNION BUILDING* at 64–66 W. Bay Street on the southwest corner of the W. Bay Street and Laura Street. Johnson's first job as a youth was working for the newspaper, earning $2.50 a week as a paperboy. He then became office boy to the noted editor Charles H. Jones, who later became editor of *The New York World*. That first exposure to journalism began Johnson's life-long fascination for journalism, which led to his founding *The Daily American*, a weekly newspaper in Jacksonville that started in 1895 and was Florida's first-known daily newspaper for blacks, as well as serving as contributing editor to the *New York Age* in 1914.

Also on the James Weldon Johnson Heritage Tour is the site of the ST. JAMES HOTEL at 117 W. Duval Street. The hotel was on the site of what came to be called the St. James Building, which was built in 1911–12 to house the Cohen Brothers' Department Store from a design by noted Jacksonville Architect, Henry John Klutho. Built in 1869 and expanded over the years to six stories, the rambling wood-framed St. James Hotel was

the place where thousands of tourists stayed during the winter months. Because of his previous experience in the hospitality business in Nassau, **James Johnson**, the father of James Weldon Johnson, rose to the prominent position of headwaiter at the St. James Hotel. The young **James Weldon Johnson** frequently visited the hotel while his father worked there.

The TOLBERT HOUSE at 1665 Pearce Street is where **Susie Ella Middleton Tolbert** lived and worked for other African Americans after she moved from her birthplace in Chicago. She organized the Willing Workers Club and the Christian Endeavor Organization for her church, New Bethel AME. Her Garden Club efforts also beautified black neighborhoods around the city, and she provided needy students at nearby Edward Waters College free room and board. In 1951, fifty years after her death, school officials changed the name of New College Park Elementary School to SUSIE E. TOLBERT ELEMENTARY SCHOOL #128 at 1925 W. 13th Street to honor her.

The Ritz Theatre at 825 Davis Street between State and Union Streets northwest of downtown Jacksonville had an Art Deco style and neon lights which may have been among the earliest such fixtures in the city. Opened in 1929, at the time of the Depression, the theater contained spaces for shops and offices. The six-hundred-seat theater in the LaVilla neighborhood became the center for the arts, entertainment, and shopping activities of the black community. The theater, which closed in 1972 and was mostly demolished, has become part of the RITZ THEATRE AND LAVILLA MUSEUM, which is open Tuesday through Sunday. Phone: (904) 632-5555.

The CATHERINE STREET FIRE STATION #3 in Metropolitan Park, which used to be at 12 Catherine Street, replaced the nearby Fire Station #3, which the devastating fire of 1901 had destroyed. Opened in 1902, the new station with its large, arched door that was large enough for horse-drawn fire wagons was manned by black firemen until 1905, when an all-white crew took over. Officials decommissioned the unit in 1933 and began using the building as a storage facility for the Fire Department. Workers were to tear down the building in 1972 to make room for a new police administration building, but historians pointed out the significance of the site and convinced the authorities to build the new building around the old one. It then became a museum for the city's firefighting history. Tours by appointment. Phone: (904) 630-0618.

According to a four-page brochure available at that museum, "Black Firefighters: Jacksonville, Florida, the Early Years" by Ruth Graham Ray, twenty-two African Americans organized the volunteer Duval Hose Company in 1876 on Pine (now Main) and Ashley Streets. A paid department, Station Three, which was sometimes called Eastern Station-Regulars (colored), was organized in 1886 on E. Bay Street between Washington and Catherine Streets; the fire of 1901 destroyed that building, but workers rebuilt it in 1902 on Catherine Street. This account is from an inaccessible work entitled *Black Firefighters in Jacksonville, Florida 1850–1905* by Ruth Graham Ray and Jamie R. Graham.

The **AFRO-AMERICAN LIFE INSURANCE COMPANY** at 101 E. Union Street was built in 1956 and houses the offices of the company that **A. L. Lewis** helped found in 1901. As the oldest life insurance company in Florida and one of the most successful black businesses in the state, it helped thousands of blacks over the years. Other locations of the company have been 722 Main Street and 105 E. Union Street.

The importance of that insurance company and other similar ones throughout Florida and the South cannot be underestimated. According to the *Encyclopedia of Southern Culture*, the insurance companies established by blacks and catering to them "formed the heart of black financial networks, the cultural beginnings of which can be traced to mutual benefit societies and the church."

The burial insurance that such companies offered blacks superseded that which was offered by fraternal lodges and religious organizations. Not only did such insurance provide peace of mind to people who did not want their own deaths to pose serious financial hardships on their survivors, but the blacks who invested their own capital in such firms often profited, which led to a better life style, bigger homes, etc.

The **A.L. LEWIS MAUSOLEUM** in Memorial Cemetery on Moncrief Road near Edgewood Avenue was for the family of **Abraham Lincoln Lewis** (1865–1947), one of the founders of the Afro-American Industrial and Benefit Association, which later became the Afro-American Life Insurance Company, one of the largest black-owned businesses in Florida. Born into poverty in Madison, Florida, at the end of the Civil War, he moved with his family to Jacksonville, where

A.L. Lewis was the president of the Afro-American Life Insurance Company. *Florida State Archives*

The Old City Cemetery had a separate section for the burial of African Americans.

he began working in a lumber mill and saving his money. He worked there for over twenty years, eventually saving enough money to buy part of a shoe store. In 1901, he and six other blacks contributed $100 each to establish an insurance company to provide low-cost health and burial insurance to poor blacks in the city. Lewis also helped found the Negro Business League and the Negro Insurance Association and provided recreational facilities at American Beach on Amelia Island (see Chapter Forty-five). With the wealth he earned from his different companies, Lewis contributed generously to many funds, including scholarships for black students. He is honored with a Great Floridian plaque at Community Connections, A.L. Lewis Center, 3655 Ribault Scenic Drive.

Several black cemeteries in Jacksonville should be mentioned here. OLD CITY CEMETERY, which is bounded by E. Union, Ionia, Jessie, and Washington Streets, opened in 1852 and was the primary burial place for Jacksonvillians before 1880. Different segments of the population had separate sections, for example African Americans, Catholics, Confederate soldiers, Freedmen, Jews, and Masons. Some of the pioneer African Americans, such as **Clara White** and **Eartha M. M. White**, are buried there. The only mausoleum in the cem-

etery is for an African princess, **Laura Adorkor Kofey**. An early follower of **Marcus Garvey** and his Universal Negro Improvement Association, Mother Kofey formed a rival organization before she was murdered in Miami in 1928. Some seven thousand followers accompanied her funeral procession from Miami to Jacksonville.

MEMORIAL CEMETERY, SUNSET MEMORIAL CEMETERY, and PINEHURST CEMETERY on the north side, which are near Moncrief Road around Edgewood Avenue West and Avenue B, were developed between 1909 and 1928 and were owned by Memorial Cemetery Association, which A.L. Lewis formed to provide plots for blacks who were excluded by segregation from being buried in white cemeteries. **James "Charley Edd" Craddock**, the owner of the famous Two Spot nightclub on Moncrief Road and 45th Street, developed MOUNT OLIVE CEMETERY south of the other three cemeteries in 1946; his own mausoleum is in Sunset Memorial Cemetery. Those four cemeteries declined with neglect and with the opening of integrated cemeteries in the 1960s.

CITY CEMETERY is in the Oakland section of Jacksonville, a historic African American neighborhood dating back to 1869, when freedmen settled in the downtown part of the city where there was inexpensive housing and job opportunities. It stayed fairly independent until the city of Jacksonville annexed it and other African American neighborhoods like Brooklyn, Hansontown, and LaVilla. In the last quarter of the nineteenth century, many African Americans moved out of Oakland north to the community of Campbellton or Campbell's Addition to East Jacksonville.

One of the main churches in Oakland is the **ST. JOSEPH UNITED METHODIST CHURCH** at the southeast corner of Spearing Street and Jessie Street, just east of downtown Jacksonville. The church dates its beginnings to the influx of Northerners of different religious denominations who came South after the Civil War to minister to the educational and social needs of the freed slaves and impoverished whites. A minister from the Midwest who arrived even earlier, in 1864 during the war, was Rev. **John S. Swaim** who is also credited with establishing an African American congregation initially called Zion Methodist Episcopal Church, now **EBENEZER UNITED METHODIST CHURCH** at 9114 Norfolk Boulevard.

That last church is on the James Weldon Johnson Heritage Tour. Founded in 1881, Ebenezer United Methodist Church was originally located at 432 W. Ashley Street, near the intersection of W. Ashley Street and Clay Street adjacent to Old Stanton High School. During his youth in LaVilla, **James Weldon Johnson** frequently visited the church with his maternal grandmother, **Mary Barton**, a member of the church who encouraged young James to enter the ministry. Her daughter, **Helen Louise Johnson**, the mother of James Weldon Johnson, later joined the church and used her musical talents as choir director. James and Rosamond were members and musicians at Ebenezer United Methodist Church and shared their musical talents at Bethel Baptist Institute.

Ebenezer United Methodist Church became the church of Johnson's mother, **Helen Louis Johnson**, after being rebuffed at St. Johns Epis-copal Church on the northeast corner of E. Duval Street and N. Market Street. Having been a member of the Christ Church Cathedral in the more racially tolerant Bahamas, Johnson's mother attended a worship service at the local St. Johns Episcopal Church, where her beautiful soprano voice clearly stood out. After the service, other members of the congregation told her politely but insistently that she should worship elsewhere. After that, she never returned to any Episcopal Church and joined her mother, **Mary Barton**, at Ebenezer United Methodist Church.

Other churches in Oakland and later Campbell's Addition included **FIRST BAPTIST CHURCH OF OAKLAND, MOUNT OLIVE AME CHURCH, PLEASANT GROVE PRIMITIVE BAPTIST CHURCH, TRIUMPH THE CHURCH**, and **MOTHER MIDWAY AME CHURCH**, which many consider to be the oldest (1865) AME congregation in Florida. As segregation became widespread after Reconstruction, those and other African American churches became even more important in their communities, often functioning as the most significant social and cultural institution in the community and providing much-needed services in education and welfare.

Among the distinguished residents of Oakland and Campbell's Addition are several that should be included here.

The **JAMES JOHNSON BIRTHPLACE** on the northwest corner of Lee and Houston streets is where one of Florida's most distinguished blacks was born: **James Weldon Johnson** (1871–1938). His father, **James Johnson**, had arrived from Nassau, the Bahamas, in 1869 and bought a large lot with a wood-framed house at that site in the town of LaVilla. James Weldon Johnson was born in that house on June 17, 1871. In another house on the same site—a house that his father built there—James Weldon Johnson collaborated in 1899 with his brother **John Rosamond Johnson**, to produce the famous song *Lift Every Voice and Sing*, later recognized as the Negro National An-

James Weldon Johnson was an important educator, composer, and diplomat from Jacksonville. *Florida State Archives*

them. The brothers had produced the piece as part of a community celebration in honor of Abraham Lincoln's birthday on February 12. A chorus of five hundred school children were reportedly the first performers of the song, but where the performance took place is unknown, although it may have been at Old Stanton High School, Ebenezer United Methodist Church, Bethel Baptist Institutional Church, or the Florida Baptist Academy.

Young James Weldon Johnson attended Stanton Grade School and Atlanta University before returning to Jacksonville to serve as teacher and principal of Stanton High School; during his tenure there, Stanton became the first accredited black high school in Florida. He also became a lawyer, writer, newspaper man who started in Jacksonville *The Daily American* (the nation's first daily newspaper for blacks), U.S. consul to Venezuela and

Nicaragua, co-writer with his brother of a song entitled "Lift Every Voice and Sing" (which became the Negro National Anthem), and secretary of the National Association for the Advancement of Colored People (NAACP) (1916–1930). His most famous work, *God's Trombones: Seven Negro Sermons in Verse*, and his novel, *Autobiography of an Ex-Colored Man* (first published anonymously in 1912) were published in 1927. Johnson's poetry and American Negro spirituals continue to be the basis of African American theater productions. A plaque at Old Stanton High School, 521 W. Ashley Street, notes that he was named a Great Floridian in 2000. Johnson is honored today by the James Weldon Johnson Heritage Tour, an itinerary around Jacksonville of places associated with one of the city's most distinguished citizens.

Near the Johnson birthplace is another site on the James Weldon Johnson Heritage Tour: **OLD UNION TERMINAL** at 1034 W. Bay Street. As a young adult, Johnson used the terminal to ride the train to and from his home in Jacksonville to attend school in Atlanta and later to join his brother Rosamond in New York City. James Weldon Johnson's autobiography, *Along This Way*, notes how on those train trips he commented on changing racial attitudes in the South regarding public transportation. On one 1896 trip back to Jacksonville, he boarded a first-class car out of Charleston, South Carolina, but was told, when the train crossed into Georgia, to move to the segregated "Jim Crow Car" since Georgia had laws that outlawed whites and blacks riding in the same railroad car. When Johnson commented that a white sheriff and his criminally insane (white) prisoner occupied the segregated car, the conductor was forced to move the sheriff and his prisoner to the first-class car, much to the annoyance of the other passengers.

OLD STANTON HIGH SCHOOL at 521 W. Ashley Street is where **James Weldon Johnson** attended school and where he served as principal. Established in 1868 as the first public school for

James Weldon Johnson was principal at Stanton High School. *Florida State Archives*

black children in Jacksonville and named for Edwin M. Stanton, an abolitionist and President Lincoln's Secretary of War, the school began when the blacks of Jacksonville bought the land from Ossian B. Hart, the tenth governor of Florida and son of Jacksonville's founder. In 1869, financing from the Freedman's Bureau built a school there. Fires destroyed that structure, first in 1882 and then in 1901, but insurance money was enough to rebuild it each time, although at a lower level than before. While Johnson served as principal there from 1894 to around 1904 or 1905, he and the staff added an additional grade each year until the school became the only high school for blacks in Jacksonville.

When trustees of the school realized the facility was no longer adequate for its students, they sued the Board of Public Instruction in 1915, at which time the board agreed to build a new, three-story school, which was finally finished in 1917. It served as the place where many blacks of Duval County received their education. A 1965 court ruling ended segregated schools in the county, and the building was closed down in 1971, later becoming a multi-use community building.

Another site on the James Weldon Johnson Heritage Tour is **SHILOH METROPOLITAN BAPTIST CHURCH** at 1118 W. Beaver Street and one of the largest Baptist Churches in Jacksonville. It began in 1875 and moved into a small wooden building in LaVilla about a decade later. From 1881 until the late 1890s, James Johnson, the father of James Weldon Johnson, served as minister of the small congregation at 115 Davis Street, which was in the "red light district" of the city and therefore a place where few other ministers were willing to serve the spiritual needs of sick and dying prostitutes in nearby houses.

While James Weldon Johnson was teaching, he spent eighteen months studying law under local attorney, Thomas A. Ledwith, at his offices located at the Law Exchange Building across from the courthouse. With Ledwith's encouragement, Johnson took and successfully passed the Florida Bar examination held under the direction of Judge R. M. Call at the Old Duval County Courthouse, located at the northeast corner of N. Market Street and W. Forsyth Street. The building was eventually replaced by the Duval County Courthouse and Armory (the Lanier Building) at 107 N. Market Street. Although other African American lawyers were in practice in Jacksonville at that time, Johnson was the first black to be admitted to the Florida Bar through an open examination in a state court.

Another local site on the James Weldon Johnson Heritage Tour is the **OLD DUVAL COUNTY ARMORY** at 851 N. Market Street. Completed in 1916, the armory had two incidents mentioned in Johnson's autobiography, *Along This Way.* Soon after it opened, some African Americans made plans to attend a performance of Samuel Coleridge-Taylor's *Hiawatha* that a group of local white women was sponsoring. Johnson arranged with the local organizing committee for the group of citizens to attend the performance in the large auditorium of the new armory. Unfortunately the armory's local military commander, who stated that blacks should not be allowed in the auditorium, vetoed that arrangement even though, ironically and probably unbeknownst to the officer, *Hiawatha* was the work of an African American composer. Johnson returned to the armory a few years later during a Liberty Bond drive, where both white and black speakers addressed a mixed audience to gain support for the First World War, which was fought to make the world, in the words of President Woodrow Wilson, "Safe for Democracy."

Sharon Coon and her late son, **James Lee Coon Jr.**, established the James Weldon Johnson Heritage Tour in 1997 to honor a man who played a major role in the history of African Americans in Jacksonville. Ms. Coon also helped convince state officials to induct Johnson into the Florida Artists' Hall of Fame, which occurred in 2000. She established the James Weldon Johnson National Arts Institute in 1997 to preserve and present the rich cultural heritage of Johnson. She and her son James also established TOTS 'N' TEENS THEATRE, Inc., in 1985 to enrich the lives of African American children and youth through the arts and academics. (For group tours call (904) 353-7350.)

Another African American newspaper man associated with Jacksonville is **John Willis Menard** (1838–1893), who was born in Illinois, worked at the U.S. Department of the Interior during the Civil War, moved to New Orleans (1865), and was elected to the U.S. Congress (1868), but was prevented from serving his term by bigoted white members of the Congress. He moved to Jacksonville in the early 1870s, served in the Florida House of Representatives (1874) and as a Duval County justice of the peace (1874–77). He had a collection of poems, *Lays in Summer Lands*, published in 1879, then moved to Key West (see Chapter Forty-four). There he became inspector of customs, and in 1882 took over a newspaper, *Key West News*, which he later renamed *Florida News* and relocated to Jacksonville when politicians removed him from his Key West post in 1885. He changed the name to *Southern Leader* and continued working on it until he died in Jacksonville in 1893.

Another important school was the BOYLAN-HAVEN SCHOOL, which the Missionary Society of the Methodist Episcopal Church founded in 1886 as Boylan Home School. It provided black girls educational and cultural opportunities and fostered Christian character. Miss Harriet Emerson, a white missionary from New Hampshire, organized the school and became its first director. The school was named after an early donor from Newark, New Jersey, Ann Degroot, whose maiden name was Boylan. At first it taught practical homemaking skills like cooking and sewing to a small group of girls, and then later added elementary and high school classes. Miss Artell Beaver from Montana became the second director.

The school, which at one time occupied the entire south side of the 900 block of W. Duval Street and was called the Boylan Industrial Home and School, moved in 1910 from the LaVilla section of Jacksonville to a block bounded by Odessa, Bridier, Franklin, and Jessie Streets in East Jacksonville. In 1932, the school merged with Haven Home of Savannah, Georgia, to become Boylan-Haven School and continued to attract black girls until it closed in 1959 and moved to South Carolina, where it merged with Mather Academy, a coeducational preparatory school.

The broad curriculum of the Jacksonville school included basic subjects like Bible study, English, foreign languages, history, math, and music, as well as cooking and sewing. Its alumnae include many successful college administrators, creative artists, journalists, lawyers, physicians, public officials, and teachers.

One of the graduates of Boylan-Haven School

Mary Littlejohn Singleton. *Florida State Archives*

was **Mary Littlejohn Singleton** (1926–1980), who also graduated from Florida A&M University in Tallahassee and became a teacher. In 1967, three years after her husband, **Isadore Singleton**, died, she ran for the Jacksonville City Council and won, one of the first African Americans, along with **Sallye Mathis**, to sit on the City Council in over sixty years. In 1972, Ms. Singleton was elected to the Florida House of Representatives and worked hard for educational issues. In 1976, she was appointed to the post of Florida State Supervisor of Elections. In 1978, former governor Claude Kirk asked her to run as his lieutenant governor, but they did not win the election. In 1979, she became the director of the state's Banking and Finance Division, a position she held until her death in 1980.

The school building was torn down in 1971 and is now the site of the Oakland Terrace Apartments at Jessie and Franklin Streets.

The emphasis on personal hygiene and train-ing for the general care of the sick, which the Boylan School inculcated in its students, led to the founding of **BREWSTER HOSPITAL** and the **BREWSTER HOSPITAL SCHOOL OF NURSING** in 1900. Originally situated at 915 W. Monroe Street, the hospital and school of nursing were the first such institutions for African Americans in Florida and two of the earliest in the South. The site was origi-nally the home of Hans Christian Peters, a meat dealer. His family sold the house in 1901 to the Women's Home Missionary Society of the Meth-odist Church, which used a $1,500 gift from Mrs. George A. Brewster to establish the hospital and school of nursing. The hospital moved to other, larger facilities in the Oakland section of East Jacksonville in 1910. It finally closed in 1966, two years after the 1964 Civil Rights Act, which opened the city's other hospitals to blacks. One can still see the beautiful Victorian gingerbread porches on the building, which was built in the nineteenth century, is on the National Register of Historic Places, and today serves as a private resi-dence. In 2005, workers relocated the building to the northeast corner of W. Monroe Street and N. Davis Street.

The **CLARA WHITE MISSION** at 611–13 W. Ashley Street honors **Clara English White** (1845–1920) and her daughter, **Eartha Mary Magdalene White** (1876–1974). Eartha, herself the eldest daughter of a former slave, nursed sol-diers during the Spanish-American War in 1898, taught school in a poor country school in Duval County, worked for the city's Afro-American Life Insurance Company, and encouraged construc-tion of the first public school for African Ameri-cans in the community of Bayard in Duval Coun-ty. After the terrible 1901 fire which destroyed much of the city, Ms. White became a social worker in the black community and started the Union Benevolent Association to help those in need. In 1922, she honored her mother by open-ing the Clara White Mission, which helped many during the Great Depression. In 1936, she helped

Eartha M. M. White. *University of North Florida*

secure a tuberculosis rest home for blacks and also helped obtain better prison facilities for inmates. The three-story framed building at 613 W. Ashley Street is a living memorial to two great women. A plaque there notes that Eartha was named a Great Floridian in 2000. Phone: (904) 354-4162.

A nearby building is GENOVAR'S HALL at 638–644 W. Ashley Street. Built between 1891 and 1895 for the grocery store of Minorcan descendant Sebastian Genovar, the three-story building has housed African American businesses like the Lenape Tavern/Bar and the Wynn Hotel.

Another site associated with Eartha M. M. White is the large building attached to a feed-store building at 7420 Roscoe Avenue. It used to be BAYARD SCHOOLHOUSE, where Eartha White taught school for several years, beginning in 1899. She convinced Bartolo Genovar to donate land, organized black volunteers into building a schoolhouse, and had others contribute building materials. That one-room wooden schoolhouse, the oldest public school building in Duval County, served many black students for decades before it became a church and, in 1985, part of the feed-store building.

Reverend Samuel B. Darnell and Rev. Alfred Cookman are honored in the name of DARNELL-COOKMAN MIDDLE SCHOOL at 1701 Davis Street North. Rev. Samuel B. Darnell and a group of northern Methodists began the DARNELL INSTITUTE on the corner of Beaver and Hogan Streets in 1872 as the first school in Florida established by the Methodist Episcopal Church's Freedmen's Aid Society. The Freedmen's Bureau, which had been established after the Civil War to set up schools for those slaves whom Emancipation had freed, provided the funds for such schools. That particular institute/school was closely allied to Ebenezer Methodist Episcopal Church. Rev. Darnell lived in the parsonage of the church.

Associated with Georgia's Clark University, Cookman was one of the first institutions for the higher education of African Americans in the state and for a long time was the only school of its kind in Florida. The students included thousands of young black men and women, some of whom were ex-slaves. When the 1901 fire destroyed all of the buildings, officials moved the location of the campus outside of town for safety. A friend of Rev. Darnell, Mr. Cookman, who visited Jacksonville each winter, provided money to Rev. Darnell to buy the property where Darnell-Cookman School is today. In thanks for the funds, officials named the school COOKMAN INSTITUTE. Around 250 students attended the new school, which had classes through high school.

Many students trained there to become teachers and ministers and professionals. Among the school's many distinguished graduates were AME Bishop **Abram Grant**; **L.W. Livingston**, U.S. Consul to Haiti; pioneer funeral director **Lawton**

L. Pratt; **A. Philip Randolph**, founder of the Brotherhood of Sleeping Car Porters and an important figure in the Civil Rights movement (see Chapter Fifty-four for more about him); and **W. S. Sumter**, founder of the Union Mutual Insurance Company. (For more about another graduate of Cookman Institute, **James Dean**, see Chapter Forty-four.) In 1923, the school merged with the Daytona Normal and Industrial Institute of Daytona Beach and the two became Bethune-Cookman College.

The Duval County Board of Public Instruction later purchased the property and built the current Darnell-Cookman Middle School. Ms. **Eartha M. M. White** suggested the name of the new school, Darnell-Cookman, which kept alive links to the former school there.

Ms. White also recommended that the name of Franklin Street School be changed to MATTHEW GILBERT. That school at 1424 Franklin Street, now a middle school, was built in 1926 in the Italian Renaissance style to serve the students in Oakland and East Jacksonville communities and was the second high school built for African Americans in Duval County, after Old Stanton High

School. One of its graduates is **Robert "Bullet" Bob Hayes**, who won two Olympic gold medals in track and played professional football for the Dallas Cowboys (1965–74). The Florida Baptist Academy, founded in the 1890s by Bethel Baptist Institutional Church under the pastorate of Reverend **Matthew W. Gilbert**, had first occupied the site. The music director of the academy was **J. Rosamond Johnson**, brother of **James Weldon Johnson** (see more about the Johnsons on page 54). During his visit to Jacksonville in 1905, President Theodore Roosevelt visited the Florida Baptist Academy and gave a speech to an assembly that included several thousand African Americans from the community.

The Florida Baptist Academy later moved to St. Augustine to become the Florida Normal and Industrial Institute (see Chapter Fifty-five), before relocating to Dade County in 1962 to become Florida Memorial College (see Chapter Forty-three).

Once known as Barrs Field, the Myrtle Avenue Ball Park, and Joseph H. Durkee Athletic Field, JAMES P. SMALL MEMORIAL STADIUM at 11200 W. 8th Street on the corner of N. Myrtle Avenue has

Matthew Gilbert School.

James P. Small Park.

had sporting events for the past hundred years. Organized professional, semi-professional, and amateur baseball teams have played there since 1911. Baseball teams such as the professional Philadelphia Athletics and Brooklyn Dodgers used it for spring training, and later teams like the Jacksonville Red Caps of the Negro Southern Leagues played there. City officials bought the field in 1926 from **J. H. Durkee**, nine years later built a steel and brick grandstand, and then expanded that facility in 1937 to what it looks like today. The field and grandstand are the oldest such sports facilities in Jacksonville and one of the oldest in Florida.

Under an earlier name, **DURKEE FIELD** was one of the earliest sites where minor-league baseball in the South was integrated. Before then, though, segregation reigned. For example, in 1946, a year before he broke the color line in modern major-league baseball, **Jackie Robinson** played for the Montreal Royals, a farm team of the Brooklyn Dodgers. Because he was on the roster of the Montreal Royals, Jacksonville officials would not allow the team to play at Durkee Field.

In 1953, the Jacksonville Braves, along with the Savannah team, was the first team in the Class

A-South Atlantic League to break the color line in minor-league baseball when the new team owner, Samuel Wolfson, hired three African American players: **Henry "Hank" Aaron**, **Horace Garner**, and **Felix Mantilla**. So many fans turned out to see Aaron and his black teammates that the team set attendance records, especially for black fans, who took great pride in the integration of the league. Durkee and the other ball fields were segregated, but the excellent play by Aaron and the other two blacks helped get people used to the integration of the league.

The nineteen-year-old Aaron had to endure a full season of verbal abuse from bigots and had to stay in private homes apart from the white ballplayers, but he excelled on the field, hitting twenty-two home runs and achieving a .362 batting average. He led the Braves to win the pennant that season and was named Most Valuable Player in the league. He also married a Jacksonville woman. The next year, 1954, he went to the Milwaukee Braves and eventually broke Babe Ruth's career home run record by hitting 755 home runs in his career.

Horace Garner never made it to the majors, but Mantilla did, playing for the Milwaukee

Hank Aaron played for the Jacksonville Braves in 1953.
Florida State Archives

of the 1890s was the Roman Cities, which had as a pitcher **James Weldon Johnson**, who would go on to a distinguished career in education and international service (see page 55).

Just to the south of where Durkee Field is today was a section of Jacksonville begun by black veterans of the Civil War. Founded by a surgeon, Dr. **Daniel D. Hanson**, and known as HANSONTOWN, the communal farming operation enabled the blacks to grow crops, market them for a good price, and then pool their resources to buy more land.

Between Hansontown and the St. Johns River was the section called LAVILLA, a mile-square section that has deteriorated due to neglect and poverty. Historian Patricia Kenney points out that the settlement, which took its name in 1851 from a nearby plantation house called LaVilla, began with the arrival of emancipated slaves after the Civil War. Some of the first black residents were ex-slaves who had escaped or been freed by Northern troops and then joined the Union forces to fight against the Confederacy, even occupying Jacksonville for a time. When the war ended, some of those soldiers stayed in Jacksonville and brought their families to begin a new life. During the years of its incorporation (1869–87) LaVilla prospered and allowed the local blacks to elect their own officials, build a decent infrastructure, and land good jobs. After annexation to Jacksonville, the section began a slow, steady decline because of a lack of political power and the loss of jobs.

South of LaVilla and along the St. Johns River is another place on the James Weldon Johnson Heritage Tour: MEMORIAL PARK in the 1600 block of Riverside Avenue. Right after the 1901 fire which destroyed much of downtown Jacksonville, Johnson, who was working at a commissary to serve victims of the fire, agreed to an interview by an African American female writer with a very light complexion who was writing about the fire and its effects on the black population. Johnson arranged for the interview to take place away from

Braves (1956–61), New York Mets (1962), Boston Red Sox (1963–65), and Houston Astros (1966).

In 1985, officials changed the name of the field to honor Stanton High School instructor and coach **James P. Small**.

Baseball has always been popular in Jacksonville, which hosted the first major-league exhibition game in Florida and the first spring-training site (both in 1888). In 1883, the city had a black team, the Athletics, who were good enough to be invited by the national Colored Baseball Association to play a tournament in Savannah, Georgia. In 1891, Jacksonville hosted the first annual convention of the Southern League of Colored Baseball, which had a series of games to determine the state champion. The major local black team the downtown area and in the cooler confines of the new waterfront park recently purchased by the city. Mistaking the writer as white, the street-car conductor that delivered them to the Riverside neighborhood reported their presence to the militia patrolling downtown. A hostile group of soldiers quickly surrounded Johnson and threatened to kill him on the spot, but, fortunately, the officer in command quickly established control, and the provost marshal later released Johnson and his companion. That incident greatly disturbed Johnson for weeks and contributed to his leaving Jacksonville for good.

A section of Jacksonville near Jacksonville University, Arlington, is the site of a unique facility in Florida: a film studio that made movies featuring African Americans. When several major movie studios established their winter headquarters in Jacksonville in the early twentieth century to take advantage of the warm climate and relatively inexpensive costs, they began making silent films. Although most of those film companies soon moved west to California, one white filmmaker, Richard Norman, bought the bankrupt Eagle Film Studios complex in Arlington across the river from downtown Jacksonville.

Between 1920 and 1928 the **NORMAN STUDIOS** produced at least eight features starring black actors. Wishing to capitalize on the growing African American market, he changed one full-length movie of his, *The Green-Eyed Monster*, a popular romance set in the railroad industry, from an all-white cast to an all-black cast. Unlike other filmmakers, who often made racist movies about blacks, Norman treated his actors with respect and depicted blacks, not as stock characters that were stereotypical and unflattering, but as ordinary people in different situations.

The "race" movies, as they were known, that Norman wrote and produced, like those of his African American contemporaries such as the Lincoln Motion Picture Company and Oscar Micheaux, were different from racist films. Instead of degrading racist travesties, these were positive stories featuring black actors described in Norman's publicity as "splendidly assuming different roles."

One of his films made in Arlington, *The Flying Ace* (1926), was an action-romance filmed in the Arlington studios that took advantage of the widespread interest in black aviators such as **Eugene Bullard** and **Bessie Coleman**. Unfortunately, Coleman, the first black woman licensed pilot, died that year in a fiery crash over Jacksonville.

The Norman Studio, located at 6337 Arlington Road in the Arlington section of Jacksonville, is on at least one tour of Black Jacksonville.

Among the county personages recognized in The Great Floridians 2000 program, which recognized distinguished individuals throughout the state, was **David H. Dwight Sr.** (1882–1959), who led the way for African Americans in Jacksonville to become part of the Boy Scouts of America. His leadership led to African American Scouts being granted the right to participate in scouting activities, attend camp, and wear the official Boy Scout uniform. The first Boy Scout camp in the state, initiated during his tenure, served African American Scouts in Jacksonville and throughout Florida. As a Scout, he achieved the position of assistant regional director of scouting activities for the southeast region. He was the first African American in America to receive the Boy Scouts of America's highest council award, the Silver Beaver, in 1936. Dwight was one of the founders of the National Alliance of Postal Employees in 1912. In the 1940s he founded the Duval County Democratic Alliance, which aided voter registration in Jacksonville. His Great Floridian plaque is located at the North Florida Council, Boy Scouts of America, 521 S. Edgewood Avenue.

A schoolhouse in nearby Jacksonville Beach is the **JACKSONVILLE BEACH COLORED SCHOOL** at 4th Avenue and 4th Street South. That 1939 building was once the only school for African Americans east of the Intracoastal Waterway in the area and may have been the outgrowth of a school begun there by a former slave. The building serves today as an educational facility, museum, and genealogical center.

Just north of Jacksonville at the northern end of Fort George Island off Highway A1A is the **KINGSLEY PLANTATION STATE HISTORIC SITE**. As one of the few remaining examples of the plantation system of Territorial Florida, the plantation has a large house where Zephaniah Kingsley (1765–1843) directed a group of slaves in growing sea island cotton, sweet potatoes, sugarcane, and citrus from 1813 until 1839. Kingsley was married to an African princess, **Anna Madgigine Jai**, but later freed her, and she became the owner of her own farm and twelve slaves. She had four children with Kingsley and managed his planta-tion for twenty-five years. When Florida became part of the United States in 1821, conditions became much worse for her, and she took her children to Haiti, where her husband had established a refuge for free blacks. At the site above Jacksonville one can take a guided tour of the main house and see the slave cabins. Guides can explain details of nineteenth-century plantation life, including stories of whites, slaves, and free blacks. The grounds are open daily (except for New Year's Day, Thanksgiving, and Christmas) 9 A.M.–5 P.M.; free admission. Phone: (904) 251-3537.

The Kingsley Plantation is a good example of what the plantation system was like in nineteenth-century Florida.

16.

Escambia County

Escambia County, along with St. Johns County, was one of the first two counties established in Florida in 1821. The name Escambia probably goes back to the Native Americans, but its meaning is unknown. It had a population of 294,410 in the 2000 census, 63,004 (21.4%) of whom were African Americans.

Pensacola

One of the oldest settlements in Florida, Pensacola traces its European background to Don Tristan de Luna y Arellano, whom the Spanish appointed Governor General of Florida. He established a small settlement in the area in 1559, but a hurricane, famine, and poor leadership caused the settlers to give up and leave. A century later the Spanish returned to establish a stronghold there, and the English also settled there in the late 1700s.

The first blacks to live in the Pensacola area probably came with the Tristan de Luna expedition in 1559. Over the next few centuries blacks settled in the area to work as soldiers or as farmers, fishermen, and laborers. During Spanish rule in West Florida, those blacks who were free owned property, operated businesses, worked at different trades, and experienced less discrimination than did slaves. Many blacks worked in the lumber industry, building Spanish fortifications and much later, when the United States took over Florida, the buildings and houses of the Americans. Life was hard for blacks and much discrimination existed.

One abolitionist who tried to help them was Jonathan Walker, a man from Massachusetts who came to Florida in the 1800s to try to help the slaves. He took a group of slaves in his boat from

Pensacola, Florida, to try to make it to freedom in Nassau, but was captured near Key West in July 1844. Officials took him back to Pensacola where the letters "SS" for slave stealer were burned into his right hand. The New England poet, John Greenleaf Whittier, wrote a poem entitled "The Branded Hand" about that incident.

Blacks also worked in the bricklaying industry, building structures like Fort Pickens, and eventually as physicians, attorneys, and journalists. By 1900 43% of the total work force in Pensacola was black. The city had two private black schools, black barbers who served both races, and many black professionals. The races seemed to be getting along well.

One of the city's best-known blacks was **Matthew M. Lewey**, the owner and publisher of *The Florida Sentinel,* at one time the South's largest black newspaper. He had established the *Sentinel* with **Josiah Walls** in Gainesville in 1887 and took it with him when he moved to Pensacola in 1894. The newspaper, which he published in Pensacola and sent throughout the South, eventually became the *Tampa Sentinel-Bulletin* and is the oldest black paper published continuously in the state. He served as the first president of the Florida Business League, an association that was geared to help blacks in business.

The association invited Dr. **Booker T. Wash-**

ington to Pensacola in 1913, and he was so impressed by the city that he wrote in his book, *The Negro in Business*, that the city was a "typical Negro business community" with its many opportunities for blacks. Among the black businessmen were **Sam Charles**, who owned a shoe store on Palafox Street; **D. J. Cunningham**, who owned the Excelsior grocery; and **G.B. Green**, who operated a furniture store.

When the city suffered an economic slump and a doubling of the white population forced workers to compete for a dwindling number of jobs, a bitterness between the races rose up to destroy any good feeling that had existed before. The city council passed a Jim Crow ordinance for streetcars, restaurants, and railroad cars, and downtown merchants forced black businesses to relocate to the Belmont-DeVilliers area.

Blacks had many restrictions placed on them in Pensacola. Historian James McGovern wrote, "In a city where people associated primarily on the basis of similarities of wealth, status, residence, ethnic make up and color, blacks became Pensacola's most restricted and publicly ghettoized group. . . . Local businessmen, who hoped to put politics on a more efficient basis, preferred to minimize political participation by Negroes."

Booker T. Washington was the namesake of two important schools in Pensacola. The first, BOOKER T. WASHINGTON HIGH SCHOOL at 1421 E. Cross Street, played an important role in the education of young African Americans in the twentieth century. Among its graduates, one in particular needs to be mentioned here: **William E. Allen** (1903–1981). After being born on N. A Street in Pensacola and graduating from Booker T. Washington, he went on to earn his B.S. and M.D. degrees from Howard University. Among his accomplishments were these: was the first black to be certified in radiology by the American Board of Radiology (1935); was the first black Fellow elected by the American College of Radiology; created the first residency for the School

Older residents like this woman at a school in Pensacola in 1935 learned how to read and write for the first time late in life. *Florida State Archives*

of Radiologic Technology at Homer G. Phillips Hospital; was the first black officer from the city of St. Louis to enlist in the U.S. Army; was the first certified black radiologist in military service; was one of the first two blacks to be appointed as a consultant to the Secretary of War; was responsible for the first cobalt treatment unit to be introduced in Western Africa (1974); and was the first black to receive the American College of Radiology's highest honor, the Gold Medal. After retiring from the teaching staff at both St. Louis and Washington universities, he died in St. Louis in 1981.

Booker T. Washington was commemorated in the naming of BOOKER T. WASHINGTON JUNIOR COLLEGE, which began in 1949 as the first black junior college in Florida when the Escambia County School Board added a thirteenth grade to Booker T. Washington High School. One of the black men who helped inspire the school was Dr. **Simon W. Boyd**, the first dentist in the city to use gas for oral surgery and one who had a biracial practice. The School Board combined the junior college and the senior high school under one administrator and called it the Washington School Center. It served the black students in the community and on the naval base. The naval base and other government facilities, in fact, were powerful forces behind the founding of the two-year college because officials there needed skilled workers and artisans. The founding president of the junior college was Dr. **Garrett T. Wiggins**, formerly dean of the graduate school at Texas State College (now Texas Southern University) and the only educator in northwest Florida with an earned doctorate. He served as principal of Booker T. Washington High School and dean of the junior college, which had six teachers. About seventy-five percent of those enrolling chose the college parallel program rather than the vocational program, which included homemaking and business courses.

In 1965, just before the school merged with Pensacola Junior College (PJC), a white school that had been founded in 1948—one year before the black junior college—Booker T. Washington Junior College had 361 students. The enrollment figures, which included college parallel courses and vocational courses, for Washington Junior College were as follows:

    1957–58: 232 students
    1958–59: 205 students
    1959–60: 208 students
    1960–61: 212 students
    1961–62: 235 students
    1962–63: 233 students
    1963–64: 272 students
    1964–65: 361 students

When the school merged with Pensacola Junior College in the mid-1960s, the seven faculty of Washington Junior College joined the integrated college staff or the local public school system, and Dr. Wiggins, the president of Washington, became the Director of Research at PJC. While the faculty were able to find places of employment, the black students at Washington, as at other newly integrated junior colleges in Florida, declined in numbers. In 1968, state officials became so alarmed at the falling numbers of black college students that they sent a memo to all junior college presidents urging that they recruit more black students. In many cases the integrated colleges had not had an effective recruiting office or programs geared to minority students.

Part of that decline in numbers may have been due to a reluctance on the part of the black students to enter the white college world or a poor academic preparation in their own high schools or financial difficulties that precluded their attending the new school. Those integrated junior colleges that took a personal interest in minority students, who placed them in part-time jobs, and who instituted a wide student financial program did well in attracting minority students, but it took a concerted effort on the part of the colleges to begin such programs.

Only in the 1970s and 1980s, with the passage of federal civil rights laws and the efforts of public officials did relations between the two races improve. In 1991, for example, the Society for the Preservation of Pensacola Black History helped sponsor the first annual Enshrinement Ceremonies for Pensacola's Black Americans. The African American Heritage Society, Inc., has exhibits and programs throughout the year dealing with African Americans.

The 2000 census indicated that Pensacola had a population of 56,255, of whom 17,203 (31%) were black.

Among the places in the city associated with African Americans are several that should be mentioned here. The **JULEE COTTAGE MUSEUM** at 210 E. Zaragoza Street in the heart of the Historic Pensacola Village was the home of a free black woman, **Julee Panton**, who used the money she earned from land speculations to help other blacks obtain their freedom. Local historians have

The Julee Cottage Museum is the Center for Black Heritage in Pensacola's Seville Square Historical District.

moved the cottage, one of the city's oldest surviving wooden buildings, from its original location on W. Zaragoza Street and turned it into the Center for Black Heritage, complete with exhibits, documents, and photographs, to tell the little-known story of blacks in Pensacola. The cottage is part of the city's Preservation Board's "living village" in the Seville Square Historical District, which mixes businesses, residences, and museums in the heart of old Pensacola.

Julee Panton bought the cypress house, which was probably built between 1790 and 1800, in 1808, which was in the last Spanish period and thirteen years before the United States acquired Florida from Spain. Blacks continuously owned the house until the Civil War and then after the war until the 1970s, at which time the Preservation Society acquired it. Displays in the museum-cottage show how Pensacola blacks differed from plantation blacks, how the former were craftsmen, tailors, ironworkers, and bricklayers. Hours of operation are 10 A.M.–3:30 P.M., Monday through Saturday; (904) 444-8586.

SAINT MICHAEL'S CREOLE BENEVOLENT ASSOCIATION HALL at 416 E. Government Street is

an 1896 building that housed a benevolent association established by Creoles in 1878. Since the mid-nineteenth century the term "Creole" designated one of a racially mixed background, usually black with French or Spanish. The association gave members financial help during sickness, paid doctor bills and expenses for medicines, and provided death benefits to the family members of those enrolled. Members dissolved the association in 1971 when their numbers were dwindling. Workers restored the building in 1972, but it is a private residence today that is not open to the public.

The **DANIEL "CHAPPIE" JAMES JR. BIRTHPLACE** at 1606 N. Alcaniz Street is the place where the country's first black general in the Armed Services was born. In that house his mother also ran a school for black children. **Daniel "Chappie" James Jr.,** (1920–1978) grew up in Pensacola, the naval aviation capital of the United States, and dreamed of flying in one of the airplanes he saw every day. After graduating from high school, he attended Tuskegee Institute in Alabama, where he played football and basketball. While there, he joined a Civilian Pilot Training Program and eventually the Army Air Corps. He flew as a fight-

The site of the birthplace of General Daniel "Chappie" James, Jr.

A memorial to General James in Pensacola.

er pilot in the Korean Conflict and the Vietnam War and became the Commander of the North American Air Defense Command. In 1975, he became the first black four-star general in our history. A plaque honoring him is at the **DANIEL JAMES STATE OFFICE BUILDING**, 160 Governmental Center.

Today all that remains of the house where he was born are three concrete steps with the words "Chappie's First Steps" painted on them. Those steps led to the house where his mother raised him and where she taught many black children of the area. An article entitled "Miss Lillie's School" by a local author described how **Lillie James** operated her school, the Lillie A. James School, from the 1930s until the late 1950s. Among those who attended the school were doctors **Ralph Boyd, S. W. Boyd, E. S. Cobb**, and **Thomas James**; Mrs. **Lillie Frazier**, Mrs. **Pansey Harris**, Mrs. **Mamie Hixson**, Mrs. **Glorida Hunter**, Mr. **Lawrence**

Scott, and Dr. **Robert Walker**; and countless other teachers and business leaders, all of whom heard Mrs. James repeat over and over again, "Never let anyone your size beat you doing anything." Alcaniz Street is one of the major streets in the city and is between I-110 and Davis Street. The site of "Chappie's First Steps" is on the east side of Alcaniz Street between Mallory and Moreno Streets, eight blocks north of Cervantes Street (U.S. 90). A plaque honoring Lillie A. James is at the "Chappie James" Judicial Building, Governmental Center.

The **MOUNT ZION BAPTIST CHURCH** was organized in 1880 at Number Two Hall on Tarragona Street, Pensacola. After Rev. **Joseph Cook** conducted services for about a year, Rev. **Daniel Washington** became pastor. As the congregation grew in number, the members raised enough funds to buy from the St. Luke Society a lot on Alcaniz Street, west side, between Gregory and Wright.

Under the guidance of pastors **James Banks, C. J. Hardy, G. W. Raiford**, and others, the congregation increased to over six hundred and built a large building. The church is located at the northeast corner of the intersection of W. Jackson Street and Coyle Street eleven streets above Main Street, two streets below Cervantes Street (U.S. 90), and six blocks west of Palafox Street. It is the second oldest African American church in Pensacola.

Other sites of importance to blacks are the ELLA JORDAN CITY WIDE WOMEN'S CLUB BUILDING on the corner of C and La Rua Streets, a building founded by Mrs. **Ella Jordan** in 1930 and used as a safe haven for homeless girls in the area and also a meeting place for black women's clubs in the city; the BELMONT-DEVILLIERS NEIGHBORHOOD, where black businesses flourished during the time of Jim Crow laws; ST. JOSEPH'S CATHOLIC CHURCH, established for blacks and creoles; and the CORRINE JONES RECREATION CENTER, which honors a woman who inspired many local black youth.

The AFRICAN AMERICAN HERITAGE CENTER at 200 Church Street has exhibits and cultural programs, as well as being a resource center for promoting African American heritage and culture. The building that houses it was built in 1895. Open Monday–Friday, 10 A.M.–4 P.M. Phone: (850) 469-1299.

JOHN THE BAPTIST CHURCH at 101 N. 10th Avenue is the only surviving evidence of Hawkshaw, an African American community. The church building dates back to 1847, before the American Civil War.

The first members inducted into the Northwest Florida Afro-American Hall of Fame in 1989 were a distinguished group: **Zebulon Elijah**, the first black member of the Florida House of Representatives (1871–73) and the first black Pensacola postmaster (1874); former Florida A&M University football coach, **A. S. "Jake" Gaither**; General **Daniel "Chappie" James Jr.**; civil rights activist **H. K. Matthews**; retired educator Dr. **Vernon McDaniel**, who sought equal pay for black teachers; **John Sunday**, a wealthy community leader who had served as a first sergeant in the Union Army, Escambia legislator (1874), and city alderman (1878–80); and **Thomas deSaille Tucker**, an attorney appointed by the governor in 1887 to serve as superintendent of the Normal School for Colored Students, the forerunner of Florida A&M University.

More recent black Pensacolans who have done well on the national scene are athletes **Emmitt Smith** of the Dallas Cowboys football team, **Roy Jones Jr.,** a boxer; pianist **Ida Goodson**; and saxophonist **Wally "The Cat" Mercer**.

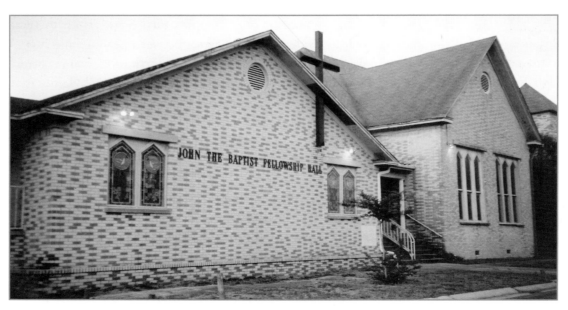

John the Baptist Memorial Hall. The church dates back to 1847.

17.
Flagler County

Flagler County, established in 1917 and honoring Henry Flagler, the great developer of the east coast of the state, had a population of 49,832 in the 2000 census, 4,385 (8.8%) of whom were African Americans. The county is one of the fastest-growing in the country, mostly due to the growth of the city of Palm Coast, which has about sixty thousand residents and which may have as many as 250,000 when it stops growing.

Interestingly, the county delegation that went to Tallahassee when the county was being established wanted to name it Moody County in honor of the Moody Brothers, who helped develop the county. Because the brothers did not want the name of the county named after themselves, they convinced the delegation to name it after their friend, Henry Flagler. Although Flagler never visited the county that would bear his name, he did buy up the narrow-gauge railroad tracks that were there, changed them to standard gauge, and continued the railroad to Ormond and then points further south.

Bunnell

Local officials built a school for African American children in the late 1950s, the CARVER SCHOOL, in an area south of the present courthouse. The school had twelve grades and consolidated many smaller black schools in the county, except for the one in Espanola (see below). In the early 1960s, officials built a gymnasium near the school. Today the school is gone, having been torn down when it began to deteriorate from lack of use, but the gym remains as an after-school safe haven for all the children of Bunnell and as the site of the Boys and Girls Clubs. The gym is located on Drain Street, which is four blocks south of the S.R. 100 intersection.

In the mid-1960s, when courts ordered the integration of schools, some African American parents sent their children to the previously all-white Bunnell High School (BHS), and a few white parents sent their children to the previously all-black Carver School. When problems persisted, for example when white parents refused to take black athletes to compete in out-of-town meets, at least one white woman became a certified bus driver and did the driving of the entire teams: black and white children. The coach of the girls' basketball team at BHS, in order to ease integration in the schools, chose twelve girls—six white and six black.

A fire in 1970 destroyed the main building of Bunnell High School (BHS) and necessitated the transfer of all its students to Carver School. The facility at BHS is today Bunnell Elementary School. School officials eventually built Flagler Palm Coast High School around 1975, and that school accepted all the high school students of the county.

The AFRICAN AMERICAN CULTURAL CENTER at 4422 U.S. 1 North, built in 2001, has seven thousand square feet of offices, classrooms, and a reference library. Private citizens and businesses took ten years to build the center. Open weekdays, 10 A.M.–2 P.M. Phone: (386) 447-7030.

The African American Cultural Center is just north of Bunnell.

BULOW PLANTATION RUINS HISTORIC STATE PARK, which is 3.5 miles south of S.R. 100 on Old Kings Road, has the remains of slave quarters for the slaves who worked in and around the sugar mill. A ranger can point out the remains of the cabins, which now consist only of stones in the ground. The cabins were part of 2,200 acres, which Major Charles Bulow cleared in the 1820s with slave labor. During the Second Seminole War Native Americans burned that plantation and others in the vicinity. All that is left today of the plantation are the coquina ruins of the sugar mill, several wells, a spring house, and the foundation of the mansion. The forest has reclaimed most of the land.

Bunnell, the county seat, has had three African American city commissioners: **Louis Jackson** in the 1970s; when he died in office, **Annie Johnson** replaced him and finished his term of office. **Daisy Henry** became a city commissioner in the late 1990s. There have been no African Americans on the county commission.

Espanola

Many black families moved to the town of Espanola to the northeast of Bunnell in the nineteenth century because of the opportunities for work, for example in the turpentine industry. The town declined when the nearby Dixie Highway was replaced by such highways as U.S. 1 and I-95, and only about seven miles of brick remain from the Dixie Highway.

Today the town has one African American church, **ST. PAUL MISSIONARY BAPTIST CHURCH**. Next to the church off Railroad Street is the site of the **ESPANOLA SCHOOL**, a school for African American children in the days of segregation. The teachers of that school were Mrs. **Geneva Smith**, Mrs. **Melissa Heard**, and Mrs. **Essie Mae Giddens**. The county furnished furniture and electricity for the building, which housed eight grades, all in the same room with one teacher. The number of students ranged between twenty-five and thirty. When the school closed in 1957, the children were transferred to schools in Bunnell. The Espanola school building then became a community center and a pre-kindergarten center. Rev. **Frank Giddens** of St. Paul Missionary Baptist Church opened an African American museum in the building in 2006.

The **MASONIC CEMETERY**, which is located 1.1 miles north of S.R. 100 on the right of Old Kings Road, is an African American cemetery run by the black Masonic lodge in Bunnell: Espanola Lodge 161. Old Kings Road is about five miles east of Bunnell on S.R. 100. The cemetery, which has been in use since about 1946, has several hundred African Americans buried on its five acres.

The Masonic Cemetery near Old Kings Road is an African American cemetery run by the black Masonic lodge in Bunnell.

18.

Franklin County

The Florida Legislature established Franklin County in 1832 and named it after statesman Benjamin Franklin. The county had a population of 11,057 in the 2000 census, 1,802 (16.3%) of whom were African Americans, which is a higher percentage than the 14.6% for Florida as a whole.

Africans and African Americans have visited or lived in Franklin County for a long time, but have not had the same negative experiences that blacks in other Florida counties have had, probably because the county has had few problems with integration. One of the first non-Native Americans in the area may have been a Moor named **Estevanico the Black**, one of just a handful of survivors of the ill-fated **Narváez** expedition of 1528 that sailed in make-shift rafts from below Tallahassee along the Florida coast to eventually reach Mexico.

In the seventeenth and eighteenth centuries slaves played an important part in the economy of the South, including Florida, as they worked in cotton fields and rice plantations. However, Franklin County differed from other Florida counties concerning slaves because it never had the large cotton plantations that used dozens of slaves in the nineteenth century. Therefore the county had relatively few slaves, a fact that would lessen the difficulties of integration in the 1960s. The few slaves that the town did have were able to hire themselves out as laborers and earn money for their work. In the twentieth century, African Americans were able to work in the seafood industry, dealing with oysters or shrimp, two important staples in the local economy.

A typical example of the "freedom" that slaves had in Apalachicola in the nineteenth century was

a woman known as **Aunt Susan**, a faithful servant who belonged to the prominent Raney family of the town. After a group of white women had spent time in the Raney house making beautiful garments, Aunt Susan would take the finished products from house to house, selling them to the local housewives. The money produced from the sale went into the Auxiliary Guild of Trinity Episcopal Church. When Aunt Susan died, she was interred in the Raney plot in Chestnut Cemetery.

Most of the African Americans in Franklin County and elsewhere before the twentieth century did not learn how to read and write since customs and laws forbade such teaching. Even free blacks were restricted in their movements. In the 1830s, blacks who did not have the proper, written passes in Franklin County could be punished with twenty strikes from a rawhide whip.

Before the start of the Civil War in 1861, conditions began to change for everyone. Slaves, who might have seen a loosening in the strict laws that restricted their movement, had to feel the tension of a nation breaking asunder under the weight of slavery. Even those African Americans who were free, such as the sailors who frequented the little port of Apalachicola in Franklin County, found their freedom curtailed; they were not allowed to enter the town, but had to remain at a distance.

When the Civil War ended in 1865, one of the Union troops occupying Apalachicola was

African Americans shucking oysters in Apalachicola. *Florida State Archives*

African Americans also worked peeling shrimp in Franklin County. *Tampa Hillsborough County Public Library System*

the 82nd United States Colored Infantry under the command of Major General Alexander Asboth. In those difficult years after the war, many former slaves stayed in Franklin County to raise their families and work at jobs for pay. Some of them were accepted into the community and took up positions of authority. A former slave of the Cook family, Frank, for example, took "Cook" for his last name and served for a time as a vestryman of Trinity Episcopal Church. Many African Americans began attending St. Paul African Methodist Episcopal Church after it was built in 1913.

Apalachicola

During the Reconstruction Period after the Civil War, African Americans in the area established several churches and by 1880 had integrated the two-man police force in Apalachicola. African Americans operated businesses in the area, including two of the main hotels in Apalachicola: the Spartan Jenkins (which served only whites) and the Fuller (which served blacks and whites); the Fullers (**Mary Aldin Fuller** and her husband) ran the hotel until they died. A local African American, **Emmanuel Smith**, served on the Franklin County School Board and as the local postmaster, eventually to be replaced in the latter post at his retirement by the famous botanist, Dr. Alvan Chapman.

The town also had a black sheriff, **Henry Hutchinson**, who in turn had a black deputy, **James Gulliam**; that deputy died of yellow fever when he was sent to Jacksonville to bring back some prisoners, but instead contracted the deadly disease there, died, and was buried there. Hutchinson, whom Governor Ossian Hart had appointed in 1874 after replacing a popular white incumbent, became so effective and popular with county voters that he remained in office until 1877, six months after the end of Reconstruction.

When the twentieth century began, the local newspaper, the *Apalachicola Times*, had a column devoted to news of the local African American community. One of the popular brass bands was the Colored Odd Fellows. Finally, many African Americans are buried in the small cemetery on 12th Street, as well as the cemetery at the south end of 7th Street, the same street that had a funeral home at the north end—thus the common saying among the African American community: "You lived, died, and were buried on Seventh Street."

During World War II, one of the first four draftees from the county was an African American named **Mose Langston**. At Camp Gordon Johnston near Carrabelle many African American troops trained for amphibian landings, although the African American soldiers there felt discriminated against in the poor facilities they were supplied with and in the Jim Crow segregation laws they faced in Tallahassee, where they went on leave.

When integration of facilities occurred in the 1960s, partly as a direct result of the Civil Rights Act of 1964, the county experienced relatively few racial incidents, partly because Apalachicola did not have the sharp residential demarcation of the races that other towns had. While most African Americans lived in the northern section of town called "The Hill," whites also lived there, and other African Americans lived in other parts of the town. The Hill, so called because of the slight rise of the area from the surrounding streets, consisted of ten streets, from 5th Street to 14th Street and from Highway 98 to Avenue M. Eight churches served the residents there. Today, almost a thousand African Americans live there.

Among the more famous local African Americans from Apalachicola is **Frederick Humphries**, who earned a Ph.D. in physical chemistry from the University of Pittsburgh and later became president of Tennessee State University and then Florida A&M University (FAMU) in Tallahassee. In 2001, he helped FAMU win a $2.5 million per year grant for three years from the National Oceanic and Atmospheric Administration (NOAA) to conduct research in Apalachicola Bay. After Dr. Humphries stepped down from the presidency of FAMU in 2001, he became the president of the National Association for Equal Opportunity in Higher Education. His sister, **Mona Humphries**, became school superintendent in Seattle, Washington.

Other prominent African Americans from the area are Dr. **George Hilliard**, a physician; **William Kornegy**, who became the Student Placement Director for General Motors; Mrs. **Mattie Edwards Murrell**, the Postal Inspector of New York City; Dr. **Ben Sealey**, the Director of Finances at Decatur Community College in Decatur, Georgia; and **Charles Wilson**, the vice president of the Jim Walter Corporation.

One of the buildings in town that an African American owned is the **O. E. CONE BUILDING** at 67 Commerce Street. Constructed after the 1900 city fire, it once had a barbershop, laundry, and wood yard. Another important building is the **ODD FELLOW HALL**, located between Avenues G and I on the left side of 6th Street going south; the Odd Fellow Lodge, which had a Woman's Auxiliary named the Households of Ruth, was an African American fraternal organization. The **MASONIC HALL** was located on 6th Street between Avenues I and J going north on the right side of the street. Other similar organizations were the Knights of Pythias, Young Men's Progressive Club, Cream of the Crop, the Owl's Social Club, and the Social Lites.

Beginning around 2000, local African Americans began an annual African American History Celebration sponsored by H'COLA (Hillside Coalition of Laborers, Apalachicola). The festivities include a parade, informational booths, and food vendors.

The **ST. PAUL AFRICAN METHODIST EPISCOPAL (AME) CHURCH** at I Avenue and 6th Street is on the National Register of Historic Places. The congregation was organized in 1866, right after the Civil War, when members bought the land on which the church stands. They recorded the church's name on the deed as "Methodist Episcopal Church for Colored People." Soon afterwards, the congregation built a small, wooden building there, which served them for seventy-four years.

In 1874, the church changed its name to St. Paul African Methodist Episcopal Church and became affiliated with the AME Church, which had been founded in Philadelphia in 1816. The

St. Paul AME Church in Apalachicola.

present large, red-brick structure is the third one on the site, dating back to 1921. The building is known for its two brick towers with their metal steeples, peaked Gothic windows at the front, and stained-glass windows throughout that were made in Germany especially for St. Paul's. Since then, fire has struck the structure twice, but it has been rebuilt each time.

Apalachicola in the 2000 census had 815 African Americans, 35% of the total population of 2,334.

Fort Gadsden

Twenty miles north of Carrabelle on S.R. 65 and situated on the Apalachicola River is FORT GADS-DEN STATE PARK. The first fort on this site dates back to 1814, when the British built a fortification on the east bank of the Apalachicola River at a place called Prospect Bluff to encourage the Seminole Indians to ally themselves with England against the United States in the War of 1812. Part of the force that the British raised for an attack on New Orleans consisted of about 170 blacks recruited from runaway slaves and those whom the British had freed in Pensacola.

After the defeat of the British and their withdrawal from the fort, a large group of blacks and their Choctaw allies remained behind in the fort, which came to be known as "The Negro Fort." Under the leadership of a man named **Garcon** or **Garcia**, the blacks established farms along the river and raised corn. The location of the fort on the Apalachicola River gave it a strategic importance as the natural highway into southern Alabama and Georgia, especially because so few good roads existed in the region at that time.

The Negro Fort, situated high on a steep hill overlooking the river and protected from a land attack by a swamp at its back and fortified with artillery the British left behind, effectively controlled commerce up and down the river at that point. Because of its threat to commerce on the river, General Andrew Jackson ordered his troops to destroy it.

When residents of the Indian villages along the river heard of the approaching soldiers, they took refuge in the fort. Lieutenant Colonel Duncan Clinch led a group of 116 soldiers and 150 friendly Creek Indians down the river; he rendezvoused with two gunboats sent up from Apalachicola and made plans to attack the fort and force its black commandant and his three hundred men, women, and children to surrender. In late July 1816, the boats moved into position, and one of them fired a cannon ball into the fort directly into the powder magazine. The ensuing blast destroyed the fort and killed 207 of the 334 men, women, and children and maimed the rest.

Two years later General Jackson led a band of soldiers down the Apalachicola and had Lieutenant James Gadsden of the Engineer Corps build a new fort on Prospect Bluff as a supply depot or base. General Jackson named the new site Fort Gadsden in honor of the engineer. It later played a minor role in the Civil War and faded into obscurity until the Florida Park Service developed Fort Gadsden State Park in 1961. Today the fort, including the remains of the Negro Fort, are part of the Apalachicola National Forest. Both are National Historic Landmarks maintained by the U.S. Forest Service. Open sunup to sundown.

19.

Gadsden County

Florida's fifth county was established in 1823 and named for James Gadsden (1788–1858), an aide-de-camp to General Andrew Jackson during the 1818 campaign in Florida, a campaign that showed how weak the Spanish hold on the territory was. Gadsden would become more famous when he negotiated a boundary dispute with Mexico that resulted in the acquisition by the United States of lands that are now part of Arizona and New Mexico.

In the 1820s, Gadsden was one of five counties, along with Jackson, Jefferson, Leon, and Madison Counties, in which slaves made up more than fifty percent of the population. North Florida's so-called "black belt" region had a rich soil that enabled plantations to thrive, although at great personal cost to their black slaves.

Gadsden County had a population of 45,087 in the 2000 census, 25,745 (57.1%) of whom were African Americans. It was the only Florida county where the majority of residents were African Americans, but it was not until 2004 that the county elected its first African American sheriff, **Morris Young**.

Quincy

The town of Quincy, which today has a population of 7,444, of whom 4,565 (61%) are black, is the county seat of Gadsden County, northwest of Tallahassee. Quincy was named after John Quincy Adams, who was secretary of state of the United States when the town was founded in 1825.

Slaveholders established the county in the nineteenth century and used slaves to cultivate tobacco, cotton, sugar cane, and corn. The soil there, unlike that in the southern half of the peninsula, was fertile for plantation owners to prosper, and so they used slaves extensively to till the land up until the Civil War. The first census of the county, which was taken in 1825, showed that slaves made up 41% of the total population. Thirteen years later that figure rose to 57% as more and more slaves were brought in to work the fields. Tobacco became so important that it earned $400,000 just before the Civil War began. After the Civil War freed the slaves, many of them stayed in the area to raise their families on their farms. The percentage of blacks has remained consistently high over the years.

ARNETT CHAPEL AME CHURCH at 209 S. Duval Street represents an important step in the religious history of local blacks. Before the American Civil War slave owners used religion as a means of controlling their slaves and teaching them the values of western civilization. The overseers discouraged slaves from practicing African religions, especially in the African languages the slaves had brought with them, on the theory that those religions were pagan and the slaves might be fomenting rebellion in languages unknown to the overseers. In order to keep the slaves in view, even during their religious worship, and therefore less liable to conspire among themselves to

Arnett Chapel is the county's oldest black church that still exists today.

revolt, overseers insisted that the slaves attend the churches that whites established in each township. Because slaves were not allowed to sit with the white parishioners, architects built separate slave galleries in the churches. The records of plantations in Gadsden County, where Quincy is, sometimes noted each slave with the letter "B" for believer or "S" for sinner, presumably based on whether the slave went to church or not.

Once the Emancipation Proclamation and the end of the Civil War freed the slaves, they began establishing their own churches. The African Methodist Episcopal (AME) church and the African Methodist Episcopal Zion (AME Zion) church began in the North, in Philadelphia and New York City respectively, unofficially in the late eighteenth century, formally in 1816, and expanded throughout the South after the Civil War. Ministers, missionaries, and freedmen worked in Florida and established many parishes among the former slaves.

In 1866, some Quincy blacks established the **ARNETT CHAPEL AME CHURCH**, which at first met in members' homes or even outdoors. In 1867,

two years after the Civil War ended, members spent $100 for a plot of land about one-fourth of an acre in size. This church is the county's oldest black church that still exists today. The date of the construction of the first church is not known, but the second structure was built on the southeast corner of DuVal and Clark Streets in 1898–89 and named in honor of Reverend **Benjamin W. Arnett**, the Presiding Bishop in Florida from 1888 to 1892. The congregation met in that structure until 1938–39, at which time another building was begun. The first services were held there in the new building in 1940.

In the **HARDON BUILDING** at 16 W. Washington Street **William Hardon**, a black from Quincy, owned one of the town's earliest ice and electric plants. Ice would have been very important for a product closely associated with Quincy—Coca-Cola. In 1922, local farmers invested some money in a relatively new company in Atlanta, the Coca-Cola Company. Eventually the Quincy State Bank had shares worth more than $15 million, money that has greatly benefited the town, although many of the blacks have remained in poverty to the present day. The Hardon Building, which was built around 1900, now houses an office-supply business.

The **MASONIC LODGE** at 122 S. Duval Street has served as the meeting hall for black Masons since 1907. The Masonic order, which is the oldest such group in the Western world, stresses friendship, morality, truth, charity, and prudence. Because Freemasonry does not allow members to discuss religion or politics within its temples, the organization was able to survive during such divisive times as the American Civil War. In many states the Masons operate homes for orphans, the aged, and the infirm, and specialize in treating crippled children and burn victims. The place where the Masons meet is called a lodge. The Masonic Lodge in Quincy where black Masons have met is a simple two-story building with an open hall on the first floor. Unlike some Masonic lodges in large cities, which are often elaborate and adorned with large columns, this Quincy lodge, which was moved from its original site in 1976 and remodeled, is simple and practical.

The **WILLIAM S. STEVENS HOSPITAL** on the corner of Roberts and Crawford Streets, which is now a private residence, was where Dr. **William Spencer Stevens** practiced medicine in Quincy for more than fifty years. The hospital treated patients through both the yellow fever outbreak of 1906 and the influenza epidemic of 1918. Dr. Stevens, who also had a clinic and a drug store, used this two-story building to treat many of the local black people.

Dr. Stevens (1882–1949) was born in Tallahassee, graduated from Florida State Normal and Industrial College, and received a medical degree from Meharry Medical College in Nashville, Tennessee. He returned to Florida and became the first African American to open a medical practice in Quincy. In 1906, he opened Stevens Drug Store in downtown Quincy. In 1914, he was named supervisor of the Quincy City Schools. In 1925 he began a four-year process to expand Dunbar

School, and, when the new building was finished, officials renamed it **W. S. STEVENS HIGH SCHOOL**. The Rosenwald Foundation, which helped construct well-designed schools for African Americans throughout the Southeast, originally built Dunbar School in the 1920s for all twelve grades. The L-shaped, one-story red brick building still operates as a school. Stevens Park is adjacent to the school building, and a plaque at the W. S. Stevens School, 1004 W. 4th Street, honors him.

One of the principals of the Stevens School was **Witt A. Campbell**, who was born in 1910 in Quincy. He attended Florida A & M University for two years before joining the U.S. Army, finished his undergraduate degree at Bethune-Cookman College, and returned to Quincy, where he worked in the public school system for forty-four years. He served as principal of East Quincy School (1942–43), Midway High School (1951–53), and the Stevens High School and Elementary School (1955–70), as well as assistant principal of Chattahoochee High School (1970–77) and principal of Gretna Elementary (1982–83).

During the Civil Rights movement of the 1960s, Campbell registered voters in Gadsden County. In 1983 he was elected to the Gadsden County School Board. He served as financial secretary to the Good Shepherd Lodge of the Order of Emancipated Americans until his death June

A group of students in the early twentieth century in Gadsden County. *Florida State Archives*

30, 1996. His Great Floridian plaque is located at that lodge at 1001 4th Street, Quincy.

Several African Americans who played pivotal roles in the history of Florida were associated with Quincy. **Robert Meacham** (1835–1902), who fostered the establishment of churches and schools in Jefferson and Leon Counties (see Chapters Thirty-two and Thirty-six), was the son of a Gadsden County physician and a slave woman. At an early age, he learned to read and write and also attended a local educational institution: QUINCY ACADEMY. In the early 1850s, he served as a house servant in Tallahassee, where he taught other slaves how to read and write. While there, he established his own congregation toward the end of the Civil War, leading members from the Tallahassee Methodist Episcopal Church South into their own church.

One of the leaders that came from Quincy was **Richard Moore** (1907?–1994), a man who was born in Quincy, attended school there, and eventually went on to become the third president of Bethune-Cookman College in Daytona Beach in 1947. He held that position for twenty-eight years until his retirement in 1975. In his career he was an instructor of social studies and athletics coach at Pinellas High School in Clearwater (1932–34), principal of Union Academy in Tarpon Springs (1934–37), principal of Rosenwald High School in Panama City (1937–44), principal of Booker T. Washington High School in Pensacola (1944–45), and State Supervisor of Black Secondary Schools (1945–47).

Another African American who worked in the area was **Alexander C. Lightbourn Sr.** (1846–1908), who was born in Nassau, taught school in Tallahassee, and served as sergeant-at-arms of the Florida House of Representatives (1869–70). Governor Harrison Reed appointed him a justice of the peace in Gadsden County, where he worked until 1874. In Quincy he helped establish the AME church, worked as a county Republican leader, and then worked as a railroad postal employee (1877). In the mid-1880s, he moved with his family to Jacksonville, then later to Cocoa, Palm Beach, and Miami. (For more about him see Chapter Forty-three.)

One of Quincy's most distinguished African Americans was Dr. **Lasalle Doheny Leffall**, who was born in 1930 in Tallahassee and later lived at 11 S. 9th Street in Quincy. After graduating summa cum laude from Tallahassee's Florida A&M University at the age of eighteen, he received his M.D. degree from Howard University.

He went on to become the president of the American Cancer Society, president of the Society

Dr. Lasalle Leffall's house in Quincy.

of Surgical Oncology, a member of the editorial boards of the *American Journal of Surgery* and *Archives of Surgery*, and on the board of governors of the United Way of America. He was also the civilian aide-at-large to the Secretary of the U.S. Army. Different organizations honored him for being an outstanding doctor. He once said, "I hope my greatest contributions are being a good teacher and surgical oncologist who provides his patients with the best care."

The 1841 UNION BANK BUILDING across the street from Tallahassee's downtown Old Capitol Museum has an oil portrait of Dr. Leffall, the first black physician to lead a national surgeons' group (see Chapter Thirty-six).

Among the more famous local blacks was one of the state's most renowned attorneys, **Simuel Decatur McGill**, who was born in Quincy in 1878; in 1940, he went on to secure the release of four innocent men who had spent four years on death row.

20.

Gilchrist County

Gilchrist County had a population of 14,437 in the 2000 census, 1,011 (7%) of whom were African Americans. That number (1,011) tied Lafayette County for the fewest African Americans in a Florida county. African Americans in Gilchrist County were spread out throughout the area; only 326 resided in Trenton, and only seven in Bell, the two main population centers of the county.

The last Florida county established (1925) honors Albert Gilchrist, governor of Florida (1909–13). When residents in the western part of Alachua County decided to break off from their neighbor to the east, they did so for various reasons. They were tired of making the long trip to Gainesville to conduct official business, especially in the days when the sandy roads made it an all-day trip for their Model-T cars. They felt neglected by the Alachua County Commission, which spent more time and money on the county seat of Gainesville. And they believed they would be better off financially, especially because a new county would receive an equal share of the state's racetrack revenue, which the state distributed each year.

The citizens who wanted to form a new county decided to call it Melon County to commemorate the many watermelons grown in the area. African Americans found steady work in the watermelon fields during harvest season and could earn between two dollars and five dollars a day, depending on the type of work they did. They would transport the melons to trains, but later the boxcars were replaced by piggybacks, big trailers that could be pulled to the fields for loading and then returned to the shipping ramp

to be loaded onto flatcars, each of which could handle two piggybacks. Railroads began using piggybacks for faster shipping in order to compete with the trucks that were beating the trains to northern markets.

Instead of choosing Melon for the name of the new county, however, the Florida Legislature at first chose Wilson County to honor the late President Woodrow Wilson (1856–1924), but then decided to name it after ex-governor Albert Gilchrist, who was ill at the time in a New York hospital.

As governor, Gilchrist had worked to pass laws that provided hospital care to the state's poor children and prohibited the practice of leasing out convicts to road contractors and work camps. One action that made him popular with African Americans was his unsuccessful effort to make Abraham Lincoln's birthday a state legal holiday. Schools in Gilchrist County, as elsewhere in Florida, were segregated until the 1960s. Trenton had the John Morse School for African Americans until the mid-1960s, when federal officials ordered the county to desegregate its schools for the 1966–1967 school year. The school board voted to consolidate the all-black John Morse School, named after its principal, with Trenton

High School and reassigned two of the four teachers at the John Morse School to Trenton and two to Bell.

But then, the school board reversed its decision and decided not to close down the John Morse School. It did allow eleven of its African American students to transfer to Trenton High School, which occurred without any serious incidents. In 1968, when the federal government accused the school board of not moving fast enough on school desegregation, the school board decided to finally phase out the all-black school, which it did that year. The principal at the all-black school, **John Morse**, then became assistant principal at Trenton High School.

The county had relatively few racial incidents over the years and in fact has elected African Americans to local offices, beginning in 1979 with the election of **Bill Hogan**, the first black man elected to serve on the Trenton City Commission.

African Americans worked long hours in the melon fields of north Florida. *Florida State Archives*

21.
Glades County

This county, named for the nearby Everglades, was established in 1921. Glades County had a population of 10,576 in the 2000 census, 1,110 (10.5%) of whom were African Americans. That number (1,110) was the third-lowest number of African Americans in a Florida county.

Moore Haven

A 1985 book, *Glades County, Florida History*, described subdivisions just north of Moore Haven, which were called Keederlee, Lakeview, and Latum, as the place where many African Americans settled after the Civil War. They worked on building the railroad in south Florida or in farming the lands there. The descendants of those first blacks, **Gus Days**, **John Huggins**, and **William Tobias**, still live there. Around 1919, others arrived, for example farmers **Julius Castor**, **Arthur Huggins**, **Charles** and **Louise Latum**, **Will Smith**, and **John Henry Williams**, as well as grocers **William** and **Ella Tobias**.

A booklet commemorating the William and Ella Tobias Community Center notes that African American parents established a school in the local Baptist Church located on the site of the McPhersons' home on the corner of Gamble Street and Central Avenue. The school later moved to the Methodist Church as more and more students sought admission. The Baptist Church had grades one to four, while the Methodist Church had grades five to eight.

In the 1920s, parents built a one-room schoolhouse to put all grades under one roof. Twenty years later, when the schoolhouse became too small, classes were held in a new First Baptist Church. As more and more students sought

The facilities of the Booker T. Washington School are used as the Glades County Child Development Center.

admission, officials began building Booker T. Washington School for kindergarten through the twelfth grade in 1950 and finished it in time for the 1951–52 school year.

Robert Gamble, who had served in the U.S. Army Air Force, became the school's first and only principal, a position he held for eighteen years until the school closed in 1969. In 1967, **Ella Tobias** donated money for a gymnasium at the Booker T. Washington School. The William and Ella Tobias Gymnasium still exists at the site and is used as an after-school facility. When integration took place in Glades County in the late 1960s, Gamble became assistant school superintendent and did much to ease the transition to integration of local facilities. In the 1960s, he sponsored a contest to name the community as part of a beautification program. The winning name was Washington Park.

Today, the facilities of the Booker T. Washington School are used as the Glades County Child Development Center under the supervision of **Eliza Brown**.

22.
Gulf County

The sixty-sixth and next-to-last county established was created in 1925 and named for the Gulf of Mexico, which borders the southern part of the county. Gulf County had a population of 13,332 in the 2000 census, 2,253 (16.9%) of whom were African Americans.

Port St. Joe

One local man who became a war hero was **Clifford Chester Sims**, who was born in Port St. Joe on June 18, 1942. After graduating from Washington High School, he joined the U.S. Army, trained at Fort Jackson in South Carolina, and went with his fellow soldiers to Vietnam in 1967.

Two months later, he was leading his squad of soldiers against the enemy, when a booby trap caught his foot. Realizing that the bomb was about to explode, he called out a warning to his men and threw himself onto the bomb in order to protect his fellow soldiers. By taking the full force of the explosion, he gave up his life in order to save the lives of the men he was leading. For his heroic deed, the U.S. Government awarded him the Medal of Honor, the highest honor awarded to a soldier. Sims is buried in Barrancas National Cemetery in Pensacola, Florida, and is honored in the **MEDAL OF HONOR PARK** near Sebring, Florida (see Chapter Twenty-seven).

A tragedy that occurred in 1963 involved two African Americans, **Freddie Pitts** and **Wilbert Lee**, who were falsely accused of murdering two white gas-station attendants near Port St. Joe. All-white juries twice convicted the twenty-seven-year-old Pitts and the nineteen-year-old Lee of the crime and they were sentenced to death, but

Clifford Chester Sims from Port St. Joe won the Medal of Honor for bravery during the Vietnam War. *State of Florida, Dept. of Military Affairs*

their convictions were overturned when a white man finally admitted to the murders and passed a lie-detector test. When Gene Miller wrote the Pulitzer Prize–winning book entitled *Invitation to a Lynching*, Florida Governor Reubin Askew ordered an investigation into the murder and eventually granted both men full pardons. After years of hesitation, the Florida Legislature in 2004 passed a bill compensating Pitts and Lee with $500,000 each for the initial travesty of justice.

Money Bayou

One beach in Gulf County, Money Bayou, became a favorite with African Americans from north Florida, south Georgia, and Alabama in the days of segregation. According to local legend, a black man (**Damon Peters Sr.**) and one of his white friends (Raymond Driesbach) overcame the segregationist policy of not allowing blacks to own beachfront property by negotiating in secret and late at night to buy thirty acres of virgin beach, called Money Bayou, in the office of a local white attorney (Alfred P. Andreasen). Before the segregationists realized what was happening, the two men had bought the land in Port St. Joe.

Two African Americans, Freddie Pitts and Wilbert Lee, were falsely accused of murdering two white gas-station attendants near Port St. Joe. *Florida State Archives*

23.

Hamilton County

Florida's fifteenth county was established in 1827 and named for Alexander Hamilton, the first U.S. Secretary of the Treasury. Because the land in that area of Florida was so conducive to the growing of cotton, the plantation owners there relied on slaves to till the land, at least up until the Civil War.

The county had a population of 13,327 in the 2000 census, 5,024 (37.7%) of whom were African Americans.

Jasper

This town has a one-acre **HERITAGE VILLAGE** at 501 NE 1st Avenue with two houses that were once part of the black residential area called Cox Quarters. The location of the Quarters is now the site of the Southern Railroad station office. The original building of the so-called "Colored School" was torn down in 1860, but a structure that represents that building dates to 1941. The structure, called the **SPRING BRANCH BAPTIST CHURCH,** served as a church on Sunday and then as a school Monday through Friday. The same teacher taught all twelve grades of the school.

The **E. LEWIS VAUGHN SHOP** dates back to 1910, when the Vaughn family settled in Jasper in 1910. **Lewis Vaughn**, whose outstanding skill as a blacksmith was recognized and highly valued, set up his shop in the center of town. As the town grew, he moved his blacksmith shop seven blocks north to 604 Hartley Street. His son **Joseph** took over the shop in 1954 and inherited his father's craftsmanship, designing and making tools for his customers, such as the Alligator Hook, which hunters used to snare alligators and which is still on display at the shop. In modern times, the blacksmith shop has evolved into a welding shop, which is owned and operated by the third generation: **E. Lewis Vaughn**, who has served as a Hamilton County Commissioner.

We should mention here a white author, Lillian Smith, the daughter of a leading white Jasper civic and business leader. Ms. Smith was the author of *Strange Fruit* (1944), a controversial novel set in a small town that resembles Jasper, where she grew up. Smith, born in 1897, became one of the most liberal and outspoken white Southern writers on issues of social and racial injustice, boldly calling for an end to segregation at a time when most white Southerners were opposed to racial change.

The **JASPER POST OFFICE** was built with WPA funds in the 1930s and still displays a set of murals high on the walls, a reminder of the Depression Era, when artists were commissioned to paint scenes of local interest in public buildings. One of the Jasper murals, painted by Pietro Lazzari, depicts black workers tending a turpentine still, cutting timber, and harvesting tobacco. The pictures are enduring tributes and reminders of the dignity and worth of these African American laborers.

White Springs

The only site in Hamilton County on the original Florida Black Heritage Trail is the STEPHEN FOSTER FOLK CULTURE CENTER STATE PARK on U.S. 41 North, three miles east of I-75. The nearby Suwannee River became famous when Stephen Foster (1826–1864) wrote about it in his song, "The Swanee River (Old Folks at Home)," which the Florida Legislature adopted in 1935 as the State Song. When Foster wrote the song in 1851, he had never seen the Suwannee River, and in fact first had Pedee River in the song, but he liked the sound of Suwannee, which he changed to "Swanee," a name he picked from an atlas. Some of the words that he wrote, for example "Way down upon the Swanee River/Far, far away/That's where my heart is turning ever/That's where the old folks stay" and "All up and down the whole creation/Sadly I roam/Still longing for the old plantation/And for the old folks at home," were interpreted in the Post-Reconstruction era (1870s–1890s) as meaning that the blacks yearn to go back to the plantation, where they were better off. However, others interpret the song to mean that no matter how far we travel or what heartbreaks we suffer, our hearts yearn for the best memories of childhood, the security of a family and parents ("old folks"), the familiarity of home.

On Memorial Day weekend in May, the annual Florida Folk Festival is held at the Stephen Foster Park, and since its beginning more than fifty years ago African Americans have performed as storytellers, musicians, and gospel singers, and have shown their skills at quilting, carving, and other crafts. Food delicacies of the Upper Suwannee River region, strongly influenced by Caribbean and African tradition, are also celebrated at the festival. Delicious home-cooked favorites such as sweet potato pie, Bar-B-Que, Hoppin' John, chicken pilau, and gumbo are prepared and served by members of local black churches.

EASTSIDE CEMETERY on Adams Memorial Drive in White Springs is the final resting place of the ancestors of local black families. This well-tended burial ground near the White Springs Historic District honors veterans, family patriarchs and matriarchs, and past generations of the African American community of south Hamilton County.

The Stephen Foster Folk Culture Center State Park has displays of life in north Florida. *Florida State Archives*

24.
Hardee County

This county was established in 1921 from DeSoto County and named for Cary Augustus Hardee, Florida governor from 1921 until 1925, during which time Hardee County was created.

Hardee County had a population of 26,938 in the 2000 census, 2,236 (8.3%) of whom were African Americans.

Among the sites of interest to the history of African Americans are two cemeteries: the **MAGNOLIA MANOR CEMETERY,** behind the Missionary Baptist Church on Martin Luther King Jr. Boulevard below Wauchula, and an unnamed cemetery on County Line Road just north of Bowling Green. Near the church and cemetery is **ZOLFO LODGE #223**, whose members are all African Americans.

Directions to Magnolia Manor Cemetery: Go south on U.S. 17 1.4 miles from Main Street in Wauchula, the county seat; go left (east) on Will Duke Road .4 miles to Martin Luther Jr. Boulevard; turn left, and the cemetery is on the right behind the Missionary Baptist Church.

Directions to unnamed cemetery north of Bowling Green: from Main Street in Bowling Green go north .5 miles on U.S. 17, turn left (west) on County Line Road, and the cemetery is .7 miles on the right.

The Cracker Trail Museum at the corner of S.R. 64 and U.S. 17 in Zolfo Springs has exhibits about the history of Hardee County, but has none dealing with the African Americans who have lived there.

The Magnolia Manor Cemetery behind the Missionary Baptist Church has many gravesites spread out over a large area.

The unnamed cemetery on County Line Road just north of Bowling Green has relatively few gravesites.

25.
Hendry County

The Legislature established this county in 1923 and named it for Captain Francis Asbury Hendry, an officer in the Confederate Army and later a local cattle rancher. The county had a population of 36,210 in the 2000 census, 5,323 (14.7%) of whom were African Americans.

Throughout the nineteenth century, very few non-Native Americans lived in the area that became Hendry County, mostly because the district was relatively inaccessible and inundated with water. Over half of the area was in the Everglades. The military had established several installations, for example Fort Denaud and Fort Thompson on the Caloosahatchee River, which were used during the Seminole Wars. Captain Francis Asbury Hendry was an early visitor to southwest Florida; in 1854, he noted that he could not find a single settler or trace of civilization in the area.

The Caloosahatchee Valley did not attract immigrants until after 1881, when the Atlantic and Gulf Coast and Okeechobee Land Company began draining the swamps there. Hamilton Disston, the man who controlled the company, had bought twenty-five million acres of southwest Florida for twenty-five cents an acre and tried to drain much of it for cultivation and the raising of cattle. Captain Hendry may have been the first to graze cattle south of the Caloosahatchee River.

LaBelle

The city of LaBelle was a pioneer town in the early 1900s. There may have been only one black family there in those early decades, a farming family outside of town. In the 1920s, when the town imported 1,200 African Americans to build the streets, officials housed them at a camp with a dormitory and commissary. The white community was suspicious of such a large group of strangers, and tensions resulted. One woman in particular was fearful because her first husband had been killed elsewhere in a dispute with a black man. When a black man came to her door in June 1926, possibly to ask for a glass of water, she panicked, threw a hot iron at him, and called her husband. He then organized a group of white men, who caught the black man and took him to the Everett Hotel (where trials were held while the courthouse was being built), but he escaped from his captors and fled. Some of the men shot him dead near the intersection of today's Highways 29 and 80, then took his body and hung it from a tree outside of town.

Authorities arrested a dozen of the men involved in the crimes and put them on trial at the Everett Hotel, but the judge released them all, reasoning that the black man's corpse had so many bullets in him that it would be impossible to determine which bullet actually killed him. The whole incident frightened the African Americans on the road crew so much that they all deserted the camp and left town.

The trial of the men suspected in the killing of the African American man was held at the Everett Hotel, but the judge let them all go free. *Florida State Archives*

26.
Hernando County

This county was established in 1843 and named for Spanish explorer Hernando de Soto. His last name was chosen for the name of the county seat, although it was later changed to Brooksville. Hernando County had a population of 130,802 in the 2000 census, 5,363 (4.1%) of whom were African Americans. That percentage (4.1%) is the third-lowest among all Florida counties.

Brooksville

The largest town, Brooksville, has 1,548 African Americans or 21% of the total town population.

A white man, Frank Saxton, built the **BETHLEHEM PROGRESSIVE BAPTIST CHURCH** at 661 S. Brooksville Avenue in 1861 for his former slaves. Eight years later, fifteen black Baptist churches in Florida formed the Bethlehem Baptist Association.

Frank Saxton built the Bethlehem Progressive Baptist Church in 1861 for his former slaves.

Also in and around Brooksville are several African American cemeteries, for example **FORT TAYLOR CEMETERY** off Culbreath Road south of the city; that cemetery has the final remains of Fort Taylor's African American community, which began in the late 1800s to work in the local timber business.

Directions to cemetery: To reach Culbreath Road, go south on U.S. 41, turn left (east) on Elgin Boulevard, then right on Culbreath to just below C.R. 576, where a sign on the right points to the cemetery.

Fort Taylor Cemetery has the final remains of the local community's African Americans.

Other nearby black cemeteries are **LANG MEMORIAL** at WPA Road and Mondon Hill Road; **RUSSELL HILL CEMETERY** at Brittle Road northwest of the city; and **OLD SPRING HILL CEMETERY** off W. Fort Dade Avenue five miles west of Brooksville. South of Brooksville in Masaryktown at the blinking light on U.S. 41 heading south is **ENVILLE CEMETERY**, a privately owned lot that has the gravesites of African Americans employed in the lumber and turpentine industries from 1890 to 1915.

27.

Highlands County

This county was established in 1921. Its name alludes to its elevation. Though no land in Florida is very high, the highest point in Florida is only 345 feet above sea level. The county had a population of 87,366 in the 2000 census, 8,125 (9.3%) of whom were African Americans.

Avon Park

O. M. Crosby of Danbury, Connecticut, established this town around 1885. As president of the Florida Development Company, he recruited settlers to the area, including several from England's Stratford-on-Avon who gave the town its name. Situated in the geographical center of the state and blessed with many clear lakes, the town has had a history of growing oranges and grapefruits despite some devastating freezes.

Crosby began a newspaper, *The Home Seeker*, which successfully lured new residents with such racist advertisements as this one: "Can you imagine a spot where there is no swamp, no malaria, no frost, no mosquitoes, no Negroes, and no liquor sold, and all the people are busy Northerners? Such is Avon Park."

Despite Crosby's intentions to keep them out, blacks began settling in the area in the early part of the twentieth century to work in the lumber, turpentine, and railroad businesses, although they were segregated in the southeast part of town called "The Quarters." On page 94 of his book, historian Horace Fenton quotes the following 1916 city ordinance that created that section:

Ordinance No. 46, for preserving the peace and preventing ill feeling between the White and Colored Races by providing separate areas for White and Colored

people for residences, churches, etc.

1. Be it enacted that it shall be unlawful for any white person to settle in any part of Marsh's Subdivision of Lot 4, Block K, Section 26, Township 33, Range 28 East.2.3.4. Be it enacted that it shall be unlawful for any colored person to settle in any part of Avon Park save in that section mentioned and described in Article 1 of this ordinance.

In the days of segregation, black children had a school of their own, Hopewell, which had grades one through eight. Historian Leoma Bradshaw Maxwell wrote that the school's name came from the children's repetition of "hope we'll win, hope we'll win" when they entered some exhibits in a local fair. The principal of Hopewell, **Earnest E. Sims**, had moved to Avon Park from Fort Meade when he was a child; after attending Florida Memorial College, A&T College in North Carolina, and Columbia University, he taught in his adopted town for thirty-five years, eventually becoming assistant principal of the Avon Park schools after integration. He later served as assistant principal of the middle school until his retirement in 1971.

The **SIMS/COX CENTER/HOPEWELL PUBLIC SCHOOL** is the site of the first public school for African Americans in Avon Park, Hopewell Public School. The school has since been renamed the Sims/Cox Center and houses the Highland Boys and Girls Club and the Redlands Migrant Christian Association (RCMA).

MT. OLIVE AME CHURCH at 900 S. Delaney Avenue is one of the most important churches for blacks in Avon Park. Church members raised donations in 1940 to build the structure, whose first pastor in 1920 was Rev. **A.M. Wardell** (or Wadell), and did much of the actual construction themselves. The church is about ten blocks south of E. Main Street on the corner of E. Green Street and S. Delaney Avenue, which is one mile east of U.S. 27 off E. Main Street.

One of its residents that Avon Park honors with a street named after him was Kansas City Royals baseball star **Hal McRae** (1945–). After attending and playing baseball for Douglas High School in Sebring, he went to Florida A&M University in Tallahassee, where he played baseball for the Rattlers. He then went on to play professional baseball for nineteen years, first with Cincinnati (1968, 1970–72) and then with Kansas City (1973–87). He played in four World Series

and three All-Star Games and also managed the Royals in the 1991 season. He led the American League in doubles (54) in 1977 and runs-batted-in (133) in 1982, all of which helped lead to his induction into the Florida Sports Hall of Fame in 1986.

The 2000 census indicated that Avon Park had 2,513 African Americans or 29% of the total town population.

Sebring

The **E. O. DOUGLASS SCHOOL** on School Street, built in 1957, was an all-black school named for a local president of the First National Bank. The school was originally on Harris Street. After integration of schools, the facility on School Street became the headquarters for the county school administration. A plaque on the School Street site marks a favorite gathering place for students and the site of a yearly class reunion.

FIRST MISSIONARY BAPTIST CHURCH on Lemon Street was organized in 1913, when **John**

Mount Olive AME Church in Avon Park.

Grady, the city's first black carpenter and second black policeman, made specially designed concrete blocks with a hand-block press and used them for the building. The church is one of the oldest black churches in the city.

HOME OF CLARENCE MARION at 829 Lemon Street was where **Clarence Marion**, the first black principal in Sebring, lived while serving as principal of the E. O. Douglass School. The building is being restored by the Highlands County Minority Economic Development Council to house a museum and community meeting center.

LAKESIDE CEMETERY on Cemetery Road at Lucas Lake was the first black cemetery in Sebring.

Southwest of Sebring on U.S. 27 is the **MEDAL OF HONOR PARK** 2.5 miles south of U.S. 17. This park commemorates each Florida winner of the Congressional Medal of Honor with a tree and a plaque listing the birth and death dates of each honoree. The Medal of Honor is the highest honor our nation can award a soldier. Two of the men so honored are black: **Clifford Chester Sims** and **Robert H. Jenkins Jr.** (For more about Sims see Chapter Twenty-two; for more about Jenkins see Chapter Fifty-four.)

The Medal of Honor Park near Sebring has two plaques that honor African Americans.

28.

Hillsborough County

This county was established in 1834 and named for Wills Hills, the Earl of Hillsborough (1718–1793), an Irish peer who served in England as secretary for the colonies. Hillsborough County had a population of 998,948 in the 2000 census, 14,984 (15.0%) of whom were African Americans.

Plant City

The **BING ROOMING HOUSE** at 205 Allen Street offered accommodations to African Americans during the days of segregation when other hotels would not do so. **Jane** and **E. L. Bing** built the house in 1926, and Mrs. Bing operated it until 1975. She also operated the Seminole Restaurant nearby, but it no longer exists. Her grandson, **James Bing**, still lives in the house and is helping to restore it.

Directions to Rooming House: From I-4 take the Alexander Street exit, go south through three traffic lights past the hospital, go left on Martin Luther King Jr. Boulevard, go east through town, cross two railroad crossings, go about 6–8 blocks, turn right on Allen Street and go to 205 Allen Street.

The Bing Rooming House in Plant City offered accommodations to African Americans during the days of segregation.

The one-room Glover School served African American students from Bealsville and other areas.

Bealsville

Freed slaves from plantations in Hopewell, Knights, and Springhead settled an area called Howell's Creek, seven miles south of Plant City, in 1865. They built their homes from logs cut from trees cleared for future farmland. **Alfred Beal** and **Bryant Horton** planted orange seeds, which started orange production in what came to be called Bealsville after Alfred Beal. They built five churches, the first of which, Antioch Baptist, began in 1868 and had a school. Beal (1859–1948) was honored in the naming of the community because of his efforts to keep ownership of property in the area in local hands. For example, he bought foreclosed lots and sold them back to Bealsville residents, and he donated land for a church, school, and cemetery.

The only structure still standing in Bealsville that is associated with Alfred Beal is the house of his daughter, **Beulah Estelle Beal Holloman**, at 5604 Horton Road.

The settlers moved into the phosphate-mining industry and raised $1,100 from fish fries and musicals to build a wood-framed building in 1933: the **GLOVER SCHOOL**, named after **Wil-**liam Glover, who created a community school. The one-room schoolhouse, which seldom had running water or a full supply of books or desks, served African American students from Bealsville and other areas like Knights Station, Keysville, and Coronet. The parents added a concrete-block addition in 1945 and another building in 1949. The school finally closed in 1980 when the school board complained about its physical inadequacies, but the community transformed the building into a community center that continues to serve the people there. One can visit the school, which is on the National Register of Historic Places, at 5104 Horton Road.

Directions: Go south from Plant City on S.R. 39 for 5–6 miles, turn left on S.R. 60, go 2.7 miles, watch for the sign on the right, go left on Horton Road .7 miles, and Glover School is on the right.

Tampa

Long before the Spanish arrived in the Tampa Bay area in the sixteenth century Indian tribes like the Calusas lived there, taking advantage of the good fishing and rich farmlands. The European exploration of the area began in the early 1500s when Spanish adventurers like Panfilo de Narváez arrived and headed inland to see if they could find any gold or silver. The name of Tampa may come from an Indian phrase meaning "near it" or "split wood for quick fires" or from a Spanish version of an Indian name, "Tanpa." When white settlers began moving into north Florida in the early nineteenth century, the federal government forcibly moved many Indians and the runaway slaves who had taken refuge with them to south Florida, including reservations around Tampa Bay. In 1821, a band of Creek Indians led by men with ties to General Andrew Jackson burned and plundered a settlement of blacks near Tampa Bay and destroyed what may have been the first black colony on Florida's west coast.

Tampa can trace its origins to the establishment of Fort Brooke by federal troops in the early 1820s in preparation for the Seminole Indian War. After the wars with the Indians were over, the town developed into a port for the shipping of cattle, but still depended on slaves for domestics, carpenters, and army scouts. Unlike north Florida, which developed a cotton-growing economy dependent on slaves, Tampa had a more diversified economic base, but slaves still made up one-third of the county's population right before the Civil War and were instrumental in building the settlement.

Tampa went into an economic slump after the Civil War and declined in population to 720 by 1880. Many ex-slaves stayed in the area to farm and homestead the land. A group of them established the community of Bealsville near the Alafia River, while many others moved into an area of Tampa called the Scrub, which was northeast of Oaklawn Cemetery. The blacks often had to take unskilled jobs, a situation that contributed to their poverty. **John Williamson** opened a black school in 1871, at about the same time that the Ku Klux Klan began operating in the area. Some twenty years later many blacks joined Cubans and

Italians to establish West Tampa, a thriving area that the city of Tampa incorporated in 1925.

A few blacks served in political office during that time, despite the harassment of the Klan. In time Tampa became a stronghold of Cuban resistance and a cigar-making center around Ybor City, which today is east of the intersection of I-4 and I-275. The black Cubans who went to Tampa for the cigar-making business felt excluded from other ethnic groups in the city, for example the Spaniards, the Italians, and even the American blacks. Black and white cigar makers had been part of the same mutual aid society, but Florida laws against integrated social clubs made them split in 1900, and so the black Cubans established LA UNIÓN MARTÍ-MACEO. In 1908, they built a two-story brick building, which lasted until urban renewal demolished it in 1965. Members secured another building at 1226 E. 7th Avenue that was built in 1950 and continued their meetings at the gateway to Ybor City and just east of Nuccio Parkway. The organization worked to promote heritage preservation activities in Ybor City and served black Cubans whom other Cuban and Spanish clubs excluded. Those black Cuban cigar makers became very involved in early Cuban independence activities in the town, especially with José Martí. One of the black Cubans who helped Martí was **Paulina Pedroso**, who is honored with a plaque at the José Martí Park on the corner of 13th Street and 8th Avenue in Ybor City at the site

Black Cubans established La Unión Martí-Maceo in Tampa.

where her boarding house stood.

The racist movie, *The Birth of a Nation* (1915), which had high praise for the Ku Klux Klan, led to a black movie, *The Birth of a Race*, which was filmed in the Sulphur Springs area of Tampa in 1917–18. The latter film, most of which has been lost, was supposed to be the story of mankind and emphasized equality among all races in the world.

Among the important blacks who helped other blacks in the city was **Christina Meacham** (1865–1927), who taught for forty years and became the first black woman principal of a Tampa school; the **MEACHAM EARLY CHILDHOOD CENTER** at 1225 India Street honors this woman, who was the daughter-in-law of **Robert Meacham**, a post-Reconstruction black leader in Florida.

The **HELPING HAND DAY NURSERY**, which has had several locations in Tampa, is one of the city's oldest African American-owned businesses. For over seventy-five years it provided a safe place for the children of working black families. It was organized by one of Tampa's most famous African Americans: **Blanche Armwood Beatty** (1890–1939).

She came from a background of achievers.

The governor had appointed her grandfather to the Hillsborough County Commission in 1875; her father was Tampa's first black uniformed policeman, a school supervisor, and a deputy sheriff. Young Blanche passed Florida's teacher exam at age twelve, successfully argued in court the following year for a friend's acquittal, graduated with honors from Spelman Seminary in Atlanta at sixteen, and began teaching third-graders in Tampa. Around 1915, she began working for Tampa Gas Company and instituted a program to teach domestic workers how to cook on gas stoves. In 1922, she became supervisor of black schools in the county and served well for eight years. She convinced school board authorities to build new schools for blacks, improve the poor conditions of the older schools, organize parent-teacher associations in the black community, begin a vocational school for blacks, and extend the school year for black students from six to nine months. She then organized a school of household arts attended by one thousand homemakers and cooks who learned how to balance diets, plan and serve meals, and do other domestic tasks. She is buried in L'Union Italiana Cemetery in Tampa, on land her family once owned. The **BLANCHE ARM-**

African American workers in Hillsborough County often lived in shacks along dirt roads. *Tampa-Hillsborough County Public Library System*

WOOD HIGH SCHOOL at 12000 U.S. 92 in Seffner is named after her.

Segregation became a way of life for Tampa blacks in the twentieth century. Even when they became sick, they had to go to segregated facilities, for example the CLARA FRYE MEMORIAL HOSPITAL, which was named after a black nurse who had begun taking in black patients to her home in Tampa Heights in the early 1900s and who ran the private seventeen-bed facility for twenty years. The hospital opened in West Tampa in 1938 and served thousands of blacks until the formerly all-white hospitals began treating blacks after the Civil Rights Act of 1964 outlawed segregation. That hospital, which was located where Tampa Presbyterian Village is today (721 W. Green Street), shut down in 1967 and was demolished in 1973. In 1991, Tampa General Hospital renamed a nine-floor patient-care wing the Clara Frye Pavilion in honor of this great woman.

Even those black soldiers stationed at Tampa's MacDill Field at the beginning of World War II found that segregation kept the races apart in the city, just as it did in the Armed Forces at that time. Officials actually worked up a contingency plan to establish martial law in Tampa in case racial violence occurred.

What helped many blacks endure segregation was the religious faith they had and the churches established to help them. For example, ST. PAUL AFRICAN METHODIST EPISCOPAL CHURCH at 506 E. Harrison Street, built between 1906 and 1917, has been important as a religious site and also a leader in the fight to integrate the city. The church traces its history back to 1870, when Rev. T. W. Long walked from Brooksville, Florida, to Tampa to establish a mission. On the night of his arrival in Tampa, Rev. Long began preaching and received his first three members. The next day Rev. Long and his new members began building a mission, called Brush Arbor Mission, out of palmetto thatch leaves. When Rev. Long went on to south Florida to establish more missions,

Rev. (Rabbit) Thompson stayed behind to work in Tampa. When the cold of winter set in, a Mr. Jones offered the use of an old log house between Franklin Street and Florida Avenue for services.

After a yellow fever epidemic of the 1890s forced the closing of this building, members bought a lot on Marion Street between Harrison and Fortune Streets and there built a church, called Mount Moriah. Storms destroyed that building and another one that replaced it, but members built a new church, called St. Paul A.M.E. In 1917, the three-hundred-member congregation completed the building of the present Gothic Revival structure at 506 E. Harrison Street. As the largest black-owned building in the city and one located on a major street and close to downtown, the church was a good meeting place for different black organizations, especially during the civil rights movement of the 1950s and 1960s.

Another church with a long history is GREATER BETHEL MISSIONARY BAPTIST at 1206 Jefferson Street North. Its stately brick building, built in 1949, towers over a walled-in cemetery. The church can trace its origins back to 1893, when its few members pitched a tent near the present building and called the church Ebenezer Missionary Baptist, to be changed later to Bethel Baptist and later to Greater Bethel Missionary Baptist.

ST. PETER CLAVER SCHOOL at 1401 Governor Street had its beginnings in 1883, when William Tyrell, S.J., pastor of Tampa's St. Louis Church bought the Methodist church on Morgan Street to establish a school for black children. He had workers make necessary changes, and then in 1894 two sisters of the Order of the Holy Names began classes for sixteen children. Less than two weeks later arsonists burned the school down. Undaunted, Father Tyrell bought some property on the corner of Governor and Scott Streets and had the classes resume in October of that year. By the end of the school year eighty students were attending classes. The school was so good that just seven years after its founding the first of its many

African Americans and others without a good education had to be content with jobs like sorting flowers, as these women did in Hillsborough County. *Tampa-Hillsborough County Public Library System*

graduates passed the teachers' examination and was certified by the Board of Public Instruction.

When students outgrew the old wooden building, benefactors financed a new brick building in 1929. An annex was built in 1952. In 1970, the school eliminated the seventh and eighth grades because a nearby Catholic school had expanded its junior high program enough to take in St. Peter Claver's junior high students. St. Peter Claver is the oldest parish school in the Diocese of St. Petersburg.

The Dobyville area in Hyde Park was founded by **Richard C. Doby**, a black man who accumulated a large plot of land after he settled along the railroad tracks in Hyde Park at the end of the nineteenth century. He also donated land for what became known as **DOBYVILLE ELEMENTARY SCHOOL**

at 307 S. Dakota Avenue. Doby was a trash collector who had his own workers and trucks. He lived at 201 S. Oregon Avenue and later at 1403 Azeele Street in Tampa. Throughout the twentieth century much of Dobyville was lost because of development, including construction of the Lee Roy Selmon Expressway, a road that was named after **Lee Roy Selmon**, an African American star for the Tampa Bay Buccaneers football team and a generous contributor to humanitarian causes in the area.

Tampa's oldest black school, **MIDDLETON HIGH SCHOOL** at 4302 N. 24th Street, became a middle school during desegregation. It honors in its name **G. S. Middleton**, an African American who served the community for many years. Among its graduates were Hillsborough County

Commissioner **Sylvia Kimbell** and State Representative **James Hargrett**. A 1940 graduate of the school, **Robert W. Saunders**, became field secretary for the Florida NAACP in 1952 after the murder of **Harry T. Moore** (see Chapter Five) and served during the crucial years of the civil rights movement, 1952 until 1966. His wife, **Helen Saunders**, became president of the Tampa Branch of the NAACP in 1976 and launched a voter registration drive that was called the most effective in the nation.

In 1946, **Robert Saunders** worked for the city's weekly black newspaper, the *Florida Sentinel Bulletin*, the oldest black paper continuously published in the state. It had been established as the *Gainesville Sentinel* by **Matthew Lewey** in 1887, had its name changed to the *Florida Sentinel* when he moved to Pensacola in 1894, moved to Jacksonville in 1914, and was sold to **W. W. Andrews** in 1919. The Andrews family still publishes in Tampa today.

For the first three decades of the twentieth century Tampa had the dubious distinction of leading the state in lynchings. In the 1930s conditions for blacks had improved a little, but local whites still lynched a black man, **Robert Johnson**, for supposedly having robbed and raped a white woman; despite having been exonerated by the police, he was still kidnapped by white vigilantes and killed.

In the 1950s tensions arose as blacks tried to desegregate restaurants and public facilities. In 1959, Mayor Julian Lane formed Tampa's Biracial Committee, the state's first such committee, consisting of blacks such as Tampa resident and president of the Florida NAACP Reverend **A. Leon Lowry**, pastor of Beulah Baptist Church, and **Perry Harvey Sr.**, the president of the International Longshoreman's Union, which employed many blacks. White leaders joining them included attorney Cody Fowler and port developer Robert Thomas. Another important black leader was **C. Bythe Andrews**, publisher of *The Florida Sentinel*

Bulletin, the city's black newspaper. The following year saw a sit-in at Woolworth's by **Clarence Fort** and about sixty students. After seven months of negotiation, local stores agreed to eliminate their "whites only" eating policy and officials agreed to desegregate movie theaters and municipal facilities.

The city's tranquility was broken in 1967 when a police officer shot a robbery suspect, an action that triggered a race riot which destroyed much of the Central Avenue black business area. Twenty years later another race riot erupted in College Hill, one of the city's poorest housing projects, when the police killed a black man with a choke-hold. However, in 1983, Tampans elected their first black state legislator and their first black city councilman. In 1992, developers proposed a pirate museum for the city, but many blacks were angry that the museum would center around the *Whydah*, a former slave ship; the Coalition of African-American Organizations (CAAO) opposed the project, and it died.

In 2000 Tampa, had 69,871 blacks (25%) out of a total population of 280,015.

29.

Holmes County

The legislature established this county in 1848 and named it for Holmes Creek, the eastern boundary of the county. The county had a population of 18,564 in the 2000 census, 1,207 (6.5%) of whom were African Americans. That number was the fourth-lowest of Florida counties.

E. W. Carswell's *Homesteading: The History of Holmes County, Florida* describes how African Americans went to the county in the beginning of the twentieth century to work in the naval-stores industry, one that demanded very hard labor under difficult working conditions for low pay. Operators went into the county with black laborers who were skilled at working on the pine trees there. The operators of the naval-stores facilities built two-room cabins for the African American workers near the actual work sites. The cabins, built at a cost of about $200, had a life expectancy of up to twenty years. However, the cabins were seldom screened and did not have indoor plumbing. The only source of water was a nearby shallow well or spring. The workers obtained fuel for cooking and heating from wood they could gather in the woods. Life was very hard for them.

When the forest industry declined in the second quarter of the twentieth century, many of the black workers went elsewhere for work, reducing the number of African Americans in the county to little more than three percent of the total.

African Americans who remained in the county had separate schools in the towns of Bonifay, Eleanor, Esto, Limestone, Noma, and Ponce de Leon, for a total enrollment of 1504. For example, a new Bayview High School for black students was built in Bonifay for $54,294, and last-ed more than a decade until integration. When integration put an end to the segregated schools in the mid-1960s, the schools were deactivated.

Carswell noted that in 1986 there were three black churches in Holmes County: Bethel AME and Mt. Zion Baptist, both in Bonifay, and St. Marks AME in Noma.

Many African Americans have attended tent revivals over the years. *Tampa-Hillsborough County Public Library System*

30.

Indian River County

By the time the Florida Legislature established Indian River County in 1925, many blacks had settled there and were supporting their families by fishing and raising citrus and vegetables. The county had a population of 112,947 in the 2000 census, 9,262 (8.2%) of whom were African Americans.

The Ais Indians inhabited this part of Florida long before the Spanish explorers arrived in the sixteenth century with diseases and deadly weapons. Indian middens found along the Indian River testify to the presence of the Native Americans, who lived and buried their dead near the river.

A Spanish treasure fleet was shipwrecked off the coast there in 1715. Salvors found much of the treasure from that shipwreck in the twentieth century and helped give the area the nickname of "Treasure Coast."

One of the earliest white settlers was George Fleming of St. Augustine. The King of Spain granted him almost one thousand acres on both sides of the St. Sebastian River in 1790 in what came to be known as the Fleming Grant. More and more settlers moved in over the next century. Even before the end of the Civil War in America, runaway slaves and a few free slaves settled in the area in the hopes of living in peace and raising their families. The Seminole Indians who were already there befriended many of the blacks and taught them how to hunt, fish, and farm.

After the American Civil War, new settlers moved in and founded such towns as Sebastian and Roseland. Pelican Island became the first National Wildlife Refuge in the United States when President Theodore Roosevelt established the site in 1903.

While most settlers arrived in the region in the nineteenth century by boat, workers built railroads there in the early twentieth century, and that brought in many more people. African Americans helped build the railroads and then settled down themselves after its completion in order to raise their families and earn a living. One of the first letter carriers in the region was a black man named **Peter White**, who delivered the mail from Titusville to the Indian River area by boat.

Fellsmere

The town of Fellsmere to the southwest of Sebastian was developed and named by Nelson Fell, who planned to drain 118,000 acres at the headwaters of the St. Johns River, sell the reclaimed land to farmers, and become rich in the process. He helped found the town of Fellsmere, a name that combined his own with "mere," meaning "a great watery place." His idea failed when World War I began, torrential downpours flooded the land, and an economic depression hit the country.

Today, around three hundred African Americans live in Fellsmere. For years the cemetery they buried their dead in was Fellsmere's Brookside Cemetery east of I-95 and just north of the intersection of County Roads 512 and 510. The cemetery actually has two parts separated by a creek: one for the whites, which is better cared for, and another one that the blacks used for many years. The black cemetery, which some people incorrectly refer to as Old Sebastian Cemetery, has the black gravestones at the back over a small bridge at the western edge.

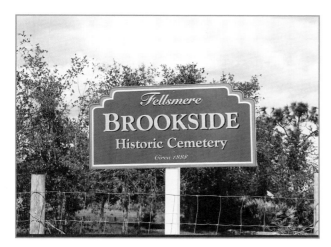

Brookside Cemetery near Fellsmere had a separate section in the back for the burial of African Americans.

Relatives of the deceased used to go to the cemetery to take care of markers and stones, especially on Memorial Day, when families would gather at the creek for a picnic and a grave clean-up. A group of young people from Fellsmere, Young Blacks In Action, has cleaned up the cemetery, but it will take much care to keep it that way.

Alvin Thomas was the first black to be elected mayor of Fellsmere (1983). Several African Americans were elected to the city council before Mr. Thomas, including **Andrew Clayton**, **Obie Smith**, and **Jonathan Washington**.

Gifford

William Brown was one of the first blacks to settle in the area, after he moved from Georgia and obtained a U.S. government homestead grant for sixty acres along the Indian River in 1896. He planted citrus in the rich soil and became a prosperous grower. A small settlement, Brownsville,

honored him, but the name later became Gifford, the last name of an early white settler, Henry Gifford.

The East Coast train depot was in Gifford, and that is where several black-labor camps developed. African Americans helped extend the Florida East Coast Railway down the east coast of Florida until it eventually reached Miami.

The Gifford area used to have many citrus groves, but they have been replaced by trailer parks and modest homes, with sections of upscale homes built by African Americans, some of whom worked in menial jobs, saved their money, and slowly worked their way up the economic ladder.

Among the local leaders who helped ease the integration of schools in Indian River County in the twentieth century was **Walter Jackson**, the first black elected to the School Board of Trustees. He and his brother, **Theodore**, organized a group of blacks in 1967 into Industrial Growers Incorporated, which owned and sold real estate, managed citrus groves, and built and managed the first modern supermarket in Gifford.

When more and more black people settled in the Sebastian area, they established the MACEDONIA BAPTIST CHURCH, which stood for many years on Bob Circle off Main Street behind today's post office west of U.S. 1. Murray E. and Sarah Braddock Hall, a white couple, donated the land for the church in 1907, for which **Mose M. Hill**, **Sebrose P. Norris**, and **Syd Norris** served as trustees of what was first called the Colored Baptist Church of Sebastian, built in 1908. The Sebastian Methodist Church donated to the new church benches and also a bell which had once called slaves in from the fields in Louisiana. The congregation, which grew so large that its members often had to stand outside the little church and lean in the open windows to take part in the service, named the church the Macedonia Baptist Church. The pastors of the church included Reverends **Thomas**, **Jones**, **Stagles**, **Sheddick**, and **Matthis**.

When the church building deteriorated badly in the 1990s, county officials threatened to tear it down, but local leaders raised $8,000 to move the building to 45th Street in Gifford. Of particular interest is the darkened century-old wooden board displayed in a window frame in the building's front; it reminds visitors of a time when the church was the only house of worship for blacks in what is today Indian River County.

Directions: The church is .4 miles west of U.S. 1 and on the northwest corner of 45th Street and 28th Court, just past Gifford Middle School on 45th Street.

The Macedonia Baptist Church in Gifford was moved from one section of town to another.

That church is just one of about thirty black churches in the county, churches that represent a strong part of the community. Ministers of such churches in this country have often commanded respect, even by white politicians who want their support. One can argue that the black church in the United States, especially in the South, was the center of protests against the injustices of slavery and segregation, that the leaders of the black community have often been ministers, who spoke eloquently and were able to solidify the disparate elements of the black community to speak as one.

Gifford was also the site of the earliest black school in the county. Around 1901, Mr. W. E. Geoffrey donated land for such a school and a park in Gifford. Before then, those few blacks who could read and write may have taught other blacks those skills in the local churches, but black children were not allowed to attend the first white school built in 1898. The small school that was built for the blacks later became part of Gifford High School; children could attend their first school for grades one through six. And the black children attended school only three months of the year, when there were no crops to pick. If the children wanted an education beyond the sixth grade, they had to go to another county. That was very difficult financially for the families.

Education helped many African Americans secure decent jobs at a time when the uneducated had to settle for menial jobs. And while many African Americans at the beginning of the twentieth century worked as railroad laborers, sawmill workers, and domestics, little by little their descendants were able to do better. After World War II, when more and more tourists came to the county, African Americans worked as cooks, dishwashers, and bellhops in the new hotels.

In the 1950s, African Americans moved into semi-skilled jobs and self-employment positions like barbers, carpenters, beauticians, and masons. The Civil Rights Movement of the 1960s opened up more opportunities, including state and government jobs. By the 1970s, even more opportunities presented themselves, especially for those with a good education. Piper Aircraft, for example, hired skilled and semi-skilled workers to build airplanes there. By the late 1970s, Dr. **Thomas A. Jackson** of Gifford became the first black doctor to open a successful medical practice in the county, and **Blayne Jennings** was the first black to open a law practice in Gifford. **Dallas Yates** became the first black deputy sheriff in the county. Today, there are black medical doctors and lawyers throughout the county. In education and law enforcement and business, many African Americans are working in the county.

Sebastian

Spanish explorers named the river in the area in honor of St. Sebastian. A small settlement that grew up along that river was first called New Haven in 1882, but later became Sebastian in 1884 because of its proximity to the river. The little town became an important fishing and trading center that used the river steamers to take products to and from other towns. A cut through the barrier island on the Indian River to the ocean increased the prosperity of the town, but workers had to dredge it several times to keep it open.

Black people moved to the area in the nineteenth century, although census records seemed to ignore most of them. The 1885 Florida State Census, for example, showed only one black in the area, **R. Hamilton**, a laborer. When Henry Flagler's Florida East Coast Railway came to the Roseland-Sebastian area in 1893, many black men arrived to lay the tracks and then stayed behind to maintain the line. They brought their wives, who worked as vegetable pickers, domestics, and launderers for white families.

The first resident physician in Sebastian was Dr. David Rose, who began practicing medicine there in 1910. The white doctor treated white patients inside his house at 1063 Louisiana Avenue, but treated black patients on the outside porch. The house burned down around 2001, but the property can be seen on the southwest corner of Palmer Lane and Louisiana Avenue.

Wabasso

Twelve miles north of Vero Beach is Wabasso, where many blacks lived while they worked in the turpentine camps and sawmills. They attended the first African American church in town, Beulah African Methodist Church, which became the Allen Chapel African Methodist Episcopal Church. Their children attended the first black school in Wabasso, Douglas Elementary.

One of the streets in Wabasso, Broxton Road, commemorates a black man, **John Broxton**, a brick mason who built many of the early brick homes in the county. He bought a ten-acre tract of land, built a home there for his family, and donated land for part of 64th Avenue, which honors him today in its name: Broxton Road. He felt so strongly about education that he sent his children to Daytona Beach to attend Bethune-Cookman School up to ninth grade. He saved enough money to buy a used car to transport six children to Fort Pierce to finish high school and later bought a bus to take more children to Fort Pierce to attend high school. County officials, realizing what an unselfish act that was, agreed to pay for the gas and later paid a bus driver to do the driving up until the mid-1930s.

The history of African Americans in this particular county, along with those in Martin and St. Lucie Counties, is well documented in *Treasure Coast Black Heritage: A Pictorial History*, a book that other counties should emulate.

31.

Jackson County

Florida's third county, established in 1822, was named for General Andrew Jackson, the first governor of the territories of East and West Florida and later the President of the United States. In the 1820s, Jackson was one of five counties, along with Gadsden, Jefferson, Leon, and Madison Counties, in which slaves made up more than fifty percent of the population. North Florida's so-called "black belt" region had a rich soil that enabled plantations to thrive, although at great personal cost to their black slaves.

The county had a population of 46,755 in the 2000 census, 12,437 (26.6%) of whom were African Americans.

Jackson County was similar to other counties in what came to be known as Middle Florida (Gadsden, Hamilton, Jackson, Jefferson, Leon, and Madison) in that the early churches established there had among their small congregations both white and black parishioners. The blacks had to sit apart from the whites in the segregated churches and, in fact, often had a separate, side entrance. The whites could tolerate the situation because they often believed that church-going slaves would be easier to subject to the rule of the overseer, especially when white ministers preached to the slaves how important it was for them to respect their "betters," i.e. subject themselves to the whites. Slaveholders were increasingly reluctant to have preachers from the North, who were sometimes abolitionists spending time in Florida for their health, preach to the slaves for fear that those preachers would foment rebellion.

The Spanish had thought they could rely on Native Americans to work the fields and produce income during the first Spanish period of rule there (1565–1763), but European diseases and inhumane treatment led to the demise of the Native Americans. To replace them, the Spanish imported slaves to Middle Florida to work on early plantations, not only because the use of slaves was much cheaper than bringing in European workers, but the former could more easily be forced to work in the heat, high humidity, mosquito-infested fields, and dangerous conditions than could European workers. Those slaves were forced to work, not only in the fields, but also in the Spanish forts, building new fortifications, repairing older ones, and building new ships from the Florida timber resources.

The morality of slavery, however, became an important issue among different sects throughout the eighteenth and first half of the nineteenth century. From the time of the American Revolution, a movement that stressed the freedom of Americans from tyranny, religious leaders in this country argued that slavery was wrong, that it violated religious principles. Such an idea (freeing one's slaves) was particularly difficult for the clergy to defend, not only in relation to others, but especially for those clergy who owned slaves.

Marianna

Marianna, the county seat of Jackson County,

was established in 1823 and named by the original site owners for their two daughters, Mary and Anna or for the wife, Anna Marie, of the town's founder. A Scottish immigrant laid out the town in 1827, and little by little businesses and families moved there. A Civil War skirmish, called the "Battle of Marianna," took place nearby, with the result that Union troops seized six hundred slaves from the area's plantations. Throughout the nineteenth century and into the twentieth century farmers grew peanuts and cotton, crops that demanded hard work, much of it performed by black workers.

In 2000 the town, which lies near U.S. 90 and I-10 in the state's Panhandle, had a population of 6,292, of whom 2,422 (39%) were black. For more about one of the town's blacks, see the section on St. Augustine on page 242: the Cary A. White Complex.

The Joseph W. Russ, Jr. House used to be a plantation house.

The **JOSEPH W. RUSS JR. HOUSE** at 4318 (formerly 310) W. Lafayette Street is now a private residence, but it used to be the main plantation house near where a famous black journalist was born a slave: **Timothy Thomas Fortune** (1856–1928). When the Civil War ended, he joined adults and other children of Marianna in a small church, where two Union soldiers taught them how to read and write. Later he began working at a local newspaper, *The Marianna Courier*, and

learned skills he would keep with him the rest of his life. When his father was elected to the Florida Legislature, the local Ku Klux Klan threatened the Fortune family, and so they had to move to Jacksonville. There young Timothy worked on another newspaper, *The Daily Union*, and learned more about the power of journalism.

He later went on to Howard University and to New York City, where he worked on several important black newspapers: *The New York Globe*, *The Freeman*, *The New York Age*, and *The Negro World*. By the time he died in 1928, he was known as the dean of black journalism and had established the National Afro-American League, one of the earliest equal rights organizations and a predecessor of the National Association for the Advancement of Colored People, to fight for the rights of blacks in this country. His published books include *Black and White: Land, Labor, and Politics in the South* (1884), *The Negro in Politics* (1885), and *Dreams of Life* (1905).

Directions: The large, wooden Russ House is on the north side of W. Lafayette Street just west of Russ Street and between Russ and Daniels Streets west of Jefferson and Caledonia Streets and east of Guyton and Smith Streets.

Timothy Thomas Fortune became a well-known journalist in the early twentieth century. *Florida State Archives*

Fortune would have been pleased with an educational institution established in Marianna in 1961 near the Jackson County Training School for blacks: JACKSON JUNIOR COLLEGE, one of twelve black junior colleges in Florida. Its first president was **William H. Harley Sr.,** the principal of the black high/training school there. The facility attracted African American students from Calhoun, Jackson, and Washington Counties, and prepared many for transfer to Florida A&M University in Tallahassee. In the mid-1960s it merged with Chipola Junior College, which was founded in 1947 as the state's third junior college.

The enrollment figures for Jackson Junior College were as follows:

1961–62: 47 students
1962–63: 83 students
1963–64: 97 students
1964–65: 333 students
1965–66: 443 students

Two tragic events associated with the COURT-HOUSE in the middle of Marianna show how difficult the plight of the black was in the twentieth century. The first event was the 1934 lynching of a black man, **Claude Neal**, who was accused of raping and murdering a white woman, the daughter of one of his employers. After authorities arrested Neal and took him to a jail in Alabama for his protection, a mob of angry whites found out where he was, kidnapped him, returned him to the scene of the murder, tortured him, and then lynched him. They then hung his corpse from a tree on the ground of the courthouse in Marianna. The horror of that torture and execution so incensed much of the country that lynching began to decline in popularity in the U.S. Lynching had become a means by which white racists, who lynched almost three thousand blacks since the 1880s, were able to control the blacks after the Civil War.

The other tragic event associated with the courthouse was the second trial of two black men, **Freddie Pitts** and **Wilbert Lee**, who were falsely accused of killing two men in Port St. Joe in 1963. The first trial of the two innocent men that year sentenced the men to death, but the Florida Supreme Court ordered a new trial in 1971 because the state had suppressed evidence and excluded black jurors in the trial. The Marianna Courthouse was the scene of the second trial, seventy-four miles north of Port St. Joe, but another all-white jury convicted the two black men even though another man had already confessed to the crime. Pitts and Lee spent nine years on death row, but Governor Reubin Askew and three other Cabinet members believed the men were innocent and pardoned them in 1975.

Around eight miles northeast of downtown Marianna is RENAISSANCE PARK at 5989 Hartsfield Renaissance Park, a forty-acre park with artifacts and items from early rural life in Florida. In September and December each year, African American artisans demonstrate their trades for the public.

32.

Jefferson County

The legislature established this county in 1827 and named it for President Thomas Jefferson, who had died on July 4th of the preceding year. In the 1820s, Jefferson was one of five counties, along with Gadsden, Jackson, Leon, and Madison Counties, in which slaves made up more than fifty percent of the population. North Florida's so-called "black belt" region had a rich soil that enabled plantations to thrive, although at great personal cost to their black slaves.

Jefferson County had a population of 12,902 in the 2000 census, 4,941 (38.3%) of whom were African Americans.

Festus

The old post office at Festus, one-quarter mile east of Ford Chapel AME Church on W. Lake Road and now on private property, served as a place where mail was delivered between 1904 and 1911 for the Junious Hill and Ford Chapel communities. The postmaster was an African American, **Stepney Thomas Tillman**, minister for the Junious Hill Missionary Baptist Church. The mail carrier, **Puliston Kirksey**, rode a horse to make deliveries.

Monticello

HOWARD ACADEMY HIGH SCHOOL at 665 E. Chestnut Street was originally built as a public school for African Americans. In 1936, officials consolidated grades one through twelve from the Masonic Lodge, Bethel AME Church, and Miss Leonora Mills's store for the new school. The original building became the elementary school in 1940, while a second building became the high school. Today that second building houses the Boys and Girls Club.

ELIZABETH SCHOOL in the Dills Community on Old Salt Road across from Elizabeth Church was originally established in the Elizabeth Church, but later moved to a Masonic Hall, Mount Pleasant Church, and Ruth Hall. **Miles Groover** and his wife, **Daisy Black Groover**, donated two acres of land for the school, and the parents of the children donated money to build it. Workers in the Works Progress Administration (WPA) finished the project. In 1938, students transferred from the Masonic Hall to the three-room school. Today, the Quins Club, an African American women's community-service organization, uses the building.

For more about a native of Monticello who practiced midwifery in Collier County for twenty-five years, see Chapter Eleven.

Among the schools set up for African Americans after the Civil War were several on plantations. Although the Freedmen's Bureau encouraged the establishment of schools for the ex-slaves and in fact built one in Monticello, the organization did not have much money to support such facilities and relied on local planters to supply the schools. **Robert Meacham**, who was the pastor of the first African American church built in the

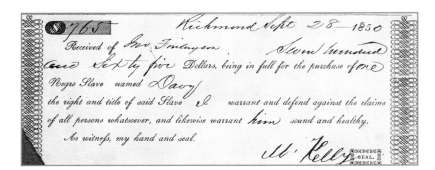

The receipt of a slave purchased in Virginia for a man in Jefferson County, Florida, in 1850. *Florida State Archives*

county, opened the first school for freedmen in his AME church in 1866. The teachers, one male and one female, charged one dollar tuition per pupil, but were able to collect only about one-third of the amount due them. Meacham also served as voter registrar in the county (1867, 1868) and as a member of the constitutional convention (1868) and Florida Senate (1868–79). He also worked as Monticello's postmaster, clerk of the circuit court, and superintendent of schools.

An owner of one of the largest plantations in the county, John Bradley, donated two acres of his land north of Lake Miccosukee and helped support a school for freedmen. William Scott supported a small school for freedmen on his plantation near the same lake. Burton Bellamy helped establish St. Johns School for freedmen near the Aucilla River. Mrs. Edward Henry conducted a similar school at Mount Zion Church on the Gadsden Plantation. Finally, Robert Gamble helped fund a school at Welaunee. With such individual efforts, many African Americans received the rudiments of education in the county.

Washer-women in Jefferson County in the 1870s. *Florida State Archives*

33.
Lafayette County

This county was established in 1856 and named for the Marquis de Lafayette (1757–1834), a Frenchman who had supported the cause of American independence from Great Britain, not only by contributing much of his own money, but also by serving as a major general in the American Revolutionary Army.

The county had a population of 7,022 in the 2000 census, 1,011 (14.4%) of whom were African Americans. That number (1,011) tied Gilchrist County for the fewest African Americans in a Florida county.

Mayo

In the early 1960s, before integration took place, the county had African American schools, for example **KERBO ELEMENTARY SCHOOL** at 696 Willow Street in Mayo. The enrollments in the school's grades in 1963 were as follows: first, seventeen students; second, twelve students; third, twenty students; fourth, ten students; fifth, ten students; sixth, six students; seventh, nine students; and eighth, eight students. The county provided transportation for eight African American students to attend high school in Madison, and offered transportation to any African American students who wanted to attend Suwannee River Junior College in Madison (see Chapter Thirty-nine for more about the black college). Kerbo Elementary School is abandoned today and is badly deteriorating.

Directions to the School: In Mayo, turn left after Mayo Town Park onto C.R. 300 .3 miles west of the town center. Go one block, then turn left on Martin Luther King Jr. Boulevard, then take your first right onto SW Willow Street, and proceed to the end of the dead-end street.

Kerbo Elementary School, which used to serve African American students, is now abandoned and badly deteriorating.

34.

Lake County

The legislature established this county in 1887 from Orange and Sumter Counties and named it for the many lakes within its boundaries: over five hundred named and unnamed of over ten acres apiece. The county had a population of 210,528 in the 2000 census, 17,474 (8.3%) of whom were African Americans.

Clermont

The **TOWNSEND HOUSE** on W. Osceola Street was the original home of **James** and **Sally DeVaughn Townsend**, the first black residents of Clermont.

Eustis

The **ACE THEATRE** at 1609 Bates Avenue was built in the late 1940s and served African American moviegoers in the area. After integration, the community used the building as a church, but later abandoned it.

Groveland

After World War II, when black soldiers returned to Florida from military service, they found that little had changed in terms of race relations. Lake County, for example, which grew much citrus, depended on black workers to work in the fields for low wages and resented any attempts to have them better their lives with fair wages and job opportunities. Two black veterans, **Walter Irvin** and **Samuel Shepherd**, returned to their parents' homes in Groveland after serving in the Army, but refused to endure the inhumane conditions being foisted on them by white owners of citrus groves.

In 1949, a local white woman accused those two young black men and two others of rap-ing her. A white mob then went on a rampage through the town's black neighborhood, and the National Guard had to be called out to restore order. Three of the men (Irvin, Shepherd, and **Charles Greenlee**) were caught and put in jail, while the fourth one fled the county. A posse led by Sheriff Willis McCall caught and killed him. Civil rights' activist **Harry T. Moore** uncovered evidence that the Groveland defendants had been brutally beaten while in the custody of McCall, but a jury convicted the three Groveland defendants, then sentenced Greenlee to prison and Irvin and Shepherd to death.

Two years later, the U.S. Supreme Court overturned that conviction, and Lake County officials immediately prepared to try them again. In November 1951, while Sheriff McCall was driving defendants Irvin and Shepherd back to Lake County for a pre-trial hearing, he shot them, killing Shepherd and critically wounding Irvin. McCall claimed that the handcuffed prisoners had attacked him while trying to escape, but Irvin claimed that the sheriff had simply pulled them out of his car and started firing at them. The shooting created a national scandal.

In the second trial, Irvin was represented by future Supreme Court Justice **Thurgood Marshal**; the venue was changed to neighboring Marion County, but again the jury found Irvin guilty. The case was appealed, but in 1954, the United

States Supreme Court declined to hear it. Acting Governor Charley Johns rejected an appeal for clemency and scheduled Irvin's execution. Irvin won a last-minute stay of execution from the U.S. Supreme Court and—after voters did not re-elect Johns—the new governor, LeRoy Collins, asked for a report on the case and eventually commuted Irvin's sentence to life in prison. In 1962, Greenlee was paroled, moved to Tennessee, and never returned to Florida. Authorities released Irvin in 1968, after which he moved to Miami, but returned in 1970 to Lake County, where he died of a heart attack. Voters continued to reelect Willis McCall despite charges of corruption and abuse, but Governor Reubin Askew finally suspended him from office after a black prisoner was kicked to death.

Leesburg

This town in Lake County was named by Calvin Lee, an early resident who named it after himself. The Lee family came from Alabama in the 1840s to take advantage of the rich lands and the lakes.

In the 1949–1966 period, blacks of Florida wanted an institution of higher learning below the university level to provide a post-secondary education. The twelve black junior colleges established in Florida allowed those Floridians who were not able financially to attend Florida A&M University in Tallahassee or out-of-state colleges to live at home and attend the first two years of college at minimal cost.

JOHNSON JUNIOR COLLEGE was one of those twelve black junior colleges in Florida. Established by legislative act in 1961 to serve black students in Lake and Sumter Counties and offering classes for the first time in the fall of 1962, the school had as its first president Mr. **Perman E. Williams**, then the Supervisor of Negro Education in Lake County. Like the other eleven black junior colleges and white junior colleges, Johnson was to have courses both for those who wanted to transfer to a four-year university and for those who wanted to learn a technical trade. The college began meeting in two portable classrooms on the campus of Carver Heights High School and shared the facilities of the high school. President Williams paid for a school bus out of his own pocket, and the bus enabled students from places between Orlando and Leesburg to attend the school. The enrollment figures for Johnson Junior College showed that it served a good number of students:

1962–63: 250 students
1963–64: 318 students
1964–65: 397 students

In 1965, when the college merged with Lake-Sumter Junior College, local officials did their best to employ the black faculty from Johnson in the integrated college or in high schools. As was often the case in Florida, administrators at the black school had to settle for reduced responsibilities in the integrated college; the president of Johnson Junior College, for example, became the dean at Lake-Sumter Junior College.

In 1996, officials dedicated a building in honor of President Williams on the campus of Lake-Sumter Community College, some thirty years after the merger of the black and white colleges.

As mentioned in Chapter One, **Virgil Darnell Hawkins** was a man who helped integrate the University of Florida (UF). He was born in Okahumpka, Florida, in 1906, eventually graduated from college, worked as a teacher and principal in Daytona, worked at Bethune-Cookman College, and then applied in 1949 to the law school at UF. Four other African Americans also applied to UF at that time, but they went elsewhere to school. UF, citing the 1885 Florida Constitution ("White and colored children shall not be taught in the same school, but impartial provision shall be made for both" [Fl. Constitution, art. 12. #12]), denied admission to all of the applicants, but did forward their papers to Florida A&M. UF could cite the 1896 decision by the U.S. Supreme Court

The Virgil Hawkins Memorial near Leesburg.

The final resting place of Virgil Hawkins.

in *Plessy v. Ferguson* that announced the "separate but equal" doctrine.

Black students who wanted to pursue graduate work had to go out of state. That was especially true for Hawkins since the state of Florida had no other law school at that time. Even though officials offered money to Hawkins in the form of a scholarship, he did not want to leave the state and therefore refused the offer.

Florida officials claimed that it had fulfilled the doctrine of "separate but equal" by establishing Florida A&M, although that college did not offer a law school or, in fact, any graduate or professional programs of study. When the state's Board of Control authorized a law school for Florida A&M in 1949, it did not provide funds for the school and so it did not really function. Hawkins argued that the non-functioning law school was not adequate and filed several suits with the Florida Supreme Court and the U.S. Supreme Court. The FAMU law school was finally established in 1951, and it lasted until 1968, eventually to be re-established by the Florida Legislature in 2001.

The U.S. Supreme Court ordered the Florida Supreme Court to reconsider its decision against

Hawkins in light of the historic 1954 *Brown v. Board of Education* case that overruled the "separate but equal" doctrine of *Plessy*. The Florida Supreme Court refused that demand by the higher court, citing three arguments: that Florida A&M College had a law school for black students; that the *Brown v. Board of Education* case did not apply to Hawkins because he was a 48-year-old adult, not a child; and that admitting Hawkins to UF would cause a disruption to other students at UF.

The Florida Supreme Court adopted delay tactics by appointing a circuit judge to take evidence and determine when and under what circumstances UF could accept black students without disrupting university life. Hawkins again appeared before the U.S. Supreme Court, which again ordered Florida to admit him to the UF law school, but once again Florida officials refused.

Frustrated by the continual refusal of Florida officials to obey the law, the fiftyish Hawkins withdrew his application to UF in exchange for a court order which would later desegregate Florida's public universities. Hawkins then went to the Portia Law School (now the New England School of Law) in Boston, from which he graduated in

1965 and returned to Florida. Because that law school was not accredited, he was not allowed to take the Florida bar examination. Instead he settled in Leesburg, where he worked as a schoolteacher, insurance salesman, public-relations specialist, and director of a community action agency. By the mid-1970s, times had changed dramatically in Florida. Public schools were integrated. Black students had been admitted to UF's law school and had graduated and become practicing attorneys. The Florida Supreme Court had as one of its members **Joseph Hatchett**, an African American. Finally, the Florida Supreme Court allowed the seventy-year-old Virgil Darnell Hawkins to become a practicing attorney in Florida in 1976, twenty-eight years and six petitions after he had first applied to UF's law school.

When Hawkins died in 1988 at age 81, he was praised as a pioneer in promoting the efforts of black students to be treated equally in Florida. In 1998, UF President John Lombardi, with the family of Mr. Hawkins in attendance, unveiled a plaque on the wall of Bryan Hall, the old law-school building up until 1969. The plaque commemorates the state's fortieth anniversary of desegregation in higher education and the fact that the federal court desegregation order was issued on June 18, 1958, three months before the first black UF student, **George Starke Jr.**, was admitted to the law school.

UF's College of Law has an annual Virgil Hawkins Summer Program, which allows students who are accepted for the fall term at the law school a chance to participate in an intensive four-week program with mini-courses about law. A portrait of Virgil Hawkins hangs in UF's Levin College of Law Civil Clinic dedicated to him as the Virgil Hawkins Civil Clinic.

In 2001, UF granted Virgil Hawkins a posthumous Doctor of Laws, the first time the university had awarded such a posthumous degree.

Directions to the Virgil Hawkins Memorial and Cemetery outside Leesburg: To reach both, traveling south on U.S. Highway 27/441, approximately five miles south of Leesburg, turn right on County Road (C.R.) 48 West; a gas station is on one corner and a grocery store plaza is on the other. Go west on CR 48 approximately 1.5–2 miles to the traffic light at the intersection of C.R. 33. To reach the memorial, cross over C.R. 33; the first paved road to the right is Virgil Hawkins Circle, where the memorial is. For the cemetery, where Mr. Hawkins is buried: before reaching C.R. 33, turn right on a clay road near the entrance of which is a fernery. Go about one-quarter to one-half mile, and the cemetery is on the right.

After the FAMU law school graduated its last class in 1968, two years after a law school opened up at nearby Florida State University (FSU), most of the FAMU law library books were transferred to FSU, increasing that school's book collection by over thirty percent. To commemorate the history of the FAMU law school and to honor Virgil Hawkins's role in desegregating legal education in the state, those FAMU books have bookplates designating them as part of the "Virgil D. Hawkins Collection."

Mount Dora

In 1898, local African Americans established the **WITHERSPOON LODGE OF FREE AND ACCEPTED MASONS, NO. 111**, which is today one of the oldest functioning African American lodges in Florida. **Prince Hall** (1735–1807), a firm opponent of racial oppression in New England, founded the first African American lodge in this country. In 1903, the Witherspoon Lodge bought the vernacular building at 1420 Clayton Street in Mount Dora and has been meeting there ever since. The building also houses the Order of the Eastern Star, the Masonic women's auxiliary. When fire destroyed the city's one-room segregated school for African American children (Public School No. 66, which had been established in 1886), the Witherspoon Building served as a schoolhouse until the building of the Milner-Rosenwald Academy, as well as a temporary meeting place for two churches.

Clayton Street is .1 mile west of Highland Street. The Lodge is 1.3 miles east on Clayton Street from the town.

Lodges such as the one in Mount Dora have been an integral part of black life in the South and date back to the days of slavery, when clandestine societies needed to hide their activities from the eyes of the slave master. The Black Masons, begun in 1787, and the Odd Fellows, begun in 1843, developed when mainstream white societies excluded blacks. Other black counterpart groups, like the Elks and the Knights of Pythias, were begun after the Civil War. Such societies were usually third in the hierarchy of black loyalty, after their family and church. The societies provided reasonably priced insurance against disasters as well as recreational facilities that allowed the participants to escape the monotony of work.

A plaque at 1560 Highland Street (one of the main streets in the town), the former site of the **MILNER-ROSENWALD ACADEMY** and the present site of a Head Start facility, notes the role that the academy played in the community. Julius Rosenwald, one-time president of Sears, Roebuck and Co. and the founder of the Rosenwald Foundation, provided the funds to build some 5,300 Rosenwald schools in the South and Southwest from 1918 to 1932 in order to educate African American children. Rosenwald, the son of German Jewish immigrants, believed that racial prejudice could be very destructive and wanted to do something to help those who were afflicted.

The Milner-Rosenwald Academy in Mount Dora, built in 1926, served the children of the community until 1962. The elementary school also served as a facility for fellowship and community gatherings and housed the city's first kindergarten, the East Town branch library, the youth center, and, later, the Head Start program. The success of that school led to the building of another local Milner-Rosenwald school at 1250 Grant Avenue, one that was dedicated in 1955 and renamed Mount Dora Middle School in 1970. They were just two of 125 such schools built in Florida with Rosenwald grants, including ten in Lake County. The Northeast Black History Committee, Mount Dora, Inc. helped establish the state marker as a reminder of an important part of the black history of the town.

The 2000 census indicated that Mount Dora had 1,806 African Americans or 19% of the total town population.

The Witherspoon Lodge of Free and Accepted Masons, No. 111, is in Mount Dora.

35.
Lee County

The legislature established this county in 1887 and named it after Confederate General Robert E. Lee. The county had a population of 440,888 in the 2000 census, 29,099 (6.6%) of whom were African Americans.

Fort Myers

In the nineteenth century, this city on the southwest coast was the site of a military outpost, from which authorities shipped Seminole Indians to western reservations. Right before the Civil War, Major James S. Evans, a surveyor, brought in slaves from his Virginia plantation to cultivate the land, but the war disrupted life there, and it wasn't until the war ended and the telegraph line reached Fort Myers in 1869 that settlers began arriving in greater numbers. The first free black to settle in the area seems to have been **Nelson Tillis**, who arrived in 1867; more than one hundred of his descendants still live in Lee County.

When Fort Myers was incorporated in 1885, the area had only five hundred people, twenty of whom were black, but the coming of the railroad in 1904, connecting Fort Myers with Tampa and the North, attracted more people and increased the prosperity of farmers who could ship their perishable crops to northern markets. Blacks worked on farms, in hotels, and in the lumber mills, prospering until the Depression of the 1930s put many out of work. Fort Myers and the surrounding Lee County experienced a population explosion in the twentieth century as more and more people moved south to take advantage of the area's semi-tropical climate. The 2000 census indicated that Fort Myers had 16,095 African Americans or 33% of the total city's population.

From those early days, black families wanted the best education possible for their children. The minutes of the area's first school board meeting, held in 1887, stated that "the colored people shall be encouraged to organize a school district and receive equal benefits as sub-district No. 3 in New Prospect." According to some records, the school board hired a black teacher, **Wesley Roberts**, and paid him $20 a month to teach a three-month term in the black district of North Fort Myers near Hancock Creek. The next year the school board named **Prince Robinson** as trustee of another black school district in Fort Myers. By 1900 the school-age students in the area were as follows:

	Male	Female	Total
White	395	396	791
Blacks	17	15	32
Indians	16	16	32

Eight years later seventy black students were attending school there.

The **PAUL LAWRENCE DUNBAR SCHOOL** at 1857 High Street off Dr. Martin Luther King Jr., Boulevard (formerly Anderson Avenue) was opened in 1927 and served as the school for the predominantly black Dunbar community. The school was named for black poet **Paul Lawrence (or Laurence) Dunbar** (1872–1906) of Ohio and had for its first principal **James Robert Dixon**; it became so well known for its excellence that

The former Paul Lawrence Dunbar School now offers adult classes.

children from as far away as Lakeland attended it to complete their high school requirements. In 1963, officials built a new high school one mile away on Edison Avenue and named it Dunbar High School. It remained an all-black high school until 1969, when it became associated with the present Riverdale High School and then a middle school for grades six to eight. Today it serves as the Dunbar Community School for adult classes and other community activities.

At the Dunbar School are buildings belonging to the former **WILLIAMS ACADEMY**, which opened in 1913 as a black school and later became known as Williams Primary. The first Williams Academy (1913) was a two-story structure built between Lemon Street and Anderson Avenue. After fire destroyed the second floor of the building, workers moved the first floor to the Dunbar campus be-

tween 1935 and 1937. They moved the building to the present location in 1995. Its first teachers were **K. D. Wilson** and **Sadda Ford**; among its graduates was **Edgar Leo Barker**, the first graduate to return to Lee County to teach and who later served as principal of Dunbar High School. Located on the northern side of Anderson Avenue at Cranford Avenue, extending back to Lemon Street, the two-story school with classrooms on both floors and a name which honored **J. S. Williams** (the Superintendent of the Colored Schools) closed in 1927, when the Dunbar School opened. Its buildings have been altered and moved to the Dunbar School site.

WILLIAMS ACADEMY BLACK HISTORY MUSEUM at 1936 Henderson Avenue has a Living History Classroom, representing conditions in the 1940s, and exhibits about the many contributions of African Americans to Southwest Florida over the years. It is the first black museum in that area of Florida. Open Tuesday through Friday, 10 A.M.–4 P.M. Phone: (239) 332-3587.

Directions to the museum: From I-75 take exit 23 west to Henderson Avenue; go north on Henderson Avenue. The museum is on the left about one block from there.

The Williams Academy Black History Museum is housed in the Lee County Black History Society building.

One of the long-time teachers at Dunbar Elementary School was **Evelyn Sams**, who retired in 1971 after a forty-seven-year career in education. **Jessie Bennett Sams** wrote an autobiography, *White Mother*, about growing up in the black section of Fort Myers. A black educator who was appointed to the Florida Board of Regents by Governor Lawton Chiles was **Audrea Anderson**, a professor of English at Edison Community College.

One section of Fort Myers that attracted many blacks over the years was Harlem Heights, which is southeast of McGregor Boulevard, east of San Carlos Boulevard, and south of Gladiolus Drive. Dr. **Marion Johnson**, a black physician who built a settlement for migrant farm workers in the 1940s, named this site after the country's most famous black neighborhood. Today the area, which consists of eleven streets and around seven hundred residents, has a growing number of Hispanics.

MCCULLUM HALL at the northeast corner of Cranford Avenue and Dr. Martin Luther King Jr. Boulevard (formerly Anderson Avenue) served for many years as the entertainment center for the black community and hosted such entertainers as **Count Basie**, **Duke Ellington**, and **Louis Armstrong**. During World War II many black soldiers went to the USO there from nearby Page and Buckingham Fields, where they were training for overseas duty. Today one can reach the site, which was built in 1938 and is today a store and rooming house, by going south on U.S. 41 just over the Caloosahatchee River and turning east on Dr. Martin Luther King Jr. Boulevard for about eleven blocks.

The **ETTA POWELL HOME** at 2764 Lime Street used to house black major league baseball players who trained at Terry Park, but were not allowed to stay at area hotels in the days of segregation. The hospital for blacks, **JONES-WALKER HOSPITAL** on High Street, honored in its name Mrs. Melissa Jones and Candis Walker, who worked hard to raise money for the facility; it operated from the late 1920s until a federal edict closed it in 1965. Finally, the **DR. ELLA PIPER CENTER** at 1771 Evans Avenue honors **Ella Mae Piper** (1884–1954), who established the first beauty parlor and chiropody (for foot problems) office in Fort Myers.

MOUNT OLIVE AFRICAN METHODIST EPISCOPAL CHURCH at 2754 Orange Street is one of the oldest churches in the Dunbar Community, dating back to 1895. The congregation was originally organized in the Lee County Courthouse. The congregation built the present structure at Palm Avenue and Orange Street around 1929.

Sanibel Island

Sanibel, which is twelve miles long and about three miles wide at its widest point, and Captiva, which is only five miles long and about half a mile wide at its widest, are barrier islands off the southwest coast of Florida.

The Calusa Indians inhabited the islands in the sixteenth century and resisted the Spanish explorers seeking gold and converts. After the Spanish weapons and diseases killed off the Calusas, pirates inhabited the islands and, eventually, lighthouse keepers at the lighthouse at Point Ybel on Sanibel, farmers, fishermen, visitors, and those who liked isolation. The building of a bridge and causeway to the mainland in 1963 brought in many more settlers and thousands of visitors, effectively changing the islands forever and driving up land values.

A few black families settled on the islands in the early part of the twentieth century, but work was hard to come by. Men like **Isaiah Gavin**, who established the first black family on Sanibel, worked for a dollar a day when he could find work. The isolation meant no electricity and no running water, but his family and others preferred the peace and quiet of the islands. The families would fish in the Gulf; farm tomatoes, squash, and eggplant; and then hunt a rabbit or pheasant for dinner. Hurricanes did much damage; for example, the 1926 storm flooded the island with salt water and ruined much of the farmland. After such hurricanes, some of the blacks and whites decided to move to the mainland where they could more easily earn a living.

When many of the whites left after that storm, their Baptist church became vacant, and so James Johnson, a farmer and the owner of the land on which the church stood, offered it in 1927 to the remaining black families for a school, SANIBEL COLORED SCHOOL. Up until that time the black children on the island had not had a school. Today the Schoolhouse Gallery at 520 Tarpon Bay Road occupies that site and has housed an art gallery since 1973, but it stands as a memorial to the school that once served as a school for blacks. In 1929, Lee County bought the building, which had been built in 1909 or 1910, from the Florida Baptist Convention for $1,500. The first principal was Miss **Angelita Stafford Swain George**, and Miss **Hazel Hammond** was a teacher who taught there until 1933.

Other teachers included **Helen V. Goodman** and **Agnes Thompson** (1933–34), **Ernestine Mims** (1934–35), **Wardell Salters**, and **Lossie Pearson** (1947–48). Although closed from 1940 until 1946 for World War II, when the black children may have been bused to Fort Myers, the building was used by the black children until 1963, when officials opened up Sanibel Elementary, the first integrated school in Lee County. Officials named the school an historic landmark in 1991, a designation that will protect the building from relocation or alteration without city approval.

Directions to the old schoolhouse: Turn west on Periwinkle Way just after crossing the toll bridge from the mainland. Periwinkle runs into Tarpon Bay Road, and the school is just to the left of the intersection and north of W. Gulf Drive and south of Sanibel Captiva Road.

In 2000 Sanibel had only sixty blacks (1%) out of a total population of 5,468, and Captiva had none. The high cost of living, especially as high-rises and condominiums spread over the island, has kept many blacks away. Among the present black families are the **Gavins**, the **Jordans**, the **Prestons**, and the **Walkers**, many of whom are descended from the original pioneer black families.

36.
Leon County

Florida's seventh county was established in 1824 and named after Juan Ponce de León, the Spanish explorer who gave Florida its name. The county had a population of 239,452 in the 2000 census, 69,681 (29.1%) of whom were African Americans. That number has decreased significantly from 1860, when the authors of *Landmarks & Legacies* estimate that Leon County had nine thousand slaves and sixty free blacks, compared to only three thousand whites.

Tallahassee

The name of Tallahassee goes back to an Apalachee Indian word meaning "old fields" or "abandoned villages." Spanish adventurers like Pánfilo de Narváez and Hernando de Soto explored the area in the sixteenth century, but white settlers, for example Catholic missionaries, did not move into the area to live until the next century. Farmers began establishing farms in the early eighteenth century, but the real impetus to establish a town in the vicinity came with the decree of the Legislative Council to have the capital of the territory midway between Pensacola and St. Augustine in the 1820s. It had been too difficult and time-consuming for delegates to the territorial legislature, which alternated meeting between Pensacola and St. Augustine, to travel to the two settlements at the west-east extremities of Florida. The town and surrounding Leon County grew steadily over the next century despite an outbreak of yellow fever in 1841 and a disastrous fire two years later.

During the Civil War units from Tallahassee took part in the nearby Battle of Natural Bridge, at which the Confederates successfully defended their city. Many of the Union soldiers were blacks. The war ended for the city in 1865 when Union troops raised the stars and stripes on May 20th, a day that local blacks celebrated as their day of emancipation for years to come. The hopes that blacks had during the Reconstruction period dissipated as white legislators slowly eroded the rights of the blacks and effectively disenfranchised them. Many blacks had to become tenant farmers on cotton and corn plantations, a situation that kept them in poverty for decades.

From 1840 through 1940, blacks outnumbered whites in the area, but in 2000 blacks made up 29% of the city's total population of 124,773, numbering 36,276. Blacks slowly achieved economic and political gains in the twentieth century, although it took a black boycott in 1956–57 against the city's segregated transit system, as well as sit-ins in the 1960s to integrate local stores.

Before the Civil War black Methodists in the South worshipped at white churches, but after the war the black members either formed Colored (later renamed Christian) Methodist churches under the guidance of the old white organizations or they followed the African Methodist Episcopal or African Methodist Episcopal Zion movements. The latter movement began in the North apart from any white sponsorship. An example of a church in this movement in Tallahassee is **BETHEL A.M.E. CHURCH** at 206 W. Virginia Street; in 1865, Rev. **William G. Stewart** organized this church, called by historian Robert

Hall "one of the most politically and socially active churches in Tallahassee" after the Civil War.

The end of the Civil War led many African Americans throughout the South, including Florida, to establish their own churches free from the domination of the white churches to which many slaves had belonged for generations. The new churches allowed African Americans to incorporate their own traditions and culture, but also became the dominant centralized force in the lives of their congregations, encouraging them to use the ballot box to change their living conditions, social functions to encounter similar-believing people, and, later, the pulpit to galvanize the Civil Rights Movement. The central role that black churches played in the lives of thousands of Floridians, as was true elsewhere, from birth to baptism to marriage to death, made them the single most important force in the twentieth century and beyond.

ST. JAMES CHRISTIAN METHODIST EPISCOPAL CHURCH at 104 N. Bronough Street, at the corner of Bronough Street and Park Avenue, is the oldest black church still standing in Tallahassee. The black members of the Methodist Episcopal Church bought the present-day site from Trinity Methodist Church in 1853, but did not gain title to the property until they formed in 1868 a separate organization, St. James Colored (later Christian) Methodist Episcopal (C.M.E.). White bishops at Jackson, Tennessee, consecrated the first black bishops of the C.M.E. Church in 1870. Three years later St. James C.M.E. Church hosted the first session of the Florida Conference of the C.M.E. Church in America, followed by another state conference there four years later; Rev. **James Smith** was the minister during that time. St. James C.M.E. later relocated to 1037 Richmond Street.

St. James may also have been the first public school for black children of the city; **Robert Meacham** and **Henry Matthews** taught many of them there, as did Mrs. **Lydia Smith** much later. The congregation built the present building in 1899 on a site that had had two earlier structures.

During the Civil War the church served as a hospital for soldiers wounded in the Battle of Olustee and during Reconstruction as a school for black children. In 1948, the congregation remodeled the 1899 structure to make the present Gothic Revival design. Today, it is the home of a government-watchdog agency, Florida TaxWatch.

A prominent member of the congregation was **John Gilmore Riley** (1857–1954), a successful black businessman, prominent civic leader, and long-time educator. Riley lived at 419 E. Jefferson Street in a house that still stands a few blocks away from the state capitol. From an early age John Riley chose to be an educator, a goal that culminated in his becoming principal of Lincoln Academy, the first local school for blacks. He died in 1954, the year that the U.S. Supreme Court banned segregation in public schools. His heirs lived in the RILEY HOUSE until 1973, when the city bought the property. Five years later officials placed the house on the National Register of Historic Places. Today, it is a research center and museum. Phone: (850) 681-7881.

The RILEY HOUSE CENTER/MUSEUM FOR AFRICAN-AMERICAN HISTORY AND CULTURE is responsible for producing the second edition (2002) of the *Florida Black Heritage Trail*, which was financed in part by a grant from the Division of Historical Resources, Florida Department of State. The first edition (1991) was the product of the Study Commission on African American History in Florida, which the Florida Legislature established in 1990 to increase public awareness of the contributions of African Americans to the state. The commission recommended sites for a Black Heritage Trail, including buildings and places that should be preserved and promoted as tourist attractions.

LINCOLN HIGH SCHOOL, of which **John G. Riley** was principal, was established as Lincoln Academy by the Freedman's Bureau in 1869 as one of two schools in Florida that could provide advanced instruction to black students. The

Chamber of Commerce today occupies the site of the original school. The first staff consisted of one man and one woman, both white. After a few years the first black teacher, **John G. Riley**, began teaching there. Fire destroyed the original structure in 1872. After a temporary move to a site on Copeland Street, the school found a permanent home on the corner of W. Brevard and Macomb Streets. The W.P.A. during President Franklin Roosevelt's administration replaced the original wood with brick. The principals after John Riley included **T. B. Dansby**, **W. Dabney**, **Noah Griffin**, **Cecil H. Walker**, **Gilbert Porter**, **James Abner**, **R. Frank Nims**, and **Freeman D. Lawrence**. After 1967, during the initial stages of school integration, the Lincoln High School facility was not used. The third Lincoln School structure of the school today serves as a community center. Phone: (850) 891-4180.

One of those principals, Gilbert Porter, was important for black education in several Florida sites. Born in Kansas in 1909, he went on to become a science teacher at Booker High in Sarasota (see Chapter Fifty-eight), in 1933 the teaching principal at Tivoli High School in DeFuniak Springs, in 1937 the principal of Tallahassee's Lincoln High, and in 1954 the executive secretary of the Florida State Teachers Association (FSTA), a black teachers' organization that merged with the Florida Education Association in 1966. In that role with the FSTA Porter worked hard against the racial firing of black teachers. In 1965, he went to Dade County to be special assistant to the deputy superintendent, **E. L. Whigham**. **GILBERT PORTER ELEMENTARY SCHOOL** at 15851 SW 112th Street in Miami honors him. A very fine history of the schools in Leon County is *A History of African-American Education in Leon County, Florida: Emancipation Through Desegregation, 1863–1968* (see Further Reading).

The **FIRST PRESBYTERIAN CHURCH** at 102 N. Adams is the only Tallahassee church from territorial days that is still standing and is the city's oldest building for public meetings that is still be-

The First Presbyterian Church is the only Tallahassee church from territorial days that is still standing. *Florida State Archives*

ing used. The ties between Presbyterianism and Florida government go back to at least 1826, five years after the U.S. took over Florida from Spain, when Presbyterian minister Rev. **Henry White** became chaplain to the Legislative Council. Organized in 1832, the Presbyterian congregation began the present building in 1835 and finished it three years later. They financed the $13,371 church by the sale of forty of the forty-four pews for a total of $12,500. In the early days the slaves, who were allowed to be members but had to sit apart from their masters, sat in the north gallery. Prominent early families that belonged to the church included the **Butlers, Gambles, Perkins, Shines, Wards,** and **Wilsons**. In 1932, during the centennial of the church, some members argued for a larger building to house the increased congregation, but fortunately they agreed to keep the old building and renovate it.

Another important black church is BETHEL MISSIONARY BAPTIST CHURCH at 224 N. Martin Luther King Jr. Boulevard. Founded by an ex-slave from Virginia and the first ordained black Baptist minister of Florida, Rev. **James Page**, it had its beginnings at Bel Air (or Bellaire) six miles south of Tallahassee when the minister and his wife, **Elizabeth**, founded the Bethlehem Baptist Church. When many of those two hundred members moved to Tallahassee in 1870, the new congregation called itself the Bethel Missionary Baptist Church. Because whites usually controlled the black schools, this and other churches became the meeting place for black community leaders, fraternal organizations, and civic groups. When the congregation finally outgrew its church building, they built a new one in 1976. After Rev. Page other pastors followed: **Horace C. Bailey, J. B. Hankerson, J. P. West, A. L. Pettis, C. T. Stamps, Harry Jones, Jerome B. Harris, William Burns,** and **Charles Kenzie Steele.**

Rev. James Page was born in 1808 into slavery in Richmond, Virginia. At about the age of twenty, he and his wife came to Leon County with their master, Colonel **John H. Parkhill**, settling on a plantation named Bel Air. Parkhill's religious devotion influenced Page to take up the ministry. In 1851 at Newport, Florida, a white Baptist minister ordained Page as Florida's first and only African American minister at that time. In the same year he founded the Bethlehem Missionary Baptist Church of Bel Air. Reverend Page served as a Leon County delegate to the Republican Convention (1867), a Leon County commissioner (1869–70), and legislative chaplain of the Florida Senate (1868–70). In 1870, he ran unsuccessfully for the State Senate, but returned to public office in 1872 when Governor Hart appointed him Leon County's Justice of the Peace. Reverend Page died March 14, 1883. A Great Floridian plaque honoring him is located at the Bethlehem Missionary Baptist Church, 3945 Museum Drive, Tallahassee.

The willingness of the Baptists to ordain James Page and to allow him to establish an all-black church whereas the Methodists were unwilling to do that might have led to an increase in both the number of black preachers and all-black churches, but even the Baptists were hesitant about going that way. Black Baptists in fact had a minority, subservient role in their church and could not vote and therefore could not really run the business of their churches, even if they were a majority in those churches.

Rev. **Charles Kenzie Steele** (1914–1980) became an important civil rights activist at a time when many people looked to him for leadership. At 111 W. Tennessee Street a C. K. MEMORIAL, consisting of a statue and marker, commemorates the work of this great man. Born in West Virginia as the son of a coal miner father, Charles decided at an early age to become a minister. After graduating in 1938 from Morehouse College in Atlanta, Georgia, he became a minister at a Baptist church in Montgomery, Alabama. In 1951, he moved with his family to Tallahassee, where he became a minister at the Bethel Missionary Baptist Church.

Rev. Charles Kenzie Steele was an important civil rights activist. *Florida State Archives*

He also became president of the local chapter of the National Association for the Advancement of Colored People (NAACP), president of the Inter-Civic Council, and charter member and first vice-president of the Southern Christian Leadership Conference (SCLC).

In 1956, he helped lead a boycott, begun by students at Florida Agricultural & Mechanical University (FAMU), against the local bus company that practiced segregation. He and other local organizers may have been encouraged by the success of the first such boycott, the 1955–56 one in Montgomery, Alabama, which succeeded in uniting the black community there and forcing the local bus company to end its segregation policies. The passive nature of the bus boycott was inspired by the preaching of Rev. **Martin Luther King Jr.**, who in turn was influenced by the nonviolent movement in India that Gandhi had led.

Steele kept the boycott nonviolent despite having his house attacked by the Ku Klux Klan. The year-long bus boycott succeeded in integrating the bus system, but Rev. Steele continued fighting for the complete integration of hotels, restaurants, and movie theaters in the city. The **C. K. STEELE BUS TERMINAL** at 111 W. Tennessee Street commemorates this great leader.

One of the important educational institutions of the city and the whole state is **FLORIDA AGRI-CULTURAL & MECHANICAL UNIVERSITY** (FAMU), a multiracial school that has given the state and the nation many important black leaders and is the oldest historically black university in Florida. The school on S. Adams Street had its beginnings in 1887, when the Florida Legislature established in the city the State Normal College for Colored Students in order to train black teachers for schools throughout the state. Beginning with just fifteen students that first year, it had as its first president **Thomas DeSaille Tucker** from Sierra Leone, a graduate of Oberlin College (1886) and a practicing attorney in Pensacola before arriving in Tallahassee (1887). In 1909, the school became a four-year college with a new name: Florida Agricultural and Mechanical College. In 1953, it became Florida A&M University and joined the state university system. Two recent presidents are **Frederick Humphries** and **Fred Gainous**.

The FAMU Marching Band is famous around the country. *Florida State Archives*

Alonzo "Jake" Gaither was the long-time football coach at FAMU. *Florida State Archives*

Humphries, president from 1985 to 2001, attracted many outstanding faculty and students to the school, including more National Achievement Scholars than any other university. Gainous, who became president in 2002, continued strengthening the university. Today FAMU, the state's only historically black public university, has over 450 full-time faculty and an enrollment of about thirteen thousand students.

Among the buildings on campus is the **SOUTHEASTERN REGIONAL BLACK ARCHIVES RESEARCH CENTER AND MUSEUM** in the Carnegie Library Building, the oldest building on campus and one that attracts over 100,000 people a year to its exhibits, which include tribal masks, African artifacts, and slave irons. The founder, curator, and director of the center was the late **James N. Eaton Sr.** (1930–2004). Research facilities, a repository of manuscripts, and an oral history laboratory provide scholars materials for documenting the history of blacks in the United States, especially Florida. The library, built in the Neo-Classical style in 1907 and now on the National Register of Historic Places, was the first Carnegie Library built at a black land-grant college. From 1908 to 1944 the building housed the offices of college presidents **N. B. Young** and **J. R. E. Lee**. The building is in the middle of campus northeast of Coleman Library and just south of Gamble Street. In 2003, the Florida Legislature approved naming the new archives and museum building on campus for **James N. Eaton Sr.** and retired U.S. Rep. **Carrie Meek**. Open weekdays 9 A.M.–5 P.M. Phone: (850) 599-3020.

Carrie Meek grew up near FAMU, attended elementary school, high school, and college there, graduated from FAMU with a degree in biology and physical education, and began teaching at Bethune-Cookman College in Daytona Beach. She later taught at Miami-Dade Junior College in Miami before running for public office when state legislator **Gwen Cherry** was killed in a car crash in Tallahassee in 1979. (For more about Carrie Meek, see Chapter Forty-three.)

On the campus on S. Adams Street is the **GIBBS COTTAGE**, constructed in 1894 and used as a home by **Thomas Van Renssalaer Gibbs**, a member of the Florida Legislature who introduced in 1887 the bill that established what would become the university. (For more about President J.R.E. Lee, see Chapter Forty-three.)

Near the campus is the **LUCY MOTEN ELEMENTARY SCHOOL** at Gamble Street and S. Martin Luther King Jr. Boulevard. Built in the early 1930s with the help of the Julius Rosenwald Foundation, the school was at first FAMU's training center for teachers. It honors in its name **Lucy E. Moten** (1851–1933), a well-known African American educator and proponent of educational opportunities for African Americans. Today the building houses FAMU's Developmental Research School. Originally established in 1887 as a teacher training school for FAMU, it served students at the grammar school or Colored Normal School. In its early years it served only elementary students and was located in temporary quarters at 424 Osceola Street. It later moved its three intermediate grades to the junior high school building at Gamble Street.

The **KNOTT HOUSE** at 301 E. Park Avenue, which was built around 1843, was owned by the Thomas and Catherine Hagner family through the 1880s and is one of the few remaining structures in the city dating back to the Territorial Period (1821–1845). In 1865, the Commander of the Union troops in Tallahassee, General Edward McCook, used the house as his official headquarters and residence. On May 20th of that year, he reissued President Abraham Lincoln's Emancipation Proclamation from the house's front steps in order to inform the former slaves, many of whom did not realize that they were already free, that in fact they were no longer slaves. As a result of that action by General McCook, blacks in Leon County celebrate May 20th as Proclamation Day. Today the house-museum, called "The House

That Rhymes" because owner Luella Knott wrote poems about her house and possessions, belongs to the state and has exhibits that illustrate the history of Tallahassee and Leon County. Phone: (850) 922-2459.

The African American carpenter who built the Knott House was **George Proctor**, who built several other important buildings in the city. He bought and then married a slave woman, **Nancy Proctor**, with whom he had eight children. One of those children was **John Proctor**, who became a state legislator, educator, and customs officer at St. Marks, Florida. George Proctor went to California in the 1849 Gold Rush and never returned to Tallahassee. At that time, his family was sold back into slavery by a white family.

The **UNION BANK BUILDING** at the corner of Apalachee Parkway and Calhoun Street dates back to 1841, thus making it the state's oldest bank building. It originally stood on S. Adams Street and served as a bank for territorial planters. In those early days the bank took slaves as collateral for loans. When the borrowers could not repay the loans, the bank sold the slaves to recover its money. The bank later failed because of poor management. When the bank reopened under federal supervision as the Freedman's Bank for newly freed slaves, some may have noticed how ironic it was that a bank built by slaves for slave owners later became a bank that was to help freed slaves handle money. But poor management led to its failure, causing many blacks to lose whatever savings they had accumulated in the bank. The building later was used as a church, a beauty parlor, city offices, and a dental laboratory. A black shoemaker, **Willis Jiles Sr.**, rented the building in the 1920s and trained many workers to make and repair shoes. In 1970, Mrs. T. Aubrey Morse bought the building from the First Baptist Church; Mrs. Morse later donated the building to the state, which moved it to its present site east of the Old Capitol in 1971. In 1984, after a complete restoration, the bank opened to the public as a museum of Florida history. Among its exhibits is an oil portrait of Dr. **Leffall**, a surgeon from nearby Quincy (see Chapter Nineteen). The bank is open to the public Tuesday through Friday, 10 A.M.–1 P.M.

The **MCKINNEY HOUSE** at 438 W. Georgia Street, now an art gallery and gift shop, was built in 1945 by Nathaniel and Lucille McKinney. Its present owner, **Annie Harris**, is the second female African American assistant principal of Leon County schools. Next door at 448 W. Georgia Street is the **TAYLOR HOUSE**, the birthplace of the first female African American assistant for the county's school system, **Acquilina Howell** (deceased). The city's Urban League owns the house today.

The **TOOKES VILLA/TOOKES HOTEL** at 412 W. Virginia Street was owned by **Dorothy Nash Tookes**, founder of the Bond School for African American children in the 1930s. Because African American travelers could not stay in ordinary hotels during the days of segregation, she added three rooms to her home in 1948 to accommodate those travelers. Personages such as **Nat Adderley**, **James Baldwin**, **Cab Calloway**, **Ray Charles**, and **Lou Rawls** stayed there. Today the building houses a rehabilitation program.

That hotel was part of **FRENCHTOWN**, which took its name from French immigrants who settled there in the early 1830s after the failure of a 36-square-mile plot of farmland in the county established by General Marquis de Lafayette after the American Revolution; because the general hated slavery, he operated the farm without slaves, a rarity in the South at that time. After the American Civil War, former slaves migrated there to make a thriving African American neighborhood with homes, churches, schools, and businesses. Among the establishments were the Laura Bell Memorial Hospital, Campbell Clinic, Capital Theater (owned by **Margaret Yellowhair**, who required her patrons to stand and sing the National Anthem before shows), the El Dorado Cafe, Modern

Cleaners and Twine Cleaners and Laundry, and Tookes Villa (mentioned above). The main thoroughfare was Macomb Street. Frenchtown, which declined in the 1960s, extended from Tennessee Street to Brevard Street, and from Martin Luther King Jr. Boulevard to Copeland. Today, only a few landmarks remain in the pretty neighborhood across from Florida State University.

OLD CITY CEMETERY at Martin Luther King Jr. Boulevard and Park Avenue, the city's first public cemetery, served blacks and whites as early as 1829, but laws required blacks to be buried in the western half of the cemetery, thus keeping segregation in effect. A 1936 city ordinance forbade the sale of plots to blacks. From then on, most African Americans were buried in Greenwood Cemetery (see below), then later in Southside Cemetery. Among the African Americans buried in Old City Cemetery are **Thomas Van Renssalaer Gibbs** (Reconstruction legislator and educator), **William Gunn** (one of Florida's first black physicians), **James Page** (founder of Bethel Missionary Baptist Church), **John Proctor** (educator and politician; see page 132), and **John G. Riley** (educator; page 126).

GREENWOOD CEMETERY at Old Bainbridge Road and Tharpe Street began when a 1936 city ordinance forbade the burial of blacks in Old City Cemetery (see above). Seven African Americans, led by **J. R. D. Laster**, the city's first black funeral director, bought sixteen acres on Old Bainbridge Road and established the cemetery in 1937. It became the burial site of many local African Americans.

HENRY HILL PARK at the corner of Centerville and Hillgate Roads was established from one hundred acres bequeathed in 1883 by the will of slave owner Benjamin Lewis to **Edward Johnson**, probably one of the slaves of Lewis, for meritorious service to Lewis by Johnson. The park, a private five-acre estate established in 1979, is owned by Gertrude Hill Williams, the Hill family matriarch. Debbie Edwards began an Emancipation Day Celebration in 1865, and that celebration is still observed on May 20th at Henry Hill Park, hosted by the Hill-Williams family.

SMOKY HOLLOW was a community, established in the late 1800s, that included many black families and black businesses. The widening of the Apalachee Parkway in the 1950s and the construction of the Department of Transportation Building in 1966 led to the destruction of many houses in the Smoky Hollow community. Some of the former businesses included Bob Nims Meat Market on Lafayette Street and Lena Cook's Diner. One of the residents was **Wallace Amos**, creator of the Famous Amos cookie line. What is left of the community is on the National Register of Historic Places.

37.

Levy County

Florida's twenty-sixth county was established in 1845 and named for David Levy Yulee, a member of Florida's first constitutional convention (1838–1839), the elected territorial delegate to the U.S. Congress (1841), and the state's first U.S. senator after Florida became a state (1845). The county had a population of 34,450 in the 2000 census, 3,790 (11.0%) of whom were African Americans.

Rosewood

In the early 1920s, this small town ten miles east of Cedar Key and about forty miles west of Gainesville was home to 150–200 people, many of whom were blacks who worked for the railroad, the turpentine industry, or a sawmill company. On January 1, 1923, a white woman in nearby Sumner claimed that a black man attacked her, a charge that led to one of the worst tragedies associated with blacks in Florida. Some local blacks believed that the woman was lying to cover up the fact that she had quarreled with a white lover who beat her and that she was trying to protect herself. Nevertheless, word of the alleged attack by the black man spread quickly, and a mob of angry whites gathered to seek revenge. The blacks fled into the nearby swamp of Gulf Hammock, trying to escape the revenge-seeking mob. The whites ran through the Rosewood-Sumner area searching for any blacks, killing at least six of them and destroying the homes, churches, and meeting hall of the blacks, effectively driving away forever those blacks who had been living there.

All that remains today are scattered bricks from destroyed buildings and the house of John Wright, one of the few white residents in the community and a man who had tried to help the blacks defend themselves against the mob. Although other communities in Florida and the Deep South experienced such bloodbaths against blacks, Rosewood was the only community that mob violence completely destroyed. In the spring of 1994, the Florida Legislature passed and Governor Chiles signed a bill to compensate the survivors and descendants of that massacre.

A mob burned down the homes of African Americans in Rosewood in 1923. *Florida State Archives*

38.

Liberty County

The legislature established this county in 1855 and named it for the goal that the founders of the United States were striving for. Liberty County had a population of 7,021 in the 2000 census, 1,292 (18.4%) of whom were African Americans. That number (1,292) was the sixth-lowest for a Florida county. Blacks used to live in both the eastern and western parts of the county, but today for some reason live only in the western part. Liberty County is the smallest county in Florida in terms of population.

Located between two rivers, the Ochlockonee on the east and the Apalachicola on the west, the rural county is mostly made up of the Apalachicola National Forest in the bottom two-thirds and farmland in the upper one-third. St. Joe Paper Company, which has owned much of the northern part of the county, has been selling more and more of its property to private landowners in order to earn capital for developing property closer to the Gulf of Mexico.

African Americans had their own school, Bethune Cookman School, which had twelve grades. When integration took place in the mid-1960s, the school was closed. It would later become the Latch School for after-school child care, but is today closed and vacant.

Although the county has no black officials today, it has had two on the County Board of Commissioners. **Earl Jennings** served for twelve years beginning in the early 1990s. He was defeated by another African American, **Stanley Dawson**, who served for only one term. The lack of more black officials may be due to the fact that Liberty County is one of the few counties in the state, and possibly the nation, where the courts ruled against single-member districts so that today commissioners are elected at large rather than from a particular district.

There are four African American cemeteries in Liberty County that have been documented. Three are near Bristol, and the fourth is near Telogia.

1. **ST. STEPHENS CHURCH AND CEMETERY**

   Directions: Go north from Bristol on Hwy. 12 for 4.1 miles; turn left on Hwy. 270. Then travel four miles to a large cemetery on the left, across the road from St. Stephens Church.

2. **BETHEL CHURCH AND CEMETERY**

   Directions: From St. Stephens Church, as described above, go 3.2 miles and turn left on Bethel Road to the church and cemetery on the right.

3. **ROCKYVILLE CHURCH AND CEMETERY**

   Directions: From Bethel Church, as described above, continue on to Hwy. 271. Turn right, go about two miles, then left again on Hwy. 270. Go to Rockyville Road 1.8 miles away, turn left, and the church is on the right about a half-mile down the road. From the left edge of the churchyard, there's a dirt lane off to the left through the woods to the cemetery.

4. **HUMILITY CHURCH AND CEMETERY**

   Directions: Go south from Bristol on Hwy 12 and travel 8.5 miles to Hwy. 333. Turn right on that road and go four miles to Humility Church. Its unmarked cemetery is 2.5 miles further on.

Bethune Cookman School in Bristol became the Latch School.

Humility Church is one of the African American churches in Liberty County.

39.

Madison County

The county (established in 1827) and town (established in 1838) honor in their name James Madison, the fourth president of the United States.

In the 1820s, Madison was one of five counties, along with Gadsden, Jackson, Jefferson, and Leon, in which slaves made up more than fifty percent of the population. North Florida's so-called "black belt" region had a rich soil that enabled plantations to thrive, although at great personal cost to their black slaves.

The county had a population of 18,733 in the 2000 census, 7,549 (40.3%) of whom were African Americans.

Many of the African Americans who lived in Madison County in the nineteenth century were engaged in working on the large cotton plantations that planters from Virginia, the Carolinas, and Georgia cultivated after their own lands became depleted with overuse. Many of the Florida lands were relatively unoccupied before then after the Native Americans died from disease and battles with the Spanish. The rich lands of what became known as Middle Florida enticed many immigrants to the territory, and with them came many slaves to work on the land.

Madison

In the first half of the nineteenth century the county had many slaves—2,688 slaves out of a total population of 5,490 in 1850. Whites and blacks worshiped together even in the days of segregation—for example, of the forty-six members of the Hickstown/Madison Baptist Church in 1851, thirty-eight were white and eight were black, probably slaves. After the Civil War, the two races often worshiped in different churches. In 2000 the town had 1,194 blacks (36%) out of a total population of 3,360.

An early Spanish explorer in the area was Panfilo de Narváez, who led a group of some four hundred men in 1528 through Florida. One of the members of that group and one of only four who survived Indian attacks, shipwreck, and an eight-year journey to Mexico was a slave, **Estevanico the Black**, who originally came from Morocco in Africa. He was the first black man to travel through Florida and much of the southwestern part of the present-day United States.

Another black who was not from Madison County, but who made a significant contribution to the county, was **David Montgomery**, whom Governor Harrison Reed appointed sheriff of the county in 1868. Montgomery, a New Yorker who had worked as a bricklayer and mason in Key West and Tallahassee since 1857 and who had become a political ally of Governor Reed, served for four and a half years as the state's first black sheriff, then became a member of the Florida House of Representatives in 1873. Three years later, Republicans nominated him for lieutenant governor, but he did not win the election and moved to Jacksonville and then New York, where he died in 1878.

One black from Madison who went on to become well-known was **Abraham Lincoln Lewis** (1865–1947), a founder of the Afro-American Industrial and Benefit Association, which later became the Afro-American Life Insurance Company, one of the largest black-owned businesses in Florida (see Chapter Fifteen). After being born into poverty in Madison at the end of the Civil War, he moved with his family to Jacksonville, where he worked hard and slowly built up enough money to buy part of a shoe store. In 1901, he joined other blacks to establish an insurance company to provide low-cost health and burial insurance to poor blacks in the city. Lewis also helped found the Negro Business League and the Negro Insurance Association and provided recreational facilities at American Beach on Amelia Island (see Chapter Forty-five).

Another black from Madison was **Marshall Williamson**, who was born there in 1890, graduated from Georgia State College, went to Larkins in Dade County, and became the first black man to buy land there. (For more about him, see Chapter Forty-three.)

Another black who grew up in the county was singer **Ray Charles**, who moved to Greenville in Madison County a few months after his birth in 1930. When he went blind at age seven, he went to St. Augustine to the State School for the Deaf and Blind, where he learned to play the piano and the clarinet. He would eventually go on to become one of this country's best-known musicians.

A mural in the post office in Madison depicts a dozen African Americans working in a cotton mill while a white overseer inspects a roll of cotton. Several years ago, the mural sparked local

Singer Ray Charles moved to Madison County a few months after his birth in 1930. *Florida State Archives*

controversy when a new black postmaster tried to remove the mural because it represented racial stereotypes. Local residents, however, successfully opposed that recommendation on the grounds that the mural is historically accurate.

SUWANNEE RIVER JUNIOR COLLEGE (SRJC), which was established in 1958, was one of twelve black junior colleges in Florida. **James Gardener**, who at the time was principal of the Williston Vocational Technical School in Williston, served as the first president of the school, which enrolled the most students, 402, in the 1964–65 school year. The school served African American students in Hamilton, Jefferson, Lafayette, Madison, and Taylor counties, but others came from as far away as Bradford, Clay, and Dixie counties and even some south Georgia towns when the students learned that the credits they earned at the junior college would be accepted at other institutions of higher learning.

When Mr. Gardener took a job in Broward County in 1961, Mrs. **Jenyethel Merritt**, then Dean of Instructions at SRJC, became president of SRJC, the first female president of an institution of higher learning in Florida. In 1967, the school, which had several buildings near the Madison County Training School, merged with North Florida Junior (later Community) College, at which time Mrs. Merritt became vice-president of the integrated junior college and the director of the Learning Resources Center, which has her name.

The enrollment figures for Suwannee River Junior College were as follows:

1959–60: 90 students
1960–61: 170 students
1961–62: 234 students
1962–63: 202 students
1963–64: 261 students
1964–65: 402 students
1965–66: 250 students

40.
Manatee County

The legislature established this county in 1855 and named it for the marine mammals that live in the oceans around Florida, or manatees, an endangered species. The county had a population of 264,002 in the 2000 census, 21,648 (8.2%) of whom were African Americans.

Bradenton

The town of Bradenton is near the site where Spanish explorers Juan Ponce de León (1521), Panfilo de Narváez (1529), and Hernando de Soto (1539) landed to begin exploring Florida. Five hundred years before them, the Timucuan Indians had lived there. The DeSoto National Memorial honors the third of those explorers.

The site may also have been where free blacks and escaped slaves lived in a community known as **ANGOLA**. Those settlers may have been joined by Seminoles. If so, they probably used a tabby house for a trading post. The blacks may have settled there, near the mouth of the Manatee River, between 1812 and 1821. When white soldiers found the settlement of over seven hundred residents, they forcibly returned the slaves to their owners throughout the South.

Other blacks there escaped in the 1820s by heading south to Cape Florida on Biscayne Bay, then across the Gulf Stream to Andros Island in the Bahamas. The small settlement of Red Bays at the isolated northwestern tip of Andros Island provided them with safety and security, although hurricanes destroyed that settlement and forced them to move about three miles south of the original site. Historian **Rosalyn Howard**, who wrote *Black Seminoles in the Bahamas*, about the site, found that about three hundred descendants of those escapees live in Red Bays today.

White settlers began moving into the area of present-day Manatee County in the middle of the nineteenth century to take advantage of the closeness to the Gulf of Mexico, the rich soil, and good pasture land. The town of Braidentown grew up there, honoring but misspelling the name of a Dr. Joseph Braden, one of the first white settlers and a man who had ninety-five slaves to work his 1,110-acre plantation. Another slaveholder was Robert Gamble, who had 102 slaves in 1850 to work the labor-intensive sugar cane production he had on his 3,450 acres along the Manatee River.

Blacks eventually moved into the area as free men after the Civil War, but they often had to be content with menial, back-breaking jobs. One of those jobs dealt with sugar cane. Black workers would feed sugar cane into a crude mill to extract the juice from which they would make sugar. The black smoke spewing forth from the sugar mill chimneys told everyone from miles around that workers were busy making the sugar. At the site black youngsters would help out by leading the horses around and around the crude machine that extracted the juice from the cane.

Ex-slaves living in the area might have felt strongly against Judah Benjamin, who used the Gamble Plantation in nearby Ellenton as a hiding place at the end of the Civil War. Benjamin, the secretary of state for the Confederacy, was fleeing the United States for England when he stopped at the plantation to hide.

In the twentieth century conditions for blacks improved, but it took a pair of collectors from Detroit to begin to amass the records for a better understanding of those conditions. For much of the twentieth century Fredi and Ernest Brown collected everything they could find about American blacks, including hundreds of books, magazines, photographs, and recordings about black accomplishments, especially the stories of ordinary citizens. Ernest Brown served as chairman of the Michigan Civil Service Commission, and Fredi was the Equal Access/Equal Opportunity officer for Manatee Community College in Florida. When they retired to Bradenton, they wanted to make their huge collection accessible to the public and sought the right place to house it.

In 1990, the Browns opened the **FAMILY HERITAGE HOUSE** resource center in an air-conditioned trailer behind the Head Start Center at 1707 15th Street East. Today the house is at 5840 26th Street West in Bradenton and is a wing of the Manatee Community College Library. Open Tuesday through Thursday, 11 A.M.–6 P.M.; Saturday by appointment; (941) 752-5319. The house has a good collection of books, newspaper clippings, magazines, photographs, and audio cassettes about the cultural and economic life of African Americans.

According to the 2000 census, 49,504 people lived in Bradenton, plus many more in the winter season; the official black population was 7,481 (15%). The black baseball players on the roster of the Pittsburgh Pirates, who hold spring training in Bradenton, may well be role models for many of the youth who are seeking a way out of low-income jobs. Another role model is Dr. **Jesse L. Burns**, who was born and raised in Bradenton and went on to become the twenty-fifth president of Jacksonville's Edward Waters College (see Chapter Fifteen); he received his Bachelor of Science and Master of Business Administration degrees from Stetson University and his Doctor of Business Administration from the University of South Florida and worked as a top resource management and development official with Tropicana Products.

Gamble Mansion near Bradenton is the only surviving plantation house in south Florida.

41.

Marion County

The Florida Legislature established this county in 1844 and named it for General **Francis Marion**, the so-called "Swamp Fox" of the American Revolutionary War, who was from South Carolina, a state from which many people moved to Marion County, Florida. The county had a population of 258,916 in the 2000 census, 29,775 (11.5%) of whom were African Americans.

Marion County has grown rapidly in the last hundred years as more and more people moved in to take advantage of the rich farmland, good horse-grazing facilities, and natural beauty. In 2000, Ocala had a population of around 42,045, of whom 10,060 (24%) were black.

Blichton

Northwest of Ocala on Highway 27 is the tiny settlement of **BLICHTON**, the place where **Jesse J. McCrary Jr.** was born in 1937. When Governor Reubin Askew appointed him Secretary of the State of Florida in 1978, McCrary became the second black to serve in the Florida cabinet (the first was **Jonathan Gibbs**, who served during Reconstruction—see Chapter Fifty-two). McCrary's father, a Baptist minister, had hoped his son would also become a minister, but instead Jesse Jr. went to law school after graduating from Florida A&M University in 1960. He then worked in Miami as assistant attorney general, in which position he became the first black to represent Florida before the U.S. Supreme Court. In 1971, he headed a commission to study the causes of riots in Opa-Locka's black community before resuming his law practice.

Butlersville

The former black settlement of Butlersville near the present-day **SILOAN BAPTIST CHURCH**

Jesse J. McCrary, Jr. of Blichton became Secretary of the State of Florida in 1978. *Florida State Archives*

at 12977 NW 35th Street in Ocala existed from around 1870 to 1895. It took its name from the inhabitants there, for example **Harriet** and **Hinson Butler**, who had been born slaves in South Carolina but made their way to Marion County. The Butlers made a living by grazing cattle and raising crops like corn, cotton, oats, sugar cane, and sweet potatoes. Other black families included the **Burtons, Chisolms**, and **Menchans. Harriet Butler** donated land at the westernmost boundary of Butlersville for a church, which became Siloan Baptist Church. A nearby cemetery has the gravesites of many of the early residents, including Harriet Butler.

Dunnellon

When Albertus Vogt discovered phosphate in Dunnellon in 1889, hundreds of workers poured into the area hoping to take advantage of the find. Many of those workers were blacks from Georgia and Alabama who had been lured to Dunnellon with the promise of wages and a sharing of the phosphate wealth. At one point, according to Gene Burnett, half the population was black, but "they shared little if any voice in its affairs, even while contributing greatly to its prosperity. They toiled long hours in the mines at subsistent wages—always lower than a white man's—and had to live in the flimsiest of shacks." One black doctor who ministered to the health needs of local blacks was Dr. **James F. Sistrunk**, who moved to Fort Lauderdale in 1921 to become the only black doctor in the city's black community (see Chapter Six).

Racist whites formed lynching mobs to try to control the blacks in Marion County, who in turn secretly formed their own Anti-Mob Lynchlaw Society to protect themselves and fight against a particularly racist marshal of the town. The discrimination became so bad that many blacks finally left town and did not return. In 2000 Dunnellon's blacks made up just 12% (192 people) of the population of 1,624.

The **SECOND BETHEL BAPTIST CHURCH**, now the Annie Johnson Senior Service Center, was originally a school which served the black community. Completed in 1888, it later became Second Bethel Baptist Church. Its first pastor, Rev. **Henry Shaw**, established the church in an old house, borrowed chairs and boxes for seats, and began ministering to blacks working in local sawmills and at turpentine facilities. In time the church moved from the east side to the west side of old U.S. 41; then, when the new U.S. 41 needed room, workers used a mule team to move the church further west to its present location on Test Court.

The church building also served as a school for black children four months a year. Students would kneel on the floor and use the church benches as desks. One of those students was **Annie W. Johnson**, who later earned degrees from Booker T. Washington High School in Miami, Florida Normal College in St. Augustine, Florida A&M University in Tallahassee, and Columbia University in New York City. She spent thirty-three years teaching in Dunnellon and Citrus Counties, including time at Hernando Elementary School in the latter county. After her retirement in 1974, she established the **ANNIE JOHNSON CENTER** that now uses the building of the Second Bethel Baptist Church. With contributions from sources like United Way the Center provides help to the elderly and others in need. In 1976, the congregation left for a new, cinder-block chapel across C.R. 488. A $20,000 grant in 1987 helped restore the original church building, which serves today as a Human Resource Center for south Dunnellon.

Directions: Although Dunnellon is part of Marion County, the Second Bethel Baptist Church is actually in Citrus County just below Dunnellon. The turnoff to the original building of the Second Bethel Baptist Church is west of U.S. 41, just south of the Withlacoochee River.

The Annie Johnson Senior Citizen Service Center is near Dunnellon.

Ocala

The 1860 census indicated that 62% of the 8,609 residents of Marion County were slaves, a fact that worried those whites who thought that Union sympathizers might incite the blacks to attack their owners, especially because so many white men were away at war. That did not happen, but it pointed to a reason for distrust between the races.

When the Civil War ended in 1865, more and more people, including African Americans, moved to Florida to take advantage of the opportunities here for making a living and raising families. In the Reconstruction period after the war officials organized a company of black soldiers to enforce the rulings of the local administrator and placed ex-slaves in county offices. Ex-slaves like **Singleton Coleman**, **Scipio Jasper**, and **Samuel Small** represented Marion County in the Florida Legislature for several years and also served as chairmen of the Board of County Commissioners. **Henry Wilkins Chandler** (1852–1938), a black educator from Maine, represented the county in the Florida Senate (1880–88), served as city clerk in Ocala (1883–84) and on the town council (1886–93). The second African American to win an election to the city council was **James C. Cun-**

ningham, who won the seat in 1975. (For more about another African American born in Ocala who excelled in law, **James Dean**, 1858–1914, see Chapter Forty-four).

The **WEST OCALA HISTORIC DISTRICT** between I-75 and Pine Avenue on Silver Spring Boulevard has over one hundred buildings associated with the African American community that flourished there between 1886 and 1920. The original focal point was **HOWARD ACADEMY,** established in 1886. Some of the prominent African Americans who worked there were **Gibbs Crompton, F. P. Gadsden**, and Dr. **L. R. Hampton**.

The Freedman's Bureau, with financing from northern benefactors, organized **HOWARD ACADEMY** as a school for black students in 1867. It honored in its name either James H. Howard, a former slave-owner who donated the land for the school in the block bounded by Osceola, Orange, 6th, and 7th Streets, or General Otis Howard, the ex-Federal officer who was in charge of the Freedman's Bureau and was interested in the education of blacks. By 1880 a group of black teachers replaced the white teachers of the school. After fire destroyed the original building on Orange Avenue in 1935, workers built a new one at Academy and Adams Streets. The school was phased out in

The former Howard Academy is today a community center.

1969 and today serves as a community center at 306 Northwest 7th Avenue.

One of the graduates of the school had a major effect on the integration of Marion County: the Rev. **Frank George Pinkston Sr.**, who graduated from Howard Academy in 1953 and Virginia Union University in Richmond, Virginia, in 1958 with a degree in English and then in 1961 with a master of theology degree. While in Richmond, he helped lead African American students in 1960 on a crusade to desegregate the former capital of the Confederacy. As he was being led away to jail, Pinkston urged on his followers, "The students have set the flame. Now we challenge you to put some oil on it and keep a blaze going." The end result was the establishment of the Campaign for Human Dignity which led to the integration of Richmond. He later returned to Ocala to teach English at Howard. He organized college students in the county to desegregate facilities, built the building at Mount Moriah Church, and organized and implemented the first Headstart Program in Marion County.

Among the people associated with Howard Academy was Dr. **R.S. Hughes**, who in 1925 opened the American National Thrift Association Hospital, the only facility to treat African Americans for hundreds of miles. Located on W. Broadway Street and Pine Street, the hospital served residents of West Ocala and all of Marion County. Dr. **Nathaniel Hawthorne Jones** and Dr. **Ernest Lamb** also had their offices on W. Broadway Street during the 1920s. The first man is honored in the naming of **DR. N. H. JONES ELEMENTARY SCHOOL** at 1900 SW 5th Street. Before he was murdered by a home invader, Dr. **Nathaniel Jones** was much beloved in his community. (For more about him, see Chapter Sixty-one.)

A student who attended Howard Academy and went on to become the first black female physician to practice in Florida was **Carrie Effie** (or **Effie Carrie**) **Mitchell Hampton**, who was born in Fernandina in 1886, grew up in Ocala, attended Orange Park School for girls at Orange Park after Howard Academy, received her medical degree from Meharry Medical College (1908), set up her practice in Ocala, and also owned and operated a drug store on W. Broadway Street for many years. She practiced medicine there until her marriage in 1915 to the first African American dentist in

Ocala, Dr. **Leroy R. Hampton Sr.**, and in the following year served as secretary for the Florida Medical, Dental and Pharmaceutical Association. (For more about Dr. Leroy Hampton Sr., see page 148.)

Meharry Medical College, where Carrie Hampton studied, was extremely important in the training of southern blacks in the medical field. Founded in 1876, the Nashville, Tennessee, school was responsible by the early 1980s for training almost half of all black physicians and dentists practicing in the United States.

Black-run businesses extended west from Magnolia Street to 16th Avenue. One resident of West Ocala, Mrs. **Mattie J. Shaw**, started *The Florida Watchman* newspaper in 1925 and ran her own printing presses. At the time, she was the only African American woman in Florida who solely owned and operated a printing business. The newspaper was originally housed in a build-

ing located to the north of 4th Street, across from Howard Academy.

MOUNT ZION AME CHURCH at 623 S. Magnolia Avenue or the northeast corner of SE 7th Street and S. Magnolia Avenue is on one of the major north-south thoroughfares of Ocala. Reverend **Thomas W. Long**, a circuit rider who traveled by horseback throughout Florida for the African Methodist Episcopal Church, helped establish the church in 1866, as did Reverend **S. Morgan** two years later. In 1891, the congregation decided they wanted a new brick building so that it would be more secure from fires such as those that destroyed much of Ocala in 1883. Rev. **J. W. Dukes** and then Rev. **John H. Dickerson** formulated the plans for the construction, the men of the congregation donated their time, and the women raised money by giving dinners and holding bazaars. Black architect and builder **Levi Alexander Sr.** was the architect of the building, the first brick

Mount Zion AME Church was the first brick church owned by black people in Ocala. *Kevin McCarthy*

church owned by black people in Ocala. Other groups have held many functions there, for example Howard Academy and Howard High School commencements, concerts, and other activities of the black community. The fine acoustics and large seating capacity (up to six hundred persons) of the building have made it an ideal location to hold functions. The church, which is the only surviving nineteenth-century brick, religious structure in Ocala and stands behind the site of the original white-frame building, is now on the National Register of Historic Places.

Another early church was **MOUNT MORIAH BAPTIST CHURCH**, founded in 1866 under the leadership of **Samuel Small**. Before the Civil War blacks had attended services of white congregations, usually sitting in galleries reserved for blacks. After the war they established their own churches so they no longer had to tolerate segregated churches. Rivers and Brown point out in their important study of the black church in Florida, *Laborers in the Vineyard of the Lord*, that Mount Moriah traces its beginnings to a log cabin at Daisy in 1860.

HAMPTON JUNIOR COLLEGE, which opened in 1958 at 1014 N. 24th Street, was one of twelve black junior colleges in Florida. Its first and only president during its eight years of operation was Mr. **William H. Jackson**, principal of Howard Senior High School, a school in northwest Ocala that would share its facilities with the new junior college; the high school honored in its name a white person who had donated land on which the black high school had been built. Originally called Howard Junior College, the school changed its name to Hampton to honor a local black dentist, **Leroy R. Hampton Sr.**, who was born near Santos and encouraged educational opportunities for black youth. Dr. Hampton's son, Dr. **Leroy R. Hampton Jr.**, was the chairman of the college's advisory council from its inception until the school merged with the local white college. Many blacks of Marion County opposed the establishment of the black junior college, arguing

that the University of Florida (UF) in nearby Alachua County should be forced to integrate, but at that time UF had not admitted a single black undergraduate student and would not do so for some time (see Chapter One).

As was true elsewhere in the state, the black junior college shared the facilities of a local black high school in order for the facilities of the college to revert back to the high school at the time of the merger/integration of the black and white colleges, which meant that the integrated high schools would be able to use the buildings that the segregated colleges had used. President Jackson continued serving as supervising principal of Howard High School for three years after becoming president of Hampton Junior College.

Unlike other black junior colleges that relied on hiring the faculty of local black high schools—a practice that led some local activists to criticize the junior colleges—Hampton Junior College hired faculty from other colleges, especially from outside the state. When it merged with the predominantly white Central Florida Junior (later Community) College in 1966, half the faculty of the black college transferred to Central Florida and the other half transferred to Marion County public schools. President William Jackson became Associate Dean of Academic Affairs, eventually retiring in 1985 as Director, Institutional and Sponsored Research.

The enrollment figures, which included college parallel courses and vocational courses, for Hampton Junior College, which served African Americans in Citrus, Levy, and Marion Counties, were as follows:

1958–59: 146 students
1959–60: 193 students
1960–61: 366 students
1961–62: 407 students
1962–63: 426 students
1963–64: 699 students
1964–65: 890 students
1965–66: 778 students

The number of graduates during those years (1958–66) was 317 out of a total of 3,905 students who attended the school, or about 8%.

A school to the northwest of Ocala and south of Reddick, Lowell, and Martin is FESSENDEN ACADEMY at 4200 NW 90th Street, now being used as an integrated elementary school, but for 123 years it was an important institution for the county's black students. When a number of black families settled in the suburb of Martin, they went before the county school board and asked for a school for their children. The school board granted their request and hired a northerner, **Emma Hodd**, to be the teacher of what was called the Union School. The students attended class in a small log cabin, beginning in 1868, and had white instructors until 1877. As more and more students wanted to attend the school, a larger building was built. During the winter of 1889, Ferdinand Stone Fessenden of Boston, a sickly man who had traveled to Florida to try to regain his failing health, was staying in Martin on the advice of his doctor. When he visited the Union School one day, he noticed how poor the facilities were for the 250 black students and resolved to do something about it.

Mr. Gilbert Maynor donated two acres of land a mile south of Martin for a new school, and by 1890 workers had completed the building. On the recommendation of Mr. Fessenden, the American Missionary Association in New York City placed the school under its auspices and began emphasizing domestic science for girls and industrial training for boys. The school opened with Miss **Mattie J. Brydie** as principal. When she resigned in 1896, Mr. **J. C. McAdams** from Kentucky took her place, to be succeeded two years later by Mr. **Joseph Wiley** of Nashville, Tennessee. Before Mr. Fessenden died in 1899, he requested that his body be buried on the grounds of the school he had helped build and which changed its name from Union School to FESSENDEN ACADEMY to honor him.

The first class of five young ladies graduated in 1903. In 1916, Rev. **H. S. Barnwell** became principal for five years, to be succeeded by **W. H. Kindle** of New York City. Later, **John M. Moore** of Mississippi became principal for six years, during which time officials raised the school curriculum to the junior college level and organized a band. In 1928, **A. S. Scott** of Mississippi became principal for one year, to be followed by Rev. **Leonard F. Morse** of Mobile, Alabama, who served from 1929 to 1932. **Ripley Simms**, a graduate of Alabama's Talladega College, served as principal from 1933 to 1938 and was succeeded by **Josie B. Sellers** (1938–41) and **John A. Buggs** (1941–51). In 1952, the Marion County Board of Public Instruction purchased the school for use as a public school. Later it became Fessenden Elementary-Middle School and in 1975 became Fessenden Elementary School, which it remains today. The school is on NW 90th Street west of Highway 25A and just north of Highway 326, which has an exit on I-75 to the west.

The SILVER RIVER MUSEUM AND ENVIRONMENTAL EDUCATION CENTER at 1445 NE 58th Avenue in Ocala has a one-room schoolhouse, built in the 1930s and used up to the late 1950s as a public school primarily for black students through the fifth grade. Museum is open Saturdays and Sundays, 9 A.M.–5 P.M.; fee: $4/car; phone (352) 236-5401.

In the first quarter of the twentieth century, African American businessmen did well in Marion County and owned, for example, many of the businesses on W. Broadway Street in Ocala from Magnolia Avenue to 16th Avenue. They owned METROPOLITAN NEGRO BANK at the corner of S. Magnolia Avenue and 2nd Street, one of the few African American banks in the South at that time. It began in 1914, but went out of business in the economically hard times of 1928. Nearby was the ST. GEORGE HOTEL, also owned by African Americans. The Great Depression made it difficult for many African Americans to pay their property taxes, and so many of them lost their homes and businesses and moved away.

Santos

The small town of Santos six miles south of Ocala on Highway 441 was settled by the South American family of John A. Cole, who named it after their Brazilian hometown. The family had two slaves, **Benedict** and **Sirea Cole**, who worked for them in the Florida town. The first school for black children in the area was a two-room, two-story, unpainted building with an outside stairway. The school, called Roper Farm School, was named in honor of a black minister, Reverend **London Roper**, and was located near a Methodist church. A Mr. **H. R. Burrell** served as principal of the school for many years. In the early 1930s, the school was consolidated with the Mount Royal School of Belleview and Clearwater School of Oklawaha to become the **BELLEVIEW-SANTOS HIGH SCHOOL**. Mrs. **Fannie Butler** was the first principal of the consolidated school.

The town had four black churches: an African Methodist Episcopal Church, which was discontinued in the 1920s; the Holiness Church, which no longer functions there; the **CALVARY BAPTIST CHURCH** at 10515 SE 115th Avenue in Santos, which traces its history to 1874, but which moved to its present location one mile north of the original site because of its location in the path of the ill-fated Cross-Florida Barge Canal; and the **LITTLE CHAPEL UNITED METHODIST CHURCH** at 2381 SE 73rd Street, a facility named in honor of an early land donor (**Charles H. Little**) and one that was also moved because of the Cross-Florida Barge Canal.

A popular gathering place for African Americans was the **BLUE SINK**, which is west of Chestnut Avenue and near **BURRELL MEMORIAL CEMETERY**, which was named in honor of the donor of the land, Professor **W. H. Burrell**. The former **FELDER WELL** was a meeting place there where the local women would meet and wash their clothes. A nearby tree was used as a trading post, where people who wanted to trade something would put it in a bag, hang it from a low limb there with instructions about what they wanted, and later retrieve the new object if someone else agreed to exchange something for it.

42.

Martin County

Florida's sixty-fourth county, established in 1925 out of northern Palm Beach County, commemorates Governor John W. Martin, possibly because the promoters of the county wanted to name it after the current governor in order to prevent a gubernatorial veto. Martin had served as mayor of Jacksonville for three terms and was governor of the state for one term (1925–29). The county had a population of 126,731 in the 2000 census, 6,717 (5.3%) of whom were African Americans.

The first blacks probably arrived in the 1800s, brought as slaves by whites moving in from other Southern states to take advantage of the rich soil for growing pineapples and vegetables. Other blacks came over from the nearby Bahamas after the American Civil War, eager to start new lives in a relatively unpopulated place. They worked for white families who wintered on Sewall's Point, labored in the pineapple fields near Jensen Beach and the citrus field of Indiantown, and fished the rich waters off Port Salerno and Jensen.

Early black communities included Banner Lake, Booker Park, East Stuart, New Monrovia, Pettway Park, and Tick Ridge. Blacks chose to live in what became Martin County, especially when places like Palm City had conditions as the following in its real estate contracts in 1914: people were "not to sell any land at Palm City Farms or Palm City to a Negro."

Today, at least two dozen black churches serve the communities of Martin County. Some of those churches date back to the late 1800s, including Peaceful Valley Christian Methodist Episcopal Church in Banner Lake (1890), Saint Paul African Methodist Episcopal Church in Stuart (1907), New Mount Zion Baptist Church in

Gomez (1909), Allen Temple African Methodist Episcopal Church in Gomez (1911), Mount Calvary Baptist Church (1916), and Union Baptist Church (1923). The churches often began in small, wooden shacks or outside under the trees, but they remained an important part of each community and served as schools and community centers, even as gathering places for fostering civil rights.

The struggle to have adequate schools for African American children in Martin County, as elsewhere, took the concerted efforts of many parents, students, and local black leaders, but they made education their top priority and slowly achieved the schools they deserved. After the Civil War, the Florida Legislature levied a state tax of $1 on all black men between the ages of twenty-one and forty-five, plus a fee of fifty cents a month per student, in order to support black schools, but the money was seldom spent on black schools. In the early twentieth century, most schools for black children were in churches or private homes.

Stuart

The county seat of Martin County takes its name

Saint Paul African Methodist Episcopal Church in Stuart has been serving the local congregation since 1907.

from Samuel Stuart, the first telegraph operator and station agent for the Florida East Coast Railway when a new bridge enabled the railroad to cross the St. Lucie River in 1893. Black workers on the railroad line sometimes chose to settle in the area, but they experienced discrimination and segregation early on.

To provide accommodations to those blacks who would otherwise not have found lodging, **Emma** and **George White**, who had gone to Stuart around 1919 to obtain fifteen acres of farmland under Florida's Homestead Act, built a six-bedroom, two-story home at 613 E. Church Street in 1922. After George died in 1933, Emma opened the house to any blacks who needed temporary shelter, whether church leaders or new teachers or students competing in local athletic meets. After

she died in 1967, the house was abandoned and slowly deteriorated.

An early development in the education of blacks in the county occurred with the construction of Lincoln Park School (later called Stuart Training School) in Stuart, as well as a one-room schoolhouse in Port Salerno where Murray Middle School is today. The man who became principal of Stuart Training School in 1945, **Robert G. Murray**, had gone to Stuart as a business partner with his brother, **C. E. Murray**, in mortuary science. Robert opened up in Hobe Sound the first school in Martin County for African Americans and also taught school in Wabasso in Indian River County. Integration of the public schools finally occurred in 1965 with relatively few incidents. The elementary part of Stuart Training School was renamed East Stuart Elementary School, then J.D. Parker Annex, and finally Spectrum Junior Senior High School, an alternative-education and community school. Educator **Felix A. Williams**, who was named Teacher of the Year for the State of Florida in 1957, was honored by having **FELIX A. WILLIAMS ELEMENTARY SCHOOL** named for him when the school opened in 1994.

That same Felix A. Williams became the first African American to run for political office in Martin County in 1963 when he ran for city commissioner. Although he lost by only twelve votes, he helped galvanize the efforts to register African Americans. Before then, roadblocks were put in the way of their attempts to vote, for example the state poll tax (which the Florida Legislature repealed in 1937), the whites-only primary system (which the Supreme Court outlawed in 1944), at-large elections that excluded blacks, and the ignoring of them by white political parties.

Robert Hall became the first black elected to the Stuart City Commission (1969), the first black elected to a political office in Martin County, and the first black to become mayor of Stuart (1974). **David L. Anderson** became the first black elected to the Martin County School Board,

Felix A. Williams Elementary School honors a local Teacher of the Year and a politician.

while **Joyce Hobson** became the first black female School Board member. She would later (1995) be appointed Director of Business and Citizen Partnerships for the State of Florida.

Early African Americans to the county worked in the pineapple and bean fields, but also started their own businesses. For example, **Willie Pettway** arrived in 1909 in Gomez on the east side of the Florida East Coast Railway and became the first black to own a business and the owner of the first grocery store. **Theresa Clark** owned the first store in New Monrovia. Black business entrepreneurs there, as elsewhere, had many obstacles to overcome, including the reluctance of white businesses to deal with African Americans, the difficulty of getting bank loans, and overt racism. For example, when out-of-town African Americans arrived in Stuart by train, the white sheriff would pick them up and transport them to the city limits with an admonition to keep going. Local blacks had a midnight curfew.

Medical services were difficult to find for African Americans in Martin County for a long time. Blacks usually had to go to Fort Pierce in St. Lucie County for medical or dental needs because

Martin County had no black doctors. The first black male nurse in the area was **Charley Green**, who also bought land west of Stuart for $25 an acre and started a junkyard. Many of the streets in Rio, a black community north of Stuart on the St. Lucie River, are named in his honor since he sold much of the land there to the families still living there. Today, conditions are much different, but black business owners have to compete with white-owned businesses, and therefore the challenges are different than in the past.

Finally, among the Martin County African Americans of the last half-century who should be mentioned for achievements are these: **Marlon Brown**, who revived interest in the NAACP in 1992; **Eula Clark**, who helped establish the Martin County Black Heritage Association for keeping alive the culture of African Americans and for sponsoring the annual Black Heritage Festival; **Ralph Clark**, who organized demonstrations in the 1960s against the unfair treatment of blacks in Martin County; **Willie E. Gary**, the first black attorney in the county and one of the most successful attorneys in Southeast Florida; **Willeva Holmes**, who organized an after-school homework assistance program; **Willie Jay Thompson**, who became the first teacher in the county to integrate an all-white school, the winner of the "Outstanding Elementary Teacher of America" award, and the founder of the East Stuart Community Choir; **Leroy Washington**, the first black to advance to captain in the Stuart Police Department and the first one to become deputy police chief; **Thelma Waters**, the unofficial mayor of Booker Park, who obtained grant money to build the town's first group of block houses and who is honored in the naming of the Thelma Waters Infant Child Care Center for her work in getting such a center established in the county.

In recent years, as an indication of how political times have changed, the Martin County Commission, at the urging of Commissioner **Elmira Gainey**, voted in 2002 to spend over $600,000 to extend water lines to around 150 homes near a polluted site on Cove Road in Port Salerno. The site was polluted by a company that made microwaves and electronic parts there, but never cleaned it up before leaving. The predominantly African American neighborhood successfully lobbied for help and got it.

43.
Miami-Dade County

Dade County was established in 1836 and named for Major Francis Dade, the commander of 110 men who were ambushed and killed by Seminole Indians in 1835 near present-day Bushnell. That massacre began the Second Seminole War. Dade County became Miami-Dade County in 1997 after voters approved the name change.

The county had a population of 2,253,362 in the 2000 census, 457,432 (20.3%) of whom were African Americans. This county has the highest number of African Americans among all sixty-seven Florida counties.

Caesar's Creek and Caesar's Rock

Two sites near Key Largo in the Florida Keys are of interest here: Caesar's Creek and Caesar's Rock, named in honor of the infamous pirate **Black Caesar**. According to legend, in the early slave-trading days in the Caribbean, slave traders captured a huge African chief and transported him and other slaves across the Atlantic. When the slave ship approached Florida, a storm sank the ship, drowning many of the crew and most of the slaves shackled down below. By some means Black Caesar and a mate who had befriended Caesar escaped from the ship and made it to land. From there, they began preying on ships passing off the Florida Reef. The two pirates were very successful in their attacks and accumulated many goods and jewels on their island.

When the two men eventually had an argument, Black Caesar killed his friend and continued carrying on his piracy as a one-man band. He soon enlisted more pirates and used larger boats to attack the passing ships. When his crew had to hide from danger, they would escape into Caesar's Creek (near Elliott Key) and other inlets between Old Rhodes Key and Elliott Key. There they would run a strong rope through a metal ring embedded in a rock (today called Caesar's Rock), heel the boat over, and hide it in the water until the patrol boat went away. Or they would lower the mast and sink the ship in shallow water, hidden from prying eyes; later they would cut the rope or pump out the water, raise the boat, and continue with their raids.

Although piracy was wrong and hurt many people, it offered escaped slaves like Caesar a liberty they could not have obtained at that time. In the early 1700s, Black Caesar left Biscayne Bay to join the more infamous **Blackbeard**, Captain **Edward Teach**, to prey on shipping up and down America's east coast, especially around North Carolina. In 1718, government forces finally defeated and killed Blackbeard near Ocracoke Island off the tip of Cape Hatteras. The British took Black Caesar to Virginia for trial and hanged him in Williamsburg.

Coconut Grove

In south Miami near the Vizcaya Museum and Gardens is Coconut Grove, one of the oldest settled parts of the area. With a name that recalls a time when the site had coconut palms, Coconut Grove today is the Greenwich Village of Miami-Dade County and also the site of the first black community in Miami.

The area can trace its history back to the late 1880s, when blacks began arriving from the Bahamas by way of Key West to work as chambermaids, washerwomen, and carpenters at the now-defunct Peacock Inn, the first hotel in the Miami area and originally known as the Bay View House. The first black to arrive, **Mariah Brown**, lived on the inn property, but, when more and more blacks arrived from the Bahamas, they settled in a small settlement not far away known as Evangelist Street, later Charles Avenue. One of the remnants of that first settlement is the 1890 MARIAH BROWN HOUSE at 3298 Charles Avenue. Her house is in the CHARLES AVENUE HISTORIC DISTRICT just below Grand Avenue and the site of the first black community on the south Florida mainland. A marker at Charles Avenue and Main Highway states the following:

The first black community on the south Florida mainland began there in the late 1880s when blacks primarily from the Bahamas came via Key West to work at the Peacock Inn. Their firsthand experience with tropical plants and building materials proved invaluable to the development of Coconut Grove. Besides private homes, the early buildings included the Odd Fellows Hall, which served as a community center and library; Macedonia Baptist Church, home of the oldest Black congregation in the area; and the A.M.E. Methodist Church, which housed the community's first school. At the western end of Charles Avenue is one of the area's oldest cemeteries. So many Bahamian blacks came to the area that, according to historian Melanie Shell-Weiss, "Through the 1920s, Miami was home to a greater percentage of foreign-born black persons than any other city in the United States." Among the many contributions of those Bahamians to the local whites was how to cope with the insects and heat, which fruits and vegetables they could safely eat, and how they could clear the formidable Florida pine tree from the land.

A structure there that honors Dade County's first black millionaire is the STIRRUP HOUSE at 3242 Charles Avenue (now a private residence). **Ebenezer W. F. Stirrup**, a native of the Bahamas, went to Key West in 1888 and later moved to Cutler, fourteen miles south of the Miami River. He worked in the pineapple fields during the day and then at night cleared the land in the area, sometimes being paid in land instead of cash since money was scarce at that time. After returning to

This is one of the very old houses in the historic Charles Avenue District.

The Stirrup House was the home of Miami-Dade County's first black millionaire.

the Bahamas at age twenty-one to marry **Charlotte Jane Sawyer**, his childhood sweetheart, he brought her back to Cutler, where they worked in the fields and began building small houses on their property.

At age twenty-five, Stirrup moved his family to Coconut Grove and began slowly buying more and more land until he owned much of what became the downtown. He built over a hundred homes to rent or sell to other Bahamian blacks who came to Coconut Grove around 1900; many of their descendants still live in some of those houses. In 1897, he used tough Florida pine to build **THE STIRRUP HOUSE**, his own two-story structure, which still stands today. Although Mr. Stirrup could barely read and write, he insisted that his children, ten of whom were born in south Florida, acquire as much education as possible. In turn they became productive, influential members of the community. In 1976, the Model

City Development Corporation dedicated twenty-six proposed townhouses in Coconut Grove to Stirrup's memory as a memorial to the many houses he built there. Situated off Main Highway at Franklin Avenue and Royal Road, the houses were called the Stirrup Grove Townhouses.

Although Mr. Stirrup, who worked for some time for Charles Deering, the man who bought the town of Cutler and developed it into a beautiful estate, lost much land and money during the Florida real estate bust, he died a very wealthy man in 1957 at the age of eighty-four. In a 1976 interview, three of Stirrup's daughters recalled what it was like growing up in the Grove in the early part of this century. One of them, **Kate Dean**, said, "The thing that we liked in Coconut Grove in those early days of growing up is that everybody seemed to want to take care of everybody else." She continued, "Coconut Grove was and still is one of the few black areas not separated [from the rest of the community] by a railroad track."

In the Coconut Grove area, Bahamian men built homes that had broad gables and ornate porches running along the front of the houses; some of their descendants still live there today. More and more blacks went to that part of the state in the nineteenth century to begin a new life as they developed farms and businesses and later worked on Henry Flagler's railroad, in the fields and hotels, and in the homes of white settlers. The chance to own their own land in a mild climate was very attractive to Northern blacks, especially because they had often experienced racial discrimination in long-established, tradition-bound areas of the North. The newness of the south Florida area held out the opportunity of prosperity based on how hard the people worked. The problem was that, as more and more whites moved into the Miami area, they made the longtime residents from the Bahamas feel unwelcome, just as the Native Americans were made to feel unwelcome there.

In the first half of the twentieth century the

Grove attracted more and more people of different races, many of them with jobs in Miami. Artists like Augustus St. Gaudens and Maxfield Parrish and writers like Virgil Barker and Hervey Allen moved in and helped make the place an artists' colony with a subsequent rise in land values. However, the section where blacks tended to live deteriorated badly. In the late 1940s officials discovered that 3,000 residents lived in 777 structures in that section, many of them without indoor plumbing; those residents relied on a truck they called the "Honey Wagon," which would collect the excrement each night. Determined to improve the living conditions of those living in the area, many local residents formed the biracial Coconut Grove Committee for Slum Clearance and by 1951 had removed all outdoor privies, connected each residence to water lines, increased police protection in the area, and begun a fund for establishing a day nursery.

Blacks in the Grove joined with whites in 1891 to worship in a nondenominational Christian chapel, the Union Chapel, but three years later had their own church. Macedonia Missionary Baptist Church at 3515 Douglas Road was the site of Dade County's first Baptist church for blacks. It began around 1894 when the Rev. **Samuel A. Sampson**, a black Bahamian, organized the church and called it the Fifty-Six Baptist Church because it had fifty-six charter members. After meeting at the home of **Edith Albury** on Williams Avenue, the congregation built the first church building on Charles Avenue in 1903 and changed its name to ST. AGNES MISSIONARY BAPTIST CHURCH. In 1922, they changed the name to Macedonia Missionary Baptist Church. Workers completed the present structure on the corner of Douglas Road and Charles Avenue in 1948. In 1993, officials dedicated several historical markers there to commemorate the many contributions that Bahamian and black pioneers made to the area.

Another old black church in Coconut Grove is CHRIST EPISCOPAL CHURCH (often called Christ Church) at 3481 Hibiscus Street. Dating back to 1901 and built by Bahamians to resemble the ones they knew back home, the church was first administered by clergy from a white Episcopal church, Trinity Church, as was St. Agnes Church. When the 1926 hurricane destroyed Christ Episcopal Church and the parish church, parishioners quickly rebuilt them, using stronger, local materials like coquina. Noted civil rights' advocate Father **Theodore R. Gibson** (1915–1982) served as its pastor during the 1960s and succeeded Father **John Culmer** as the city's most important black leader. Father Gibson was partly responsible for having the black section of Coconut Grove connected to the city sewage-disposal system, fought for school desegregation and more jobs for blacks and Hispanics, was president of the Miami chapter of the NAACP and of the Florida Council of Churches, served on the Miami City Commission, cast the deciding vote to reform the city's civil-service laws, and worked tirelessly for the betterment of the city's African Americans. He is honored in the naming of GIBSON SENIOR PLAZA and the GIBSON BUILDING.

COCONUT GROVE CEMETERY, between Charles Avenue and Franklin Avenue and between Douglas Road and Hibiscus Street, was developed in 1913 by the Coconut Grove Colored Cemetery Association. That cemetery was actually the second one in the black Grove; the first one was further east on Charles Avenue and lasted from 1904 to 1906, at which time city officials shut it down for health reasons. At least seven hundred, maybe as many as 1,200, people lie buried in the Coconut Grove Cemetery, but weather and time have obliterated many of their names. Among those buried there are **Willie Bullard**, the area's only black casket maker; **James Summons**, the first black in Coconut Grove to obtain a real estate license; and **John E. Sweeting**, founder of the early black settlement called Sweetingtown located near what is now S. Dixie Highway and Douglas Road.

In order to restore and maintain that important cemetery, members of area churches filed articles of incorporation as the Coconut Grove Cemetery Association in 1989. Under the guidance of local historian Esther Mae Armbrister, this association helped place seven historical markers in Coconut Grove to recognize the contributions of Bahamian and other early black settlers to the area. Two other cemeteries nearby, the **CHARLOTTE JANE CEMETERY** and the **CHARLOTTE JANE ANNEX**, have also been the burial sites of many of the black Grove's early residents who were not allowed to be buried with whites.

The George Washington Carver Elementary School was one of the last remaining schools that were all black before integration.

The Charlotte Jane Cemetery is the burial site of many of the black Grove's early residents, who were not allowed to be buried with whites.

Among the other places in Coconut Grove that honor blacks are **FRANCES S. TUCKER ELEMENTARY SCHOOL**, which honors **Frances S. Tucker**, an early elementary school principal at George W. Carver Elementary and the school which bears her name; **GEORGE WASHINGTON CARVER MIDDLE SCHOOL**, formerly a senior high, and **SCOTT-CARVER HOMES HOUSING DEVELOPMENT** named after **George Washington Carver** (1859–1943), famous for agricultural research at Tuskegee Institute, especially concerning the peanut. **GEORGE WASHINGTON CARVER ELEMENTARY SCHOOL** at 4901 Lincoln Drive. Built in the 1920s, the school shares a five-acre site with the **GEORGE WASHINGTON CARVER MIDDLE SCHOOL**,

which was built in the 1950s. In 1991, the city's Historic Preservation Board unanimously declared both schools historic. One former student remembered how it was attending the elementary school in the 1930s, "I remember the stone water fountain in the courtyard and how on a cold day the teachers would bring the students out into the sunshine because we had no heat in the building. But we still thought it was the greatest school around." It was one of the last remaining schools that were all black before integration.

Coconut Grove is the setting for the Miami/ Bahamas Goombay Festival each June. The week-long party that transforms Grand Avenue into Nassau's Bay Street has brilliantly costumed junkanoo groups in the streets, dancing to Caribbean rhythms to the accompaniment of different kinds of musical instruments that range from drums and whistles to cowbells and combs. Junkanoo is a street parade with music, which occurs in many towns across the Bahamas every Boxing Day (December 26) and New Year's Day. A wide variety of arts, crafts, food, and drink from several hundred vendors on Grand Avenue attracts thousands of visitors.

African and Bahamian descendants also have a Junkanoo Festival in Miami, using goombay drums (metal containers with goatskins), tom-toms (drums), cowbells (one or more in each hand), whistles, and wind instruments called foghorns. The musicians perform at the annual Goombay Festival each June in Coconut Grove and at the Martin Luther King Jr. Day parade in West Perrine. Because the Junkanoo events in the Miami area and the Bahamas occur on different dates, many musicians from both sides of the Florida Straits can perform in both places.

Coral Gables

Coral Gables may have been the second planned city in the United States, after Washington, D.C. George E. Merrick spent much time and money designing the city, including what became the University of Miami, which opened in 1926. To promote the planned community, he used the oratorical skills of William Jennings Bryan in the mid-1920s; Bryan, who had been President Woodrow Wilson's Secretary of State and a three-time Democratic Party nominee for President, gave impassioned speeches around Merrick's fabulous Venetian Pool, encouraging visitors to buy and settle in the planned community.

The city never had a large number of blacks, and in 2000 only 3% (1,348) of the total population of 40,091 were black.

MACFARLANE HOMESTEAD SUBDIVISION HISTORIC DISTRICT is a black enclave within the city of Coral Gables. It is bordered by Oak Avenue, S. Dixie Highway (U.S. 1), Brooker Street, and Grand Avenue east-northeast of the University of Miami. The district takes its name from **Flora MacFarlane**, who homesteaded 160 acres of land there and in Coconut Grove in 1892. Some of the houses in the district predate the expansion of the Gables in 1925 and 1926, while others were built in the 1930s at a time when blacks were not allowed to build in the wealthier parts of Coral Gables. One of the early structures, ST. MARY'S BAPTIST CHURCH, was built in 1927. Most of the homes in what is called the black Gables are small, single-story homes built from Dade County pine. Many of the blacks worked in the homes of the

wealthy white residents or in the construction of such buildings as the City Hall and the Biltmore Hotel. The area is changing rapidly today, with many large homes being built.

Key Biscayne

In 1497, long after the Vizcaynos Indians had lived in the area, explorer John Cabot sailed to the site that became Key Biscayne and returned again in 1498. In 1513, Spanish explorer Juan Ponce de León visited the area, which Spanish cartographers called "Cabo Florida," Cape Florida. In the sixteenth century Spanish treasure fleets sailed north in the Gulf Stream near Cape Florida and sometimes wrecked on the offshore reef. Pirates frequented the area, including **Black Caesar** (see page 155).

In the early nineteenth century, escaped slaves and black Seminole Indians came to Cape Florida, especially after the United States took control of the territory from Spain in 1821, to try to escape by boat to the Bahamas. During the Civil War blockade runners used Biscayne Bay to bring in supplies for the Confederacy, and in the twentieth century rumrunners brought in illegal liquor from the Bahamas. Many wealthy people, including President Richard Nixon, have built homes on the bay and transformed the site into a popular beach. In 2000, Key Biscayne had a population of 8,854, of whom twenty-six (less than 1%) were black.

At the southeastern tip of Key Biscayne in the Bill Baggs Cape Florida State Recreation Area stands the only lighthouse in Miami-Dade County and one that saw an act of great bravery by a black man in 1836. Workers built CAPE FLORIDA LIGHTHOUSE in 1825, just four years after the United States gained control of Florida from Spain. Soon after the Second Seminole War started in the mid-1830s, Indians attacked the two men stationed at the lighthouse, intent on driving them and other whites in the area out from south Florida. The lighthouse keeper and his assistant, a black man named **Aaron Carter,** or just **Henry**, rushed into the lighthouse, bolted the door, and fired on the Indians from the window of the tower. When the Indians set fire to the door and then burst through, the two men inside quickly climbed up the ladder, cutting it out from beneath them to prevent the Indians from pursuing them. The Indians aimed their muskets up at the fleeing men, killing the brave Henry and wounding the keeper. U.S. troops eventually rescued the keeper from the top of the tower and probably buried Henry in the area, but records of this are hard to find. The lighthouse is open from 8 A.M. to sunset each day.

Off the northern edge of Key Biscayne is **VIR-GINIA KEY**, a place that played an important role in the history of blacks in the 1950s. At that time blacks were not allowed to enter Miami Beach or Palm Beach unless they had identification cards that indicated they were employees who worked there. Those black workers could work at the beaches, but were not allowed to swim there. They were allowed to swim at nearby Fisher Island in the 1920s because Mr. **Dana A. Dorsey**, Miami's first black millionaire, had bought the whole island in order to provide blacks with a place of their own. However, he had to sell the island in the mid-1920s because of rising property values and taxes.

In the following decades blacks were continually denied access to public beaches in the Miami area. They finally became so angry over the official policy that would not allow them to use the public beaches that they staged protests and peaceful demonstrations. Many white people who had not known that blacks could not go to any public beach also pressured officials to solve the problem. **L. E. Thomas**, a lawyer who later became a municipal judge, tried in 1944 to be arrested at Baker's Haulover Beach in North Dade in order to make a test case out of it, but the police refused to arrest him, instead handing the problem over

to the Dade County commissioners, who in 1945 finally designated part of Virginia Key as a black beach. Before then, in March 1944, the U.S. Navy conducted the training of African Americans on that beach because black enlisted men could not be trained on the other beaches. Until a causeway to Virginia Key and Key Biscayne was completed in 1947, the Dade County commissioners arranged for a ferry to take the blacks to and from Virginia Key.

Miami

This city of 362,470 (according to the 2000 census), of whom 80,858 (22%) are black, developed in the last hundred years after hosting an earlier army outpost on the Miami River, Fort Dallas. Today, the site at NW 2nd Street near the County Courthouse has **LUMMUS PARK**, marking the place where William English had a plantation with slave quarters dating back to 1844. As many as one hundred slaves worked the citrus groves and plantations near the Miami River. Today the English plantation is near the house where white pioneer William Wagner and his Creole wife lived. The Wagner House has been relocated to Lummus Park as part of an effort to preserve historical sites in the area. Author and activist William Keddell wrote a play entitled "Love and Slavery" about the plantation house and slave quarters; local students at Troy Community Academy first produced the play in 2004.

In 1849, the U.S. Army took over the cabins at Fort Dallas until abandoning them in 1858. The coral-rock structure there is called the "Long House" because soldiers used it for barracks during the Seminole Wars.

When Henry Flagler brought his railroad to Miami in 1896, Miami's first land boom began. Among the blacks who played a significant role in the city's early history were Rev. **A. W. Brown**, who dug the first hole in the building of Flagler's Royal Palm Hotel in what is now the Dupont Plaza area; **W. H. Artson**, the first person to sign the original city charter on July 28, 1896; and the 162 black voters out of a total of 368 pioneers who voted to create the city of Miami. John Sewell, Flagler's head of the work gangs that extended the railroad to Miami and beyond, referred to his black workers/voters as his "Black Artillery," and in fact their vote for the city of Miami gave a big boost to Flagler's railroad.

Many of those black pioneers are buried in the CITY OF MIAMI CEMETERY at 1800 NE 2nd Avenue. Among them are Father **Theodore Gibson**, who served as a Miami City Commissioner and local president of the NAACP; Judge **Lawson E. Thomas**, Miami's first black judge; and **Alexander C. Lightburn** (or **Lightbourne**) **Sr.**, who helped establish the Bethel A.M.E. Church. Lightburn represented the county at the state Republican convention in 1896 and the state Republican executive committee and in 1897 supervised what were called the "Colored Schools of Miami."

Miami grew rapidly in the twentieth century, especially after World War II when so many of its sons and daughters returned to live after serving in the Armed Forces, and many of the soldiers who had trained in the area decided to live there also. The population of the area nearly doubled between 1940 and 1950 and then nearly doubled again the following decade. Many returning soldiers used the G.I. Bill of Rights to attend the fledgling University of Miami, transforming it into a major educational institution. Black veterans moved to segregated subdivisions like BUNCHE PARK in North Dade and Richmond Heights in South Dade. Bunche Park honors **Ralph Bunche** (1904–1971), undersecretary of the United Nations (1955–71) and the first black to win the Nobel Peace Prize (1950); Richmond Heights changed the name of its main thoroughfare from Lincoln Boulevard to **Olivia Love Edwards** Boulevard to honor the generous pharmacist who operated a drug store along that street for thirty-four years. In time, blacks entered the Miami work

force as policemen, mail carriers, and attorneys, slowly making gains as integration provided more opportunities.

That history has been clouded in recent decades by racial riots and unrest. In 1980, after insurance executive **Arthur McDuffie** was allegedly killed by police and an all-white jury acquitted white Dade County police officers of his death, black residents of the city rose up in disgust and rioted, with the result that fifteen more people died and more than $100 million in physical damage scarred the city.

When South African leader **Nelson Mandela** visited the city in June 1990 to address a labor union convention, no local official publicly welcomed him. That led to a tourism boycott by black attorneys that spread to much of the black community and, after lasting 1,030 days, eventually resulted in gains by blacks in the community. In 1992, voters elected **Alcee Hastings** and **Carrie Meek**, along with **Corrine Brown**, as the first blacks elected to Congress from the state since Reconstruction.

When state legislator **Gwen Cherry** died in an automobile accident in Tallahassee in 1979 at the age of fifty-six (see Chapter Fifty), Carrie Meek decided to run for office. She won the election in 1978 and went on to represent the 17th congressional district in Miami-Dade County and won five more terms before retiring in 2002, at which time her son, state senator **Kendrick Meek**, won election to the seat. At that time Ms. Meek returned to Miami and established a foundation to help the poor and underprivileged, something she had done during her years as a legislator. Among her firsts was being the first black woman elected to the State Senate (1982) and among the first blacks elected to Congress from Florida since Reconstruction.

Among the sites of importance to blacks is the VANGUARD in the Historical Museum of Southern Florida, 111 Flagler Street. The Urban League of Greater Miami, Inc. commissioned a mural

Carrie Meek was the first black woman elected to the State Senate and among the first blacks elected to Congress from Florida since Reconstruction. *Florida State Archives*

entitled "The Vanguard—Black Miami's Mural of Purpose" to commemorate the twenty-fifth anniversary of the passage of the 1965 Civil Rights Bill. Miami artist Carl Latimore created the mural with photographs of the city's black personages, past and present, all of whom made important contributions to the city's black progress in the past twenty-five years. To prepare the mural the artist conducted oral history interviews, did research in the archives, and used high technology to create a unique collage of photographs and images.

When Henry Flagler was building his railroad down to Miami, and eventually to Key West, in the 1890s, he needed a place for his workers to live. At that time, because blacks were not allowed to live within the white community, the land west of the railroad tracks within the city limits of Miami between today's NW 6th and 12th Streets

was called "Colored Town" and became the basis of what later would become **OVERTOWN**. By 1915, the area had most of the city's five thousand blacks, although some lived in other so-called "colored districts" on what is now SW 8th Street, in Coconut Grove (see above), and near Lemon City. It did not take long before many churches and businesses flourished in Overtown. However the poor conditions contributed to an area that reeked with poverty, disease, and crime.

Avenue G (now NW 2nd Avenue) was the main street of Colored Town, which had more than one hundred black-owned businesses and a Colored Board of Trade which encouraged blacks to own their own stores. Six doctors, several pharmacists, an attorney, nine ministers, and many grocers, tailors, dressmakers, repairmen, and two undertakers provided services for the black community. As World War I erupted, many black Miamians enlisted in the armed forces; residents would often hold a parade down Avenue G before sending off a group of its young men to begin their training at Tuskegee Institute in Alabama. Several decades later, in 1935, **ST. FRANCIS XAVIER CATHOLIC SCHOOL** opened as south Florida's first private school for blacks.

By 1930, most of the 25,000 blacks of Miami lived in the fifty-block area of Overtown. Because of the poor working wages of those blacks and the poor economy of the country as a whole during the Great Depression, the residents lived in poor so-called shotgun houses and slums. The racial zoning practices of white Miami kept the blacks confined to Overtown and a few other sections.

In the 1930s, another Miami suburb developed for blacks northwest of Overtown, the result of a New Deal public housing effort for blacks called Liberty Square five miles northwest of the central business district. The whites in power saw the availability of federal funds for such a project as a way to move the blacks out of the downtown area and thus make way for businesses to expand there. Such an idea was coupled with a so-called

"Negro resettlement plan," which would remove as many African Americans as possible from the downtown area to three "model Negro towns" on the outskirts of Miami on land that was primarily agricultural to the west.

Although those plans were never carried out, agencies like the Home Owners Loan Corporation and the Federal Housing Administration did change neighborhoods by redlining, the illegal practice of discrimination against a particular racial group by real estate lenders or insurance companies by which money lenders or insurance companies decide certain areas of a community are too high risk and refuse to give a mortgage to buyers who want to purchase property in those areas, regardless of their qualifications or creditworthiness. Insurance companies who redline refuse to insure consumers who live in certain neighborhoods. Such practices led to the physical neglect and decay of the inner-city area of Miami.

Liberty City, the new name for the Liberty Square housing project, took the overflow from Overtown and developed the first public housing in Florida, the Liberty Square Housing Project between NW 12th and 15th Avenues. Among the places in Liberty City that honor blacks is LILLIE C. EVANS ELEMENTARY SCHOOL, named after a longtime teacher and principal of the Washington Graded School; and the ALONZO KELLY PARK, named after one of black Miami's first real estate developers. One of the places that visiting black entertainers stayed at was the GEORGETTE TEA ROOM at 2550 NW 51st Street, once a meeting place/guest house for black celebrities and entertainers and today a private residence on Dade County's list of historic places.

The building of I-95 right through the middle of Overtown in the 1960s succeeded in tearing apart that African American community. Thousands of people and businesses were forced to relocate. Over thirty thousand black residents of Overtown moved out to make way for the expressway and its interchanges, leaving behind fewer than ten thousand blacks in what had been referred to in its heyday as the Harlem of the South.

One particularly successful black businessman was **Dana Albert Dorsey** (1872–1940), who came to Miami in the late 1890s to farm. He slowly began to buy property in the area, often for only $25 a lot, and his real estate holdings eventually included an island, which later became Fisher Island, which he developed as a black bathing beach until selling it in the 1920s. He opened the first black hotel and the first black bank, was chairman of the Colored Advisory Committee to the Dade County School Board, served as registrar for black men during World War I, and gave land for a black high school, DORSEY HIGH SCHOOL, at NW 71st Street and NW 17th Avenue. Before he died in 1940, he had become the area's first black millionaire. Named in his honor are Dorsey High, which is now the DORSEY SKILLS CENTER in Liberty City, and DORSEY PARK and DORSEY AVENUE (also NW 3rd Avenue), both in Overtown. Miami's Heritage Conservation Board has had erected at the site of the D. A. Dorsey House at 250 NW 9th Street a replica of the house, which has been destroyed. A plaque that mentions his being named a Great Floridian 2000 is located at 100 NW 17th Street in Miami at what was named DORSEY MEMORIAL LIBRARY, on land donated by the millionaire.

Another successful businessman was **Henry Ethelbert Sigismund Reeves**, who came to Miami from the Bahamas in 1919. As a former printer for the *Nassau City Press*, he wanted to stay in the newspaper business, and so he joined with Rev. **Samuel Sampson**, Dr. **Alonzo P. Kelly**, and **M. J. Bodie** to form a printing company and publish a newspaper, the *Miami Sun*, for the black community. After publishing the newspaper for eight months, they had to suspend operations because of the lack of newsprint caused by World War I. In 1923, Reeves began another black weekly newspaper, *The Miami Times*, which is today the

South's largest black weekly in circulation. **REEVES PARK** in Overtown honors him to this day. His son, **Garth C. Reeves Sr.**, and grandson, **Garth C. Reeves Jr.**, have continued the newspaper over the years. Another business that Henry Reeves began, the Magic City Printery, did well enough to tide the newspaper over during the difficult times of the Depression. Other black newspapers in Overtown, all of which were owned by blacks and served their interests, were *The Industrial Reporter, The Miami Journal, The Biscayne Messenger, The Tropical Dispatch*, and the Florida edition of the *Pittsburgh Courier. The Miami Times* is the only one that survived. The **GARTH C. REEVES SR. HALL** at Miami-Dade Community College honors the man who served as chairman of the Board of Trustees of the college.

More recent black newspapers include the *Coptic Times* published by the Ethiopian Zion Coptic Church in Miami Beach; *Liberty News*, which claimed to be "Miami's largest circulated Afro-American Daily"; *Newsletter of African American Activist* about the Miami riots; *The Orthodox Messenger—The Voice of Washington Heights*, "A Negro Catholic Monthly" and the "Official Organ of the Southern Jurisdiction of the African Orthodox Church"; *Yahweh*, published by Yahweh Ben Yahweh Temple of Love Publishers; and *Haiti en Marche*.

Well-known black entertainers like **Count Basie, Cab Calloway, Nat King Cole, Ella Fitzgerald, Aretha Franklin**, and **Billie Holiday** had to stay in Overtown when they performed in white nightclubs on Miami Beach or in Miami, but they also performed in Overtown places like Sir John Hotel (formerly at NW 6th Street and NW 3rd Avenue), the Mary Elizabeth Hotel (NW 2nd Avenue and NW 7th Street), and other nightclubs. Vacationers in Overtown included distinguished Americans like author **W. E. B. DuBois**, folklorist **Zora Neale Hurston**, boxer **Joe Louis**, and baseball players **Roy Campanella** and **Jackie Robinson**.

A center of entertainment which opened in 1919 at 819 NW 2nd Avenue was the **LYRIC THEATER**, a building whose theater, movies, and meeting space were frequented by many people. Advertisements for the theater, which **Gedar Walker** owned, called it the "most beautiful and costly playhouse owned by colored people in all the Southland." Today this masonry building is all that survives of what was known as "Little Broadway" that prospered in the 1930s and 1940s. When desegregation and the construction of an expressway through the district led to many black families moving out, the area deteriorated, but officials have plans to revive the district. The Black Archives bought the Lyric Theater in 1988 and has progressed greatly in its restoration work on it. The fact that the Lyric was not made of wood explains why it survived the fires that ravaged much of Miami's black community.

ST. JOHN'S BAPTIST CHURCH at 1328 NW 3rd Avenue dates back to 1906. Its current building, designed by the black architectural firm of McKissack and McKissack, was finished in 1940. The two-story masonry building exhibits an architectural style known as Art Moderne.

The first school for black children in Miami's Colored Town was a wooden building that stood on NW 8th Street between NW 2nd and 3rd Avenues where the Berrien Hotel later stood. Started around 1896, "Old Washington," as it was called, had only grades one through six. Later the Fort Dallas Land Company gave the land on NW 12th Street for a new school building where Douglass Elementary School now stands.

BOOKER T. WASHINGTON SENIOR HIGH SCHOOL at 1200 NW 6th Avenue was the first school in south Florida that allowed black students to complete the twelfth grade. When the school board acquired land on NW 6th Avenue in the mid-1920s for Booker T. Washington High School, some white residents in the area protested; concerned blacks then took turns guarding the site at night. The school finally opened

Booker T. Washington Senior High School was the first school in south Florida that allowed black students to complete the twelfth grade. *Florida State Archives*

in early 1927 for 1,340 students and had its first graduation for six students the following year.

Over the years the school expanded its activities and facilities. For example, it played its first football game (1928), became A-rated (1934), organized its first band (1941), and organized its first School Supply Store (1947). The last senior class was in 1967, just before integration took place. In 1970, the school had only the ninth grade and was paired with Ada Merritt Junior High School for the seventh grade and Citrus Grove Junior High School for the eighth. Among the many graduates of Booker T. Washington who went on to success was **John D. Johnson**, who became a judge in Miami. The original high school now serves as a middle school.

Booker T. Washington High School might have been expected to share facilities with a black junior college that might be established in the area. Throughout Florida officials had established twelve black junior colleges, despite the fact that the 1954 Supreme Court had outlawed segre-

gated schools. When the Dade County School Board began attempts to establish a local black junior college, the local NAACP chapter objected, arguing that establishing such a junior college would be a continuation of segregation. Although enough liberal, forward-thinking citizens lived in Dade County to support an integrated junior college, the local school board feared that a segregationist legislature in Tallahassee would punish the local school system for establishing an integrated junior college. The school board also worried that the lack of good preparation among black students at the segregated high schools would not prepare them for college work.

The school board decided to open a separate branch of Dade County Junior College (Northwestern Center) rather than establish a separate black junior college. The faculty at the center would be black, but would share the advisory committee and administration of the main campus (Central Center). This may have been the first time in the nation that such an arrangement was attempted. When several black students requested admission to the all-white Central Campus of the junior college, the school board allowed seven of them to register in the fall of 1960, thus becoming one of the first desegregated public schools in Florida and the whole Southeast.

By the early 1960s officials closed down the black center and transferred its black students and eleven black teachers to the main center. The Greater Miami Urban League gave the college, Miami-Dade Junior College, an award for totally integrating itself in two years. Little by little black students became more and more involved in activities on the central campus, including the student newspaper, and all extracurricular activities became integrated. The 1966 election of a black to be student body president indicated that the integration of students was succeeding.

The **GREATER BETHEL AME CHURCH** (nicknamed Big Bethel) at 245 NW 8th Street is a Mediterranean Revival style church in Overtown that was built during the difficult times of Florida's Real Estate Bust and subsequent Depression (1927–1942). Miami's oldest congregation, the Greater Bethel AME Church was organized in 1896, even before the city was incorporated, but at a time when developer Henry Flagler was extending his railroad to the tiny settlement on Biscayne Bay that would later become the state's most populous city. One of the church's lay leaders, **Alexander C. Lightburn Sr.** (or **Lightbourn**), was one of the city's founding fathers. The first building, called "Little Bethel," was a simple frame structure with a dirt floor; built before 1899, it was moved to NW 8th Street that year. Congregation members began the present structure in 1927 with a building fund of $7,000. Adopting a "pay-as-you-go" policy, members did not finish the structure until 1942, at a total cost of $150,000. Engineers designed the building well so that the thick walls, small windows, and high ceilings keep the inside of the church cool without the use of air conditioning.

One of the active members of the Greater Bethel AME Church was Dr. **William A. Chapman Sr.**, the first black appointed to the Florida Department of Health and possibly the first black doctor to travel through Florida with an education program about communicable diseases; from Tallahassee to Key West he met with groups in

The Greater Bethel AME Church dates back to 1896.

churches, schools, and homes to explain about health issues. His Overtown home, CHAPMAN HOUSE at 526 NW 13th Street, out of which he practiced medicine for a while and which the city declared a historic site in 1983, is of special significance to the history of blacks in Florida and therefore became the site of the Chapman House Ethnic Heritage Children's Folklife Educational Center, a facility which emphasizes the city's diverse cultural influences. The school board took over the property in 1984 as part of a new campus for the rebuilt Booker T. Washington Middle School. It is available through the Office of Cultural Diversity: (305) 995-1275.

MOUNT ZION BAPTIST CHURCH at 301 NW 9th Street was established in 1896 by the Rev. T. M. Trammell, first at the corner of Avenue G and Cherry Street (now NW 2nd Avenue and Flagler Street) and then, two years later, to its present location.

The HAMPTON HOUSE at 4200 NW 27th Avenue was built in 1953 as Booker Terrace and became the social center of the area. The twenty-room hotel, each with a private kitchenette and bathroom, had a swimming pool, patio, restaurant, and nightclub that attracted such black performers as **Cannonball Adderley, Muhammad Ali, Count Basie, Cab Calloway, Duke Ellington, Ella Fitzgerald, Jackie Robinson,** and **Malcolm X.** Dr. **Martin Luther King Jr.** gave an early version of his "I have a dream" speech there.

On the grounds where the Chapman House and the Joseph Caleb Community stands in North Miami is the BLACK ARCHIVES, HISTORY AND RESEARCH FOUNDATION OF SOUTH FLORIDA at 5400 NW 22nd Avenue. Dr. **Dorothy Jenkins Fields** established and incorporated it in 1977 to preserve manuscripts, photographs, and documents about the black experience in Miami-Dade County. It exhibits art about Overtown and other historic sites. Open 1 P.M.–5 P.M. daily; research hours by appointment; phone: (305) 638-1231.

Other early black medical doctors to practice in Miami included a **Dr. Rivers**, who practiced medicine in the city in 1896 before moving to Tampa; Dr. **J.A. Butler**, who also owned The Magic City Drug Store on the corner of Avenue G and NW 5th Street; Dr. **Solomon Frazier**, who arrived in 1904 and began a practice that lasted for over sixty years in the city; and Dr. **William B. Sawyer**, who arrived in Miami in 1903 and later joined others in 1918 to start the first hospital for blacks in the city, Christian Hospital—complete with twelve bedrooms in a wooden structure—which cared for blacks after other hospitals refused to do so. Dr. Sawyer also built and ran the MARY ELIZABETH HOTEL and ALBERTA HEIGHTS, the first residential development in Miami that blacks owned. Dr. Sawyer's daughter, **Gwendolyn Sawyer Cherry**, was the first black woman elected to the Florida House of Representatives.

Overtown was renamed Culmer-Overtown in 1967 to honor Father **John Edwin Culmer** (1891–1963), an early civil rights leader from the Bahamas; beginning in 1929, he served as pastor of Overtown's ST. AGNES EPISCOPAL CHURCH, Miami's oldest black Episcopal church, having been established in 1897 by a white clergyman and named after St. Agnes Church in Nassau, Bahamas, where many of the first parishioners were from. Rev. Culmer led the church out of financial difficulties after he became pastor in 1929. He became one of the city's most important and influential black leaders in the 1930s and 1940s, a fact that led to increased membership in his church. CULMER LIBRARY and CULMER COMMUNITY CENTER also honor him.

Other places in Overtown that honor blacks are DOUGLASS ELEMENTARY SCHOOL named after **Frederick Douglass** (1817–1895), a leading spokesman for blacks in the 1800s; DUNBAR ELEMENTARY SCHOOL named after **Paul Lawrence Dunbar** (1872–1906), a famous black poet and novelist; PHYLLIS WHEATLEY ELEMENTARY SCHOOL, named after the first famous black woman poet in America (1753–1784); and the **WILLIAMS PARK AND POOL**, named after **Charles Leofric Williams**, a well-liked principal of Booker T. Washington School.

Another place there is **ATHALIE RANGE PARK** at 525 NW 62nd Street. It honors a woman long considered the matriarch of Miami politics and the city's first African American commissioner. Born in 1915, she experienced the segregation in Miami. Her political career began when she became involved in the Parent Teachers' Association (PTA) of her children's schools in the 1940s and tried to have better facilities built for the children. She was elected president of the school's PTA and then convinced the school board to begin building new schools in predominantly black neighborhoods. In 1953, Range and her husband, **Oscar Range**, started Range Funeral Homes in Liberty City. When her husband died unexpectedly, Athalie enrolled in the New England Institute of Anatomy and Embalming to obtain her funeral home director's license and continued running the family business, one of the longest-running, most successful black-owned businesses in the region. In the mid-1960s, she became the first black Miami city commissioner. In 1970, Florida Governor Reubin Askew appointed Range Secretary of the Department of Community Affairs and she became the first black person to serve as head of a Florida state agency. In that position, she helped the area receive more than eight million dollars to survive a drought. She was elected to the Florida Women's Hall of Fame in 1997.

The black activist clergymen **Edward T. Graham** and **Theodore R. Gibson** succeeded **Athalie Range** in the 1970s on the Miami City Commission.

Among many places in Miami named after blacks are the following: the **BELAFONTE TACOLCY CENTER**, a youth activity center in Liberty City, which honors singer and actor **Harry Belafonte** (1972–); the **JOSEPH CALEB COMMUNITY CENTER** at 5400 NW 22nd Avenue; the **ANNIE M. COLEMAN GARDENS** at 2610 NW 48th Street, a housing complex which honors a woman who did much to establish a local library and have the police department hire black officers; **CHARLES HADLEY ELEMENTARY SCHOOL** at 8400 NW 7th Street; **KELSEY L. PHARR ELEMENTARY SCHOOL** at 2000 NW 46th Street, which honors a man who came to Miami in 1914 and later established a funeral parlor for area blacks; and the **LINCOLN MEMORIAL PARK** at NW 46th Street and NW 30th Avenue. That last place, which opened in 1924 and served for decades as the cemetery for blacks, includes the final resting place of **Dana A. Dorsey** (Miami's first black millionaire) and **Gwendolyn Sawyer Cherry** (the first black woman to serve in the Florida Legislature).

The first black man to buy land in present-day South Miami, then called Larkins, was **Marshall Williamson**, who arrived in 1912. He donated land for what became **J. R. E. LEE OPPORTUNITY SCHOOL** at 6521 SW 62nd Avenue, a school named after Dr. **John Robert Edward Lee**, president of Florida Agricultural and Mechanical College (1924–44). The original J. R. E. Lee Elementary School, built in 1924, was replaced by the present building in 1955. Williamson also donated land for the **ST. JAMES AME CHURCH**, the first church for blacks in south Miami.

In recent decades, Miami-Dade County has had a huge influx of black Cubans and black Haitians seeking better opportunities than in their countries. Often settling in places like Little Havana and Little Haiti, the immigrants, many of whom illegally entered the United States, brought in the Spanish and Haitian Creole languages, as well as ethnic foods and customs from their islands.

Opa-Locka

This city in Miami-Dade County, which has a name that comes from an Indian phrase meaning "big swamp," had a population in 2000 of 15,283, of whom 10,654 (70%) were black. That figure is all the more amazing when one realizes that the first city codes established segregation as official policy, a policy that was meant to keep out blacks. The settlement began when Glenn H. Curtiss, an early aviation pioneer, joined with James H. Bright to develop it in the 1920s land boom. They designed the place to resemble a city from *Tales From the Arabian Nights* and thus it has minarets and domes on some of its buildings and street names like Oriental, Arabia, Sultan, Sahara, Sesame, and Aladdin. Some sixty-five of the original one hundred buildings in a Moorish Revival architectural style remain in what is called the **OPA-LOCKA THEMATIC DEVELOPMENT**, a predominantly black community. The city might have had more buildings in this Middle Eastern style, but the Depression of the late 1920s and the devastating 1926 hurricane that hit the area curtailed many of the plans that Curtiss had made.

Several buildings deserve mention here. The **HARRY HURT BUILDING** with a central dome and minarets at 490 Alibaba Avenue was built in 1926 and served as a shopping center with offices, apartments, and a social hall on the second floor. After World War II it became the Opa-Locka Hotel. The **OPA-LOCKA CITY HALL** at 777 Sharazad Boulevard has domes, minarets, and watchtowers that resemble Middle Eastern architecture, and the **OPA-LOCKA RAILROAD STATION** has a multi-colored glazed tile that is quite remarkable.

FLORIDA MEMORIAL COLLEGE at 15800 NW 42nd Avenue is one of the oldest institutions of higher learning for blacks in the state. This school is a private, coeducational, four-year college that can trace its history back to the Florida Baptist Institute in Live Oak, Florida, and the Florida Baptist Academy, founded in 1892 in Jacksonville. The two schools merged in 1941 to become the Florida Normal and Industrial Memorial Institute in St. Augustine, Florida (see Chapter Fifty-five). Four years later it became a four-year college. After several name changes the school became Florida Memorial College in 1963. Five years later the school moved to its present location. Its early presidents included Rev. **M. W. Gilbert** (1892–94), Rev. **J. T. Brown** (1894–96), **N. W. Collier** (1896–1941), Dr. **William H. Gray** (1941–44),

Opa-Locka is the home of Florida Memorial College.

and Dr. **John L. Tilley** (1944–49). Dr. **Albert E. Smith** became the tenth president in 1994.

Among the other places in the town that honor blacks are the **WILLIE LOGAN RECREATION CENTER PARK**, named after the man from Opa-Locka who was the first black mayor of the city (1980–82) and subsequent member of the Florida House of Representatives (1982–); and **NATHAN B. YOUNG ELEMENTARY SCHOOL**, named after the man who served as president of Florida A&M University (1901–23), then later as president of Lincoln University in Jefferson City, Missouri, and Inspector of Schools for the state of Missouri. The **GWEN CHERRY PARK** at 2591 NW 71st Street in Miami honors her. (For more about her see Chapter Fifty.) The U.S. post office facility at 550 Fisherman Street, the **SEGAL-MILLER PARK** and the **HELEN MILLER MULTIPURPOSE CENTER**, both at 2331 NW 143rd Street, honor **Helen Miller**, the first black woman to serve as mayor (1982–84) of a Florida city.

Porgy Key

The small island off Caesar's Creek called Porgy (or Porgee) Key played an important role in the largely unknown history of African Americans in Florida. **Israel Lafayette "Parson" Jones**, who was born in North Carolina in 1859, survived slavery, then moved to South Florida to work as a stevedore on boats. By 1887, he had been so successful that he bought Porgy Key for $300 and moved there with his Bahamian wife, **Mozelle**, and their two sons, **Arthur** and **Lancelot**. The family lived off the land growing pineapples, Key limes, and winter tomatoes. He worked as a fishing guide and on the railroad on nearby Elliott Key, and may have established the Mount Zion Baptist Church on the mainland.

After his mother died in 1924 and his father in 1932 and after his brother went into the military, **Lancelot Jones** took control of Porgy Key and served as a fishing guide for many, including

Presidents Lyndon Johnson and Richard Nixon. He lived simply, used solar power for his few appliances, and acted as an environmentalist. Instead of selling the island for a large sum of money, he eventually sold it to the U.S. Park Service for $1.2 million, which ensured that the island will be preserved for future generations. He was allowed to stay on the island until Hurricane Andrew forced him off in 1992, five years before he died at the age of ninety-nine.

Students at Homestead Senior High School have volunteered to do research about the island and the Jones family for inclusion of Porgy Key on the National Register of Historic Places.

South Miami-Dade

In the first part of the twentieth century, as Dade County opened up to more and more settlers, African Americans moved there in increasing numbers, eager to take advantage of opportunities to prosper and raise their families. Many of the newcomers had come from towns like White Springs and Jasper in north Florida. The town of Goulds, south of Miami, attracted many of them because of the generosity of **William Randolph**, an African American landowner/resident who helped newcomers buy land at a low cost. While some of the African Americans worked for the railroad, especially as it was extended into the Florida Keys, and others worked for white landowners, still others farmed their own land.

Mr. Randolph gave five acres of his own land to establish a school for the black children of Goulds. Two other local African Americans, **Polly** and **Arthur Mays**, helped create the school. In 1914, they established **MAYS SCHOOL**, which had grades one through eight. That school, the first of its kind built by and for blacks in south Dade County, later became the so-called "black high school" until integration in the 1960s.

One of the towns that attracted African Americans was Homestead, a place where they settled down while working with the railroad survey crews in 1902. The newcomers, many of whom came from north Florida, Georgia, and the Bahamas, settled in McClain's Addition, a subdivision that **Mark McClain** created from his 160-acre spread. After working for the railroad, many of them became farmers on the rich land. Those from the Bahamas, where home ownership was particularly prized, built houses. A segregated community arose in that subdivision, which included ST. PAUL'S MISSIONARY BAPTIST CHURCH, Homestead's first black church.

The HOMESTEAD COLORED SCHOOL, the town's first formal black school, opened in the 1920s and had grades one through eight. Before then, the children had lessons at home or at a small facility run by a professor named **Sapp**. If students wanted an education beyond the eighth grade, they had to go twenty-five miles away to Coconut Grove.

Discrimination and worse occurred in the Homestead community. For example, in 1923, when Homestead Town Marshall Charles Bryant was killed in the town's black quarter near U.S. 1 while investigating a disturbance, a posse of whites searched for the suspected killers, **William Simmons** and **Robert Gaines**, then caught, shot, and lynched them. The Ku Klux Klan was active in the area and took part in parades, beginning in 1929.

A black baseball team in south Dade, the Miami Clowns, entertained audiences in the 1920s as part of a black league that played in southeast Florida.

Goulds and Perrine attracted many African Americans, who tended to live apart from the whites and made up the majority of the population in each town. The Florida East Coast Railway brought in many African American workers from Georgia to clear out the dense forests and put down rails as the line headed toward the Keys. Violence erupted from time to time between the races. For example, whites lynched a black man from a tree on Silver Palm Drive near U.S. 1 in the mid-1930s, and the Ku Klux Klan was known for burning crosses in the front yard of blacks.

Many African Americans were severely affected when one of this nation's costliest natural disasters, Hurricane Andrew, struck the Homestead area in August 1992. Damages in the county reached $25 billion, and many local residents have still not totally recovered.

The story of Richmond Heights deserves more detail. A white Pan American Airways pilot, Frank C. Martin, bought three thousand acres of high land west of U.S. 1 and one mile east of the Richmond Naval Air Station in the late 1940s, cleared the land, and created a large residential black community. He also donated land that became known as SERGEANT JOSEPH DELANCY PARK and may have had the first swimming pool for blacks of the county. After Martin had finished building almost five hundred housing units, he died in a car accident in 1951. The community honored him in the naming of the new elementary school, built around 1956 and located today at 14250 Boggs Drive. In an effort to integrate during the early 1970s, the school became a sixth grade center drawing students from surrounding communities. The school remained a sixth grade center school for twenty-five years until 1997, when it once again reverted to an elementary school. Soon after that, it became a member of the Magnet Program for Language as well as the first to participate in the International Baccalaureate Primary Years Program in Florida.

44.

Monroe County

Florida's sixth county was established in 1823 and named for President James Monroe, the fifth president of the United States, because the United States acquired Florida from Spain during his eight years as president. Although Monroe County is not one of the state's largest counties today, in the second half of the nineteenth century it had many more people than much of the rest of the state, and Key West was Florida's largest city in the period right after the Civil War.

The county had a population of 79,589 in the 2000 census, 3,820 (4.8%) of whom were African Americans.

Key West

The town of Key West, at the southern end of U.S. 1, has a long history unlike that of any other American place. Isolated for most of its existence from the mainland, it finally became accessible from land when Henry Flagler extended his Florida East Coast Railway to the town in 1912. Before then this small outpost, which is only one mile long and four miles wide, attracted many hardy souls who were willing to endure the hardships of isolation, threats from hurricanes, and attacks from pirates and Indians to earn a living from the sea. That living might consist of fishing, salvaging wrecked ships along the Keys, or guiding ships among the dangerous reefs.

Key West and the other islands along the Florida Reef became the destination of many slaves brought over from Africa in the eighteenth and nineteenth centuries. Before the United States ended the slave trade around 1807, slave traders brought over millions of Africans to work on plantations in Brazil, Jamaica, and the southern United States. Whenever U.S. patrol boats would capture a slave ship near the Florida Keys, they would take the slaves into Key West, where

doctors would treat them and try to help them recover from the long trip across the Atlantic Ocean from Africa.

Sometimes those slave ships wrecked on the reef off the Keys. For example, the *Henrietta Marie*, a ship that could transport as many as four hundred slaves, sank on **NEW GROUND REEF** near Key West in 1701. The many sets of iron leg shackles and wrist shackles that divers found on the remains of the ship indicate that the slave traders kept the slaves imprisoned under the decks during the passage. In 1993, the National Association of Black Scuba Divers placed a memorial near the site of the shipwreck in memory of all those slaves who had died on ships like the *Henrietta Marie*.

In 2003, the Mel Fisher Maritime Heritage Society sponsored a visit by the *Freedom Schooner Amistad*, a re-creation of *La Amistad*, a ship involved in an 1839 slave revolt. On that original ship, fifty-three Africans, who had been captured in Africa and sold into slavery in Cuba, rebelled against the Spanish sailors who were taking the slaves to what would be a terrible life of slavery in Cuba. The slaves overpowered the Spanish and ordered that the ship be turned around for Africa.

Key West was often the destination of slave ships like this one. *Florida State Archives*

During the night the Spanish sailors tricked the slaves, turned the ship around, and sailed up the coast of North America for two months before landing on Long Island, New York. Authorities imprisoned the Africans while a two-year-long legal battle determined their fate. A judge finally ruled that the slave trade had been outlawed and therefore the Africans were to be freed. In 1841, the thirty-five surviving Africans were returned to what is now Sierre Leone, Africa, and in 1998 a ship was built to honor them and remember their struggle. The new *Amistad* was the one that called at Key West in 2003.

In the late 1850s, U.S. warships were ordered to enforce the anti-slave trade laws of this country and began intercepting slave ships on their way to Cuba and Puerto Rico. In 1860, the American ships captured three slave ships near Cuba and took 1,432 slaves to Key West, which at that time had only three thousand residents. Officials kept the slaves quarantined in barracks, but local residents visited them each day, bringing food and clothing, and the local U.S. Marshall paid for their medical care out of his own pocket because he had no government funds for such charity.

Before the slaves were repatriated to Africa three months later, 294 of them died in Key West of typhoid fever and dysentery. They were buried in unmarked graves in a cemetery that later became a public beach, **HIGGS BEACH**. A marker on Atlantic Boulevard between White and Reynolds Streets points out the site of what may be the only known slave cemetery in this country.

Because Key West remained in Union control during much of the American Civil War, runaway slaves from other parts of Florida sometimes made their way south instead of to the dangerous Confederate states to the north of the state. Some of those escaped slaves were recruited to join Union forces to fight for the freedom of other slaves. For example, historian Daniel Schafer points out that the 2ⁿᵈ South Carolina force consisted of two companies of former slaves recruited in Key West. Five of the Navy men who died during the Civil War and are buried in the Key West Cemetery were black.

By 1890, the 5,654 African Americans in Key West represented thirty-one percent of the town's population, but they did not suffer the harsh conditions endured elsewhere in the country. For example, a reporter in 1888 had written in the *New York Age* that Key West was "the freest town in the South, not even Washington excepted. There are no attempts at bulldozing and intimidation during campaigns and at elections here. No Negroes are murdered here in cold blood, and there are no gross miscarriages of justice against them as is so frequently seen throughout the South, to her everlasting shame and disgrace. A vigilance committee here would meet with the warmest kind of reception and a Ku Klux Klan member would be unceremoniously run into the Gulf of Mexico or the Atlantic Ocean."

The **BAHAMA VILLAGE**, a twelve-block area, surrounded by Whitehead, Louisa, Fort, and Angela Streets, is the chief black residential area of Key West. Persons of African descent who had arrived from the U.S. mainland, the Bahamas, and the Caribbean began settling there in the mid-1800s. Some of them came looking for freedom, while others came looking for work in the sponge and turtle industries. Most of the neighborhood houses and churches were built before 1912. Among the important blacks who had homes in the area were **Robert Gabriel** (Monroe County's representative in the state legislature in 1879) and **Mildred Shaver** (principal of the Frederick Douglass School in the early twentieth century). The DOUGLASS SCHOOL was organized in 1870, just five years after the end of the American Civil War, to educate black children in Key West. **William Middleton Artrell** of Nassau, who served on the city council (1875–76), headed up the school in its early years. He later was the principal of Jacksonville's STANTON INSTITUTE before returning to Key West, where he died in 1903.

Today, the Bahama Village is the setting for the annual African American Heritage Festival held each June as an effort by local African Americans to maintain and celebrate their history.

The CORNISH MEMORIAL AME ZION CHURCH at 702 Whitehead Street, which was built in 1903, honors **Sandy Cornish**, an early immigrant from the area of Cambridge, Maryland, who founded the congregation around 1864. Because no ordained black minister lived in Key West at the time, Sandy Cornish and another black man, **Cataline Simmons**, conducted the services. Simmons later went on to Jacksonville to be in charge of a church there. The tall, stately Cornish Memorial AME Zion Church remains today a strong force in the lives of Key West's blacks. Fires and hurricanes have destroyed the building several times, but members of the congregation have rebuilt it each time.

Cornish, who was known as the strongest man and the best farmer in Key West, was born in Maryland in the 1790s. After buying his freedom for $3,200, he moved with his wife to Florida to work on the railroad between Tallahassee and St. Marks. When his house burned down and he lost the papers proving he was free, a mob attacked him with the intention of selling him as a slave in New Orleans. Cornish beat them off with his great physical strength, but, when he learned that a bigger mob was planning on sending him off into slavery, he mutilated himself so badly (cutting the muscles in his leg and chopping off the fingers of his left hand) that the mob left him alone. Everyone had to be impressed with how much he hated slavery and how much he was willing to do to remain free. (For more about him, see Chapter Sixty-five.)

Sandy Cornish and his wife, **Lillah**, bought farmland near today's intersection of Simonton Street and Truman Avenue in Key West and prospered, raising fruit on a twenty-acre farm and selling the produce to visitors, including Union soldiers during the Civil War. He was well respected in the black community, led parades, made speeches at local events, and delivered sermons at burials. He died around 1869 and is probably buried in the City Cemetery, which interred both white and black citizens. Lillah died in the 1870s and is also probably buried in the same cemetery, although time has erased any identifying marks on their gravestones. CORNISH LANE in Key West honors Sandy Cornish and perhaps his wife.

The second-oldest black church in Key West is BETHEL AME CHURCH at 223 Truman Avenue. Reverend **T. W. Long** organized the church soon after arriving by steamer in 1870. A 1921 fire of mysterious origin burned down the original church building, established in 1878 at 712 Duval Street. Four years later, the congregation, under the leadership of Reverend **Logan**, rebuilt the church on the corner of Truman Avenue and Thomas Street.

Other important churches include the CHURCH OF GOD OF PROPHECY at 815 Elizabeth Street, which was built in the late 1920s and remodeled by **Brother Kemp** (a black Bahamian) and **John Bruce Knowles Sr.** ST. JAMES FIRST MISSIONARY BAPTIST CHURCH at 312 Olivia Street was founded in 1876 by freed blacks from Georgia, Alabama, and north Florida; the present masonry building was built around the original, wood building. ST. PETER'S EPISCOPAL CHURCH at 800 Center Street, the oldest black Anglican church in the Diocese of South Florida, goes back to 1872 when a group of black Anglican immigrants from the Bahamas decided to establish a church, began meeting in a schoolhouse, and eventually built a facility; the present church dates to 1924. TRINITY PRESBYTERIAN CHURCH at 717 Simonton Street began as Trinity English Wesleyan Methodist Church and was served by ministers from the Bahamas on a quarterly basis until it changed to its present name around 1931; both black and white Bahamians established the church and had no segregation inside. TRINITY WESLEYAN METHODIST CHURCH at 619 Petronia Street began around 1931, when the previously mentioned church joined the U.S. Presbyterian Denomination; **George W. Allen** became an ordained pastor, and his descendants have continued serving as pastors and officers, as well as members of the church. Rev. Allen's brother, Rev. **Alexander Allen**, established a church by the same name in Miami.

Another place on Truman Avenue, the LOFTON B. SANDS HOME/AFRICAN-BAHAMIAN MUSEUM AND RESOURCE CENTER at 324 Truman Avenue, was built in 1928 by electrician **Lofton B. Sands**, the first African American hired by the City of Key West. The facility housed the state's first African-Bahamian Museum dedicated to the education of the children of Key West with displays of African Bahamian settlers in the city, as well as a living Yoruba African village exhibit. (For more about a person from Key West who was born of Bahamian immigrants, see Chapter Forty-three and the piece about **Athalie Range** on page 169.)

The V.F.W. AMERICAN LEGION HALL at 803 Emma Street was built in 1951 by its members. The hall commemorates blacks killed in World War I (**William Weech** American Legion Post 168) and World War II (**Walter Mickens** V.F.W. Post 6021).

Among the places of significance to blacks in Key West is NELSON ENGLISH PARK on the corner of Thomas and Amelia Streets in Bahama Village, a recreation area named for the black civic leader who served as the postmaster in Key West from 1882 to 1886. **Nelson English** was the son of **James** and **Mary English**, who had moved from St. Augustine after 1850. James, a barber, became the first citizen of African descent elected to the County Commission (1868–77), as well as a member of the School Board. Nelson received an education at the Catholic and public schools of Key West, later became an accountant and bookkeeper, and then was appointed postmaster there at age thirty-three, the youngest African American named to that post.

Running a post office in Key West in the nineteenth century was difficult because the island was not yet connected to the mainland by railroad and therefore depended on boats arriving with mail and newspapers. The first postal service to Key West began in 1829, when sloops from Charleston, South Carolina, made regular calls; later ships came from St. Marks, Florida, a small town in the Panhandle that was closer to the Keys than was South Carolina, and brought in the mail. When Nelson English served as postmaster in the 1880s, mail came regularly by way of ship, but not as regularly as when the railroad linked Key West to the mainland beginning in 1912. Nelson English was also the leader of the Key West/Welters' Cornet Band, a group of musicians named after one of its leaders (**Frank Welters**) that became famous for accompanying funeral processions from the black churches to the cemetery. He also worked in the Customs House at a time when Key West had the ninth largest port in the country.

In 1873, Nelson married a teacher at the Douglass School, **Julia E. Post**, and raised five children who went on to have successful careers. **Irene** graduated from the Boston Conservatory of

Music and taught piano for many years. **Grace,** who married **Eddie Palacious,** taught at the Douglass School. **George** became the Chief of the Red Caps at Grand Central Station in New York City. **James** earned a Ph.D. in mathematics from the University of Chicago, served as principal of Douglass School (1914–22), then taught for twenty-five years in the New York public schools. **Leo** earned a bachelor's degree from Howard University and an M.D. from Northwestern University, then practiced medicine in Toledo, Ohio, for almost fifty years.

Nelson English served as one of three men appointed by state registrar Ossian B. Hart as voter registrars in Dade County in 1867. The federal Congressional Reconstruction Acts of 1867 established three-man boards for each county, and one of those men had to be black. Only fifteen men, two of whom were black, would register to vote that year in Dade County, but Nelson's reputation for honesty made his choice as one of the registrars a logical one.

BILL BUTLER PARK near the City Cemetery was the site of Monroe County Colored Folks Home, a home for indigent senior citizens. The city in 1986 created a park there to honor the memory of **William "Bill" Butler,** musician and founding father of the Key West Junkanoo and a member of the Welters' Cornet Band.

The **COMMUNITY POOL** at Dr. Martin Luther King Jr. Memorial Community Center at the corner of Catherine and Thomas Streets was built by the city in 1946 for African Americans at a time when the beaches at Key West were segregated.

The waters off Key West played a part in one of the most unusual trials in the state's history. In the 1840s, abolitionists, who were determined to end slavery in the South, came to Florida to try to free as many slaves as possible. One of them was Jonathan Walker, a white Massachusetts man who came to Florida in the 1800s to try to help the slaves. He took a group of slaves in his boat from Pensacola, Florida, toward Nassau, but was

captured near Key West in July 1844. Officials returned him to Pensacola, where the letters "SS" for slave stealer were burned into his right hand. The New England poet, John Greenleaf Whittier, wrote a poem entitled "The Branded Hand" about that incident (see Chapter Sixteen).

In 1888, voters in Monroe County elected **Charles F. Dupont,** the state's first popularly elected black sheriff. The Tampa native, who was a carpenter and Republican activist, served for four years and accomplished much, including saving the lives of several prisoners whom a lynch mob tried to kill. After his term of office he remained in Key West and helped establish the state's first branch of the National Association for the Advancement of Colored People (NAACP). He died in his adopted town in 1938. **DUPONT LANE** in Key West honors him.

Two other downtown streets were probably named after African Americans: **WILLIAMS ALLEY** for **Jesse** and **William Williams,** two blacks from St. Augustine who settled in Key West; and **SHAVERS LANE** between Whitehead and Duval Streets for **Charles Shavers,** a black resident of the area.

Other blacks who served in public office in the nineteenth century in Monroe County were **Robert W. Butler, James D. English,** and **Benjamin W. Roberts** on the county commission after the Civil War; and **James A. Roberts** served as sheriff (1874–77). Among other blacks elected to office were **Charles Brown** and **James A. Roberts** as county constables in the early 1870s; **Robert Gabriel** (elected in 1879) and **Charles Shavers** (elected in 1887) to represent the county in the Florida Legislature. Robert Gabriel also served as a City Commissioner (1876–78, 1905–1909) and as a Customs Inspector. The public housing project on Whitehead Street was named the Robert Gabriel Housing Project in 1958 in honor of him.

Another distinguished African American in Key West was **James Dean.** He graduated from Jacksonville's Cookman Institute (1878) and from

Howard University with a Bachelor of Law degree (1883), was admitted to the District of Columbia bar (1884), and secured a license to practice law in Florida courts (1887). Key West voters then elected him (1888) as the state's only African American county judge in the nineteenth century. Governor Francis Fleming removed Dean from the judgeship the following year under pressure from white conservatives, but Dean went on to practice law in Key West and Jacksonville, became a clergyman in the AME church, and died in Jacksonville in 1914.

Unlike most other Florida sites, Key West had a decent record of having African Americans serve in public office. For example, **John V. Cornell** served as city clerk (1875–76), and **Frank Adams** was an assessor (1886–87, 1888–89). At least ten men served as aldermen between 1875 and 1907: **William M. Artrell**, **Benjamin W. Roberts**, **Jose Juan Figueroa**, **James A. Roberts**, **Robert Gabriel**, **Charles R. Adams**, **Frank Adams**, **Washington A. Cornell**, **R. M. Stevens**, and **Charles Shavers**. (For more about an African American newspaper editor, **John Willis Menard**, who served as inspector of customs at Key West and edited *Key West News/ Florida News*, see Chapter Fifteen.)

The 2000 census indicated that Key West had 2,365 African Americans or 9% of the total town population.

About seventy miles west of Key West in the Gulf of Mexico on the sixteen-acre Garden Key lies one of the most remarkable structures in the state and one that slave labor helped to build: **FORT JEFFERSON**. Spanish explorer Juan Ponce de León had named the islands the Dry Tortugas in the sixteenth century because they had no fresh water and were full of loggerhead turtles ("tortugas" in Spanish). The seven small coral keys that make up the Dry Tortugas were isolated, barren, and mosquito-infested for centuries until the U.S. government decided in 1846 to built a huge stone fort, nicknamed the "Gibraltar of the Gulf," to prevent British and Spanish forays into the Gulf and to protect American shipping in the area.

Hundreds of workers, including many slaves, toiled for almost thirty years to build the six-sided fort; it rose sixty feet from its coral bedrock, and each side was 450 feet long and five feet thick at the top. The workers painstakingly placed 243 monstrous cannon on the fort to guard the outside sea lanes. Inside the fort, the workers built officers' quarters, barracks to house some eight hundred men, and a large parade ground. Around the fort they dug a seventy-foot-wide, ten-foot-

Slaves worked on the construction of Fort Jefferson to the west of Key West. *Florida State Archives*

deep moat (complete with sharks and barracudas) to dissuade the prisoners from escaping. Although its guns never fired a shot against the enemy, the structure did serve as a federal prison during the Civil War for many prisoners, including Dr. Samuel Mudd, the Maryland doctor who unwittingly set the broken leg of John Wilkes Booth, the assassin of President Abraham Lincoln.

Building the fort was very hard work. The workers had to endure the blazing sun, hordes of mosquitoes, hurricanes, dysentery, scurvy, and typhoid to build what turned out to be one of the most massive fortresses ever constructed in the Western Hemisphere, a structure which contained forty million bricks. While most of the skilled workers were Yankees from the North and most of the slaves did the hard, manual labor, a few well-trained slaves were able to work as masons and carpenters. When the ordinary workday was over, the thirty to thirty-five slaves on the job sometimes continued working or did some fishing in order to gain a few cents to buy some extra food. At one point in 1847, seven blacks escaped by boat into the Gulf, but very few of the others were successful in their attempts to flee.

The men worked ten hours a day, six days a week, but the harsh conditions made one officer comment that in better conditions one man could do the work of two men at Fort Jefferson. The slaves came from Key West slave owners, some of whom bought more slaves to work at the fort. The slave owners were happy to rent out their slaves to the government and also wanted their slaves isolated at the fort and away from Key West, where Northern visitors might encourage the slaves to rebel. Also the slave owners discouraged any education among the slaves, even simple reading and writing, on the grounds that ignorant slaves would be less susceptible to abolitionist ideas. The fort, which ended its usefulness as a prison in the 1870s and was virtually abandoned for decades, is now a national park and a reminder of how harsh a life slave-workers had in the nineteenth century.

Because Union troops occupied Key West during much of the Civil War, conditions there differed markedly from other Florida sites. For example, in 1862, President Lincoln signed a confiscation order that authorized Union soldiers to seize the property of anyone in active rebellion against the U.S. government, allowed Union officers to hire as much black labor as necessary, and defined slaves living inside Union lines as "forever free." That act effectively freed the slaves of Key West and allowed them to hire themselves out for work. When official word of the Emancipation Proclamation reached Key West in 1863, the blacks celebrated and paraded through the streets.

A recruiter in Key West in 1863 persuaded two hundred of the island's African Americans to join a regiment organized in South Carolina. Some of them returned to Key West as occupation troops after the war as part of the 2nd United States Colored Troops. Some of the whites of the city were angry at that action, but the large number of federal troops kept the situation under control.

Marathon

Midway between Key Largo and Key West in the Florida Keys on Key Vaca is the small town of Marathon, which received its name from the workers who used it to refer to the endurance contest or difficulties the workers overcame in building Flagler's Florida East Coast Railway to Key West. The Indians who inhabited the Keys for decades before the first Europeans arrived in the sixteenth century did not take kindly to the invaders and killed many of them, including shipwrecked sailors. When the Indians were gone from the Keys, settlers moved in, including pirates and wreckers who used the inlets and islands in the vicinity. Around 1818, local fishermen established a small village in what became Key Vaca.

Flagler began extending his railroad down

the Keys in 1905 and finally reached Key West in 1912 in a job he called the toughest he ever undertook. By the time the 156-mile Overseas Railroad reached its goal of Key West, twenty thousand men had worked on it and it cost $50 million, which would be more than half a billion in today's dollars.

Some eight hundred of Flagler's construction workers were blacks from Florida and the Bahamas attracted to the Keys by the work. Flagler's workers had a base camp at Key Vaca that they abandoned when they finished building the Seven-Mile Bridge just southwest of Marathon, and the population slowly diminished until it reached just seventeen by 1926. Little by little the town of Marathon developed between the railroad line, where U.S. 1 runs today, and Florida Bay. In the 1950s the town began to develop rapidly, acquiring its first dial-system telephones, a Florida Highway Patrol station, a volunteer fire department, and the first full-time doctor.

In the middle of Marathon is the **CRANE POINT HISTORIC AND ARCHAEOLOGICAL DISTRICT**, which contained the black pioneer settlements of Adderly Town, which developed between 1903 and 1912. The town had six people in 1910, all mem-

bers of the **Adderly** and **Curry** families. Among those blacks was **George Adderly** (1870–1958), a black Bahamian who came to Florida in 1890. In 1903, he bought thirty-two acres of land from **Annie Crain** for $100 and moved to Key Vaca, where he built his house and where he worked in sponging and charcoal making.

The **ADDERLY HOUSE** at 5550 Overseas Highway behind the Museum of Natural History of the Florida Keys is a small, white, one-story building in the Bahamian architecture style that **George Adderly** and his wife, **Olivia**, built sometime after they bought the property in 1903 on part of the thirty-two acres they owned. The house was built of tabby, a building material consisting of lime, shells, gravel or stones, and water. When this concretelike material dried in the sun, it became hard enough to withstand the hurricanes that buffeted the area over the years. The house withstood the terrible 1935 hurricane, which destroyed much of Flagler's railroad track in the Keys and made the area less accessible until the U.S. government finished the Overseas Highway in 1938. Adderly sold his property in 1950 to people who built a new winter house on Rachel Key and connected the small island to the mainland. By then all of

The Adderly House in Marathon was home to a black Bahamian immigrant who worked in the area in the early 1900s.

the blacks had left the property. George's wife died that year, and George died eight years later; they are buried in unmarked graves in the Key West Cemetery.

In 2000, Marathon had a population of 8,857, of whom 586 (7%) were black. For many years the town's blacks lived in what is known today as Marathon Beach Subdivision, a name that dates back to the 1920s, when **William A. Parrish** bought up land between 35th and 43rd Streets on the bay side of the highway. Many of the early settlers who bought land there were blacks who settled down and renamed the place "The Rock." The segregated school for black children later became the **GRACE JONES COMMUNITY CENTER**, honoring in its name the town's first black teacher.

At the southwestern edge of Marathon is Knights Key, where the famous Seven Mile Bridge begins. The bridge, completed in 1911, withstood the hurricanes that hit the Keys, including the terrible 1935 storm that destroyed Flagler's railroad. Workers then constructed the Overseas Highway using Flagler's railroad line. The bridge led to Pigeon Key, where railroad workers and their families used to live; later the University of Miami used the island for marine research. Workers built a new bridge in 1982 and cut off Pigeon Key from the main highway.

The **PIGEON KEY HISTORIC DISTRICT** at mile marker 45 off U.S. 1 has seven frame buildings which workers used while building the Overseas Railroad between 1901 and 1912. One of the buildings is a 1912 "Negro Workers' Cottage" where black workers were housed. The site is not accessible from the new bridge, but must be reached by way of the old trestle.

45.

Nassau County

Florida's tenth county was established in 1824 and named for the nearby Nassau River and Nassau Sound, which separate the counties of Nassau and Duval. The name of Nassau, which also applies to the capital of the Bahamas, goes back to the Duchy of Nassau in Germany and then to the English line of royalty down to King William III. The British brought the name to Florida during their occupation of the territory (1763–83).

Nassau County had a population of 57,663 in the 2000 census, 4,440 (7.7%) of whom were African Americans. The county is just north of the very heavily populated Duval County (population 778,879), where more than half of Nassau County's residents work and which is under increasing pressure to accommodate more people who want to move out of the congested Jacksonville area.

American Beach

Amelia Island at the northeastern tip of Florida has had a long and varied history, part of which involved slavery, but it also had a successful attempt by blacks to establish a beach of their own. Up until the United States acquired Florida from Spain in 1821, the peninsula's many inlets and islands, especially along the east coast, provided smugglers easy access to inland markets. The U.S. outlawed the importation of slaves in 1808, but, because Florida was still under the nominal power of Spain, many smugglers simply moved their operation south and used northern Florida as a conduit for bringing slaves into the U.S. from Africa. Between 1810 and 1820 smugglers brought in some sixty thousand slaves and sold them throughout the South. Amelia Island's main town of Fernandina prospered from the profits of the slave trade and attracted its share of traders, pirates, and criminals.

After the American Civil War ended in 1865, newly freed slaves homesteaded the land or bought acreage in the area; many of those homesteaders eventually received title to the land during Rutherford B. Hayes's presidency (1877–81), at a time when Florida land cost as little as fifty cents an acre. The black families that lived there earned a livelihood from fishing, farming, and ranching. After one hundred years of living there and raising their families, the descendants of those early settlers sold the land in 1972 to a development company that would eventually build the luxurious Amelia Island Plantation.

One of the earliest local black settlements was an independent community called Franklin Town, which could date itself back to the 1860s. The early inhabitants of the settlement had been slaves on a plantation run by Samuel Harrison, a South Carolina planter who had acquired the land during the time when the English controlled Florida (1763–83).

After the American Civil War and into the middle of the twentieth century, segregation throughout the country, but particularly in the South, would not allow blacks to mix with whites in public places, including beaches. Because

American Beach was one of the few black beaches in Florida.

blacks wanted a beach where they could swim in the ocean and not be subject to the harassment of whites, they settled in **AMERICAN BEACH**, a small community at the southern end of Amelia Island.

The man behind the establishment of the 200-acre American Beach was **A. L. Lewis**, the founder and president of the Afro-American Life Insurance Company (see Chapter Fifteen). In 1901, Lewis and six others each invested $100 to establish the Afro-American Industrial and Benefit Association, or the Afro as people referred to it, to enable poor blacks to pay just ten cents a week for funerals. The company eventually changed its name to the Afro-American Insurance Company and helped to provide low-cost health and burial insurance to thousands of blacks, most of whom could not obtain insurance from white companies. The insurance company prospered and by the 1950s became a $5 million corporation.

The granddaughter of **A. L. Lewis** and the great-great-great-great-granddaughter of plantation owner Zephaniah Kingsley and his wife,

Anna Madgigine Jai (see Chapter Fifteen for information on all three), the late **MaVynee Betsch**, was a long-time fixture in American Beach who succeeded in convincing the exclusive Amelia Island Plantation to donate eight acres of dune area to the local community as a park. Having performed as an opera singer in European theaters, Betsch became known for her long dreadlocks, but was effective in helping preserve the area from developers. Author Russ Rymer featured her in his nonfiction book *American Beach*. A recent movie, "Sunshine State" (2002) directed by John Sayles, was also about Ms. Betsch and American Beach.

Besides its own schools, medical staff, and recreation center, the Afro bought the beach on Amelia Island and built summer cottages for its executives and for those employees who won company sales contests. The company called the beach American to remind everyone, blacks as well as whites, that the people there were just as American as others in this country. So popular did American Beach become that up to ten thousand people would gather there on weekends and holidays. In 1935, residents built the first permanent buildings, which consisted of houses, hotels, and even a candy factory.

The street names in American Beach honored blacks associated with the company that established the resort. Lewis Street, the main street and the only one allowing beach access, was named for **A. L. Lewis** (1865–1947), one of the founders of the Afro-American Life Insurance Company. Streets that honored his relatives were Julia (for **Julia Brown Lewis**, his mother), Mary (for **Mary F. Lewis**, his first wife), and Leonard (for his grandson, **J. Leonard Lewis**). Other streets named for company officials were Waldron (for Rev. **J. Milton Waldron**, pastor of Jacksonville's Bethel Baptist Institutional Church from 1892 until 1907 and an organizer of the Afro), Gregg (for Rev. **E. J. Gregg**, pastor of Mount Zion AME Church and the first president of the Afro when officials chartered it in 1901), Price (for Rev. **Alfred W. Price**, president of the Afro after Rev. Gregg), Ervin (for **Louis Dargan Ervin**, the first full-time agent for the Afro and later its vice president), Lee (for **William H. Lee**, a vice president and secretary of the Afro), and Stewart (for **Ralph Stewart Sr.**, a company secretary).

In 1990, officials dedicated the six-acre **BURNEY PARK** at American Beach, the first such park in Nassau County to honor a black person. Open to all from 7 A.M.–7 P.M., the park honors **I. H. Burney II**, who served as president of the Afro-American Life Insurance Company from 1967 to 1975; he was the only president of the Afro who was not a blood relative or son-in-law of Lewis and his descendants.

American Beach, which is to the east of Highway A1A on the southern end of Amelia Island, suffered from major storms over the years, for example Hurricane Dora in 1964, which destroyed some of the town's buildings. Once integration opened up the country's beaches to everyone in the 1960s, the popularity of the black settlement declined. Today American Beach finds itself sandwiched between some very exclusive resorts that cater to the wealthy, some of whom would like to buy large tracts of American Beach. In fact, with more and more whites moving into American Beach, some black residents fear that the town may undergo major changes that may eventually cause people to forget the proud legacy that the town has had.

Fernandina Beach

Fernandina Beach to the north of American Beach was the home of a black photographer, **Richard Samuel Roberts** (1880–1936), who operated the Gem Studio and took many photographs of the local community. In 1920, he moved to South Carolina and continued taking photographs of the black community there. After he died, researchers discovered more than three thousand of his glass photographic plates and in 1986 published them; these photographs show a good cross-section of Southern blacks.

MACEDONIA AFRICAN METHODIST EPISCOPAL CHURCH at 202 S. 9th Street began in 1872 from the Prayer Band, which **Samuel Irving** had established several years earlier. The congregation built their church and moved into it in 1899. The church has two features of note: a wide front door to accommodate funeral processions and stained-glass windows to honor deceased loved ones, windows purchased in the 1940s. The congregation completed a renovation of the building in 2002.

Another African American church is **FIRST MISSIONARY BAPTIST CHURCH** between Centre and Ash Streets, dating back to 1874. Among its members have been **Emma B. Delaney** (see below) and Captain **Neil Frink**, the first African American to be a licensed boat captain in Florida.

PECK SCHOOL at 516 S. 10th Street was the school that African Americans attended in the days of segregation. It honors in its name **William Henderson Peck** (1859–1950), an official

Macedonia AME Church in Fernandina Beach has a wide front door to accommodate funerals.

at the school. In 1880, African Americans in Nassau County petitioned for a high school, and officials built one in 1884. The following year **Moses H. Payne** of Howard University became principal, and William Peck became his assistant. When Professor Payne died in a yellow fever epidemic in 1887, Peck took over as principal, a position he held for fifty years. By 1894, he had established a program serving students through the tenth grade and, in 1908, had a full high school curriculum. In 1911, the school, Nassau Colored School Number 1, was named Peck High School. In 1928 a new school was constructed with the same name, which served black children until desegregation in 1968. A Great Floridian plaque at the Peck Center (formerly Peck High School), 516 S. 10th Street, in Fernandina Beach, honors him.

When the school shut down at the time of integration and began to deteriorate from lack of use, **Willie May Ashley**, who had taught there for more than two decades, successfully led the fight to restore the building. In 2004, city commissioners named the auditorium at the school in her honor: the **WILLIE MAY HARDY ASHLEY AUDITORI-**

UM in the newly restored community center. The building now houses nonprofit groups like the Amelia Arts Academy, Communities in Schools, Habitat for Humanity, Head Start, Northeast Community Action Agency, and the Police Athletic League, as well as a library, computer center, and gymnasium. The community center is open Monday through Friday, 8 A.M.–9 P.M. Phone: (904) 277-7364. Ms. Ashley also wrote *Far From Home*, the biography of local resident **Emma B. Delaney**, (see below).

The Great Floridians 2000 program, which recognized distinguished individuals, honored **Emma Delaney** with a plaque at the First Missionary Baptist Church, 22 S. 9th Street, Fernandina Beach. Born in Fernandina in 1871, she completed missionary and nursing training at Spelman College, then became the first African American female missionary sent to Africa. In 1902, she helped establish the Providence Industrial Mission in Malawi. Returning to the United States in 1906, she lectured on her experiences and raised money to return to Africa. In 1912, she went to Liberia and founded the Suehn Industrial mission near Monrovia, a mission that provided education, industrial arts, home economics, and health care. In 1922, she returned to the United States and died the same year of tropical fever. Florida Baptist Churches honor her on the third Sunday in May.

Also honored as part of the Great Floridians 2000 Program is a white woman who did much to help local African Americans. Chloe Merrick (1832–1897) was born in Syracuse, New York; taught in Syracuse public schools (1854–56), and in 1863 responded to a plea to help with slaves who had fled to the Union Army lines. Arriving in Fernandina and finding more than seven hundred African Americans living on Amelia Island, she opened a Freedmen's School where she taught and helped the needy. Merrick also organized the Orphan Asylum at Fernandina and is the only educator cited by name in the Bureau of Refugees, Freedmen and Abandoned Lands monthly education reports from Florida. In 1869, she married Harrison M. Reed, governor of Florida, influencing legislation to address social problems, including education and relief for the poor. Her Great Floridian plaque is located at the Simmons-Merrick House, 102 S. 10th Street, Fernandina Beach.

An African American honored in the Great Floridians 2000 Program was **Liberty Billings** (1823–1877), who was born in Maine, ordained a Unitarian minister at age twenty-five, and later commissioned as a lieutenant colonel and second in command of the first authorized African American military unit in the U.S. Army: the 1st South Carolina Infantry Regiment. After being wounded in the Civil War, Billings was honorably discharged (1863), arrived in Fernandina (1865), and began purchasing property. He championed black rights in Florida and was a leader in Florida's Reconstruction politics. He conducted the U.S. Census in Nassau County (1870) and was a state senator, representing Nassau, Duval, and St. Johns Counties (1871–1877), before dying in Fernandina in 1877. His Great Floridian plaque is located at the family's home, **AMELIA HOUSE**, 222 N. 5th Street in Fernandina Beach.

For information on **Effie Carrie Mitchell Hampton**, who was born in Fernandina in 1886 and went on to become the first black female physician to practice in Florida, see Chapter Forty-one.

The 2000 census indicated that Fernandina Beach had 1,708 African Americans or 16% of the total town population of 10,549.

Mount Olive Missionary Baptist Church in Nassauville was a place where free blacks, Native Americans, Spanish Indians, and mulattoes could worship freely.

Nassauville

Nassauville to the west of Fernandina Beach is the site of **MOUNT OLIVE MISSIONARY BAPTIST CHURCH** on S.R. 107. Descendants of African-born **Sam Hooper** and his Native American wife established Mount Olive Baptist Church there in 1870. After registering with the Union forces stationed at Fort Clinch in Fernandina, a group of mixed-race settlers moved to this area, which was called Nassau. The small wooden structure, which had only fifty seats and was the only church west of the Nassau River until Piney, Florida, became the center of social activities of the community. It also represented a place where free blacks, Native Americans, Spanish Indians, and mulattoes could be free and could express their feelings for freedom and rights. The first structure, built a few yards from the present building, was replaced by the current building in 1920.

In recognition of its historic significance, the National Park Service put the church on the National Register of Historic Places in 1998. The plaque in front of the church was sponsored by the church founders' great-great-great-great grandchildren in 2002.

46.

Okaloosa County

This county, established in 1915 from Santa Rosa and Walton Counties, derives its name from two Choctaw Indian words: *oka* "water" and *lusa* "black," probably referring to the Blackwater River that flows through the county. The county had a population of 170,498 in the 2000 census, 15,515 (9.1%) of whom were African Americans.

Crestview

The town of Crestview, forty miles east of Pensacola on U.S. 90, is 223 feet above sea level, the second-highest altitude in Florida and the source of its name. In 1916, it became the county seat of the newly established Okaloosa County and later became even more prominent with the establishment of the nearby Eglin Air Force Base in 1944. The 2000 census indicated that Crestview had 2,719 African Americans or 18% of the total town population.

The **FAIRVIEW PARK COMPLEX** and **CARVER-HILL MEMORIAL MUSEUM** at 895 McClelland Street are dedicated to the preservation of black culture, heritage, achievements, and personal contributions of black citizens. The Okaloosa Negro Civic Club established the park in the early 1950s and later deeded it to the City of Crestview for management. The Macedonia Baptist Church also helped manage the park.

The first museum there traced its beginnings to 1954, when a new school was built in the area. The Okaloosa County School Board donated the old one-room lunchroom building to the Civic Club to become the Carver-Hill Museum, operated by the Carver-Hill Memorial and Historical Society, Inc. Carver School alumni established the museum in order to preserve the school and various memorabilia at a time when integration

was closing black schools. Since its opening in May 1979, the museum has added many items of local interest and related to the history of blacks in the area.

The Carver-Hill Memorial and Historical Society, which was chartered in 1969 as a nonprofit organization, pledged its membership and resources to support the museum by acquiring historical documents and artifacts associated with the achievements of black citizens. After establishing the museum, members of the community donated materials and labor to construct a concrete-block structure which is used today as a recreation center. Material in the museum includes photo albums from the different graduating classes, information about Crestview High School after integration, and medals won by local athlete **Houston McTear**. The Historical Society opened a new, 3500-square-foot museum building next door to the first museum in 2002.

Directions to the Museum: From I-10, go 1.2 miles north on S.R. 85, turn left on Duggan Avenue and go .6 miles, then turn right on McClelland Street and go one block. The museum is on the right across from Hayes Place. Heading south from downtown Crestview on S.R. 85, go .5 miles from Main Street and turn right (west) on Duggan Avenue before following the above directions. The museum's hours are Monday–Friday, 8 A.M.–12 P.M.; Sat. 1 P.M.–4 P.M., and at other

The Carver-Hill Museum in Crestview has artifacts and exhibits about the heritage and achievements of black citizens.

times by appointment. Phone: (850) 682-3494 or 682-6599.

Fort Walton Beach

In the last part of the nineteenth century, several schools for African Americans were established in what became Okaloosa County. One black teacher, **Arthur Hendrith**, became supervisor of Old Walton School, one such school for blacks. In 1909, residents of the Brick community petitioned the school board for a school for black children, but the school board insisted that the parents provide the land, materials, and building for such a facility, which made it very difficult for the parents.

Finally, in 1938, the first school for blacks in Fort Walton Beach was opened. At first, the school, which held classes in a private home, was called the Fort Walton Colored School. The teacher, Miss **Payne**, taught grades one through six. In 1940, classes were transferred to another private home on Washington Street, and Miss **Johnson** became the teacher. Around 1950, the school moved to Beulah Baptist Church, where two teachers did the teaching: Miss **Bessie Cor-**

bit and Mr. **Charlie H. Hill**. In 1943, Mr. Hill became principal of the school, and a teacher was hired to replace him. The next year, Mayor **Tom Brooks** donated land for a school building, and the school board built a two-room facility, called the Brooks School in honor of the mayor.

In the next decade, the number of classrooms and teachers steadily increased. In 1954, officials decided to consolidate the black schools, and so the black students attending Brooks School began going to Carver Hill in Crestview. In 1961, officials built **W. E. COMBS HIGH SCHOOL** on Lovejoy Road in Fort Walton Beach, which allowed black students in the upper grades to go to that school. Charlie Hill became principal of the new high school, and his brother, **James Hill**, became principal of Brooks School. Officials tended to neglect Combs High School, and its facilities deteriorated. As an example of how poor the supplies were, the football players at Combs had to use discarded mouthpieces from other high schools.

When integration took place in the 1960s, Brooks and Combs schools were closed, along with other African American schools. When the school board built Choctawhatchee High School for the new, integrated school, the parents of students at Combs protested and petitioned to the school board to keep Combs open, even though that would violate federal desegregation laws. The parents threatened to send their children to the still-all-black DeFuniak Springs High School, but in the end did not. However, only a few of the ninety black students who transferred to Choctawhatchee High School graduated from that school, the rest dropping out for a variety of reasons, including a reluctance to make the transition to the new school.

Carver-Hill School was closed as part of Okaloosa County's School Integration Plan at the close of the 1968–69 school year. The school, which began around 1915, had been called Rosenwald in honor of Julius Rosenwald (1862–1932), a successful American businessman, president of Sears, Roebuck and Company, and philanthropist who used much of his money to establish schools for American blacks. The name of Crestview's school was changed to Carver to honor Dr. **George Washington Carver** (1864?–1943), famed educator at Tuskegee Institute in Alabama. In 1954, local officials in Crestview added the name Hill to honor Rev. **Edward Hill**, a man who represented a group of black parents in efforts to have the school board establish a local school for black children. Until the W. E. Combs School (named for a professor) was built in Fort Walton in 1962, every black student in Okaloosa County had to attend Carver-Hill for high school.

Carver-Hill became a kindergarten center that served all of Crestview. Combs School was closed for a year, then remodeled into Combs New Heights Elementary School at 720 Lovejoy Road Northwest.

Integration of schools in Okaloosa County occurred with few incidents, probably because the schools on Eglin Air Force Base there were integrated first with no problems, and that led to a peaceful integration in the rest of the county. How it happened on the bases was that in 1955 the school board had refused to allow an integrated school on the military bases there, which resulted in the base schools being taken over by the U.S. Air Force, which hired the principal and teachers, integrated the schools, and operated independently of the public school system.

By September 1964, when integration of the county's schools was complete, schools in other counties refused to play the Niceville High School (Okaloosa County) football team because the school had a black player on the team. When three schools, DeFuniak Springs (Walton County), Marianna (Jackson County), and Port St. Joe (Gulf County), canceled its football games with Niceville High School, the latter school played several of its opponents twice in order to make a full schedule. In the following year (1965), Niceville resumed its regular-season games.

The building that houses **INDIAN MOUND LODGE #1205** and **BOOKER T. WASHINGTON TEMPLE #863** of the Improved Benevolent Protected Order of the Elks of the World (IBPOEW) at 118 Kiwi Place Northeast has historical programs, community activities, and entertainment for the area. It also has photographs about the black history of the county.

Directions to the Lodge: From U.S. 98 West, turn north in Fort Walton Beach onto Beal Parkway/S.R. 189, then right onto Hollywood Boulevard, then left onto Harbeson Avenue Northeast, then right onto Kiwi Place Northeast.

J. R. L. CONYERS LODGE #364 at 550 McDonald Street, built in 1909, is one of the oldest buildings in the area and houses the Masons and Eastern Stars groups. The building there was also used as an early school facility.

Directions from the Carver-Hill Museum to the Lodge: Continue north on McClelland Street for .2 miles, turn right on School Avenue, and then take the first left; Conyers Lodge is on the left.

The J.R.L. Conyers Lodge #364 houses several African American groups.

her home and clinic. She was featured in several national magazines, and in 1992 was honored with the Sage Femme, the highest award of the Midwives Alliance of North America. Her biography is titled *Why Not Me?* She was inducted into the Florida Women's Hall of Fame in 1994. Her daughter, **Maria Milton**, has continued the practice of midwifery in the same building where her mother had practiced.

The 2000 census indicated that Fort Walton Beach had 2,664 African Americans or 13% of the total town population.

Among the county personages recognized in the Great Floridians 2000 program, which recognized distinguished individuals, was **Chester Pruitt** (1917–1968), the first African American police officer in Fort Walton Beach. He joined the force in 1948 and served through the 1950s and 1960s. He was a mediator on many difficult issues, especially those dealing with the city's youth. A neighborhood center and park are named in his honor. His Great Floridian plaque is located at the **CHESTER PRUITT NEIGHBORHOOD CENTER**, 15 Carson Drive, Fort Walton Beach.

Laurel Hill

Gladys Milton (1924–1999) was born at Caney Creek in northern Walton County, and later became a midwife who delivered more than two thousand babies. She became nationally known in the late 1970s, when she led a legislative fight for recognition of midwives as legitimate medical practitioners. She welcomed all races into her **MILTON MEMORIAL BIRTHING CLINIC** at 952 Flowersview Boulevard in Laurel Hill, the first such institution in Florida's Panhandle. She persisted in her work despite state attempts to ban midwifery, and also endured the burning of both

47.

Okeechobee County

Florida's fifty-fourth county was established in 1917 with a name derived from two Hitchiti Indian words: *oki* "water" and *chobi* "big." (The name of Miami may have the same meaning ("big water") in another Native American language.)

Okeechobee County had a population of 35,910 in the 2000 census, 2,837 (7.9%) of whom were African Americans.

Lake Okeechobee

On Christmas Day 1837, a major battle was fought on the northeast shores of Lake Okeechobee by Seminole Indians and regular Army troops of the Missouri militia under the command of Colonel Zachary Taylor. Part of that battle was an attempt by the U.S. forces to recapture escaped slaves who had fled to Florida seeking freedom from the oppressive conditions they had suffered on Southern plantations.

Against a much larger force of troops, the Indians killed twenty-six soldiers and wounded 112, while suffering casualties of eleven killed and fourteen wounded in the battle that lasted about three hours. That largest battle of the Second Seminole War convinced the Seminoles that they could not win such a pitched battle against overwhelming numbers, and they did not engage in such a battle again. Zachary Taylor emerged from the battle as the only Army commander to beat the Seminoles in a major confrontation and eventually became president of the United States as a war hero.

Each February during Black History Month the battle is re-enacted, probably then because few people would show up on Christmas Day, the actual anniversary of the battle, and because blacks played an important part of the Seminole Wars. The Okeechobee Battlefield is on U.S. 441 and U.S. 98 South, 6.4 miles from the intersection of S.R. 70.

A directory of the county in the early twentieth century listed fourteen African American men who were the heads of families. Many of those men were employed by the Florida East Coast Railway. At the time Okeechobee had a black Baptist Church and a black African Methodist Episcopal Church. One of the earliest citizens of the town was a black man, **Will Harp**, who helped build a hardware store for a white owner in 1915.

TEN DOLLARS REWARD.

RAN AWAY from the subscriber, a *Negro man* named *Charles*, and a *Negro woman* named *Dorcas*. The man is about forty years old, and the woman thirty-eight. The man is very black—about five feet nine inches in height,—with the African marks on his face of his native country. The woman is about five feet nine inches, and rather thick set. Any person returning them shall receive the above reward. **HENRY W. MAXEY.**

Cedar Point, March 4. 1w10

Advertisement for runaway slave (from the *Jacksonville Courier*, April 16, 1835)

Advertisements like this one were an attempt to recapture escaped slaves. *Florida State Archives*

Schools for African Americans like this one were established throughout Florida. *Florida State Archives*

48.
Orange County

Florida's eleventh county was established in 1824 with the name Mosquito, not one that would endear itself to any chamber of commerce. It became Orange County in 1845 to commemorate the many orange groves in the area. Orange County had a population of 896,344 in the 2000 census, 163,135 (18.2%) of whom were African Americans.

Eatonville

This town in Orange County, just off I-4 between Winter Park and Maitland and north of Orlando, takes its name from a white man, Captain Joshua (or Josiah) C. Eaton of Maine, a retired Navy paymaster who settled in nearby Maitland after the Civil War and helped a group of blacks buy a 500-acre tract of land west of Maitland for their own community. Incorporated in 1888 as a black community, it attracted many black settlers, including **John Hurston**, a skilled carpenter, Baptist preacher, one-time mayor of the town, and father of writer **Zora Neale Hurston**.

Ms. **Hurston** was born in 1901, according to her own testimony, or 1891, according to a source in Hemenway's biography, soon after the town was incorporated. She wrote the following in her autobiography, *Dust Tracks on a Road* (1948):

"I was born in a Negro town. I do not mean by that the black back-side of an average town. Eatonville, Florida, is, and was at the time of my birth, a pure Negro town: charter, Mayor, council, town marshal and all. It was not the first Negro community in America, but it was the first to be incorporated, the first attempt at organized self-government on the part of the Negroes in America."

She also wrote about the town in novels like *Jonah's Gourd Vine* (1934) and *Their Eyes Were Watching God* (1937), shorter works like "The Eatonville Anthology" (1926), and short stories like "Sweat" (1926) and "The Gilded Six-Bits" (1933). With a background in anthropology and literature, Ms. Hurston created a literature based partly on the stories she heard growing up in Eatonville and partly on the extensive fieldwork she did in Haiti and Florida. While the growth of black literacy in America has increased her readership among African Americans, the excellence of her writing, the universal themes she touched on, and her depiction of a rural Florida long since gone explain her growing popularity in the late twentieth and early twenty-first centuries.

Her novels dealt with the oppression, poverty, and racism experienced by many blacks in the United States, but also dealt with the hope that her protagonists had in seeking a new life with new opportunities for their families.

Her family's home, long since gone, was in the area bounded today by Lemon, Lime, People, and West Streets. **Joe Clarke**'s store, where the young Zora heard many of the stories that later made their way into her writings, is now a grocery store at the northeast corner of Kennedy Boulevard and West Street; Mr. Clarke's house was next door to his store. Her father's church, the **MACEDONIA MISSIONARY BAPTIST CHURCH**, was then on the south side of Eaton Street between East and West streets; the Macedonia Baptist Church today is in a new building on E. Kennedy Boulevard and Calhoun Street. After her mother, **Lucy**, died and her father remarried, Zora went to Jacksonville to live with a brother while attending school. She later attended Morgan Academy, Howard University in Washington, D.C., and Barnard College in New York City. In the late 1920s she returned to Eatonville to collect the folklore that would appear in her *Mules and Men* (1935). The first-class stamp with Hurston's face on it that was issued in 2003 has a Florida background with the sun rising over a body of water.

The **ZORA NEALE HURSTON MEMORIAL** by the town's fire station is on the former site of a home that belonged to one of Zora's friends with whom she stayed on her returns to Eatonville. She is honored with a plaque at the Matilda Moseley House, 11 Taylor Street (see below). The Hurston family home was located on what is today a vacant lot across from the fire station. Nearby

Zora Neale Hurston. *Florida State Archives*

Hungerford Normal and Industrial School in Eatonville. *Florida State Archives*

is the ST. LAWRENCE AFRICAN METHODIST EPIS-COPAL CHURCH, the first black church in the area and dating back to 1882. The ZORA NEALE HURSTON NATIONAL MUSEUM OF FINE ARTS at 227 E. Kennedy Boulevard has works of black artists in various shows throughout the year; open Monday–Friday, 10 A.M.–4 P.M.; (407) 647-3307. An annual "ZORA!" festival honors the town's most famous writer.

The ROBERT HUNGERFORD NORMAL AND INDUSTRIAL SCHOOL, now the Wymore Career Educational Center, on Kennedy Boulevard near I-4, used to attract black students from all over Florida, including, possibly, Zora Neale Hurston. Established at the end of the nineteenth century, it first taught its students academic subjects, as well as industrial trades, agriculture, and the domestic arts. In 1950, the school became part of the Orange County Public School System and, in 1967, when desegregation took effect, part of the alternative school system that stressed vocational training and careers for those not planning on attending college. Today the Hungerford Elementary School is also on the property.

The MOSELEY HOUSE at 11 Taylor Street, which was built between 1888 and 1889, is the second-oldest remaining structure in Eatonville and one of two remaining examples of pre-1900 wood-frame structures typical of the town. The house has connections with Joe Clarke (Eatonville's founder and second mayor) and **Matilda Clark Moseley** (Zora Neale Hurston's best childhood friend and the hostess for Hurston when the latter returned to town). The house is open for tours. Phone: (407) 622-9382 or (850) 575-2522.

The 2000 census indicated that Eatonville had 2,172 African Americans or 89% of the total town population.

Ocoee

On November 2, 1920, whites in Ocoee near Orlando went on a rampage after one black person, **Mose Norman**, and possibly several other blacks had gone to the polls to vote in an election. The whites destroyed twenty-five houses and two churches of black people and killed some thirty-five blacks. The whites lynched one black man, **July Perry**. Newspaper accounts said that two whites and six blacks were killed, but unofficial counts put the black dead at sixty. All of the blacks of the town who were alive after the attack left town as quickly as they could.

It was not until the 1970s that black families began moving back to Ocoee. The 2000 census indicated that Ocoee had 1,607 African Americans or about 7% of the total town population of 24,391.

Orlando

This city may have been named after a character in Shakespeare's *As You Like It* or from a soldier, **Orlando Reeves**, who died while saving his companions in 1835. The city, the county seat of Orange County, was sparsely settled until after the Civil War. The Homestead Act of 1866 brought many into the area, including former slaves who joined a growing number of cotton and citrus farmers and cattle ranchers. From the 1870s the city and central Florida experienced several population booms, but segregation policies tended to isolate the blacks, many of whom lived in a segregated part called Jonestown, west of present-day Greenwood Cemetery.

The 2000 census indicated that Orlando had 49,933 African Americans or 27% of the total city's population of 185,951.

Many African Americans who moved to Orlando in the 1880s settled in what is now the downtown area near South Street and Bumby Avenue. At first called BURNETTE TOWN, the settlement was later called JONESTOWN in honor of two community leaders: **Penny** and **Sam Jones**. Many residents there were moved in 1940 to GRIFFIN

Callahan Neighborhood Center.

PARK, the first public housing development of blacks in Orlando. Other such communities were **CARVER PARK** and **WASHINGTON SHORES**. The African American supervising manager of such housing parks was **James B. Walker**.

The **CALLAHAN NEIGHBORHOOD**, bordered by Colonial Drive, Orange Blossom Trail, Central Avenue, and Division Street, started in 1886, when a white builder, Rev. Andrew Hooper, built the first homes in the area in what was at first called **HOOPER'S QUARTERS**. City officials renamed the area, one of the oldest continuing black communities in Orlando, to honor Dr. **Jerry B. Callahan**, a leading black citizen of the city, after he died in 1947 at the age of sixty-three. He was the first black physician to practice at the Orange General Hospital. He was also honored in the naming of Callahan Elementary School and Callahan Park. Officials changed the name of Collins Street to Callahan Street in 1940 to honor this man who helped establish Goodfellows in Orlando and who practiced medicine in the city for forty years.

The post office facility at 440 S. Orange Blossom Trail honors in its name another local man, **Arthur O. "Pappy" Kennedy**, the city's first African American city commissioner. In 1946, Mr.

Kennedy and **Z. L. Riley** organized the Negro Chamber of Commerce to promote black businesses in Orlando.

The first church for African Americans in the Callahan Neighborhood was **MOUNT ZION MISSIONARY BAPTIST CHURCH**, which opened in 1880 in a wood-frame building, to be replaced in 1962 by a brick building. The church held commencements for Jones High School, which did not have its own auditorium.

The **CALLAHAN NEIGHBORHOOD CENTER**, formerly Jones High School, at 101 N. Parramore Avenue is the site of one of the earliest educational facilities for blacks in the city. As Jerrell Shofner described in his *Orlando: The City Beautiful* (p. 162):

"Education for Orlando's black schoolchildren formally was established in November 1882, when the Orange County School Board approved a petition to open the Orlando Colored School. Located in a frame building at Garland and Church streets, the school first was headed by principal **I. S. Hankins**. Before 1900, the school moved to Jefferson and Chatham streets and was renamed Johnson Academy, in honor of its second principal, **L. C. Johnson**. Johnson Academy's third principal, **L. C. Jones**, came to the school in 1912 and helped build what is now known as Callahan School. Jones' family donated land at Parramore and Washington for the school, which opened in 1921 as Jones High School, with grades six through ten. Elementary students remained at Johnson Academy until additional wings were built at Jones. The first high-school commencement was held for graduating seniors in 1931. For years, Jones High School and Hungerford Normal and Industrial School in Eatonville offered the only formal education to blacks in central Florida."

Today the Callahan Neighborhood Center serves the community's needs for meeting facilities, after-school programs, and cultural festivals. Among the school's graduates was movie star **Wesley Snipes**.

The **DR. I. C. HANKINS HOUSE** at 219 Lime Street, which is now a private residence, was built in 1935 and was the home of Orlando's pioneer black physician, a man who worked for improved race relations and for black home ownership.

Among other buildings of note in the area is the **GABRIEL JONES HOUSE** at 50 N. Terry Street. Built in 1907 by black businessman **Gabriel Jones**, this building has been used as a rooming house for immigrants from Africa and the Caribbean.

The **HILL-TILLINGHAST HOUSE** at 626 W. Washington Street was built in the early 1920s by black builder **James Murrell** for **Viola Tillinghast Hill**, wife of pastor Rev. **H. K. Hill** of Mt. Zion Missionary Baptist Church. The house has served as a meeting place for such famous people as educator Dr. **Mary McCleod Bethune** and aviator **Bessie Coleman**. In the 1940s, young women in a sewing program used it. Today it is a private residence. Another important house in the neighborhood is the **CROOMS HOUSE** at 504 W. Washington St, where the Crooms family, early black pioneers in Orlando, lived. **Moses Crooms Sr.** and his wife, **Daphane**, built this house, today a private residence, after moving there from north Florida in 1905.

The **J. A. COLYER BUILDING** at 27–29 Church Street in downtown Orlando was the site of early black businesses. Built by **J. A. Colyer** in 1911, this building housed the Colyer and Williams tailor shop and later a pharmacy and then an Irish pub. The **RILEY BUILDING** at 571–575 W. Church Street was built in 1947 by businessman

The Riley Building was built in 1947 by Zellie L. Riley.

Zellie L. Riley, who had a tailor shop and a men's clothing store there. He was a strong advocate of African American business opportunities through the Negro Chamber of Commerce.

The **SHILOH BAPTIST CHURCH/BOOKER T. WASHINGTON LIBRARY** at Terry Avenue and W. Jackson Street served as a library for African Americans when the public library was not open to them. A branch of the main public library operated out of the rectory of the Negro Episcopal Church on Terry Avenue. The main public library was finally integrated in the 1960s. Shiloh Baptist Church at Jackson Street and Terry Avenue was organized in 1899. In the early 1920s, officials there obtained pews from the African American churches that were burned in Ocoee during a race riot in 1920.

The **OLD EBENEZER CHURCH** at 596 W. Church Street was built about 1900 by the congregation of the Ebenezer United Methodist Church. When the congregation moved, the building became the Greater Refuge Church of Our Lord. **OLD MOUNT PLEASANT BAPTIST CHURCH** at 701 W. South Street was built in 1920 after the congregation had been meeting in a rough shed in 1919. Today the building, which was the first stone church for African Americans in Orlando, houses the Tabernacle of the Enlightened Church of God. Mount Pleasant Church is now at Prince Hall and Bruton Boulevards.

Finally, Dr. **William Monroe Wells**, one of the city's first African American physicians, opened the Well'sBuilt Hotel in 1929 in order to provide lodging for visiting African Americans. The nearby South Street Casino attracted many well-known personages, and they often stayed at the hotel, people like **Roy Campanella**, **Ella Fitzgerald**, **Thurgood Marshall**, and **Jackie Robinson**. Today the hotel at 511 W. South Street is the site of the **WELL'SBUILT MUSEUM OF AFRICAN AMERICAN HISTORY AND CULTURE**, which has many exhibits and artifacts about the African American experience. Phone: (407) 297-5790.

Winter Park

HANNIBAL SQUARE HISTORIC NEIGHBORHOOD at Pennsylvania Avenue and Morse Boulevard was the area designated for the homes of the African Americans who worked in the hotels, homes, and groves of Winter Park after it developed in the 1880s. Important buildings there included Bethel Baptist Church, the Early Rising Lodge, Flowers Temple, Grant Chapel, Lake Hall Lodge, and Mount Mariah Church.

A small obelisk in the park at Hannibal Square commemorates the site, and a mural on the front of the community center depicts the history of the area. That history includes the 1887 election which had the only two African American aldermen ever voted into office in Winter Park (**Frank Israel** and **Walter Simpson**), two of the oldest churches in the neighborhood (**MT. MORIAH MISSIONARY BAPTIST CHURCH** and **WARNER CHAPEL**), and **HANNIBAL ELEMENTARY SCHOOL** (now the **WINTER PARK COMMUNITY CENTER**).

A small obelisk in the park at Hannibal Square commemorates the area designated for the homes of the African Americans who worked in the area.

49.
Osceola County

This county, established in 1887, commemorates the Seminole leader Osceola. The county had a population of 172,493 in the 2000 census, 12,764 (7.4%) of whom were African Americans.

Kissimmee

The name of this town, which is pronounced with the accent on the second syllable, may come from an Indian name that means "mulberries yonder." The town was incorporated in 1883 and four years later became the seat of government for Osceola County. When financier Hamilton Disston bought four million acres of central Florida land at twenty-five cents an acre in 1881 and began draining and developing the land, many people moved to the area, especially after the coming of the South Florida Railroad. The population of Kissimmee reached 1,086 by 1890 and 2,200 by 1915, despite devastating freezes that hurt the local citrus industry. The building of Walt Disney World in the 1960s brought more settlers to the area, a trend that has continued to the present. The 2000 census indicated that Kissimmee had 4,775 African Americans or 10% of the total town population of 47,814.

Among the blacks who made many contributions to the history of the town are two in particular: **Lawrence Silas**, a wealthy black cattle rancher who built up a large herd of cattle, and **Scipio Lesesne**, a farmer. In an article entitled "Lawrence of the River," **Zora Neale Hurston** wrote the following about the first man: "Lawrence Silas is in, and of, the cow lands. He is important because his story is a sign and a symbol of the strength of the nation. Lawrence Silas rep-

resents the men who could plan and do, the generations who were willing to undertake the hard job, to accept the challenge of the frontiers. And remember, he had one more frontier to conquer than the majority of men in America." Silas also helped establish Bethune-Volusia Beach below Daytona Beach (see Chapter Sixty-four).

One can see the name of Lawrence Silas in the cornerstone of the **BETHEL AME CHURCH** at 1702 N. Brack Street, on the northeast corner of Brack Street, two streets east of Main Street (U.S. 441), and E. Walnut Street, which is two blocks north of Vine Street (the main east-west street in town). This one-story masonry church building was constructed in 1916 by a congregation that had been founded in 1888 to serve the black community. Two other black churches in town are **ST. LUKE'S MISSIONARY BAPTIST CHURCH** on Columbia Street and **ST. JAMES AFRICAN METHODIST EPISCOPAL ZION CHURCH** on Bermuda Avenue.

Scipio Lesesne, who was born in Barbados and came to Kissimmee in 1883 from South Carolina to work on a sugar plantation, eventually cultivated a 100-acre potato farm near the present airport. He also had a farm at the northwest corner of Main Street and Vine Street; he and his family lived upstairs in a two-story building there, the first floor of which was a movie theater. While working in the Gilbert Knox Hotel across

The Bethel AME Church in Kissimmee was built in 1916.

from the railroad depot, Scipio's youngest son, **William Buster Lesesne**, started Buster's Cabs in 1941, the same year his father died. Buster later worked as deputy hotel commissioner under Governor Collins and in various positions under Governors Askew and Graham, often bridging the gap between the white and black communities.

Black students of Kissimmee were able to attend a local school up until the eighth grade, after which they had to go elsewhere for further schooling. The Federal Emergency Relief Administration took down the old school in the northeast section of town and rebuilt it where Central Avenue Elementary is located today, at 1502 N. Central Avenue. Little by little officials added grades until the school became **KISSIMMEE HIGH SCHOOL**, which had its first graduating class in 1945. Its principals, **Lamar Forte**, **S. T. E. Pinckney**, and **W. E. Patterson**, served from 1946 until the integration of schools in 1968. One of its teachers was Mrs. **Theresa Helms**, who may have been Osceola County's first native black to graduate from college; after beginning her teaching career in 1937 at Kissimmee High School and St. Cloud Middle School, she retired after thirty-five consecutive years of teaching in county schools.

50.
Palm Beach County

Established in 1909, the county was named for the many coconut palm trees on the Atlantic Ocean beach. The county had a population of 1,131,184 in the 2000 census, 156,103 (13.8%) of whom were African Americans.

Belle Glade

With a name suggested by a tourist who once remarked that the town looked like the "belle of the 'glades," Belle Glade on the southern shore of Lake Okeechobee has had a difficult history. With a population that swells from 17,000 to 25,000 during the harvest season and an extremely high AIDS rate, the town has struggled to overcome great odds. That history of bad luck goes back a long way.

In September 1928, a monstrous hurricane hit the east coast of Florida near Palm Beach and headed inland to Lake Okeechobee. The eight-foot dike at the southern end of the lake collapsed, causing floodwaters to rise from four to eight feet in one hour. That storm killed hundreds of farm workers, many of whom were black, and increased the misery of those left behind, who were also feeling the effects of the end of the Florida land boom. Many of the estimated two thousand reported dead were transient agricultural workers from the Bahamas who were never reported missing, and so the actual casualty figure will never be known.

One visitor who came to Belle Glade to work on a novel about the poor blacks who worked in the bean fields was **Zora Neale Hurston** (1901?–1960) of Eatonville, Florida. Her novel, *Their Eyes Were Watching God*, is about a young black couple who gets caught in a terrible hurricane.

A monument to the 1928 hurricane marks the site of an unmarked grave of many workers in Palm Beach County.

During the harvest season in the Belle Glade area, black schools used to be shut down so that the children could join their parents in the fields. This practice reduced the school year for black students from nine to six months. It took much effort by the Palm Beach County Teachers' Association (PBCTA), which was organized in 1941, to halt this practice.

The first high school for blacks in the area was BELLE GLADE'S EVERGLADES VOCATIONAL HIGH SCHOOL, the third school in Palm Beach County to go to twelve grades; its principals included **Britton G. Sayles** and **Alton R. F. Williams**. Another black school in Belle Glade, LAKE

African American laborers worked long and hard in the sugar cane fields of Palm Beach County. *Florida State Archives*

SHORE, won a state basketball title under coach **Arthur King**.

CBS television and **Edward R. Murrow** featured black workers and Belle Glade in a 1960 documentary called "Harvest of Shame." Local officials tried hard to show how the terrible conditions presented in that broadcast were untrue and distorted, but millions of Americans had a very negative view of the town for decades to come because of that broadcast. Local author Lawrence Will wrote a history of the town that showed how many blacks prospered by living and working in that area and how the "Harvest of Shame" documentary was not accurate.

Several black children living in Belle Glade in the 1950s served as the model for Saralee, what is believed to be the first anthropologically correct black doll mass-produced. The doll was the idea of Sara Lee Creech, a member of the Belle Glade Inter-Racial Council. **Zora Neale Hurston** wrote to the originator of the dolls after they came out: "The thing that pleased me most, Miss Creech, was that you, a white girl, should have seen clearly and sought to meet our longing for understanding of us as we really are, and not as some would have us."

The Belle Glade hotel where author **Zora Neale Hurston** stayed while doing research for her writing is now the **ROOF GARDEN HOTEL** at 416 SW Dr. Martin Luther King Jr. Boulevard, formerly Avenue E; one can reach the hotel by turning west from U.S. 441 on SW Dr. Martin Luther King Jr. Boulevard, one of the major roads in the town. The hotel, which was built in 1947 in the black part of town, has served blacks and migrant families for decades.

The 2000 census indicated that Belle Glade had 7,555 African Americans or 51% of the total town population of 14,906.

Many of those blacks have been helped by one of the town's important success stories, the Everglade Progressive Citizens, Inc., one of the largest black-owned businesses in Florida. In 1954, thirteen young men each deposited $20 with the founder of the company, **W. C. Taylor**. They each agreed to deposit $10 a month until they reached a goal of $20,000, at which point they would pay themselves an annual dividend of 5%. When news of the company began to spread, others joined them in investing, soon raised the goal of $20,000, and obtained a charter from the state. Two subsidiaries of the company, the Everglade

Progressive Finance Company and the Everglade Mortgage Company, financed many local home-improvement projects. Its assets of $800,000 included apartment buildings, vacant lots, rolling stock, and second mortgages.

Among local blacks who have had success in the political arena are **William A. Grear**, who became the first black elected official when voters selected him for the City Council in 1969; two years later he became Vice Mayor and then Mayor in 1975. The second elected black official was attorney **Dorothy Walker**, whom voters sent to the City Council in 1979. An important appointee was **David H. Hill**, whom the City Commission appointed to the Civil Service Board in 1966; he later served as chairman of that board. Also **Oris W. Walker** served as an alternate on the Board of Adjustment. Such appointments pointed out the growing influence of blacks in the governance of the city.

An organization founded in 1965 by thirteen women under the leadership of **Vivian Byrd** was the Eldorado Civic Club, which has worked to better the health and general welfare of the community, instill pride in the black heritage, and enhance the social and civic life of the residents; **Dorothy Glaze** has been one of the club's long-time leaders. Other organizations in the area which have attempted to better conditions are the Elite Community Club, the Women's Civic Club, the Friendship Women's Club, Glades Ebonique Ladies Club, Silhouettes Club, the Unity Savings Club, and COBY (Cry of Black Youth).

One modern success story in the town is **Harma Miller**, a woman who used to pick beans in the muck around the Everglades. As she grew up with her family in a one-room tin house in Belle Glade, she had to wonder what lay ahead. Against immense odds, she managed to finish school and attend Bethune-Cookman College on a scholarship. She later became a Spanish teacher at the same high school she had graduated from. For twenty-two years she taught school and somehow

found the time to earn a master's degree in linguistics from the University of Pittsburgh. When she looked around her and saw the squalor of so many of her neighbors, she resolved to do something about it.

What she did was register voters, organize protests against segregated housing, and force landlords to clean up their property. In 1985, she won an election to become a city commissioner and four years later became mayor, the second black to be mayor and the first woman to hold the office. She sums up a remarkable life this way: "The folks who knew me when I was a girl see me as an expression of hope. If I can do this—where I came from—then you can do it, too."

Among the important black churches in the area are MT. ZION AME CHURCH OF BELLE GLADE, which was begun by a midwife, Sister **Missouri Vereen**, who came to the town from Jacksonville, Georgia, in the early 1900s. When she found that the town had no Methodist church, she obtained a plot of land and organized the church. The **Ed Neal** and **Will Smith** families helped establish the ST. JOHN FIRST BAPTIST CHURCH OF BELLE GLADE in 1928; one of the later pastors, Reverend **J. B. Adams**, served the church for over thirty-two years. The NEW BETHEL MISSIONARY BAPTIST CHURCH OF BELLE GLADE, which had been organized in Chosen, Florida, in 1930, moved to Belle Glade in 1933 and was directed by Reverend **Willie Littles**. Finally, a nearby church is the BIBLE CHURCH OF GOD OF PAHOKEE, which was established in 1964 under the leadership of Bishop **Sylvester Banks**.

Boca Raton

The name of this town in Palm Beach County means "rat's mouth," referring to a hidden rock in the bay there that could cut ships' cables. In the 1870s settlers began moving into the area to take advantage of the low prices (about $1.25 an acre) and rich lands to grow citrus and pineapples. More residents moved in after Henry Flagler extended his Florida East Coast Railway down toward Miami in the mid-1890s. A local newspaper meant to attract more settlers, *The Homeseeker*, mentioned that one of the early settlers was a black man: "[**C. W.**] **Blaine** is a darkey and a good one. He is working on shares. Land and fertilizer are furnished him versus his labor. He had no capital but his two hands and a little credit. He has shipped over two hundred crates of beans, selling for $3, and for his six acres of tomatoes he will clear a good thing."

White farmers in the area depended on black laborers to do the planting and harvesting of the crops. Those black workers were sometimes former slaves who had headed to Florida after the Civil War in search of jobs and opportunities. In the absence of bulldozers the black men were hired to clear the land with grub hoes, a backbreaking task. Many of the black men lived in Deerfield Beach and would walk over to Boca Raton in the morning, work a ten-hour day, and then walk home again in the evening, having earned between 75 cents and a $1 for the day's work.

In 1915, officials surveyed and platted a section of land between 10th and 12th Streets on N. Dixie Highway that would be used for the blacks moving into the area and working on the growing of pineapples. The fifteen-acre settlement acquired the name Pearl City either from the name of the first black child born in Boca Raton or from the name of the area's chief street (Pearl Street, now NE 11th Street) or from a favorite strain of pineapples, Hawaiian Pearls.

One of the first blacks in the area was the son of former slaves, **Alex Hughes**, who arrived in 1914 and two years later built at 1100 N. Dixie Highway a house that still stands, although it has been enlarged and changed since then. As more people moved into the area, Hughes began teaching Sunday school in his house, until local residents built a bush arbor of palmettos for religious purposes and began making plans for a church. The engineer for the local developers donated a lot for the church at 128 NE 11th Street, and the black workers built the **MACEDONIA AFRICAN METHODIST EPISCOPAL CHURCH** there by 1920.

Alex Hughes also wanted to establish a school in Pearl City. The Board of Public Instruction told him that they would provide a teacher if he could find eight children for the school. When he found them, the board sent a teacher, Miss **Robinson**, and moved a school building to the south side of NE 11th Street off Dixie Highway in 1923. Later the board built a new school at Dixie Highway and NE 12th Street. A local park at 200 NE 14th

African Americans have long done back-breaking work on farms throughout Palm Beach County.

Street honors **Alex Hughes**, who died in 1977 at the age of ninety-two after many years of working for the black residents of Pearl City.

Local residents organized the **EBENEZER BAPTIST CHURCH** in 1918 and built a church three years later between NE 10th and 11th Streets on what is today Federal Highway. Because two local religious congregations could not have their own minister every Sunday, the two groups alternated having a service, but everyone attended each service. When a 1928 hurricane destroyed the Baptist church, the congregation built a new structure at 200 NE 12th Street. After several rebuildings, the new church was finished in 1957.

Pearl City is located just south of 13th Street (Glades Road) between the Dixie Highway and Federal Highway (U.S. 1). Other nearby black neighborhoods are Dixie Manor, just to the north of Glades Road, and 15th Terrace, to the north of Dixie Manor. Developers concerned about separating the black community from the white community in the 1950s and 1960s built an eight-foot-tall concrete-block wall above 15th Terrace. "The Wall" has tended to keep the black and white communities separated since then.

The 2000 census indicated that Boca Raton had 2,810 African Americans or 4% of the city's total population of 74,764. Among winter residents of the city was **Arthur Ashe Jr.** (1943–1993), the first black to win the Wimbledon men's tennis championship. Among the modern-day leaders of the city is **Wayne D. Barton**, an officer with the Boca Raton Police Department and the first black to be named that organization's "Officer of the Year"; he had an after-school program for latch-key children and used his own money to fund trips and prizes for those children who did well in school.

Delray Beach

The U.S. government built the Orange Grove House of Refuge in 1876 to give shipwrecked sailors shelter and food in an area that later became Delray Beach. In 1895, seven men from Michigan arrived to settle in the area and established a town called Linton. The name changed to Delray to commemorate the Michigan town of Delray, from which one of the early settlers came. The new town became part of the new Palm Beach County, which was established in 1909. In 1927, the city of Delray on the west side of the Intracoastal Waterway joined Delray Beach on the ocean side of the waterway, and the two towns became known as Delray Beach. Over the years blacks moved into the area and settled down to a life of hard work in agriculture and business.

In the 1990s, local officials placed on the Delray Beach Local Register of Historical Places five sites in one of the oldest and most permanent parts of the city. When this section, which is bounded on the east by NW 1st Avenue, on the west by NW 8th Avenue, on the north by Lake Ida Road, and on the south by NW 4th Street, was part of North Dade County, blacks settled it and established churches, homes, and schools.

SCHOOL NO. 4, DELRAY COLORED is on the east side of NW 5th Avenue, one hundred feet south of NW 1st Street. In 1894, when this part of Florida was part of Dade County, local blacks petitioned the school superintendent for a school and a teacher. Because no facilities existed to house the school, it did not open until October 1895. **B. F. James**, the school's first teacher, opened the four-month school term in a thatched hut on NW 5th Avenue, which is now part of the parking lot of Greater Mount Olive Missionary Baptist Church.

In 1990, officials dedicated on the east side of NW 5th Avenue, one hundred feet south of NW 1st Street, a bronze marker with a locator map showing the five historic sites mentioned here. The **B. F. JAMES & FRANCES JANE BRIGHT MINI-PARK** there honors the first two teachers of the school. The Greater Mount Olive Missionary Baptist Church and its pastor, the Rev. **L. C.**

Johnson, gave the city and the community an easement deed for this mini-park, which became part of the city's Park and Recreation Department by action of the City Commission in 1990. The inscription on the monument reads as follows:

"Late in the nineteenth century, a group of black settlers established a community in this area that became part of the Town of Linton and later the City of Delray Beach. These hardy pioneers established the cultural organization necessary to foster education, fellowship and spiritual needs, despite difficult environmental conditions and isolation.

GREATER MOUNT OLIVE MISSIONARY BAPTIST CHURCH at 40 NW 4th Avenue was organized in 1896 by a missionary, the Reverend **A. B. Williams**. Two years later, trustees of the church bought land from the Model Land Company and built what is today the third-oldest church in Palm Beach County and the oldest in Delray Beach. Mount Olive built a frame structure on the site and shared it with St. Paul African Methodist Church mentioned below. The original building, constructed in 1898 and able to seat two hundred people, was destroyed in the terrible 1928 hurricane that ravaged south Florida. A year later, workers built a new building, which doubled the size of the original. In 1959, officials completely remodeled the church and enlarged it to accommodate one thousand parishioners.

The **LA FRANCE HOTEL** at 140 NW 4th Avenue in Delray Beach was built in 1947 by **Charles Patrick.** It was one of the few hotels between West Palm Beach and Fort Lauderdale that rented rooms to African Americans.

ST. PAUL AFRICAN METHODIST EPISCOPAL CHURCH at 119 NW 5th Avenue was originally organized in 1897 as the African Methodist Episcopal Church in a packing house on the corner of NW 3rd Avenue and 2nd Street (now Martin Luther King Jr. Drive). In 1899, trustees bought a lot from the Model Land Company and shared the building of Mount Olive Missionary Baptist Church; their church, originally called Mount Tabor AME Church, changed its name to St. Paul in 1926. Officials completely remodeled and enlarged it in 1958 and put in the front yard the large bronze bell, which was part of the original building and was rung by the sexton to announce fires, other public emergencies, and deaths.

FREE AND ACCEPTED MASONS, LODGE 275 at 85 NW 5th Avenue houses one of the oldest fraternal organizations in south Florida. These masons, organized in 1899, bought a lot from the African Methodist Episcopal Church in 1904. The original building has been demolished, but the new

The LaFrance Hotel in Delray Beach was one of the few to rent to African Americans before the Civil Rights movement.

structure stands on the site of the original.

In 1911, the same year that Delray Beach was incorporated, immigrants from the Bahamas who wanted to celebrate the Anglican Episcopal service organized ST. MATTHEW EPISCOPAL CHURCH at 404 SW 3rd Street. They built the church in 1916 and remodeled it extensively ten years later.

Nearby, the SPADY MUSEUM at 170 NW 5th Avenue is a Spanish mission-style house built by **Solomon D. Spady** in 1926. A 1935 house used by the city's first black midwife, **Susan B. Williams**, was moved from NW 3rd Avenue to the museum grounds and has facilities for educating visitors about black history. It also has the offices of Expanding and Preserving Our Cultural Heritage (EPOCH). Open Monday through Friday, 9 A.M.–5 P.M. (561) 279-8883.

The Spady Museum has a plaque that honors Solomon D. Spady (1890–1966) as a member of The Great Floridians 2000 program, which recognized distinguished individuals. After graduating from Hampton Normal and Agricultural Institute in 1914, he taught there for a year, then taught physics at Virginia Union University. Through his association with the New Farmers of America, a worldwide African American youth farmers association, he met agricultural chemist **George Washington Carver**. In 1923, Spady accepted a teaching position at "Delray Colored No. 4," where he also served as principal. When he arrived, the school had an enrollment of one hundred grade school children. The school, which was later renamed S. D. Spady Elementary School, opened in 1895 for black students from places between Boynton Beach and Boca Raton. Spady was the principal there from 1923 to 1950. By 1934, enrollment had increased to 336 students in grades one through ten. His students went on to study at Hampton Institute, Atlanta University, South Carolina State, Bethune-Cookman, and Florida A&M, often on scholarships. He retired in 1957. The school was later moved and became Delray County Training School, then Carver High School, before eventually being torn down.

In 2000 Delray Beach had a population of 47,181, of whom 12,415 (26%) were blacks.

Jupiter

Two miles south of this very exclusive city was CAMP FREDERICK SMALL, possibly the only Boy Scout camp for blacks in the segregated South. Frederick Small was a resident of Palm Beach who donated $2,700 in the 1940s to buy forty acres along the Intracoastal Waterway. The Boy Scouts later sold the land for $240,000 to improve the facilities at Camp Tahna-Keeta, which was open

The Spady Museum in Delray Beach has exhibits about African Americans.

to all races. Mr. Small is also honored in the naming of Frederick Small Road in Jupiter.

Lake Worth

The first black school in Lake Worth was the **OSBORNE SCHOOL** at 1726 Douglas Street. Built in 1948, it served that purpose until 1971. Architect **William Manley King** designed the building, and local residents **Frank Jones**, **P. W. Odums**, and **Able Wilson** built it. The building reopened as a Head Start and community education facility in 1980 and is now used as an after-school training and educational facility.

The Osborne School in Lake Worth.

Palm Beach

The history of this exclusive resort on the Atlantic Ocean has involved blacks in an important way, although the 269 who officially lived in the town in 2000, according to the census that year, made up only 3% of the 10,468 residents. Before the wealthy winter visitors discovered Palm Beach and made it into one of America's prized addresses, blacks were living along what later became Sunrise Avenue. Some of them, like **Joseph Bethell**, came from the Bahamas, whereas others were escaped slaves from north Florida plantations who found a home with the Seminoles living in the area.

After developer Henry Flagler had visited Palm Beach in the 1890s, he set his eyes on developing the little town. He extended his railroad to the area and constructed a railroad bridge over Lake Worth to link the resort with the mainland. In 1894, he built the Royal Poinciana Hotel, at that time the world's largest resort hotel with its ability to accommodate two thousand people, and two years later the Palm Beach Inn, later known as the Breakers. Five years later he built the luxurious Whitehall mansion for his third wife.

As Flagler's railroad continued down the east coast of Florida, his contractors leased convicts, many of them black, from the state, as was commonly done in those days. The conditions under which those black workers labored were worse than those on plantations, involving whippings and imprisonment in sweatboxes for all kinds of infractions.

In Palm Beach, Flagler also built two baseball diamonds, one at the Royal Poinciana Hotel and the other at the Breakers Hotel. The players who played for the Poinciana and Breakers were blacks who also worked as bellhops and waiters at Flagler's hotels. Hotel owners on Long Island had discovered the popularity of baseball teams made up of waiters and other employees of expensive hotels. The Cuban Giants, for example, began at Long Island's Argyle Hotel in 1885 to entertain the wealthy white guests. When Flagler built his hotels in Florida sites like St. Augustine and Palm Beach to go along with his railroad, he also established black baseball teams for his guests' entertainment.

To run his programs, Flagler hired a former center fielder for the Philadelphia Phillies named Ed Andrews, who is honored today by Andrews Avenue in Fort Lauderdale. Historian Stuart McIver quotes from an early spectator who wrote the following in 1907:

"... I went over to the baseball game and such sport I never had in my life. Both teams are colored and composed of employees of the Breakers and Poinciana hotels, who are hired because of their baseball ability and then incidentally given employment as waiters or porters. Many of them play on the Cuban Giants team during the summer so that the quality of baseball ranked with professional white teams.

The greatest sport was in listening to the coaching and watching the antics of a full grandstand back of first base. Their sympathies were pretty evenly divided between the two teams, so accordingly, whenever either team would make a hit, then was the time to watch the bleachers. The crowd would yell themselves hoarse, stand up in their seats, bang each other over the head, and even the girls would go into a perfect frenzy as if they were in a Methodist camp meeting.

The third baseman on the Poinciana team was a wonderful ballplayer and kept the whole crowd roaring with his horseplay and cakewalks up and down the sidelines."

Andrews recruited the black players from such teams as the Cuban Giants, the Cuban X Giants, the Royal Giants, and the Leland Giants (all of whose team names showed the popularity of the New York Giants in those days). Among the players who entertained the wealthy hotel guests was **John Henry "Pop" Lloyd**, an excellent shortstop from Palatka, Florida (see Chapter Fifty-four). Also playing on those black teams were such standouts as pitcher **Smoky Joe Williams** and home-run hitters **Oscar Charleston** and **Louis Santop**. When a huge hurricane destroyed the Royal Poinciana in 1928, it also wrecked the baseball bleachers there, signaling the beginning of the end to black baseball at the resort.

Many of the workers who built Flagler's rail-

John Henry "Pop" Lloyd is one of the ballplayers who played in Palm Beach. *National Baseball Library, Cooperstown, NY*

road and his large sumptuous structures were blacks from Jamaica, the Bahamas, and Haiti. Once the buildings were completed, many of the blacks stayed on to work in the hotels; one job many of them did was to pedal around tourists in rickshawlike vehicles called afromobiles (or aframobiles). Palm Beach hotels used those afromobiles until after World War II, at which time other parts of the country labeled such demeaning vehicles as racist.

Some four hundred of those blacks lived in a shantytown on the north end of Palm Beach on Sunrise Avenue in a place they called the Styx, a name coming from Greek mythology referring to the river leading to hell. The black doctor who served the blacks in the Styx was Dr. **Thomas Leroy Jefferson** (1867–1939), a generous man who devoted his life to his patients.

A persistent rumor over the years says that, once the workers were no longer needed to build Flagler's hotels and he decided to develop the land they were on, he had the Styx burned down, which forced them to move across the shore of Lake Worth to West Palm Beach. What probably happened, according to descendants of the owners of the Styx land, is that the owner of the land gave the settlers two weeks to move out, which they did. Flagler then developed the area in Palm Beach, which today is the land along Sunrise Avenue at N. County Road.

Many of the blacks who had been living in the Styx moved to a new community on the mainland called Pleasant City.

In the mid-1920s the local government passed an ordinance that prohibited whites from setting up businesses across railroad tracks where the blacks were living. That official segregation, which lasted until the early 1960s, enabled black businesses to operate in the black area without fear of competition from larger white businesses.

West Palm Beach

Long before white or black people came to this area, Indians like the Tequestas lived around Lake Worth. Shipwrecked sailors like the Jonathan Dickinson party in the seventeenth century also passed through here, but only in the nineteenth century did non-Indians move in to settle. The first blacks in the area were probably runaway slaves whom the Seminole Indians welcomed into their tribes in the 1830s. Before the Civil War local settlers most likely had slaves with them, although those slaves may have also joined the Seminole bands when the whites fled to the north to escape the Indian uprisings. During Reconstruction after the Civil War, freed slaves and settlers from the Bahamas moved to the area. In the 1890s more black workers came to work on the construction of the railroad and in the pineapple fields. West Palm Beach was incorporated as a town in 1894.

When the owner of the Styx section of Palm Beach evicted the blacks living there at the beginning of the twentieth century (see the end of the Palm Beach section, above), they moved across Lake Worth to West Palm Beach. Many blacks continued working as domestics in the homes of the wealthy white people of Palm Beach, but the city of West Palm Beach practiced segregation at many levels. The city did not hire its first black policeman until 1948; it would be another twenty-one years before black policemen could patrol white neighborhoods. Blacks did not vote until 1947 and did not have their first black clerk typist until 1963.

The only remaining portion of the original black settlement in West Palm Beach is the **NORTHWEST NEIGHBORHOOD HISTORIC DISTRICT**, bounded by NW 2nd Street, NW 11th Street, N. Rosemary Avenue, and Douglas Avenue. Most of the original buildings in that district were built by local black builders and contractors such as **Samuel O. Major**, **Simeon Mother**, **R. A. Smith**, **Alfred Williams**, and **J. S. Woodside**. Local architect and the city's first black architect, **Hazel Augustus**, and the firm of Harvey and Clarke designed some of the buildings, especially churches.

The Dixie Movie Theater on N. Rosemary

Avenue and NW 3rd Street was built by one of the leaders in the black community, **James J. "Cracker" Johnson**, who arrived in West Palm Beach in 1900. He also bought a rooming house on Banyan Street that had pool tables downstairs and rooms to rent upstairs. He bought houses and rental properties there and across the state and willingly lent money to blacks to whom white banks would not lend. He was eventually killed in 1946 when he went to the defense of a friend being attacked by ruffians.

When a severe hurricane hit Palm Beach County on September 16, 1928, several thousand people were killed. In West Palm Beach, officials buried sixty-nine white victims in a mass grave in Woodlawn Cemetery and another 674 black victims in a mass grave in the city's paupers' burial field at Tamarind Avenue and 25th Street. Many other bodies were never found. On September 30, 1928, the city proclaimed an hour of mourning for the victims and had memorial services conducted at each of the burial sites. Two thousand people attended the service at the paupers' cemetery, where educator and activist **Mary McLeod Bethune** read the mayor's proclamation. In 1991, a Nigerian Yoruba religious ceremony was also conducted there. Today, a marker at the southwest corner of Tamarind Avenue and 25th Street marks the site of the **MASS GRAVE OF THE 1928 HURRICANE DEAD**.

In the 1980s interested individuals like **Preston Tillman** and others formed the Black Historical Preservation Society of Palm Beach County to make people more aware of the accomplishments of blacks in the community. One of the projects of that group was to preserve the **HAZEL AUGUSTUS HOME** at 615 Division Street, where the first black architect in Palm Beach County lived. **Hazel Augustus** had lived in that building in the first part of the twentieth century, but it deteriorated so much by around 1987 that it had to be destroyed.

Eva Mack and **Ruby Bullock** were elected to the West Palm Beach City Commission in 1978; Mrs. Mack was reelected four years later and became the first black to serve as the mayor of West Palm Beach. In 2000 West Palm Beach had 22,050 blacks (33%) out of a total population of 67,643.

Another important building is the **GWEN CHERRY HOUSE**, which is on the corner of 6th Street and Division Avenue near where the Augustus Home was. **Gwendolyn Sawyer Cherry** (1923–1979) was born in Miami, the daughter of the first black doctor in Dade County. After teaching science to black students in Miami for eighteen years, she became the first black to attend the University of Miami Law School, although she eventually graduated from FAMU Law School in Tallahassee. After deciding to enter politics, she became the first black woman elected to the Florida State Legislature in Tallahassee. As a legislator she concerned herself with the rights of women, children, and minorities, as well as prison reform. In 1971, she introduced the first laws for state-provided child care in Florida, a fact which later influenced officials to name the new Department of Education Child Development Center in Tallahassee after her. She died in an automobile accident in Tallahassee in 1979 at the age of fifty-six. The **GWEN CHERRY PARK** at 2591 NW 71st Street in Miami honors her.

In 1923, **PINE RIDGE HOSPITAL** at 1401 Division Avenue was designed as the only hospital admitting blacks during segregation. In the 1920s and 1930s, hospital superintendent Petra Pinn and all the nurses were medical graduates, but the hospital did not have good equipment. The facility functioned until 1956, when patients were moved to the new blacks-only north wing of St. Mary's Hospital. Pine Ridge Hospital sat vacant until 1963, when Carl Robinson bought it and converted it into an apartment building. Workers completely renovated the structure in 2000.

The **MICKENS HOUSE** at 801 4th Street on the corner of Division Avenue is a two-story, private dwelling on the National Register of Historic Places. **Haley Mickens**, who had the house constructed in 1917 soon after his marriage to **Alice Frederick** of Bartow, worked in Palm Beach for Colonel Edward P. Bradley, who owned a gambling casino there called the Beach Club. Mickens, who lived in the house until he died in 1950, was responsible for operating the bicycle-propelled wicker carriages known as afromobiles that white patrons enjoyed riding around in.

Mickens also helped establish the **PAYNE CHAPEL AME CHURCH** in West Palm Beach in 1893. It was at that church that he met his future wife, **Alice Frederick**. She had graduated from Spelman College in Atlanta, Georgia, and continued her education at the College of the City of New York and at A. and T. College of Greensboro, North Carolina, before going to West Palm Beach. She later went on to found the City Association of West Palm Beach, served as president of the Florida Association of Women's Clubs, founded the Florida Association of Girls Clubs, and served as Chairman of the U.S. Treasury Department of War Bonds. The American Negro Emancipation convention in Chicago in 1963 named her "Outstanding Woman of the Century." Officials named her an "Outstanding Floridian" in 1970.

Her interest in education, juvenile delinquency, and civic improvements brought her into contact with such leaders as **Mary McLeod Bethune**, Dr. **Ralph Bunche**, Dr. **Howard Thurman**, and **Henrine Ward Banks**. She used to have local, state, and national educators, both black and white, meet in her house and even stay there when local hotels would not allow blacks to rent rooms. Among the Florida places that honor Alice Frederick Mickens are a cottage at Lowell Correctional Institution (because of her efforts on behalf of girls who had been imprisoned with mature criminals) and the Alice Frederick Mickens Science Lecture Hall at Bethune-Cookman College in Daytona Beach.

A West Palm Beach craftsman who worked on the Mickens House, one of the oldest continuously black-owned residences in the city, was **Thomas E. Wilkens**, who also worked on the Mount Zion Baptist Church and Hilltop Baptist Church in West Palm Beach. His four sons followed him in the construction business of the county.

The **INDUSTRIAL HIGH SCHOOL** on 11th Street, which opened in 1917 and merged with Roosevelt High School in 1950, was the first high school for African Americans in Palm Beach County. A teacher at that school and an important leader among African American teachers in the county was **Charles Stebbins Jr.**, who was originally from Arcadia. In 1941, when white teachers in the county with five years of experience received a $25/month raise and their black counterparts received nothing, eighty-five percent of the black teachers established the Palm Beach County Teachers Association. When they filed a federal lawsuit, Charles Stebbins Jr. volunteered to put his name on the lawsuit. He was fired from his job, but was offered the job back with another $500 if he would drop the lawsuit, which he refused to do and for which he was blackballed throughout the state. In 1941, a federal judge in his lawsuit ruled that the county's black teachers must be paid the same amount as white teachers, but Stebbins did not benefit from that decision personally, since he was working at a restaurant in New York when the decision was reached. That decision was one of many that led to the vitally important Brown vs. Board of Education decision in 1954 that outlawed school segregation.

Stebbins moved to New York and then Washington, where he worked for the Federal Home Loan Bank Board for thirty-two years. In several of the jobs he held, including the U.S. Navy, he filed lawsuits to stop discriminatory practices, but, although the lawsuits usually failed, his actions led to better conditions for those who followed him. He died in 1991, having not profited from the anti-discrimination suits he had filed but having led the way to improved conditions for many other black employees.

Two of the original high school buildings (a barracks-style classroom and the cafeteria) are now part of **U. B. KINSEY/PALMVIEW ELEMENTARY SCHOOL OF THE ARTS** at 800 11th Street in West Palm Beach. That school honors in its name **U. B. Kinsey**, an elementary-school principal there for four decades. In 1942, he was one of four who sued the Palm Beach County School Board for equal pay for African American teachers; later the group sued to have an equal number of school days for black students.

The building of the first high school for African Americans in Palm Beach County is now part of U.B. Kinsey/Palmview Elementary School in West Palm Beach.

TABERNACLE BAPTIST CHURCH at 801 8th Street used to be called Mt. Olive Baptist Church. Eighteen members founded it in the Styx in 1893 under the guidance of Rev. **W. B. Mills**, the State Missionary. That building housed the first school for blacks in Palm Beach County. The seventy-four students who attended the school in 1984 necessitated that the superintendent have two school terms of four months each.

ROOSEVELT JUNIOR COLLEGE was one of twelve black junior colleges in Florida. Established in 1958, four years after the landmark 1954 Supreme Court decision in *Brown v. Board of Education* that outlawed segregation in schools, Florida officials opted to create a segregated college system for blacks. When the Palm Beach County School

Board announced in September 1957 that it planned to open the black junior college, despite the 1954 U.S. Supreme Court decision that outlawed separate educational facilities, local black activists strenuously protested and called the college's black advisory board members traitors who had given in to the segregationists. The activists asked Governor LeRoy Collins to use the money, not for a black college, but for efforts to desegregate Palm Beach Junior College. The governor refused and pointed to Gibbs Junior College in St. Petersburg and Washington Junior College in Pensacola as good examples of how such schools can help black students. **Britton G. Sayles**, who was principal of Roosevelt High School at the time, became Roosevelt Junior College's first and only president.

Roosevelt Junior College opened, and students began attending classes in the late afternoons and evenings in the Roosevelt High School building until workers could finish a new building for the college at 1235 15th Street in West Palm Beach. In the mid-1960s black students picketed the all-white Palm Beach Junior College for admission, and the school board finally agreed to integrate the school and close down Roosevelt. After the 1964–65 academic year, the school merged with Palm Beach Junior (later Community) College (PBJC).

The enrollment figures for Roosevelt Junior College showed that its enrollment remained steady:

1958–59: 110 students
1959–60: 208 students
1960–61: 230 students
1961–62: 283 students
1962–63: 249 students
1963–64: 245 students
1964–65: 218 students

Six of its eighteen faculty members and around one hundred of its black students moved to PBJC. One of those six black teachers was **Daniel Hen-**

drix, who in 1970 became the first black member of the county school board and the first black to be elected to a county office—and the only one for many years.

Some of the faculty at Roosevelt Junior College hoped that it would become a branch campus of PBJC, but instead it became an adult education center and then an alternative school before being torn down in 1995. The athletic field at Roosevelt Middle School is the site of the black college. The **BRITTON G. SAYLES SOCIAL SCIENCE BUILDING** on the campus of Palm Beach Community College, which was dedicated just days before Mr. Sayles died in 1994, honors that great educator, and a permanent exhibit dedicated to the black college is in the library of the community college's main campus in the town of Lake Worth.

Under pressure from federal officials to integrate all its schools, Palm Beach County established two campuses for high school students in 1970: Twin Lakes North and Twin Lakes South for the formerly segregated schools of Roosevelt High School to the north and the all-white Palm Beach High School to the south. In time, the former Roosevelt High School became a middle school. The "Twin Lakes" name probably referred to both Lake Mangonia near Roosevelt High School and Clear Lake near Palm Beach High School.

Among the county personages recognized in The Great Floridians 2000 program, which honored distinguished individuals, was Dr. **Wiley Jenkins**, who was born in Summerville, South Carolina, in 1901. He studied to become a pharmacist at South Carolina State University. After marrying **Roberta Robinson**, who was studying in Tampa, they moved to West Palm Beach in 1933 and four years later opened the Economical Drug Store, which became a popular gathering place. Their home, built in 1946, was known for its grandeur and elegance and became a meeting place for West Palm Beach's black society. The store operated until 1952. After Dr. Jenkins' death in 1950, his wife operated the store until 1952. Dr. Jenkins' Great Floridians 2000 plaque is located at the **HISTORIC JENKINS HOUSE**, 815 Palm Beach Lakes Blvd., West Palm Beach.

Also honored in that program was Dr. **Thomas Rudolph Vickers** (1879–1965), who was born in Key West and educated at Howard University. He arrived in West Palm Beach between 1912 and 1916 to begin his medical practice, and was one of seven African American pioneer physicians to practice in the city. His wife, **Alice W. Vickers**, was an opera singer and together they were known for their service, leadership, education, culture, and successful professional status. During segregation, Dr. Vickers provided medical care at affordable rates to the African American community. His Great Floridian plaque is located at the Vickers House, now restored and operated as a Community Resource Center, 811 Palm Lakes Boulevard, West Palm Beach.

Finally the **NATHANIEL J. ADAMS PARK** on Spruce Avenue between 14th and 15th Streets west of U.S. 1 in West Palm Beach honors in its name the man who established the city's first Boy Scout troop for blacks. He died in 1982 at the age of seventy-three.

51.

Pasco County

The Florida Legislature established this county in 1887 and named it after Samuel Pasco of Monticello, speaker of the Florida House of Representatives when the county was created. The county had a population of 344,765 in the 2000 census, 7,240 (2.1%) of whom were African Americans. That percentage (2.1%) is the lowest among all sixty-seven Florida counties.

Dade City

The county seat of Pasco County was named after Major Francis Dade, who was killed by Seminole Indians in 1835 at the start of the Second Seminole War. Among the sites of interest to African Americans in the city is **MOUNT ZION AME CHURCH** at 434 N. 7th Street. The congregation built the facility in 1918, the first Protestant church in the county to be built of masonry. The congregation, originally living in what was called "Freedtown" on the south of Lake Pasadena, moved into Dade City after the Great Freeze of 1894–1895.

Another church, **ST. PAUL MISSIONARY BAPTIST CHURCH**, at 405 E. Martin Luther King Boulevard dates back to 1925, when the African Methodist Episcopal Church congregation built it of brick. Next door in the Odd Fellows Hall on what was then 6th Street was a very early school for black children. Parents paid twenty-five cents a week for their children to attend the school and bought the books for their children, but the school board paid the teachers' salaries. The school had six grades and three teachers.

Education for black children in Pasco County took a large step forward in the early 1900s when **Arthmus Roberts** encouraged the establishment of a school for blacks. Roberts, an African American who could barely read and write, realized the importance of education and raised enough money to start the school, called Dade City Colored School. Roberts convinced **J. D. Moore** to go to Dade City to teach in the school and run it.

MOORE ACADEMY on Whitehouse Street at 8th Street was a school for blacks from the late 1920s to the 1950s. Constructed from the Julius Rosenwald Fund set up by Julius Rosenwald, the president of the Sears Roebuck Company, the school was the first one fully run by the Pasco County School Board for the black community. It replaced the three-room school located in the Odd Fellows Hall when the community outgrew that school. The new school was named for J. D. Moore, who donated land for the building, ran the school, and recruited teachers. In the early 1930s, he was followed by Mrs. **Etta Burt**, a graduate of Spelman College in Atlanta and the first of the teachers with a college diploma. After two years, she was succeeded by **Odell K. Mickens** as principal. The academy had only six grades because segregation did not allow black children to attend the county's junior and senior high schools.

When the school burned down soon after Prohibition ended in 1933, possibly by someone who could not get a liquor license in the vicinity of the school, teachers held classes in St. Paul and St. John churches until the school board rebuilt the school on the same spot. Principal **O. K. Mickens** organized local citizens into the School Aid Club to provide materials and furnishings for the new school. The group obtained nine hundred used desks and seats at thirty-five cents each from Blessed Trinity Catholic School in Ocala. In time, officials added grades through the twelfth. The first class graduated from Moore Academy in 1940. The school board transferred the school to the present location of Moore-Mickens School and tore down the original building of the Moore Academy.

Integration took place in 1970, but even then local businesses practiced segregation. For example, the local movie theater continued to seat blacks only in the balcony for several more years.

The **BANDSTAND** on the Meridian Avenue side of the old courthouse was built around 1925 in hopes of attracting bands like that of John Philip Sousa. The memorial there has the names of county residents who served in World War II, including the names of thirty-nine soldiers who died in the war. When the names were first included on the memorial, they were separated by race. However, in 1968 the clerk of the circuit court had the word "colored" painted over.

INDIAN LAKE CEMETERY on Indian Lake Cemetery Road outside Dade City is the burial place of many local African American pioneers.

Lacoochee

A highway marker on U.S. 301 north of Lacoochee and near the Pasco-Hernando County line honors Capt. **Charles "Bo" Harrison**, the highest ranking African American in the history of the Pasco Sheriff's Office. An unknown assailant killed Lieutenant Harrison (posthumously promoted to captain) in 2004 while he was sitting in his patrol car. Harrison was just two weeks away from retiring after a distinguished thirty-one-year career at his agency. The "Captain Charles 'Bo' Harrison Memorial Highway" honors the deputy.

Pasadena

The site of the original black community in Pasco County, called Freedtown, was near the end of Bozeman Road. Newly freed slaves founded the community around 1869, but no trace of the community remains, not even the cemetery, which was covered over. The blacks living there left after the 1894–95 freeze and moved to Dade City, where they founded the Mount Zion AME Church.

African American men worked in the sawmills in Pasco County. *Florida State Archives*

52.
Pinellas County

The Florida Legislature established Pinellas County out of Hillsborough County across Tampa Bay in 1911 and took its name from the Spanish *punta pinal* "point of pines" that described the peninsula there. The county had a population of 921,482 in the 2000 census, 82,933 (9.0%) of whom were African Americans.

Clearwater

Spanish explorers like Panfilo de Narváez in 1528 and Hernando de Soto in 1539 may have passed near present-day Clearwater, but they did not remain for long, choosing instead to push north into uncharted areas. After Spain ceded Florida to the United States in 1821 and the Second Seminole War ended in 1842, settlers began moving into the area, attracted by the rich farmlands and the fishing in the Gulf of Mexico. Early residents called the site Clear Water Harbor because of a clear spring that bubbles into the Gulf off the shore.

One of the first families to move there was the Stephens (or Stevens) family, but they did not like their land and sold it to John S. Taylor Sr. for one black slave whom her owners, the Stephens family, accused of trying to poison them. Thus, what is today downtown Clearwater was sold for the price of one unwanted slave.

From a small town in 1900 to a city of 108,787, according to the 2000 census, the county seat of Pinellas County had a black population of 10,651 (10% of the total population) in 2000. Many people have come to this beautiful city to retire, but also to live while they commute to work in places throughout the Tampa Bay area. Formerly dependent on retirees and tourists, the city nowadays attracts more and more residents who want to live and work in the area. The Church of Scientology, which owns much of downtown Clearwater, has also attracted many people.

In a 1977 history of the city, Roy Cadwell wrote that "there is no segregation in any part of Clearwater, but there is an economic segregation that makes it difficult, if not impossible, for black persons to live other than in the north Greenwood area." This section of the city is north on Greenwood Avenue and west on Palmetto Street to North Myrtle Avenue and east to Betty Lane.

The first school for black students was the Pinellas Institute on Palmetto; it later became the Clearwater Comprehensive School and was totally integrated.

The **DOROTHY THOMPSON AFRICAN AMERICAN MUSEUM** at 1505 N. Madison Avenue houses the private collection of over five thousand African American books, over three thousand records and tapes, four hundred cookbooks written by African Americans, and many newspaper articles and artifacts from the first seventy-five black families who settled in Clearwater. It has an exhibit about **Annie Sypes**, a black woman who was born in the area and lived most of her 107 years there. The museum, which opened in 1978, is open by appointment. Phone: (727) 447-1037.

The **PINELLAS COUNTY AFRICAN AMERICAN HISTORY MUSEUM & RESOURCE CENTER** under the direction of **Sandra W. Rooks** and located at 1101 N. Marshall Street in Clearwater has exhibits and resources for the study of African American history. It also sponsors historical re-creations and presentations, as well as the recording of oral histories and stories from the elders of the community. Phone: (727) 532-1698. Ms. Rooks is the author of *St. Petersburg Florida* (see below under St. Petersburg) and the co-author with **Randolph Lightfoot** of *Clearwater Florida* in the Black America series published by Arcadia.

The Pinellas County African American History Museum & Resource Center has changing exhibits about local history.

Among the other Clearwater sites that should be mentioned here is PINELLAS HIGH SCHOOL at 1220 Palmetto Street, which African American jazz pianist **Ivory "Dwike" Mitchell Jr.** attended. Mitchell, who was born in Dunedin, Florida, on February 14, 1930, attended the Chase Memorial School and played piano at the Shiloh Missionary Baptist Church in Dunedin before eventually teaming up with horn player **Willie Henry Ruff Jr.**, of Sheffield, Alabama, to create a famous and popular jazz duo, as detailed in a profile by William Zinsser.

One of the most important people from Clearwater is **Joseph W. Hatchett** (1932–), the state's first black supreme court justice. While he was growing up in Clearwater with his three brothers and sisters, his mother worked as a maid and his father worked as a fruit picker. After attending a local school, he went on to Florida A&M University in Tallahassee, spent two years in the U.S. Army, and then went to Howard University Law School in Washington, D.C. After law school, he practiced law in Daytona Beach for seven years, became an Assistant U.S. Attorney in Jacksonville (1966–71), and then a U.S. magistrate for the Middle District of Florida. When Governor Askew appointed him to the Florida Supreme Court in 1975, he became the first black to sit on the supreme court in any Southern state, and later was reelected to the position, becoming the first black since Reconstruction to be elected to a statewide office. He served on that court until 1979, at which time President Jimmy Carter chose him to serve as a federal circuit judge on the Fifth U.S. Circuit Court of Appeals.

Joseph W. Hatchett of Clearwater was the state's first black supreme court justice. *Florida State Archives*

The Union Academy was moved from Tarpon Springs to the Heritage Village in Largo.

Largo

Heritage Village at 11909 125th Street North in Largo has various displays and buildings associated with the history of Pinellas County, including **UNION ACADEMY**, an original African American school in Tarpon Springs and possibly the oldest portable classroom in Florida. Its origin probably goes back to World War I, when it was built for the military as an office, warehouse, or barracks. Later, the Pinellas County School District bought the building and moved it in 1926 to the campus of the then all-white Tarpon Springs Elementary School. In 1942, when it was no longer needed at the school, officials transferred the building and an identical structure to Union Academy Elementary, whose students were all black.

In the early 1960s, officials turned the building over to a group called the Better Boys Club, made up of youngsters who were not admitted to other clubs simply because they were black.

The club's motto was "Building boys is better than mending men." In 1968, the club had about eighty-five members, ranging in age from eight to eighteen, who paid weekly dues of ten cents, although no boy was turned away if he could not pay. When the club stopped meeting in the late 1970s, the building sat vacant, then was used as a storage area for medical equipment by a black physician, and later became a hangout for drug users.

In 2000, the building was slated for demolition until a group headed by **Elizabeth Archie**, the wife of **Samuel Archie**, who had founded the Better Boys Club, pointed out the importance of the building. Officials then had it moved to Heritage Village, where it has displays about the history of African Americans in the county. Phone: (727) 532-1698.

One of the members of that Better Boys Club was **Harry Singletary Jr.**, who later served as

Florida's Corrections Secretary (1991–98), the first African American to hold that position. He grew up in Tarpon Springs with two strong role models: his mother and father. He went to college at Florida Presbyterian College (now Eckerd College) in St. Petersburg, where he became the first African American to play basketball at a predominantly white college in Florida. In 1971, he earned his Master's degree from the University of Chicago. As a juvenile corrections officer, he spent most of his career working with young people who had broken the law, first in Illinois, then in Florida. As Secretary of the Florida Department of Corrections, he was in charge of more than 20,000 staff members, 49,000 inmates, and 100,000 men, women, and children on probation. His budget was over $1 billion.

St. Petersburg

This city, like many in Florida, is barely one hundred years old, but burial mounds and ceramic remains indicate that Indians lived here for hundreds of years before white men arrived. Those Indians, whom historians call the Tocobaga, came into contact with European explorers like the Spanish Panfilo de Narváez and Hernando de Soto in the sixteenth century. The Pinellas Peninsula remained relatively unsettled by Europeans until the eighteenth century, but runaway slaves began joining Creek Indians and formed a branch of the Seminole Indians. The nineteenth century saw a number of what historian Arsenault calls "Spanish Indians," some of whom were fugitive black slaves. After the U.S. took control of Florida from Spain in 1821, thousands of settlers poured into the territory, including the adventurer Odet Philippe, who used slaves to till his plantation.

After the Seminole Indian wars and the Civil War, more whites moved to the area, as well as a few ex-slaves like **John Donaldson**, the first black man to move to the lower Pinellas Peninsula after the Civil War. Russian-born railroad builder Pe-

ter Demens, who was responsible for the naming of Florida's St. Petersburg after the Russian city, used several hundred black workers along with his work force to bring the Orange Belt Railroad to the area in 1888. What followed were more settlers and tourists and a steady building of the city. The black workers who settled down in the town after the completion of the railroad lived on 4th Avenue South in what was called Pepper Town. Another black community on 9th Street South was called Cooper's Quarters after the local white merchant who owned their shacks, Leon B. Cooper.

In the early part of the 1900s blacks made up a sizable part of the three thousand residents and worked in the menial jobs (laborers, fishermen, domestics) that built the local economy. Many blacks lived and worked along the city's so-called "Black Belt," which was along 22nd and 16th Streets South. For entertainment they attended the Harlem Theater and the Manhattan Casino, where entertainers like **Cab Calloway** and **Dizzy Gillespie** performed. Racial violence occurred from time to time, as in 1914 when an angry white mob lynched a black man for allegedly killing a white man and attacking the white man's wife.

The **ROYAL THEATER** at 1011 22nd Street South would attract as many as seven hundred African Americans on Saturdays in the 1950s when segregation kept the races apart. The theater, which had local talent shows and other productions, closed in 1966, but now houses the Southside Boys and Girls Club.

Blacks there suffered the segregation that many other American cities had and attended separate but unequal facilities. The city has not had the violence associated with integration in other American cities, partly because blacks used legal means to redress their wrongs. For example, in 1955, after being refused entry to the Spa Beach and Pool at the city's Municipal Pier, local blacks filed a lawsuit, which they won and which finally allowed them to use the beach. Five years later, a Boycott Committee urged blacks to avoid white-owned department stores that refused to serve them food in their restaurants; it took less than a year for the lunch counters to be open for all.

In 1966, blacks entered the St. Petersburg City Hall and ripped down a demeaning mural that depicted black musicians happily strumming their banjos on a beach. The next year saw the publication of the city's first and only black-owned newspaper, *The Weekly Challenger*. Three years later attorney **C. Bette Wimbish** became the first black to sit on the City Council. More recently the city's Interdenominational Ministerial Alliance, a group of thirty black ministers, has worked hard to better relations among the races. In 2000, St. Petersburg had some 46,623 blacks (20%) out of a total population of 238,629.

Among the places of importance to blacks is the **ENOCH D. DAVIS CENTER** at 1111 18th Avenue South. This 18,000-square-foot multi-purpose center houses the James Weldon Johnson Branch Library, a large hall, three meeting rooms, classroom space, and office space for human service agencies serving the community. The building, which officials dedicated in 1981, honors Rev. Dr.

Enoch D. Davis, a long-time activist and civic leader. Young Enoch Douglas Davis, who was born in Waynesboro, Georgia, came to St. Petersburg as a teenager in 1925. Five years later he began his preaching and two years after that became pastor of Bethel Community Baptist Church, a position he held for more than fifty years. He was active in the desegregation efforts of Florida schools and in the establishment of equal opportunities for all.

GIBBS HIGH SCHOOL at 850 34th Street South honors **Jonathan C. Gibbs** (1827–1874), the black secretary of state (1869–72) under Governor Harrison Reed and later the state superintendent of public instruction in charge of Florida's schools. Gibbs improved the state's school system, adopted standard textbooks, and established many schools for blacks. In 1965, Gibbs High School became the first predominantly black institution to join the Florida High School Activities Association and then won a state championship in basketball. When court-ordered integration of schools began to take effect in 1971, local officials considered closing Gibbs High School, but blacks protested and threatened to burn down the school rather

Baseball games at Al Lang Field in St. Petersburg had segregated seating in the 1950s. *Heritage Park-Pinellas County Historical Museum*

than see it closed. It remained open. A former Gibbs principal, **Emanuelle Stewart**, in 1988 became the first black member of the Suncoasters, the committee that ran the Festival of States Parade in St. Petersburg; he also was the parade's first black grand marshal.

In 1957, the Pinellas County Board of Public Instruction established GIBBS JUNIOR COLLEGE as the first two-year college created after a 1957 report of the Community College Council. The 1885 version of the state Constitution stated that "white and colored children shall not be taught in the same school, but that impartial provision shall be made for both." Maintaining or establishing separate schools for whites and blacks in the mid-1950s was illegal since the 1954 *Brown vs. Board of Education* decision in the U.S. Supreme Court outlawed segregation in public education.

Governor LeRoy Collins, who served as Florida's governor from 1955 until 1961 and who believed that much of the state was opposed to the integration of colleges, had his Community College Council plan to establish black junior colleges on the campuses of already existing black high schools. Doing so would provide immediate facilities and administrative and academic leadership until the new colleges could stand on their own. Also, the junior colleges could more easily recruit promising students among the nearby black populations of the black high schools. Sharing facilities with a high school meant that the twelve black junior colleges had to have their course offerings from 4 P.M. until 10 P.M., when the high school buildings were not being used. Governor Collins believed that the black colleges would eventually merge with the white junior colleges, at which point the developed facilities could return to the high schools.

In the fall of 1957, the first new black two-year college opened: Gibbs Junior College in St. Petersburg on the campus of Gibbs High School at 850 34th Street South. Some local officials thought that civil rights groups, bolstered

by Northerners determined to integrate Florida's schools, especially St. Petersburg Junior College, might stage demonstrations protesting the opening of a black college, especially after the 1954 Supreme Court decision outlawing separate facilities for blacks, but those demonstrations did not materialize, possibly because local blacks had mixed feelings about whether the integration of higher education should take place immediately. The reputation of black colleges was high in that such institutions afforded blacks the opportunity of gaining access to four-year schools and of learning marketable trades and skills.

Dr. **John W. Rembert**, the only president of Gibbs, opened up the school that fall of 1957 and was pleasantly surprised when over two hundred students enrolled, one hundred more than expected. Sharing facilities with Gibbs High School did not discourage even more students from applying; by mid-year the college had over four hundred students and eleven faculty members. When Governor Collins went to St. Petersburg in 1958 to dedicate the first permanent building of the new college, one of the students was a Korean War veteran, **Walter Lee Smith**. He became the first president of the Gibbs Junior College student body; later Provost of Hillsborough Community College in Tampa; President of Roxbury Community College in Boston, Massachusetts; and President of his undergraduate university, Florida A&M University in Tallahassee.

Gibbs Junior College and eleven other such schools provided many blacks equal access to higher educational opportunities. Just before it merged with St. Petersburg Junior College in the 1964–65 school year, Gibbs had 887 students. The next year saw a name change for the formerly black college to the Gibbs Campus of St. Petersburg Junior College and later to the Skyway Campus. By the mid-1960s all Florida universities were admitting blacks. By the time the twelve black junior colleges in Florida began to be consolidated with the nearby white junior colleges in the mid-1960s, they had an enrollment of over nine thousand students. By 1966, two years after the 1964 Civil Rights Act, all twelve were gone, having been consolidated with the white schools.

The enrollment figures for Gibbs, which included students enrolled in the college parallel programs as well as the vocational programs, were as follows:

1957–58: 245 students
1958–59: 573 students
1959–60: 684 students
1960–61: 699 students
1961–62: 673 students
1962–63: 703 students
1963–64: 801 students
1964–65: 887 students

Tarpon Springs

Although this city is associated mostly with Greeks and Greek-Americans who prospered in the sponge industry, many African Americans lived there and contributed to the diversity of the city with churches, businesses, and shops. Sandra Rooks and Carol Mountain's *Tarpon Springs, Florida* in the Black America Series noted that most of the early black settlers lived in Charlestown, which extended from Alternate 19 and Levis Avenue and one block south of Tarpon Avenue to just south of Martin Luther King Jr. Drive. Gertrude Stoughton's *Tarpon Springs, Florida: The Early Years* has a chapter entitled "Black Tarponites" that describes the coming of early black families after the Civil War and how they melded into the working life of the town. Those families began their own churches, such as the African Methodist Episcopal (1887) and the Baptist (1892), as well as the Saint Safford Masonic Lodge and the Negro Odd Fellows. In the twentieth century, **Glenn A. Davis** became the first black city commissioner (1987). Stoughton concluded that the "blacks' presence and industriousness did much to shape the town and laid the basis for attempts

at mutual problem-solving by both sides."

African Americans there, however, did suffer discrimination. For example, the Atlantic Coast Line Railroad Depot in the middle of town was built in 1909 as a segregated building; to separate the whites and blacks a wall divided the main room. Because public schools remained segregated until 1962, black students who wanted to attend high school traveled by train from that segregated station to Clearwater to continue their education. Today, the Tarpon Springs Historical Society, which has been headquartered in that train station since 1976, has files and exhibits about the town's history, including the segregation of the races.

ROSE CEMETERY, which extends from Tarpon Avenue East to Jasmine Avenue North and is east of U.S. 19, is a 100-year-old black cemetery that is missing many grave markers. Researchers are hoping to identify unmarked graves with ground-penetrating radar, then use research and oral histories to identify remains in those unmarked plots. The cemetery used to be the only place where local blacks could be buried. The private, non-profit cemetery, which is east of the city-owned Cycadia Cemetery on Jasmine Boulevard, was once called Rose Hill, but had to change its name because of an older Rose Hill Cemetery in Hillsborough County. Only about six to eight burials take place a year in the 5.5-acre cemetery.

Rose Cemetery in Tarpon Springs.

53.
Polk County

Florida's thirty-ninth county was established in 1861 and named for James Polk, the eleventh President of the United States. The county had a population of 483,924 in the 2000 census, 65,330 (13.5%) of whom were African Americans.

Bartow

West central Florida in the nineteenth century was very isolated. The few white settlers who had begun moving into the area in the early 1830s, faced much opposition from the Indians who had been there for decades. Consequently the white families clustered near stockades, to which they could retreat if the Indians attacked. In the 1850s more and more cattle drovers and their families moved into the area, settling down near present-day Fort Meade, while others chose the area around present-day Bartow. Many of those white families brought along their black slaves, forcing them to make the long trip from other Southern states on foot with the livestock.

By 1861, enough settlers had moved into the area that Governor Madison Starke Perry signed the documents that established Polk County. The county seat of Bartow, which was established in the 1860s, honored Confederate General Francis F. Bartow, the first general officer on either side to die in the Civil War. In the Reconstruction Period after the Civil War, Polk County became an important citrus and cattle center and, later, a phosphate mining area. When the South Florida Railroad reached Bartow in 1884 and made the hauling of phosphate easier, many people moved there, and the town prospered.

The citrus and phosphate industries and the railroad attracted many teachers, doctors, and other professionals to the town, including black workers. Those blacks who worked in the phosphate mines in Polk County and elsewhere in Florida endured appalling conditions. They often worked from dawn to dusk for a measly dollar a day in the 1890s, and only a $1.50 a day ten years later. Before water cannons came into use in 1905, the workers used picks and shovels to scrape out the phosphate from seams near the surface, and for the phosphate in rivers they pulled dredges through the water in dangerous conditions. They also became indebted to the company stores on the premises of the mine, stores that charged high prices and kept the African Americans in constant debt. The scarred landscape and heaps of toxic materials from the days of the phosphate mine are reminders of how many lives were lost or permanently damaged in the nineteenth and early twentieth centuries.

The blacks usually lived in the southeast part of Bartow, between Parker and Bay Streets and 2nd and 10th Avenues. Churches, stores, schools, lodges, and a movie theater flourished in the area during the first quarter of the twentieth century, but most have long since been demolished.

One of the black men who came to Bartow in the 1920s was a brick mason, **Bradley Mitchell**. Like many workers, he realized the importance of education and managed to send through college his three sons and eight daughters, most of whom went on to become teachers. Two other black families, the **Hamiltons** and the **Long-worths**, joined the Mitchells in producing many of Bartow's excellent black teachers.

The two-story LAWRENCE BROWN HOME at 470 2nd Avenue is the oldest black residence in Bartow, dating back to 1884. It was the home of **Lawrence Bernard Brown**, a carpenter who invested in land around town. Brown had been born a slave in Alachua County in 1858, moved to Bartow as an adult, bought two acres along Second Avenue for $155, and built the two-story house for his family. He had a shop in front of his house from which he sold Bibles. The wood-frame residential building, located south of Main Street, west of U.S. 17/98, and north of Stuart Street, has a style called Folk Victorian. Its main features are a steeply pitched gable roof and a large veranda porch around the outside. This architectural style became popular after the Civil War as magazines featured it and praised its many beauties. The ex-

tension of the railroad to Bartow enabled builders to import building materials for such houses. This particular building has stained-glass transoms and a porch trim that made the house unique in Bartow. A plaque at the house honors Brown as a member of the Great Floridians 2000 Program.

The town's first black school, UNION ACADEMY, opened its doors in 1897 under the guidance of principal **A. N. Ritchie** and four teachers: Miss **Emma Bullard**, Mr. **J. P. Hector**, Mrs. **M. L. Norwood**, and Miss **Lula Marion Simmons**. As the only black high school in southwest Polk County for many years, it served parts of Hardee County and students bused in from Fort Meade, Mulberry, Wauchula, and smaller communities. In 1937, **James E. Stephens** became a teacher at the school and the following year became principal, a position he held for the next thirty years, at which time integration closed down Union Academy. His thirty years as principal of that one

The Lawrence Brown Home may be the oldest black residence in Bartow.

school may have been a record for Polk County. The school sent many athletes to Florida A&M University in Tallahassee in the 1940s and 1950s, but for every athletic scholarship Principal Stephens insisted that the university give one academic scholarship to an "A" student.

The **ST. JAMES AME CHURCH** on Dr. Martin Luther King Jr. Boulevard began as a small wooden structure in 1894 and now encompasses an entire corner. The church is the only remnant of a once-thriving black business district, Burnett's Quarters, which included a movie theater, meat market, and community store. The area was named after **Thomas Burnett** in the 1920s.

In 2000, some 15,340 people lived in Bartow, of whom 4,355 (28.4%) were blacks. One of the town's residents who became a leading civic and education leader was **Alice Frederick** (see the section on West Palm Beach in Chapter Fifty). Another significant resident was **George Gause** (1920–1986), the Bartow Funeral Home director who became the county's first black city commissioner in 1968 and its first black school board member, as well as the first black mayor (1971) of a predominantly white Florida town. Born in Wilmington, North Carolina, in 1920, he moved to Bartow with his family when he was eight years old. He graduated from Bartow's Union Acad-

emy, then attended Florida A&M University in Tallahassee and the Atlanta College of Mortuary Science. In 1977, Governor Reubin Askew appointed Gause to the Polk County School Board, and in 1978, he was elected to a four-year term. He did not seek reelection due to failing health. The Gause Academy of Leadership in Bartow and Gause Riverside Academy in Fort Meade commemorate him. A plaque at the Gause Funeral Home, 625 S. Holland Parkway, Bartow, honors him.

One of the most famous Bartow blacks was **Charlie Smith**, the oldest man in the United States according to Social Security records. Born in 1842 in Liberia, Africa, he was kidnapped with other blacks in 1854, brought to this country, and sold as a slave. A Texas rancher, Charles Smith, bought the young man in New Orleans as a playmate for his children and gave him his own name. Charlie later gained his freedom through President Abraham Lincoln's Emancipation Proclamation in 1863 and traveled throughout the West as a cowboy. He eventually made his way to Florida in the early part of the twentieth century, finally settling down in Bartow in 1963. After he died in 1979 at the age of 137, Bartow citizens erected a grave marker at his gravesite at the end of a row in the northeast corner of **WILDWOOD CEMETERY**

The gravesite of Charlie Smith.

that gave his name, birth and death dates, and the words "America's Oldest Man." The cemetery is open during daylight hours.

Directions to cemetery and gravesite: The cemetery is at the juncture of Stuart Street and Woodlawn Avenue, about two miles west of U.S. 17/U.S. 98. To reach the gravesite go in the cemetery entrance nearest to the corner of Vine Street and Woodlawn Avenue; go .1 miles down the main lane, turn right past the fourth rectangular series of graves, and go to the end of the back row of graves. The gravesite is the last one at the end of the row and nearest the fence.

Frostproof

An African American librarian from Arizona, **Samuel Morrison**, began the Frostproof Living Learning Library Center in Frostproof to serve migrant workers in central Florida and directed it for four years (1972–76). He then went on to work in Florida's Broward County Library System and helped establish the African American Research Library and Cultural Center in Fort Lauderdale, where he worked (1976–88) before going to Illinois to become the chief librarian for the City of Chicago (1988–90), before returning to Florida to become the director of the Broward Library System (1991–2003).

Haines City

In the 1870s and 1880s a group of settlers went to central Florida and settled in a place they called Clay Cut on the South Florida Railroad. The settlers could not convince railroad officials to put a station there until they renamed the town Haines City to honor a railroad official. Located in northeast Polk County in the center of peninsular Florida, the city, which calls itself "The Gateway to the Scenic Highlands," is near highways U.S. 27, U.S. 17, U.S. 92, and I-4. That prime location helps in the shipping of the city's primary product, citrus. The city had 4,000 people by 1940,

5,000 by 1950, 9,000 by 1970, 11,683 by 1990, and 13,174 by 2000. Of that last number, 4,197 were black, a number that represented almost 32% of the population.

The first blacks settled there in 1902, when the Malloy-Miller turpentine company relocated from Huston, Florida. The first black school opened in 1915 in St. Marks Church on 7th Street and Church Street. Two years later workers built a wooden building for the students near the site of what became **OAKLAND HIGH SCHOOL**. In 1928, Oakland School opened with the first eight grades, but students who wanted to go to high school had to travel to Bartow or Lakeland. In 1930, the school was accredited as a senior high school, at which time students came from Loughman, Davenport, Dundee, Lake Hamilton, and the unincorporated areas of northeast Polk County. The first graduating class in 1930 had four students; the second in 1931 had three. Over the years and before integration merged schools, the graduates of Oakland High School distinguished themselves as doctors, lawyers, educators, and businesspeople.

The school, which is on 8th Street near Avenues D and E near Lakes Tracy and Boomerang and west of 17th Street, is now called **BETHUNE NEIGHBORHOOD CENTER** and provides the community with recreation programs, child day-care, reading and writing programs, and other activities.

Lakeland

The **BUFFALO SOLDIERS ENCAMPMENT MARKER** at 20 Lake Wire Drive marks the spot where the 10th Cavalry, one of four all-black regiments in the regular army at the start of the Spanish-American War, camped in the spring of 1898 while awaiting transport to Cuba. The name "Buffalo Soldiers" hearkens back to the days when the soldiers won renown in their campaigns against Native Americans on the Western frontier. The local community had the marker installed in 2001.

The oldest black community in Lakeland, MOOREHEAD, lasted until 1971, when city officials told the residents of the community to leave. Using eminent domain, the government's right to force landowners to sell their property at market value, the city took over the 259-house area, which it considered a slum, then demolished the buildings and built the Lakeland Civic Center (later called the Lakeland Center) in its place.

Researcher **Lafrancine Burton** has documented the history of African Americans in Lakeland, whose officials dedicated a historical marker in honor of the city's pioneering blacks. Among the structures that the city razed was the MOUNT PLEASANT AFRICAN METHODIST EPISCOPAL CHURCH, built around 1900 as the first Methodist church for black Americans in Lakeland. Another was the FOSTER MEMORIAL (UNITED) METHODIST CHURCH, built in 1913. Another facility that is gone is the WASHINGTON PARK SCHOOL, a two-story, red-brick building where African American students could study up through the eighth grade. Before Washington Park became a high school in 1928, local black students had to travel elsewhere to complete their education.

Plaques at the Lakeland Public Library, 100 Lake Morton Drive in Lakeland, honor two people who served the African American community. **Rosabelle Blake** (1911–1973), who dedicated her life to educating students in the Polk County Public Schools, completed undergraduate and graduate degrees at Florida A&M University and did post-graduate work at the University of Cincinnati. In 1930, she began teaching at a small segregated school in Mulberry, Florida, and within a few years was named principal. In 1938, she was transferred to Union Academy, where she taught high school and served as Elementary Coordinator. In 1940, Blake was appointed supervisor of Polk County Negro Public Schools. In the mid-1960s, her title changed to Supervisor of Instruction and Migrant Activities, a post she held until her death. The Rosabelle Blake Elementary School is named in her honor.

The second person honored with a plaque there is Dr. **John Sidney Jackson** (1922–1987), who was born in Pratt City, Alabama, and later studied at Virginia State College in Petersburg, Virginia, and Meharry Medical College in Nashville, Tennessee. He served on the attending surgical staff of Lakeland Regional Medical Center; was a member of the Florida Medical, Dental and Pharmaceutical Association; Florida and Polk County Medical Associations; American Medical Association; National Medical Association; and the American Society of Abdominal Surgeons. He also served as the first African American mayor of Lakeland (1972–73). In 1970, while serving as the first African American city commissioner, he helped quell racial disturbances.

The 2000 census indicated that Lakeland had 16,682 African Americans or a little over 21% of the total city's population of 78,452.

Lake Wales

ROOSEVELT SCHOOL at 115 East Street North was the center of African American education in Lake Wales. The largest building is noted for its Masonry Vernacular construction.

54.

Putnam County

The Florida Legislature established this county in 1849 and named it for Benjamin Alexander Putnam (1801–1869), lawyer, officer in the Second Seminole War, member of the Florida Legislature, judge, surveyor-general of Florida, and first president of the Florida Historical Society. The county had a population of 70,423 in the 2000 census, 11,972 (17.0%) of whom were African Americans.

Crescent City

Crescent City in Putnam County can trace its history to the mid-eighteenth century, when white settlers began moving in to take advantage of the good soil and access to a lake. The city, which takes its name from nearby Crescent Lake, so called because of its resemblance to a crescent moon, was incorporated in 1885. Certain parts of the city were set aside for blacks. Around 1887, black residents began the Village of Whitesville, so called perhaps because of the whitewashed cabins used by the residents near Lake Stella in the southern part of the city. The 2000 census indicated that Crescent City had 612 African Americans or 35% of the total town population of 1,776.

A. Philip Randolph (1889–1979), one of the most important civil rights leaders of the twentieth century, was born in Crescent City and lived at 1004 S. Reid Avenue in a two-story house that burned in 1918. Randolph's father, **James William Randolph**, served as a minister of the African Methodist Episcopal Zion Church in town before the family moved to Jacksonville, where young A. Philip attended school. In 1911, he settled in New York City and fourteen years later organized the all-black International Brotherhood of Sleeping Car Porters, the first important black

A. Philip Randolph was born in Crescent City. *Florida State Archives*

labor union, and served as the organization's first president. He also organized two large marches on the nation's capital, one in 1941 and the other in 1963, was the first black to serve as International Vice President of the AFL-CIO (1957), and received the Presidential Medal of Freedom from President Lyndon Johnson (1964). Crescent City has a plaque in Randolph's honor at the **UNION BETHEL A. M. E. CHURCH**, 200 N. Cedar Street, and Jacksonville has the **A. PHILIP RANDOLPH NORTHSIDE SKILLS CENTER** that teaches students marketable skills.

Interlachen

Robert H. Jenkins Jr. (1948–1969) was born in Interlachen, graduated from Palatka Central Academy, joined the U.S. Marines, and was assigned to Vietnam. In March 1969, while he was serving as a machine gunner in that war, an enemy soldier threw a hand grenade into the bunker where he and his fellow Marines were stationed. At that moment, Jenkins took hold of another Marine, pushed him to the ground, and threw himself on top of the man to protect him from the exploding hand grenade. The tremendous force of the explosion wounded Jenkins so badly that he died soon after. When Jenkins had attended Palatka Central Academy, it was a segregated school that only blacks attended; after Jenkins died and integration took place, officials changed the name of the school to **ROBERT JENKINS MIDDLE SCHOOL** in his honor. He is buried in Sister Spring Cemetery in Interlachen, Florida. The Medal of Honor Park near Sebring, Florida, honors Jenkins and another black, **Clifford Chester Sims** (see Chapter Twenty-seven).

Palatka

The name of this town goes back to the Indian word "Pilotaikata," which meant "crossing" and referred to a place for crossing the St. Johns River. After the Seminole Indian wars settlers began

Robert Jenkins Middle School in Palatka honors a soldier from Interlachen who won the Medal of Honor for bravery in the Vietnam War. *State of Florida, Dept. of Military Affairs*

moving into the area to harvest and cut the cypress that grew in the area and to grow citrus, at least until the devastating freezes of the 1890s ended that venture.

The proximity of the city and county to the St. Johns River, while affording a means to transport cargo in and local produce out, also caused problems for slave owners during the Civil War. As was true of Clay County to the immediate north, runaway slaves that made it to the river would flag down Union boats, which would take them to freedom and even to recruitment in the Union army. Some of those new recruits would join expeditionary forces that sailed up the St. Johns, raiding plantations along the way and carrying off slaves, horses, salt, and whatever products they could easily transport.

The town attracted many visitors and fishermen in the early twentieth century as people discovered the beauty of this "Gem City on the St. Johns." The 2000 census indicated that Palatka had 4,859 African Americans or 48% of the total town population of 10,033.

The BETHEL AME CHURCH at 719 Reid Street is a large church in the Romanesque Revival style that members of the congregation built between 1908 and 1912 to serve the residents of the black community of Newtown. The congregation was organized around 1866, right after the Civil War, and built the first church in 1875 at the corner of Hotel and Emmett Streets. Members bought the present property around 1904–1905.

Another important church built to serve the African American community that resided west of the central business district in the 1870s and 1880s was ST. MARY'S EPISCOPAL CHURCH (built around 1883) at 807 St. Johns Avenue. The building is a beautiful Gothic Revival board-and-batten frame structure.

The FINLEY HOMESTEAD, which used to be at 522 Main Street before it was razed, was the home of **Adam Finley**, a free black who worked as a barber in Palatka. His son, **Eugene Finley**, owned Finley's Barber Shop on Lemon Street and became involved in civic activities and even formed a band at the high school. His son, Dr. **Harold E. Finley**, became a well-known protozoologist, researcher, and head of the Department of Zoology at Howard University in Washington, DC.

Another important structure is the home and office of Dr. **Napoleon Ben Hester**, at 626 Reid Street. The structure where the pioneer black dentist lived and worked has been restored by an attorney.

CENTRAL ACADEMY HIGH SCHOOL at 1207 Washington Street began in 1892, when Putnam County's board of public instruction built two buildings on Orange Street (now Reid Street): one for the white students and one for the black students. Before that time schooling for the black students took place in various halls of the city. The school for blacks was called Central Academy, and its colors were purple and gold. During the administration of Prof. **A. J. Polk** in 1936, when fire destroyed that first school, the children once again had to have their lessons in various churches and halls. Officials built a new school building on the corner of Washington and 12th Streets and opened it for classes in 1937. Between three hundred and four hundred students enrolled in the school. In the mid-1920s, Central Academy was possibly the first black high school in Florida to be accredited. After the original school burned down, a new building was constructed for the school in the late 1930s. The school board of Putnam County now uses the building as a service center.

The principals of the school have been **W. M. Berry, J. W. Holley, E. H. Flipper, E. S. Holmes, C. B. White** (who resigned to become the first black mail carrier in Palatka), **B. F. Hartwell, T. E. Debose** (the pastor of Leete Chapel M.E. Church and the one who added the ninth and tenth grades to the school), **J. A. Lockett** (who introduced football and basketball), **Clarence C. Walker** (who helped the school become accredited), **H. M. Richards, K. C. Lynon, C. W. Banks,** and **A. J. Polk** (who had to find places for the students when fire destroyed the school). By the late 1930s the school had 869 students, 26 teachers, and over 350 graduates that included ministers, physicians, businessmen, and nurses.

One of the school's more famous students, **Robert H. Jenkins Jr.** (1948–1969), was born in Interlachen, Florida, and attended Oak Grove Elementary School (1955–1963) and Palatka's Central Academy High School (1963–1967) (see the section on Interlachen in this chapter).

Palatka is also important for having given to baseball one of its more famous black players, **John Henry "Pop" Lloyd**, who was born there in 1884. Playing baseball in the Negro Leagues long before **Jackie Robinson** broke the color line in the major leagues was very hard for such players as Lloyd. The players spent much of their time traveling from town to town in order to play the games, earned little or no money, and had to stay in segregated hotels

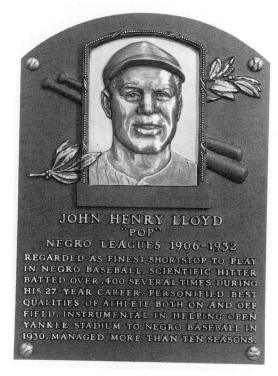

John Henry "Pop" Lloyd, who was born in Palatka, is enshrined in the Baseball Hall of Fame in Cooperstown.

Lloyd's father died when the boy was still an infant; when John Henry's mother remarried, his grandmother took over the job of raising him. He quit school before finishing the elementary grades and became a delivery boy in a store. His baseball skills became apparent at an early age, and he began playing semi-professional baseball with the Jacksonville Young Receivers before he went north in 1906 to play for the Cuban X Giants. Unlike many ballplayers then and since, Lloyd set a good example by never drinking alcohol, never cursing, and seldom if ever smoking.

Lloyd played and managed for such black teams as the Acmes of Macon (Georgia), the New York Lincoln Stars, the New York Lincoln Giants, the Chicago Leland Giants, the Chicago American Giants, the Brooklyn Royal Giants, the Columbus Buckeyes, the Atlantic City Bacharach Giants, the Philadelphia Hilldale Club, and the New York Black Yankees. He also played for Henry Flagler's hotel teams in Palm Beach (see Chapter Fifty). When some fans compared Lloyd to the great white shortstop, Honus Wagner (1874–1955), Wagner was honored: "They called John Henry Lloyd 'The Black Wagner,' and I was anxious to see him play. Well, one day I had an opportunity to go see him play, and after I saw him I felt honored that they would name such a great player after me." Lloyd, who sometimes played baseball in Cuba, where the Cubans called him "Cuchara" or "shovel" because his big hands were able to scoop up any ball hit near him, was voted into the Baseball Hall of Fame in 1977.

When asked if he had been born too soon, Lloyd replied, "No, I don't feel that I was born at the wrong time. I feel it was the right time. I had a chance to prove the ability of our race in this sport, and because many of us did our best for the game, we've given the Negro a greater opportunity now to be accepted into the major leagues with other Americans."

COLLIER-BLOCKER JUNIOR COLLEGE, which was established in 1960, was one of twelve black junior colleges in Florida. Unlike the other eleven black junior colleges, which shared the facilities of a local black high school, Collier-Blocker used a former Baptist church for its classrooms.

The school is named after Dr. **Nathan W. Collier** and **Sarah Blocker**. Dr. Collier (1872–1941) was the long-time president of Florida Normal (later Florida Memorial) College, a black school in St. Augustine from 1918 until 1968. Sarah Blocker (1857–1944), was the long-time vice president of the same school, which she helped establish in 1879 at the age of twenty-two. Ms. Blocker is an inductee in the Florida Women's Hall of Fame in the Capitol building in Tallahassee and is honored by the naming of a building at Florida Memorial College in Miami. Nathan Collier is honored in the naming of the library at the same school. (For more about their final resting place see Chapter Fifty-five.) The college attracted African American students from Clay,

Flagler, Putnam, and St. Johns Counties. (For more about one of its graduates, **Prince B. Oliver Sr.**, see Chapter Fourteen.)

The first president of Collier-Blocker Junior College was Mr. **Albert B. Williams**, then the Dean at the Florida Industrial and Memorial College in St. Augustine. Mr. Williams left after the college's first graduation and was replaced by **Fred R. Brooks** as dean and acting president, while at the same time serving as principal of Central Academy High School. The black junior college enrolled 105 students in its best year before merging with St. Johns River Junior College. The enrollment figures for Collier-Blocker are as follows:

1960–61: 59 students
1961–62: 78 students
1962–63: 105 students
1963–64: 72 students

55.

St. Johns County

Florida's first county, along with Escambia County in the western part of the territory, was established in 1821, when the United States acquired Florida from Spain. The county takes its name from the St. Johns River to the west, which in turn took its name from a Spanish mission at its mouth: San Juan del Puerto.

St. Johns County had a population of 123,135 in the 2000 census, 7,758 (6.3%) of whom were African Americans.

Much of the county away from the coast has remained agricultural, although increasing numbers of new residents are forcing dramatic changes in that make-up. The county has changed over the past two centuries: from being one of two important, settled sites in the peninsula (along with Pensacola) to being a favorite among northerners seeking relief from the winter cold to being a by-passed site as Flagler's railroad took those northerners farther south. Its main city, St. Augustine, has reinvented itself several times to attract more tourists to the city and its nearby beaches, but at the same time retain much of its distinctive architecture and charm. As more and more residents move south from Duval County to escape its congestion, St. Johns County will grow much larger, especially along the coast and Highway A1A.

Fruit Cove

The tiny town of Fruit Cove on the St. Johns River just below Julington Creek has one of the oldest buildings in the county, one that was built around 1908, although the congregation dates to 1869: **MOUNT PLEASANT AFRICAN METHODIST EPISCOPAL CHURCH** located at 726 S.R. 13. In 1990, the congregation joined with Mount Zion Church in Mandarin to become the **Philip**

R. Cousin AME Church, named in honor of the former pastor at Mount Pleasant. In 1991, a businessman purchased the former church and converted it into a screen-printing business.

Mount Pleasant AME Church was in Fruit Cove.

During the two Spanish tenures in Florida (1565–1763, 1783–1821), St. Augustine in the east and Pensacola in the west were the main centers of non-Native American population, especially St. Augustine, primarily because of its sea link to the outside world, its proximity to the thirteen English colonies north of Florida, and its accessibility to the St. Johns River, which could take people into the interior of the peninsula.

St. Augustine

When the Spanish depleted the Native American population of Florida through disease, battles, and inhumane treatment, the Spanish imported slaves to till the fields, build the forts, maintain the wooden ships, and provide the manual labor Spain depended on. At first, the slaves came from Spain, but soon the Spanish were capturing or buying slaves from the Caribbean, then Africa. Historian Jane Landers points out in "Traditions of African American Freedom and Community in Spanish Colonial Florida"(see David Colburn in Further Reading) that the Spanish used slaves to quarry coquina from Anastasia Island as just one of the onerous tasks assigned them. During times of crisis the Spanish would place the slaves in the military and force them to defend the colony.

During the seventeenth and eighteenth centuries, a number of escaping slaves from the Carolinas and Georgia made their way south, determined to flee the oppressive conditions on plantations owned by the British or Americans. Two miles north of St. Augustine, the Spanish established in 1738 a fort they called Gracia Real de Santa Teresa de Mose, what we call today **FORT MOSE** (pronounced "Moh-zay"), the first free community of ex-slaves in North America.

The Spanish gave the escaped slaves their freedom if they would join the Catholic Church and declare their allegiance to the king of Spain. About one hundred free black men, women, and children lived in the fort and helped the Spanish defend St. Augustine from the British, who wanted to recapture the runaway slaves and take them back to plantations. Fort Mose was destroyed in 1740 during the invasion led by General Oglethorpe of Georgia, but rebuilt several years later. When England took control of Florida in 1763, residents of Fort Mose left with the Spaniards for Cuba, where they established a similar community in the province of Matanzas.

Directions: Fort Mose Historic State Park is open to the public and has a boardwalk overlook-ing the fort site. The park is located at the end of Saratoga Boulevard, which is 1.3 miles north of the A1A turn-off to the east and .7 miles north of the S.R. 16 intersection and just past the New City Gates, which are about two miles north of the city. An exhibit at the city's Ponce de Leon Mall, 2121 U.S. 1 South, explains much about Fort Mose.

When the British controlled Florida (1763–1783), they established large plantations that grew indigo, rice, sugar, and sea island cotton, all of which required large numbers of workers, i.e. slaves, to make them profitable. According to Jane Landers, "Soon blacks were the most numerous element of Florida's population." When the American Revolutionary War put British outposts like Charleston and Savannah in control of the Americans, British planters moved their operations south, taking with them large numbers of slaves and making East Florida the last British haven on the east coast. Some twelve thousand people moved to East Florida, over half of them black. The slave code that the British adopted in East Florida, one that was based on that of South Carolina, made life miserable and dangerous for the blacks there.

At the end of the successful American Revolution, when Florida reverted back to Spain, many slaves either fled to the interior of the territory to find sanctuary among the Seminoles or claimed refuge with the incoming Spanish, who still had to grant them asylum if they promised to become Roman Catholic. The free black community that developed under Spanish rule in Florida adapted to changing times, accepted runaways from the colonies to the north and from the Haitian revolution, and prospered. The Catholic practice of becoming a godparent to children outside one's immediate family, for example, solidified the black community and gave it a cohesiveness.

Jorge Biassou, a black general in St. Augustine in colonial times, led a black militia out of

The courtyard of the St. Augustine Historical Society Library has a statue of two men, including that of Dr. Alexander H. Darnes (on the left), the first black doctor in Jacksonville.

Fort Matanzas south of St. Augustine. (One can visit this fort, which is located on Rattlesnake Island and is now operated by the National Park Service.) General Biassou, who had been one of the leaders of the slave uprising in Haiti and had as one of his subordinates **Toussaint L'Ouverture**, died in St. Augustine in 1801, had a funeral at the Catholic Cathedral downtown, and is buried in an unmarked grave in Tolomato Cemetery on Cordova Street.

When the United States acquired Florida from Spain in 1821, St. Augustine and Pensacola were the only towns of any significant size. That fact led to the two towns competing to become the territorial capital until lawmakers decided two years later to establish a capital midway between the two sites, in Tallahassee. The Catholic influence in both St. Augustine and Pensacola was so strong, as a result of the Spanish occupation, that non-Catholic missionaries would struggle to establish Protestant congregations, including those associated with African Americans.

After Florida became part of the United States, St. Augustine continued to have a large black population. In fact, the 1830 census indicated that blacks, who constituted almost half of the city's population, were for the most part slaves. The city had some 240 free blacks, descendants of the early colonists and of runaway slaves from Georgia. Their condition was only slightly above those of the slaves; the free blacks, for example, could not hold meetings without the permission of the white authorities, could hold only certain jobs, and had to live in one section of the city where whites could keep an eye on their activities.

The situation of the slaves was somewhat different from that of other Florida locales because the St. Augustine whites permitted slaves to hire themselves out to fishermen, lumbermen, and railroad builders. The slave owners kept most of the money the slaves earned from this practice, but allowed the slaves to keep a small amount of the money, which they used to support their own churches and clubs. The owners also allowed some of the slaves to live outside the master's residence in a separate part of St. Augustine; there the slaves had a freedom that encouraged them to express themselves.

In the CASTILLO DE SAN MARCOS federal officers imprisoned Seminole Indians, including Osceola, captured under a white flag of truce in 1837. When Coachooche (Wild Cat) escaped from the prison, then called Fort Marion, one of the prisoners who accompanied him was John Horse (or John Cavallo), a leader of the Black Seminoles. When the Seminoles and their black allies were defeated by federal forces in battle, they were sent west to Indian Territory. Finally disgusted with the bad treatment they suffered there, John Horse and some of his followers went to Mexico in 1850 to a place where slavery had already been abolished.

In the two decades before the Civil War, local white slave holders, fearful of the increasing freedom of the blacks, enacted more slave codes and sold their superfluous slaves to rural residents. St. Augustine, which came under Union control in 1862, was one of the few places where Abraham Lincoln's Emancipation Proclamation actually took effect at the time that it was issued. Slaves were gathered in a vacant lot across from **ST. JOSEPH'S CONVENT** (just south of 234 St. George Street) and told of their freedom. The site has come to be known as "Liberation Lot." When the Union army occupied the city in the Civil War, slaves from outlying areas began flocking into the city looking for freedom and protection. Union troops hired free blacks and former slaves to build defenses for the city and to help fill the ranks of the all-black regiments being formed throughout the South.

When developer Henry Flagler began building his railroad south to St. Augustine, he also built large, luxurious hotels there, for example the Ponce de Leon. Among the workers he and his designers used were twelve hundred black workers from along the St. Johns River. It would not be the last time that Flagler depended on blacks to promote his plans and cities (see Chapter Forty-three). Even after the hotel was built, Flagler's officials insisted that the blacks live in shanties at a great distance from the hotel.

The **LINCOLNVILLE HISTORIC DISTRICT** was the center of black business and residential activity in the city in the early part of the twentieth century. The 140-acre area of the southwest peninsula southwest of the downtown area consists of about fifty blocks and streets bounded on the north by DeSoto Place and Cedar Street, Riberia Street on the west, Cerro Street on the south, and

Washington Street on the east. About one-third of the 650 buildings in the district date from the nineteenth century, and many of them represent Victorian architecture. Two surviving antebellum plantation houses are Yallaha at 115 Bridge Street and a wing of Buena Esperanza at 87 Keith Street. A garage at 94 South Street is the last surviving slave cabin in the city. Most of the structures in the district are single-family residences. The area attracted former black slaves right after the Civil War. They first called the area "Africa," but soon changed it to "Lincolnville." The first settlers built homes, churches, and some businesses. After 1877, when a "Peoples' Ticket" led by political reformers including black Republican leader **D. M. Pappy** won the city elections, officials began building streets and making other improvements in the area.

The segregation that followed Reconstruction and the passage of laws meant to allow only whites to vote between 1890 and 1910 greatly limited blacks in their efforts to improve their conditions. Even when they were successful in running for office, they faced dangers. For example, in 1902, black councilman **John Papino** was shot at a meeting of the city council by the white town marshal. Papino survived his wounds, but the terror reflected by the shooting, and the failure to indict the marshal, marked the beginning of the end of black office holders until the 1970s. Papino's house still stands at 95 M.L. King Avenue.

Lincolnville lies between two bodies of water, the Matanzas and San Sebastian Rivers, and is therefore subject to flooding during heavy rainstorms, especially because of the district's low elevation. The district also suffers from real estate speculation, inharmonious zoning, and the bulldozing of many buildings to create parking lots. On the positive side, a Lincolnville Housing Project in the 1980s restored a number of old houses, and the Lincolnville Improvement Association was formed in the 1990s. Lincolnville is now listed on the National Register of Historic Places and the Florida Black Heritage Trail.

The vacant lot at 107 Kings Ferry Way was the site of the home of **Richard Aloysius Twine** (1896–1974), the city's first professional black photographer, who took many photographs of Lincolnville in the 1920s and documented the people and buildings of the area. Workers demolishing the house in 1988 found his camera and many of his glass negatives in the attic of the house, where Twine lived with his mother and two sisters in the 1920s. Twine was born in St. Augustine, grew up there, and started his photography business, which he conducted out of his studio at 62 Washington Street. In the late 1920s he moved to Miami to join his brother in the restaurant business and later died there.

When the St. Augustine Historical Society's photo curator, Ken Barrett Jr., organized an exhibition of Twine's photographs in 1990, Dr. Patricia C. Griffin and Diana S. Edwards interviewed many members of the city's black community with the help of city commissioner **Henry L. Twine**, a distant relative of the photographer. The interviewers identified people in the photographs and recorded life stories of what it was like to live in the city's black section in the 1920s.

Henry L. Twine (1923–1994) was born in Tallahassee and spent his adult life working for the betterment of the African American community in St. Augustine. He served as president of the local NAACP chapter during the 1960s Civil Rights movement, and was a member of the Democratic Party's Executive Committee. During his three terms on the St. Augustine City Commission he gained a reputation as a consensus builder. He also served two terms as the city's first African American vice mayor. His Great Floridian plaque is located at the **TWINE HOUSE**, 163 Twine Street.

Henry and his wife, **Katherine (Kat) Twine** (1925–2002), are honored in the naming of Twine Street at the southern end of Lincolnville, north of Eddie Vickers Park. Known as the "Rosa

Parks of Florida" for her participation in the Civil Rights Movement, Mrs. Twine was frequently arrested and became known for her broad-brimmed "Freedom Hat," which she wore to protect herself from the elements when confined in the treeless stockade outside the crowded jail.

Another African American who lived on Kings Ferry Way was **Idella Parker**, who worked for author Marjorie Kinnan Rawlings and authored two books about the experience. Ms. Parker's presence at 81 Kings Ferry Way is noted in a historic marker at the site.

During the 1964 civil rights demonstrations in the city Dr. **Martin Luther King Jr.** led many people in their attempts to gain better conditions. Police arrested him at the **MONSON MOTOR LODGE**, 32 Avenida Menéndez, where Dr. King led a sit-in to protest the inhumane conditions in what he called the "oldest racist city in America," lampooning the city's penchant for having the "oldest" this and that. To scare away a group of swimmers trying to integrate the facility the motel manager poured acid into the swimming pool, drained it, and stationed guards around it to keep out demonstrators. The Monson Motor Lodge, a civil rights landmark of national significance, was demolished in 2003, after a long, but unsuccessful fight to save it, so a new Hilton Hotel could be built on the site.

Officials later renamed Central Avenue to honor King, despite the objections of some white residents. Because of the danger of violence, Dr. King was moved around frequently when in St. Augustine. Places where he stayed include 81 and 83 Bridge Street and 156 M.L. King Avenue.

Among the other sites associated with those demonstrations are **TRINITY UNITED METHODIST CHURCH** at 84 Bridge Street; **ST. PAUL'S AME CHURCH** at 85 M.L. King Avenue; **ST. MARY'S MISSIONARY BAPTIST CHURCH** at 69 Washington Street; **FIRST BAPTIST CHURCH** at 81 St. Francis Street, and **ZION BAPTIST CHURCH** at 94 Evergreen Avenue.

St. Paul's, a 1904 church in the Gothic Revival style, was where many local blacks met in 1964 to hear baseball great **Jackie Robinson** call for passage of the 1964 civil rights bill passed by the U.S. Senate. Like so many churches in the South, St. Paul's was the place where blacks met to pray and also to discuss the means of attaining civil rights. Whereas whites might have met in schools or places like the Masonic lodge, blacks came to rely on their churches for communication purposes. Dr. **Martin Luther King Jr**. also spoke there; at that moment in his life, the thirty-five-year-old King was the chief spokesman for this country's civil rights movement, the winner of awards for his efforts, *Time* magazine's "Man of the Year," and the future winner of the Nobel Peace Prize.

St. Paul's AME Church has a marble baptismal font carved in the 1920s by George Leapheart of Jacksonville to honor a local black physician, Dr. **Daniel W. Roberts**, who died in 1919 after treating patients struck down by the 1918 flu epidemic that took many lives. Dr. Roberts, a native of Indiana, spent twenty years ministering to the health needs of the people of St. Augustine out of the city's first and only black hospital, **ROBERTS SANITARIUM** at 80 Bridge Street (since torn down for a city parking lot). The doctor, who lived at 124 M.L. King Avenue and 86 Bridge Street (both structures are still standing), was president of the State Medical Association and the first black doctor allowed to operate at Flagler Hospital. Stained-glass windows at St. Paul's AME Church and at Trinity Methodist Church honor that early medical pioneer.

ST. MARY'S MISSIONARY BAPTIST CHURCH resembles the late-medieval churches of Italy and has both Gothic and Romanesque styles in its architecture. This and the other black churches, with their distinctive beauty and careful workmanship, represent the important place that religion has played in the religious and social life of the blacks of the town and of the state. In the mid-1960s the churches played a major role in the political dem-

onstrations that eventually led to the enactment of landmark civil rights legislation.

Three sites in the Lincolnville section related to the Catholic Church are important in this discussion. **ST. BENEDICT THE MOOR CATHOLIC CHURCH** at 86 Martin Luther King Avenue was begun in 1909 and completed two years later. The name of the church honors St. Benedict, a Sicilian friar (1526–1589) known as "The Holy Negro" who was canonized in 1807. The name is appropriate because St. Augustine had a St. Benedict Benevolent Society before the Civil War that black Catholics of the city began. The church's red-brick rectory, built in 1915 and home for many years to the Josephite Fathers of Baltimore, was visited by Dr. **Martin Luther King Jr.** in 1964.

St. Benedict the Moor Catholic Church is in the historic Lincolnville section of St. Augustine.

The third building and the one most in need of repair is a former school building, at first called St. Cecilia and later St. Benedict. Built in 1898, it is the oldest surviving brick schoolhouse in the city. Mother Katharine Drexel (1858–1955), a wealthy Philadelphia heiress who founded the Sisters of the Blessed Sacrament for Indians and Colored People, donated the building as one of sixty parochial schools she established in the United States. Pope John Paul II canonized her in 2000. The Sisters of St. Joseph, a teaching order that came from France in 1866, operated St. Benedict School. Three of the nuns, Sisters Mary Thomasine Hehir, Mary Scholastica, and Mary Beningus—nicknamed the Three Hail Marys—were arrested in 1916 for violating a recent Florida law that made it a criminal offense for whites to teach in a black school. They were released when a judge declared the law did not apply to parochial schools. The school finally closed in 1964, when the local Catholic schools were integrated, after teaching generations of children of different faiths there.

Another site in Lincolnville at 97 Martin Luther King Avenue recalls the days of discrimination. On the side of Smith's Store and Tony's Barber Shop is a sign that has been painted over: "Lincolnville Public Library." At a time when blacks were not allowed to enter the main public library in town, up to 1964 in fact, local people established the LINCOLNVILLE PUBLIC LIBRARY, which dates back to the 1940s. Its devoted librarian, Mrs. **Dorcas B. Sanders**, a widowed educator who had served as president of the Florida State PTA, encouraged reading and did her best under trying circumstances. Many of the books in that library had the notation "Gift of the St. Augustine Alliance of New York City," indicating that they were the gifts of a group of blacks who had gone north from Florida to seek better opportunities.

A local African American barber who went on to prosper elsewhere was **James English**, the husband of **Mary English**. James, born in 1816, was a free and educated African American who had a good business as a barber in St. Augustine, but after 1850 he moved to Key West, where he became a member of the school board and the first citizen of African descent elected to the County Commission (1868–77). (For more about him and his descendants see Chapter Forty-four.)

McMillan Street above S.R. 16 and crossing U.S. 1 honors **Alexander McMillan**, a former slave born in north Florida who made his way to St. Augustine in 1876. There he worked as a carpenter, gardener, farmer, janitor, and bellman, while he saved his money and bought up much property. In the 1920s, when the high price of property made more sense to sell the land, his property went on sale, but with the proviso from the white developers that "any white person over twenty" could have a chance to win a building lot in the McMillan Subdivision, but that it "should not be sold or resold to any member of the Negro race or any association of Negroes or to any to which they are entitled to membership." Despite those restrictions, Alexander McMillan and his family continued living there until his death in 1937 at age eighty-one. Later, the Floridian Motor Lodge was built on the site of McMillan's home, a former plantation house once owned by Florida historian George Fairbanks. McMillan's name on the street sign continues to honor him.

Beginning in 1979, the Lincoln Restoration and Development Commission sponsored a Lincolnville Festival with music, food, rides, tours, and other activities.

The SLAVE MARKET in the plaza near the cathedral became a focal point of the Civil Rights marches; despite the efforts of chamber-of-commerce types to deny it, the plaza had been a place where merchants sold slaves. The PONCE DE LEON MOTOR LODGE at 4000 U.S. 1 North was the place where authorities arrested seventy-two-year-old Mrs. Malcolm Peabody, mother of the governor of Massachusetts and a Civil Rights advocate, when she tried to obtain a meal while a member of an integrated group. In 2004, this major civil rights landmark was demolished by a Jacksonville developer.

The courtyard of the St. Augustine Historical Society Library on Aviles Street, the site of the old Public Library building, has a statue of Confederate General Edmund Kirby-Smith and Dr. **Alexander H. Darnes**, the first black doctor in Jacksonville. Although born a slave, Darnes served Kirby-Smith for years, then went on after the Civil War to study at Lincoln University in Pennsylvania and Howard University Medical School in Washington, DC. The statue, whose likeness was taken from photographs from his descendants in Jacksonville, has a Masonic watch fob (showing his membership in that order) and a medical bag with his name and address on it.

The WILLIE GALIMORE COMMUNITY CENTER at 399 S. Riberia Street is a recreational center that honors **Willie "The Wisp" Galimore**, a star athlete who had played basketball and football at St. Augustine's Excelsior High School. When he attended Florida A&M University in Tallahassee, he was a three-time All American in football.

He then went on to play for the Chicago Bears in the National Football League, during which time he led the Bears in scoring (1958) and in rushing (1961), averaged 4.45 yards per carry over six seasons, and tied a Bears' record by scoring four touchdowns in one game in 1957. He was killed in a car accident in 1964 at the age of twenty-nine. The Galimore Center that honors him was the site of a 1992 Freedom Fighters Appreciation Banquet held by the Black Heritage Commission, which local residents had organized in 1983. Men and women who had participated in the marches and sit-ins of the civil rights movement of the 1960s were honored.

Willie Galimore is one of only two black athletes honored in the St. Johns County Sports Hall of Fame, whose display case is in the entrance lobby of the County Auditorium. The other black athlete honored is **Otis Mason**, who is a member

of the Sports Hall of Fame as a baseball player at his alma mater, Florida A&M University in Tallahassee. He later served two terms as Superintendent of Schools in the 1980s and 1990s, the only black person ever elected to that post in St. Augustine. He is also honored in the naming of the OTIS A. MASON ELEMENTARY SCHOOL at 207 Mason Manatee Way.

The Florida School for the Deaf and the Blind at 207 San Marco Avenue educated many students since 1885. Its most famous alumnus is musician **Ray Charles** (1930–2004), who spent his early years in Greenville, Florida; when at the age of seven he began to go blind, his family sent him to the St. Augustine School for the Deaf and the Blind, where he learned to play the piano and prepared for a successful professional career.

Another prominent black musician who attended the school is **Marcus Roberts**.

Cary White Sr. (1900–1983) became the first black deaf graduate of the school when he finished his course of studies in 1922, after which he went to work for the school. After forty-six years of faithful service there as a carpenter, mason, electrician, and vocational teacher, he retired in 1968. In 1991, officials dedicated the CARY A. WHITE SR. COMPLEX in his honor. The plaque there gives his years as a student (1907–22) and member of the staff (1922–68) and the words: "Graduate, teacher and friend of FSDB. His entire life was dedicated to helping others." Tours can be arranged by calling (904) 823-4023.

EXCELSIOR HIGH SCHOOL built in 1925 on Martin Luther King Avenue was the first public high school for blacks in St. Augustine. After closing, it served as state offices and now looks forward to a new incarnation as a museum of black history. Among the people associated with the school are two that we should mention: **Solomon Calhoun** and **Willie Irvin**. Mr. Calhoun (1905–1989) grew up in Alabama, rising at 3:30 A.M. each day to milk the cows before going to school. He did not finish fifth grade until he was

Excelsior High School was the first public high school for blacks in St. Augustine.

fifteen. He finished high school at age twenty-one and went on to earn a bachelor's and master's degree at Florida A&M University in Tallahassee, where he was a star athlete and was selected in the 1930s as a *Pittsburgh Courier* All-American, the first from FAMU. He may, in fact, be the first All-American from St. Augustine. He would later be the principal of Excelsior High School.

Willie Irvin grew up in Lincolnville and graduated from Excelsior High School before playing for the Philadelphia Eagles in the National Football League in the 1950s. He is a member of the Sports Hall of Fame in Palm Beach County, Florida.

A black school that has since moved south is **FLORIDA MEMORIAL COLLEGE**, which was located two miles west of the city and originally called the Florida Normal and Industrial Institute. It was founded in Jacksonville in 1892 and long headed by **Nathan W. Collier**, a college classmate of **James Weldon Johnson**, and **Sarah Blocker**, a member of the Florida Women's Hall of Fame. In later years it combined with the Florida Baptist Institute, which had been established in Live Oak, Florida, in 1879. Workers built the St. Augustine campus in 1918 on the site of the Old Hanson Plantation, once operated by slave labor. When famed author **Zora Neale Hurston** taught at the school in 1942, she lived upstairs in a two-story house at 791 W. King Street, just east of the campus; a historic marker commemorates that stay.

Ms. Hurston finished her award-winning autobiography, *Dust Tracks on a Road*, while living there. The school finally closed its doors and moved to a new campus in Dade County in 1968. The only surviving remnant of the once-thriving campus is the entry gate—named for black insurance millionaire **A. L. Lewis**—at the corner of Holmes Boulevard and W. King Street.

Hurston had several other connections to St. Augustine. She married **Herbert Sheen** at what is now the Wachovia Bank parking lot downtown, then the location of the St. Johns County Courthouse. In 1929, she was a patient at the old East Coast Hospital, where the St. Augustine Police Department is now located.

To the west of the city in **WOODLAWN CEMETERY**, which is north of Evergreen Cemetery and King Street, lie some important African Americans in the history of St. Augustine. **Frank Butler**, who began Butler Beach (see below), is buried near the front of the cemetery. Back from him is the gravesite of Rev. **James Harvey Cooper**, head of the Presbyterian Parochial and Industrial School, also known as Cooper's School, which was located on Martin Luther King Avenue until it was torn down in 1940. Near that gravesite is one of **Cuter Eubanks**, who was arrested in 1964 at the Ponce de Leon Motor Lodge with the seventy-two-year-old mother of the governor of Massachusetts in actions that brought national attention to the civil rights movement in St. Augustine.

Near the cemetery entrance is the gravesite of Dr. **Nathan W. Collier** (1872–1941), long-time president of Florida Normal (later Florida Memorial) College, a black school in St. Augustine from 1918 until 1968. Nearby, in an unmarked grave, is the final resting place of **Sarah Blocker** (1857–1944), longtime vice president of the same school and Collier's fellow worker from 1896 on. In 1879, at the age of twenty-two, she established Florida Memorial College, one of the jewels of African American education in Florida. Collier-Blocker Junior College in Palatka honored them in its name (see Chapter Fifty-four). They had been buried on the campus of Florida Normal College, but were moved to Woodlawn Cemetery when the school relocated to Miami. Ms. Blocker is an inductee in the Florida Women's Hall of Fame in the Capitol building in Tallahassee.

Directions to the cemetery: Go west on King Street over the San Sebastian River. Turn north on Palmer Street, then left on Evergreen Avenue to Evergreen Cemetery, then around to Pearl Street, and right on Woodlawn Street to the cemetery up on the left.

Also in West St. Augustine is a street renamed in 2003 to Dr. **R. B. Hayling** Place, honoring the black dentist and NAACP representative from the historic subdivision of Lincolnville who was the extraordinary field general of the civil rights movement in St. Augustine. In 1963, he organized a campaign against local segregated public facilities that catered to tourists, and he asked White House officials not to support the four hundredth anniversary of the founding of St. Augustine, which was to take place in September 1965. When those efforts failed, he appealed to the Southern Christian Leadership Conference (SCLC) for help.

The SCLC invited volunteers from New England universities to demonstrate in the city in March 1964 and asked Lincolnville residents to provide food and lodging. At the end of the first week of protests, police had arrested hundreds of demonstrators, including a group of rabbis and the seventy-two-year-old mother of the governor of Massachusetts. White vigilantes harassed local businesses that served African Americans.

In June, Dr. **Martin Luther King Jr.** went to St. Augustine to take part in a sit-in at the Monson Motor Lodge, and baseball star **Jackie Robinson** addressed a civil rights rally in Lincolnville (see above). The publicity surrounding those activities helped lead to Congress's passage of the Civil Rights Act on June 20, 1964.

Dr. Hayling's home at 6 Dr. R. B. Hayling Place was shot up by Ku Klux Klansmen in 1963, killing the family dog and narrowly missing Mrs. Hayling. The street is located in the Rollins subdivision, south of King Street, running east from Whitney Street.

Among the important black entrepreneurs and civic leaders in Lincolnville was **Frank B. Butler** (1885–1973), the man who developed BUTLER BEACH on Anastasia Island southeast of St. Augustine, for many years the only beach that blacks could use in the area. Butler began his meat-grocery store, The Palace Market, in 1914 near the place where he lived a good part of his life: 87 Washington Street.

In the next decade he bought real estate west of the city in what became the College Park subdivision, where many blacks built homes. In 1925, he helped establish the College Park Realty Company. Two years later he bought enough land between the ocean and the Matanzas River to establish Butler Beach, the only beach for blacks south of American Beach on Amelia Island and north of Daytona Beach. Near the ocean several blacks bought lots, built houses, and set up businesses. Butler himself had a café with fourteen rooms to rent and a nearby motel where Dr. **Martin Luther King Jr.** and his associates stayed during his widely publicized visit to St. Augustine in 1964. 5718 Rudolph Avenue is the current address of

Frank Butler (on the right) had a grocery store and real estate business besides developing Butler Beach on Anastasia Island. *Florida State Archives*

the place where Dr. King stayed.

The street names in the area honored Butler's family: Mary Street (for his mother), Minnie Street (for his wife and daughter), Mae Street (for his daughter, Minnie Mae), Rudolph Street (for his grandson), and Gloria Street (for his granddaughter). In 1958, the state bought some of the land for a state park. Five years later Butler's company gave land near the Matanzas River for a children's recreation area. In 1980, it was changed from state to local operation and became the "Frank B. Butler County Park" in honor of this distinguished man. A Great Floridian marker at the building where he used to live, 87 Washington Street, honors him. State officials established the Great Floridian program in 1997 to recognize people who have made important contributions to Florida's history and culture.

In 2000 St. Augustine had a population of 2,303 blacks (20%) out of a total population of 11,692.

Switzerland

Near the town of Switzerland is Beluthahatchee Lake, named after an Indian word meaning "Nirvana on Water." Author **Zora Neale Hurston** suggested the name to its owner, Stetson Kennedy, after noting that the word comes from the Black Seminoles. The twenty-acre lake is part of a seventy-acre spread where one of Florida's most important writers has lived for several decades. Kennedy (1916–) has written about Florida (*Palmetto County* [1942], *Southern Exposure* [1946]) and the Ku Klux Klan (*Jim Crow Guide to the U.S.A.* [1959], *The Klan Unmasked* [1990]). In the 1930s, he worked on the *Florida Guide*, a WPA Writers Project, with such writers as Carita Doggett Corse and **Zora Neale Hurston**. Kennedy was an active supporter of the civil rights movement. In 2005, the Florida Communities Trust approved the creation of Beluthahatchee Park, a state park that includes Kennedy's home.

56.

St. Lucie County

The Florida Legislature established this county in 1844 and named it for St. Lucie of Syracuse in Sicily. The name came from that of a Spanish fort near Cape Canaveral in 1565.

St. Lucie County had a population of 192,695 in the 2000 census, 29,675 (15.4%) of whom were African Americans. Despite the significant number of African Americans, the county as a whole had a reputation for resisting integration. The result was that a third of its residents lacked a high school education and the unemployment figure was twelve percent or more in the 1990s, while the poverty level was as high as twenty percent.

Fort Pierce

Fort Pierce honors in its name President Franklin Pierce's brother, Lt. Col. Benjamin K. Pierce, who built a fort there on the Indian River in 1838 to fight against the Seminole Indians. In 1843, William Henry Peck arrived with several slaves to help his father settle the land under the Armed Occupation Act of 1842; that Act induced settlers to go to former Indian territory with the promise of 160-acre plots of land. The Pecks lasted only two years, after which the Indians drove them out by murdering some of the settlers. If any of the slaves stayed behind, they probably joined the Seminoles, who took them in and sometimes even made them members of their tribe.

After the Civil War, settlers moved back into the area and began to cultivate the land and fish the waters offshore. When insecticides began to control the mosquitoes and horseflies, more people moved there, attracted by the warm climate, fertile land, and rich fishing grounds. The railroad that Henry Flagler built along Florida's east coast brought even more people, including many black workers to build the line. The outlets to northern markets that the railroad opened up encouraged many farmers, including blacks, to till the land, especially in the cultivation of pineapples, which required a lot of field labor. The blacks that came to farm the pineapple crops stayed on to become part of the early Fort Pierce settlement.

Around 1900, black families began moving to the Fort Pierce area for the economic opportunities it offered. The first families were the **Boyds**, **Highs**, **Lyons**, and **Washingtons**. They tended to live on 8th or 9th Streets. An early church, St. Paul African Methodist Episcopal Church, burned down, possibly because local whites did not want the blacks to live in the section of town now known as Marvilla. The congregation then built a church on the northwest corner of 8th Street and Avenue B. In 1926, a hurricane destroyed that building, so the congregation began again. Some of the parishioners split off and began a new church in 1903: **MOUNT OLIVE MISSIONARY BAPTIST CHURCH**. Other early churches were **MOUNT MORIAH PRIMITIVE BAPTIST CHURCH** (1911), **GOODWILL PRESBYTERIAN CHURCH** (1921), **FIRST BETHEL MISSIONARY**

Mount Olive Missionary Baptist Church is one of the black churches in Fort Pierce.

BAPTIST CHURCH (1926), and **MOUNT PLEASANT PRIMITIVE BAPTIST CHURCH** (1944).

One of the most important schools in the African American community was **LINCOLN PARK ACADEMY**, which for many years was the only school for blacks between Titusville and West Palm Beach. The school was important because in 1921 there was no full, four-year high school south of Palatka. Florida did not have an accredited Negro high school, and the entire state had only eighteen African American students in the twelfth grade in the state's three four-year high schools.

In 1923, the new school opened in Fort Pierce as a junior high school under the principalship of James A. Espy. When the local African Americans pledged to raise money for a senior high school, local officials gave their approval for Lincoln Park Academy. When the academy was accredited in 1928, it was one of four Negro schools in the state, the others being in Gainesville, Palatka, and Pensacola. One of the school's later principals, Mr. **J. Griffen Greene**, became the founder and only president of Volusia County Community College in Daytona Beach (see Chapter Sixty-four).

The parents of the students wanted their children to have a strong education. They therefore lobbied for and received approval for a junior college for blacks, a facility that would be on the grounds of Lincoln Park Academy and would serve African Americans of Indian River, Martin, Okeechobee, and St. Lucie counties. **LINCOLN JUNIOR COLLEGE** was one of twelve black junior colleges in Florida. Established in 1959, the school had as its first president Dr. **Leroy Floyd**, who was also principal of Lincoln Park Academy. The enrollment figures, which included college parallel courses and vocational courses, for Lincoln Junior College were as follows:

1960–61: 98 students

1961–62: 98 students
1962–63: 234 students
1963–64: 386 students
1964–65: 667 students

In the mid-1960s, in an attempt to desegregate Indian River Junior College, state officials applied state accreditation standards so rigidly that county officials realized the county would have to spend a great deal of money to improve Lincoln Junior College or lose accreditation. They chose to integrate the white college and merged Lincoln with Indian River Junior College. As with other black colleges throughout the state, the black faculty of Lincoln were not dismissed outright from their jobs, but were placed as well as possible in the integrated college. For example, the president of Lincoln became the administrative dean of Indian River Junior College.

Among the local blacks who were "first" in something were **Ralph Flowers**, a former band director for Lincoln Park Academy who became an attorney and then was appointed the first black municipal judge in St. Lucie County; **Gloria Morgan Johnson**, the first black woman high school principal of a St. Lucie County high school: Fort

Pierce Central High School (1993); and **Queen Townsend**, the first black woman to be appointed acting superintendent of St. Lucie County schools (1996).

Writer **Zora Neale Hurston** (1901?–1960), who grew up in Eatonville, Florida (see Chapter Forty-eight) and went on to become a well-known novelist, folklorist, and anthropologist, lived in Fort Pierce while she worked as a reporter for a weekly black newspaper, **C. E. Bolen**'s *Fort Pierce Chronicle*, and while she wrote her novel, *Herod the Great*. In 1958, she also did substitute teaching at Lincoln Park Academy, the black public school of Fort Pierce.

Dr. **C. C. Benton**, a successful medical doctor who had sold ten acres of land to the school board for a new high school for blacks, in 1957 used some of that money to build rental houses. The houses on School Court Street, which took its name from the new school one block away, were alternately yellow or green, a color scheme that has not changed over the years, and were an attempt to provide affordable, clean, and safe housing for the poor. The green, one-story, concrete-block ZORA NEALE HURSTON HOUSE at 1734 School Court Street has two bedrooms, a bath-

The deteriorating concrete-block house at 1734 School Court Street in Fort Pierce is where Zora Neale Hurston lived.

room, kitchen, and front room. Hurston was the first tenant to live in the house, now a private residence. School Court Street is off N. 17th Street between Avenue L and Avenue K about three-quarters of a mile west of U.S. 1 and about one mile north of Orange Avenue in the northern part of the city. It is close to Lincoln Park Academy, now a multiracial high school that consistently ranks in the top twenty-five such schools in the country.

Dr. Benton was Hurston's physician, but even he could not prevent the deterioration of her health. A combination of high blood pressure, obesity, gall bladder attacks, and an ulcer contributed to a stroke she suffered in early 1959. In October of that year she entered the Saint Lucie County welfare home and, on January 28, 1960, died of hypertensive heart disease.

After she died, a neighbor went through her house, took out much of the contents, and began burning them in the yard. A black policeman who was driving by saw the fire, thought that some of the burning material should be preserved, and put out the fire with a garden hose. The papers that survived the fire, although some of them were scorched, including her work on a novel about Herod the Great, were donated to the Special Collections division of the University of Florida in Gainesville, where researchers can see them today.

She had once said, "If I happen to die without money somebody will bury me, though I do not wish it to be that way." Friends raised more than $400 for her burial; even the students for whom she had done substitute teaching raised some money. At the funeral the publisher of the black newspaper she had written for, C. E. Bolen, said, "Zora Neale went about and didn't care too much how she looked. Or what she said. Maybe people didn't think so much of that. But Zora Neale, every time she went about, had something to offer. She didn't come to you empty. They said she couldn't become a writer recognized by the world.

But she did it. The Miami paper said she died poor. But she died rich. She did something."

Her friends buried her in the city's segregated cemetery, the Garden of Heavenly Rest. For a long time the exact place of her burial was unmarked. Finally, in the summer of 1973, Pulitzer Prize-winning novelist **Alice Walker**, who wrote *The Color Purple*, went to Fort Pierce "Looking for Zora," as she titled a chapter in her book entitled *In Search of Our Mothers' Gardens*. Walker found the gravesite and placed a stone on it which reads:

ZORA NEALE HURSTON
"A GENIUS OF THE SOUTH"
1901—1960
NOVELIST, FOLKLORIST
ANTHROPOLOGIST

The **ZORA NEALE HURSTON BURIAL SITE** is near the street in the Garden of Heavenly Rest Cemetery, which is at the end of N. 17th Street and Avenue S just north of the house mentioned above where she lived.

Zora Neale Hurston's burial site is in the Garden of Heavenly Rest on 17th Street and Avenue S.

A plaque at the **DR. CLEM C. BENTON BUILD-ING**, 337 N. U.S. 1 in Fort Lauderdale honors the doctor who did much to help Zora Neale Hurston. Dr. **Clem Benton** (1898–1982) was born in

Orange County, Florida, graduated from Florida A & M College (now University) and Meharry Medical College in Nashville, Tennessee, and went to Fort Pierce in 1929, where he helped establish the Fort Pierce Memorial Hospital in 1937. He served on educational committees and was a trustee for Bethune–Cookman College, Daytona Beach, and the Indian River Community College of Fort Pierce. His civic, professional and humanitarian awards included the A. H. Robbins Citizenship Award from the Florida Medical Association in 1974.

A group of black artists worked out of Fort Pierce from the 1950s on. Called "The Highwaymen" because they sold their paintings from the back of their cars as they traveled the highways of Florida, they were part of a so-called Indian River school of painting. Having been taught the basics of painting by a white man, A. E. "Bean" Backus of Fort Pierce, the young black men learned quickly and were able to get out of the back-breaking work in citrus groves and packing houses. Their paintings have become popular with collectors and with the publication of a book about them: Gary Monroe's *The Highwaymen: Florida's African-American Landscape Painters*. Several Florida Highwaymen paintings can be found at the A. E. "Bean" Backus Museum & Gallery at 500 N. Indian River Drive in Fort Pierce. Phone: (772) 465-0630.

Among the blacks who were elected to office in the city were **Jackie Caynon**, the first elected to the Fort Pierce City Commission (1967); **Havert "Coach" Fenn**, the second black elected to the City Commission (1979); **Gertrude Walker**, the first black woman to be a supervisor of elections in Florida (1984); and **Samuel Gaines**, the first and only black elected to the St. Lucie County School Board.

The 2000 census indicated that Fort Pierce had 15,326 African Americans or 41% of the total town population of 37,516.

57.

Santa Rosa County

Florida's twenty-first county was established in 1842 and named for Santa Rosa Island, which in turn was named for St. Rosa de Viterbo, a Catholic saint.

Santa Rosa County had a population of 117,743 in the 2000 census, 4,945 (4.2%) of whom were African Americans. That percentage (4.2%) is the fourth-lowest among all Florida counties.

Bagdad

This small town in Santa Rosa County one mile south of Milton may have been named after the ancient city of Baghdad or the Bagdad of the *Arabian Nights* because both places lie between two rivers on a grassy peninsula. The name may seem strange for a small town in Florida's Panhandle, but, as famous aviator Jacqueline Cochran wrote in her autobiography, *The Stars at Noon*, "Bagdad, Florida, which was my home for about two years, was not like the ancient capital of Persia. But on second thought, maybe it was because I have been to modern Persia and had a look around and for the ordinary folk it leaves almost everything to be desired."

The Florida town, which is between the Escambia and Blackwater Rivers, developed from a nineteenth-century lumber company that relied on slaves to cut trees and work in the mill on Pond Creek. Before the Civil War those slaves cut and processed the yellow pine lumber and worked in the cotton fields under very difficult circumstances. Insects, diseases like yellow fever, and poor living conditions contributed to the death of many of those workers, but after the Civil War the situation improved somewhat and former slaves were able to own their homesteads and raise their families on their own land.

The plight of the blacks worsened whenever local vigilante groups took justice into their own hands. Jacqueline Cochran later reported one such tragic incident: "Once when I was quite a small child I noticed a crowd of men going off into the woods with a Negro prisoner and I tagged along out of curiosity. The Negro was tied to a tree, wood was put all around him and after being sprinkled with kerosene it was set on fire. I was too young then to have any great feeling about the injustice or the loss of life, but I took away from that scene the very bad memory of the odor of burning flesh."

One site of importance to blacks today is the NEW PROVIDENCE MISSIONARY BAPTIST CHURCH at 4512 Church Street, one of the oldest churches in Santa Rosa County and the first church built in the county by and for the black community. **Emanuel** and **Delphia Jackson** donated the land for a church in 1874, and the sons of pastor Rev. **John Kelker Sr.** helped build it. Local residents used the original church structure as a schoolhouse because the area had no public school. The present-day wood-frame building, which was built in 1901, was moved to its present site in 1989 to serve as a community center and museum about the history of the area. The nearby shotgun-style house is an example of the housing

New Providence Missionary Baptist Church is one of the oldest churches in Santa Rosa County.

the Bagdad Land and Lumber Company provided for its white workers.

The 2000 census indicated that Bagdad had 203 African Americans or 14% of the total town population of 1,490.

Directions: Bagdad lies one mile south of Milton and about one mile north of I-10. To reach the church from I-10, take exit 8, drive north 1.8 miles on C.R. 191. Turn left onto Church Street in Bagdad; the church is 1/10 mile on the right, at the corner of Church and Bushnell Streets. If you are coming from Milton, drive 1.5 miles south on C.R. 191; turn right on Bushnell Street and go one block to the church.

Milton

This town on U.S. 90, twenty miles east of Pensacola was named after Governor John Milton of Florida or a local pioneer or was a contraction of Milltown; in any case, the name is definitely more refined than its former names: Scratch Ankle and Hard Scrabble. The town had a good location since it was on the Blackwater River, at the terminus of an old Indian and trading trail, and in the center of a forested area of long-leaf yellow pine, all of which made it a good trading and shipbuilding site. Milton became the county seat of Santa Rosa County in 1843, two years before Florida entered the United States as a slave state (1845).

The 2000 census indicated that Milton had 1,124 African Americans or 16% of the total town population of 7,045.

MOUNT PILGRIM AFRICAN BAPTIST CHURCH on the northwest corner of the intersection of Clara and Alice Streets, one block west of Canal Street and one block south of U.S. 90, is Florida's only identified work of **Wallace A. Rayfield**, one of the most important black architects in the South in the early twentieth century. Rayfield was born in Georgia in 1874, educated at Howard University in Washington, D.C., and at Pratt Institute in Brooklyn, N.Y., trained in architecture at Tuskegee Institute in Alabama, and worked in Birmingham, Alabama, specializing in designing churches, especially Baptist and African Methodist Episcopal Zion ones. Mount Pilgrim African Baptist Church in Milton was the first of his buildings outside of Birmingham to be listed on the National Register.

The church property includes the entire block bounded by Alice, Ann, Mary, and Clara Streets. The history of the church began in 1845, when the First Baptist Church of Milton was established; four years later the church had a membership of eighty-three whites and thirty-three blacks. Some of those black members may have been slaves on a nearby plantation owned by Jackson Morton, who owned 118 slaves in 1830 and by 1860 was among the one hundred largest slave-holders in Florida. In 1866, black members of First Baptist Church established Mount Pilgrim African Baptist Church. In 1880, church members bought property on Canal Street and built a frame church.

When membership continued to increase, the church trustees bought more land on Clara Street in 1911. When their 1880 church building burned down in 1916, the congregation built another church on Clara Street under the leadership of the Rev. **King David Britt**. At that time the building was the only brick church in Santa Rosa County.

Directions: To reach the church from I-10, take exit 8 and drive north 3.3 miles through Bagdad (see above) on C.R. 191. Turn left at Alice Street and go one block to Clara Street. The church is on the northwest corner of the intersection.

Mount Pilgrim African Baptist Church in Milton is Florida's only identified work of Wallace A. Rayfield, one of the most important black architects in the South in the early twentieth century.

58.
Sarasota County

Florida's sixtieth county was established in 1921 with a name that may come from Spanish for "place for dancing" (in reference to the Native American celebrations which the Spanish saw) or from the name of the daughter of Hernando de Soto or a Spanish lady (spelled Sara Sota).

Sarasota County had a population of 325,957 in the 2000 census, 13,690 (4.2%) of whom were African Americans. That percentage (4.2%) is the fourth-lowest among all Florida counties.

Laurel

The unincorporated town of Laurel south of Sarasota and north of Venice has the **Johnson Chapel Missionary Baptist Chapel** on the east side of Church Street. The structure is the only remaining rural church in the southern part of the county. Dating back to the 1910s, the chapel was built in 1915 by Bertha Potter Palmer as the Osprey Missionary Baptist Church and used to be on the west side of the Tamiami Trail in Osprey north of Laurel. When people there built a new church in 1947, they moved this one-story, wood-frame vernacular building to its present site. Since then, it has served as a church, community center, and meeting site for the Lilly White Lodge #22, an African American association that provides health care and burial benefits.

Sarasota

For many centuries before white people came to Sarasota, Indian tribes like the Timucuans and Calusas lived there. Whites did not come into the area to settle until around 1842. After the Civil War ended in 1865, more and more people moved to the area, including colonists from Scotland. The railroad, which black workers helped build, arrived in 1903, after which more and more people came to stay. John Ringling arrived in 1911 and later brought the circus and established a beautiful museum of art in 1927. The city grew rapidly and has continued to attract new residents because of its setting, cultural attractions, and mild climate.

In 2000, Sarasota had a population of 8,167 blacks (16%) out of a total population of 50,978.

The first black settler in the area was **Lewis** (or **Louis**) **Colson**, who helped survey the town of Sarasota in the late 1800s and who worked as a fisherman, land owner, and minister. More black families followed, and in 1899 **Lewis** and **Irene Colson** organized the city's first African American church, Bethlehem Baptist Church, in which Reverend Lewis Colson ministered to the people until around 1918. Later other residents, including **F. H. Haynes**, **C. H. Murphy**, **Campbell Mitchell**, and **Leonard Reid**, organized the AME Church.

Among the **Colson** children who grew up in Sarasota and prospered were **John H.** (or J. Hamilton or Hamp), who was a drayman and laborer; **James**, a waiter and laborer; **David**, a cement worker; **Ida**, a domestic worker; and **Toney** (or Tony), a fish dealer who owned and operated Colson Fish Market at 423 N. Lemon Avenue. Colson Avenue between U.S. 301 and Tuttle Avenue, east of Sarasota, honors Lewis Colson; he and his wife, Irene, are buried in ROSEMARY CEMETERY at 833 Central Avenue.

In the first quarter of the twentieth century more and more black workers came to Sarasota from the Carolinas and Georgia to work in the booming construction business. Many worked on Charles Ringling's ten-story hotel and causeway. As the city grew, the black community expanded to the north, and NEWTOWN replaced the original municipal residential area that had included Black Bottom. Later known as OVERTOWN, Black Bottom was within the area of 10th and 5th Streets on the north and south, and U.S. 41 and Orange Avenue on the west and east. Overtown had small shops, social facilities, and religious centers such as its first house of worship, Bethlehem Baptist Church. A historical marker on Central Avenue at 6th Street commemorates this first black community in the town.

Among the early black residents were **John** and **Sally Mays**, **Willis** and **Sophia** (or **Sophie**) **Washington**, **Thomas Henry "Mott"** and **Josie Washington** (who operated the Josie Grocery Store at 236 12th Street), **Leonard** and **Eddye Reid** (both of whom helped found in 1906 the city's second oldest black church, Payne Chapel AME Methodist Church; Leonard Reid Avenue one block east of U.S. 301 and north of 27th Street honors him), **Wright** and **Emma Bush** (who lived at 1723 27th Street), and **Edward** and **Rose Carmichael** (who owned and operated the Royal Palm Pressing Club on 12th Street; Carmichael Avenue east of U.S. 301 and south of 27th Street honors the family).

The LEONARD REID HOME at 1435 7th Street, built in 1926 on Coconut Avenue but later moved to its present site, was the home of **Leonard Reid**, who helped establish the city's first African American community, Overtown. Born **Leonard Sproles** in Greenwood, South Carolina, in 1881, he later took the last name of his stepfather. After studying and working in Savannah, Georgia, he met Colonel Hamilton Gillespie, a Sarasota developer and its first mayor. He worked with Gillespie until the latter's death in 1923, then continued buying land and, with his wife, **Eddye**, helped establish Payne Chapel AME Methodist Church and supported such organizations as the Odd Fellows, the Household of Ruth #3538, and the Knights of Pythias. He died in 1952, and his wife in 1970. The building now houses the Leonard Reid Learning Academy, a child-care center for minority children.

Before residents could establish a black school, **Josie Washington** taught students in her home. In 1912, trustees **Wright Bush**, **Ed Carmichael**, **J. P. Carter**, **Elbert Clark**, **Henry Clark**, **J. H. Glover**, **John Mays**, **Campbell Mitchell**, and **John Woods** established a public school, which became BOOKER SCHOOL after its longtime principal, **Emma E. Booker**. She had begun teaching blacks in Sarasota public schools in 1910, and eight years later became principal of Sarasota Grammar School, which held its classes in rented halls. For twenty years she attended college during the summers and finally earned her bachelor's degree in 1937. Because the Julius Rosenwald Fund helped fund the building of a school, which opened in 1924–25 with eight grades, at present-day 7th Street and Lemon Avenue, many people referred to it as the Rosenwald School. Under the guidance of principal **J. R. Dixon**, the school added more grades, and the first senior class of Booker High School graduated in 1935.

The first four students to graduate from Booker in 1935 were: **Annie Blue-McElroy** (see page 258); **Marthenia Riley**, who became a Sarasota teacher; **A. L. Williams**, who became a successful insurance executive in Philadelphia; and **Nacomia Williams**, one of the first black registered nurses in Sarasota County and one of

Booker School was named after a teacher who had taught many African American children in Sarasota public schools.

the first black nurses to work at Sarasota Memorial Hospital. The paintings of them and of the first five principals of Booker School, all done by 1999 graduate **Emanuel Williams Jr.**, are in the school's Gallery of Distinguished Black Educators and Alumni.

Early schools for black children in Sarasota and throughout Florida usually meant inadequate supplies, a school term lasting less than the nine months of the white schools, and teacher salaries that lagged behind those of white teachers. The dedication of the teachers to further the education of their pupils despite the poor facilities encouraged youngsters to do well in school.

As the black community expanded into the Newtown area south of the Whitfield Estates subdivision, residents saw the need for schools. In 1939, **BOOKER HIGH SCHOOL** and the Rosenwald building were relocated to a site near the present school and adjoining an elementary school. By the late 1940s, under the guidance of principal **Roland Rogers**, the Booker Grammar School was moved to its present site and the School Board of Sarasota County consolidated schools on the Newtown campus. The school received official ac-

creditation and new buildings were constructed. In 1988, the Sarasota County Historical Commission put up a plaque outside the Booker School to commemorate Emma Booker. The school and marker are at Orange Avenue at 35th Street, north of Dr. Martin Luther King Jr. Way and east of Indian Beach.

One of the school's teachers who became important in black education in several Florida sites was **Gilbert Porter**. He later served as teaching principal at Tivoli High School in DeFuniak Springs, as the principal of Tallahassee's Lincoln High, as the executive secretary of the Florida State Teachers Association (FSTA, a black teachers' organization), and as special assistant to the deputy superintendent. Gilbert Porter Elementary School at 15851 SW 112th Street in Miami honors him. (For more about him see Chapter Thirty-six.) While he worked for $50 a month as a science teacher and coach at Booker High School in Sarasota, the school lasted only five-and-a-half months and then had to close because it had no money. It has since reopened. Porter was one of the first blacks in the state to earn a Ph.D. and to receive a Rockefeller Foundation Fellowship as a public school administrator. He is also the co-author of *The History of the Florida State Teachers Association.*

The Booker High School organization called Leaving a Legacy honors its graduates and past principals by naming sites on the campus for them. For example, a literacy center in the school's media center honors the valedictorian of Booker High School's first graduating class (1935), **Annie Blue-McElroy**. After high school, she graduated from Bethune-Cookman College and spent forty-two years teaching in Sarasota County schools before retiring in 1980. She is the author of *But Your World and My World*, a history of Sarasota's black community over one hundred years. Governor Bob Graham appointed her to the Council on Distinguished Black Floridians in 1985.

The school's theater has the **Anthony B. "Tony" Major** Rehearsal Hall, named after a 1957 graduate who had a distinguished career in film, television, and theater. The school's gymnasium has the **Howard E. Porter** Hall of Champions, which honors a 1967 graduate who helped the Booker Tornadoes win the Florida Interscholastic Athletic Association (FIAA) Class-A State Basketball Championship, was a three-time All-American at Villanova University, and played in the National Basketball Association for seven years with the Chicago Bulls, New York Knicks, and Detroit Pistons.

One of the students who attended all-black schools on the north side of Sarasota, **Fredd Atkins**, was part of a 1979 lawsuit charging that the city's election system was discriminatory by making it hard for the city's large black community to be represented on the City Commission. The court agreed, and by 1985 city officials instituted a new election system that took into account representation from the city's north side, including the predominantly black Newtown community. Atkins became the city's first elected black commissioner and then the city's first black mayor.

The **GROVER AND PEARL KOONS HOUSE** at 1360 13th Street, occupied by **Grover** and **Pearl Koons** between 1927 and 1930, houses the **FLORIDA ACADEMY OF AFRICAN AMERICAN CULTURE**, which **Ruby Woodson** helped establish with an extensive library and resources about the history and accomplishments of African Americans in the United States. Open for tours; phone: (941) 360-0993.

The inside of the Grover and Pearl Koons House has artifacts and exhibits as part of the Florida Academy of African American Culture.

59.
Seminole County

The Florida Legislature established this county in 1913 by splitting off part of Orange County and named it for that tribe of Native Americans who lived throughout the state.

Seminole County had a population of 365,196 in the 2000 census, 34,694 (9.5%) of whom were African Americans.

The first African Americans to arrive in the area probably came to work on the railroad around 1885. In 1886, they built the first railroad bridge over the St. Johns River, a 3,500-foot-long drawbridge called the Thrasher Ferry Railroad Bridge, which helped link Jacksonville with Tampa. The bridge was in a location similar to today's railroad bridge over the river at that point. The Orange Belt Railway Company built a depot called Monroe Station near the bridge. Another black settlement nearby was Goldsboro.

The men who worked on the railroad and who later settled down in the area often became citrus growers, until back-to-back freezes in 1894–95 wiped out the citrus groves. The men then turned to vegetable growing, which did much better. The nearby railroad enabled the growers to ship out their produce, as well as the lumber produced from the pine forests there. Cutting timber and collecting turpentine provided jobs for a number of the black families near Monroe Station. A large turpentine camp was located where Heathrow is today, southwest of Bookertown and just west of I-4.

In 1889, white grower David Rabun established the first school in Monroe for eighteen children of black farm workers, but its location is not known. Having such a school would have been an incentive for the black families to remain

in the area. Rabun later helped establish Bookertown.

Most of the workers who worked in the celery fields were black, and they did well in the picking and processing. The blacks also helped install a sub-irrigation system of clay tiles that helped the water reach the roots of the plants directly beneath the soil.

A white storekeeper by the name of Ahearn tried to change the name of the town to Ahearn, but the blacks and others continued using Monroe. Officially, the U.S. post office called the town Lake Monroe, but locals continued to refer to it as Monroe. It became the "mother community" from which Bookertown emerged.

Monroe's first African American church was the **PROVIDENCE MISSIONARY BAPTIST CHURCH**, organized in 1917 and located at 4561 Douglas Street in Sanford. A few years later, a white farmer, Charlie Henry, donated land on Narcissus Avenue for a new church building, and it moved there to be Monroe's first permanent black church. Later, a one-room schoolhouse for black children was built nearby. It opened in 1919 as Monroe's first official African American school with Martha Scrovon from Sanford the first teacher. Children went to school in the daytime, and their parents went at night to learn to read and write and to become better educated. Today, the site of the school and church is a modern apartment complex east of White Cedar Road between Narcissus Avenue and State Road 46.

Bookertown

The small town of Bookertown to the west-northwest of Sanford, which traces its beginnings to a 1926 survey and platting of the settlement, honors the first name of famed educator/reformer **Booker T. Washington**. Some think that settlers chose his first name because other towns had already used his last name, and the use of his last name might have some people think the name was honoring the first president of the United States. The street names honor black personages like **Richard Allen** (founder of the African Methodist Episcopal Church), Rev. **Castle Brewer** (a Baptist leader), **Frederick Douglass** (African American abolitionist and reformer), **W. E. B. Dubois** (civil rights leader), and **Paul Lawrence Dunbar** (novelist).

In 1926, residents established the first official black school, which is today a community center. At first, the school had one large room divided into two sections for the teaching of grades one through six. Behind the school was a long-handled pump for water and two outhouses, one for boys and one for girls. Because the school did not have a lunchroom, the students brought their own lunch each day.

Charlie Colson and Charlie Morgan have written a very useful book, *Bookertown: A Journey to the Past*, that describes Bookertown, Monroe, and the settling of the area by the ancestors of many of Seminole County's present citizens.

Sanford

This city on the St. Johns River began during the Indian wars as a settlement around a military encampment, Camp Monroe. The site changed its name to Fort Mellon, then Mellonville, and finally Sanford after its developer, General Henry Sanford. Long before General Sanford came to the area, the Legislative Council had established Mosquito County from St. Johns County in 1824, three years after the U.S. gained control of Florida from Spain. In those early days several blacks lived there as slaves of either the white settlers or of the Indians. As federal forces defeated the Indians, more and more settlers moved into the area. In 1860, General Sanford visited the area and liked it so much that he made plans to return. In 1870, this former minister to Belgium laid out the town that would later honor him in its name. After laying out a 100-acre orange grove and finding that labor was scarce in the area, he brought in from Madison sixty black workers for clearing and tilling the land; local white people, incensed at his attempt to bring in blacks to what they considered "white man's country," drove them out with gunfire after killing one and wounding a half-dozen others.

When General Sanford later brought in more black workers, he established west of Mellonville the black neighborhood of GEORGETOWN, where his workers lived. Protected from further acts of overt violence and separated from the rest of the town by a body of water, Georgetown developed on its own. Its boundaries were 2nd Street, Mellonville Avenue, Celery Avenue, and Sanford Avenue. The black workers and their families, as well as those in GOLDSBORO, another African American community in the northern part of the county, worked in the fields, ran the steamboats, and labored on the docks of the growing Sanford town. They also opened up businesses to serve their communities.

One successful business was the Eichelberger Funeral Home, originally situated at Ninth Street and Locust Avenue.

The devastating fire of 1887 and the freezes of 1894–95 slowed down the growth of Sanford, but farmers began growing celery, making the town "Celery Capital of the United States" in the early 1900s. Many of the black workers who worked in the celery fields lived in a settlement called Cameron City.

In 2000 Sanford had 9,225 blacks (29%) out of a total population of 32,387.

Schools for blacks suffered from the deprivations of segregation. The school year for black students was shorter than that for white students, and parents had to buy books and supplies for their children. The first school for blacks, the **GEORGETOWN SCHOOL**, was at the northeast corner of 7th Street and Cypress Avenue; its principal was Mr. **McLester**, and his assistant was Miss **Hampton.** Later Mr. **Reed** and then Mr. **J. N. Crooms** served as principal. Construction on the school was finished in 1887.

Another school, **HOPPER ACADEMY** at 1101 S. Pine Avenue, was built between 1900 and 1910 on land that white people of Sanford donated. Originally an elementary school, it became Sanford High School for black students when it moved to a new site, but was later replaced by Crooms Academy. It has been restored as a community center

Hopper Academy became Sanford High School for black students.

The **ST. JAMES AFRICAN METHODIST EPIS-COPAL CHURCH** at 819 Cypress Avenue traces its beginnings to 1867, when a group of Christians began having prayer services in an old house on Mellonville Avenue. Several years later the group bought some land and moved their services to the new site. Their first pastor, Rev. **S. H. Coleman**, helped construct at Ninth Street and Cypress Avenue a small, frame church, St. James Mission, and they became part of the East Florida Annual Conference in 1880. The church's next pastor, Rev. **T. T. Gaines**, joined the church to the newly formed South Florida Conference and built a larger church. Under the pastorate of Rev. **W. H. Brown** the congregation built the new, red-brick building in 1913. During the subsequent pastorates of **R. E. Harton**, **G. J. Oates Jr.**, **C. E. Standifer**, **R. A. Thigpen**, and **K. D. White Jr.**, the congregation grew to several hundred parishoners.

Other early black churches included **ST. PAUL BAPTIST CHURCH** at 813 Pine Avenue, founded in 1878 in a bush arbor in Georgetown by the pioneer African American families in the Sanford area. **ZION HOPE MISSIONARY BAPTIST CHURCH**, organized on Mellonville Avenue in 1888, was moved from a bush arbor to 5th Street and Locust Avenue and finally to its present site at 710 Orange Avenue. **TRINITY METHODIST CHURCH**, which used to be Trinity Methodist Episcopal, was founded in 1880. The **ST. JOHN MISSIONARY BAPTIST CHURCH** at 920 Cypress Avenue dates from 1888. Also **Lawrence Williams**, **Terrell Johnson**, and **Richard McPherson** founded in Georgetown a mutual-aid society, The Friendship and Union, to support members in sickness and

The father of famed writer Zora Neale Hurston lived in this house in Sanford.

to help families in case of death.

The **JOHN M. HURSTON HOUSE** at 621 E. 6th Street was the home of the father of famed writer **Zora Neale Hurston**. The 1910 U.S. census showed the Hurstons in Sanford. After his wife, **Lucy**, had died, **John Hurston** married **Mattie** around 1905. The house today is a private residence.

Another private residence, at 611 Locust Avenue, was the home of Dr. **George H. Starke**, a black doctor who treated the sick of Sanford, both black and white, for fifty-one years. Shortly after he opened his practice in Sanford in 1927, Harvard University accepted him for a residency at Massachusetts General Hospital in Boston, one of only four black doctors to be accepted. He returned to Sanford in 1933 and practiced medicine until he died at the age of eighty. He was the first black doctor to become a member of the Florida Medical Association and the Seminole County Medical Association and the second in the American Medical Association. In 1977, city officials named a park and picnic area at 1501 West 3rd Street after him.

The **TAJIRI SCHOOL OF PERFORMING ARTS AND ACADEMICS** in Sanford provides academic tutoring, an entrepreneurial training program, and a performing arts program for children ages 3–17 years. The school's mission is to foster education, self-respect, self-discipline and self-worth through an integration of educational programs. The school, which began in 1912, features "Sanford Out of the Dust: History Still/History Alive," a tour of important sites in the area related to African American history. Phone: (407) 324-9140.

Finally, one negative in the town's baseball history was the bad experience there of **Jackie Robinson**, the first black player in major league baseball. **Arthur Ashe Jr.** reported that in 1946 Branch Rickey, the president of the Brooklyn Dodgers and the man who signed Robinson to play in the majors, "moved the entire Dodger pre-season camp from Sanford, Florida, to Daytona Beach due to the oppressive conditions of Sanford."

The Tajiri School of Performing Arts and Academics has exhibits of important sites in the area related to African American History.

60.
Sumter County

The Florida Legislature established this county in 1853 and named it for General Thomas Sumter (1736–1832) of South Carolina, an important officer in the southern campaigns of the American Revolutionary War. Many people from South Carolina had settled in the area in the nineteenth century.

Sumter County had a population of 53,345 in the 2000 census, 7,362 (13.8%) of whom were African Americans.

Bushnell

On December 28, 1835, two events happened that started the bloody Second Seminole War (1835–42). Outside Fort King, near Ocala, Indians killed an Indian agent and a lieutenant. Further south, two miles north of present-day Bushnell in Sumter County, Seminole Indians ambushed and killed Major Francis Dade and 107 soldiers; only three soldiers and one interpreter, a black man, from the two companies survived. For the next seven years the U.S. Army fought a long, bloody war to remove the Seminoles from Florida.

The black survivor of what became known as the Dade Massacre was **Luis Pacheco**, who had acted as an interpreter with the Indians for Major Dade. Pacheco (1800–1895) was born a slave on a plantation south of Jacksonville, but had learned to read and write from the daughter of his master and therefore became more valuable to his masters; he also learned some of the Seminole language. Once after visiting his wife, a former slave who had purchased her freedom, he was caught in Tampa and sold to the first of several military commanders. When Major Dade and his soldiers headed out of Tampa to march north, Pacheco went along as an interpreter who could communicate with the Seminoles, whose language he had learned as a youth.

After the Indians killed Major Dade, they spared Pacheco because of his dark color and took him with them on various missions. Because he joined or was forced to accompany the Indians after the battle, some whites accused him of having aided the Indians in setting their ambush for Major Dade's troops, but no proof exists that Pacheco collaborated with the Indians. However, he did accompany the Indians when they were sent out west to reservations by the federal government. Fifty-seven years after the Dade Massacre, Pacheco made his way to Jacksonville and located the woman who had taught him to read and write. He took her name, Fatio, and remained with her until he died in 1895.

Among those who wrote about the war and the terrible treatment of the Seminoles by the federal government was **Albery Allson Whitman** (1851–1901), a black born into a slave family in Kentucky. He wrote a 95-page work called *The Rape of Florida* (1884; republished in 1885 as *Twasinta's Seminoles*). Stanza VI of this poem describes how the slaves escaped from Georgia plantations into the Great Wahoo swamp and waited there until the Seminoles came along to take them to freedom in Florida:

The sable slave, from Georgia's utmost
    bounds,
Escapes for life into the Great Wahoo.
Here he has left afar the savage hounds
And human hunters that did late pursue;
There in the hommock darkly hid from
    view,
His wretched limbs are stretched awhile
    to rest,
Till some kind Seminole shall guide him
    thro',
To where by hound nor hunter more dis
    trest,
He, in a flow'ry home, shall be the red
    man's guest.

A museum and battlefield plaques at the **DADE BATTLEFIELD STATE HISTORIC SITE** tell the story of that ambush and the war that followed, the most brutal and expensive American Indian war in our history. The bodies of the slain soldiers were not buried by federal troops until February 20, 1836.

In 1842, troops removed the bodies of the fallen warriors and reburied them with honors in St. Augustine, just as the Second Seminole War was ending.

Part of the reason why some people thought that Luis Pacheco had collaborated with the Seminoles may have been the fact that blacks had often associated with the Indians and been accepted into their tribes. When runaway slaves from Southern plantations reached Florida in the eighteenth and nineteenth centuries, they sometimes joined the Seminoles, intermarried with them, and joined them in the fight against those who would send the slaves to plantations and the Seminoles to Western reservations.

The Black Seminoles, who had learned English on the plantations, acted as interpreters between the Indians and the whites. When the federal government forced many Seminoles to move to Oklahoma, many Black Seminoles went with them and worked as scouts for the U.S. Army. One of the Florida-born Black Seminoles, **Adam**

The Dade Battlefield State Historic Site is where a black scout managed to survive a massacre by Native Americans.

Paine, received the Medal of Honor for showing great courage in a battle with the Comanche Indians in Texas in 1874. (For more about the Black Seminoles see the section on Kettle Island below).

The site near Bushnell, Florida, about two miles southeast of I-75, is open daily, 8 A.M. until sundown. Phone: (904) 793-4781.

1,998 people lived in Bushnell in 2000, of whom 329 (17%) were black.

Kettle Island

On a small island located on the Sumter County side of the Withlacoochee River archaeologists have unearthed remains of a former settlement of Black Seminoles. There on Boggy Island (present-day Kettle Island) in the early nineteenth century, when the United States was taking control of Florida from Spain, the Seminole Indians retreated into isolated areas to escape the federal forces and to settle down with their families. In order to raise crops that would supplement their fishing and hunting, the Seminoles came to rely on those runaway slaves who had joined them. Having worked on coastal plantations in the Carolinas and Georgia and having learned some technology from their American and European owners, those ex-slaves were able to join forces with the Seminoles for their mutual survival.

Some of the blacks settled in the remoteness of the Withlacoochee Cove on Boggy Island. Having learned the languages of the whites and the Seminoles, the blacks were able to act as interpreters between the two groups. Federal forces finally drove the Indians and blacks away in order to make the area more open for white settlers.

Others blacks settled twelve miles south of Okahumpka in the town of Pilaklikaha, which was between the present-day towns of Bevilles Corner and Center Hill just east of Bushnell, near where Dade's Massacre took place (see the section on Bushnell above). Archaeologist Terrance Weik has done research in the fields there in what came to be known as Abraham's Town or Pilaklikaha. The settlement lasted for about a generation before General Abraham Eustis burned it down in the 1830s. Abraham's Town, named after a former slave of a doctor in Pensacola, was one of several areas of refuge in Florida that escaped slaves established in the seventeenth and eighteenth centuries. **Abraham** and his Seminole spouse, the widow of Chief Bowlegs, governed the town

The issue of the blacks and Seminoles was one of the most contentious in the nineteenth century. White slave-owners were rightly fearful that runaway slaves would gravitate to the Seminoles, even if the latter kept them as slaves, because the Seminole slavery system was much more lenient than was that of the whites. Historian George Klos likened the Seminole slave system to tenant farming. The black slaves lived apart from the Indians, in their own villages, and could have their own horses, cows, and hogs. Once the blacks learned the language of the Native Americans, they could serve as interpreters in dealing with whites and further increase their standing. Some of them became trusted advisers of the Seminole leaders.

Many Southern whites pressed for removal of the Indians to the West, not because of a lack of land in Florida—there was, in fact, more than enough land for whites and Indians—but rather as a way to eliminate safe havens for escaping slaves. Only when Major General Thomas Jesup allowed the blacks to go with the Seminoles on their removal to the West, rather than being returned to slavery with their former masters, did the Seminole Indian Wars come to an end.

Directions: Kettle Island is not easily reached by car. The island is located on the Sumter County side of the Withlacoochee River, about four miles west of the southern part of Lake Panasoffkee and about eight miles northwest of Bushnell.

61.

Suwannee County

The Florida Legislature established this county in 1858 and named it after the nearby river that composer Stephen Foster immortalized in "The Swanee River (Old Folks at Home)," the state song. Suwannee County had a population of 34,844 in the 2000 census, 4,216 (12.1%) of whom were African Americans

Live Oak

This town in Suwannee County has had a checkered history of black-white relations. In the 1850s, settlers arriving in the area began petitioning the Florida Legislature to establish a new county, which finally happened in 1858. One of the first legal documents entered into the records of the new county was the transfer of title to a male slave; the slave's owners, Margaret and John Demere, sold **Adam** for $1200. The county's first census of 1860 listed 1,467 whites, 835 slaves, and only one free black. By the end of the Civil War in 1865 all of the blacks were freed. Many of them stayed in the area because the Suwannee Valley region had rich soil to grow tobacco and cotton. By 1893, the town also had a black, **Thomas Harris**, as postmaster.

In 2000, Live Oak, the county seat of Suwannee County, had a population of 6,480, of whom 2,440 (38%) were African American.

One might-have-been for the town was the plan to establish **BROWN THEOLOGICAL INSTITUTE** there after the Civil War. In 1870, the African Methodist Episcopal Church of Florida planned to build the school in Live Oak for the newly freed slaves on 640 acres of land donated by friends of the church. The marble cornerstone had these words: "Erected for Educational Purposes July 4, 1872 by the A.M.E. Church[,] Rev. Charles H. Pearce, P.E. Founder." When a school

official absconded with the money, authorities had to wait another decade to build the school, which became Edward Waters College (see Chapter Fifteen), in Jacksonville.

The **AFRICAN MISSIONARY BAPTIST CHURCH** at 509 Walker Avenue Southwest, two blocks south of U.S. 90, traces its history to the First African Baptist Church, the oldest church for blacks, which was organized in January 1868, three years after President Abraham Lincoln's Emancipation Proclamation went into effect. The first church building was located on the corner of Parshley Street and Houston Avenue on land donated by Mrs. Nancy Parshley, a wealthy white woman. Workers later moved the building to its present site on Walker Avenue. One of its most important pastors was Dr. **George P. McKinney Sr.**, who began his twenty-six-year tenure as pastor there in 1890. He also served as editor of such denominational publications as *The Florida Baptist*, *The Florida Baptist Herald*, and *The Florida Baptist Watchman*.

Mrs. Parshley also gave land for another black church, the **EBENEZER AFRICAN METHODIST EPISCOPAL CHURCH** on the corner of Parshley Street and Houston Avenue. This church also began in 1868; five years later congregation members built the first building. Rev. **Frank Sylbel** and a small band of members held their first services in a small, frame house at the site of the present

This was a typical home of African Americans in Suwannee County in the 1930s. *Florida State Archives*

church. In 1892, the congregation built a brick structure on land they purchased. In 1973, Rev. **T. E. Shehee** and congregation members built the present structure.

DOUGLASS HIGH SCHOOL, which was renamed the **DOUGLASS CENTER**, on Douglass Street in Live Oak has served as an educational center from 1868 until the present. The high school was originally located on Houston Avenue; later the New Douglass High School was built on 10th Street, which was renamed Douglass Street. The original building, which had just one door and was built in 1868, operated for only four months a year: June through September. In 1949, a new school was built to house grades one to twelve and had 680 students. The enrollment jumped to 889 after the consolidation of rural schools. The school was renamed Suwannee Middle School in 1969. In 1990, a new middle school was built, and the school was renamed Douglass Center.

Two African Americans from Live Oak need to be mentioned here. **Sarah Ann Blocker** finished her education and then, at the age of twenty-two in 1879, founded Florida Memorial College (see Chapter Fifty-five for more about the college). She was inducted into the Florida Women's Hall of Fame in 2003 for her establishment of the college.

The other African American, **Nathaniel Hawthorne Jones,** was born there in 1897, the son of **William** and **Mellie Mattor Jones**. He attended many services at the Ebenezer AME Church there, later graduated from Florida Memorial College and Morehouse College in Atlanta, Georgia. He then entered Meharry Medical College in Nashville, Tennessee, where he earned his medical degree in 1926. Two years later, he began practicing medicine in Ocala, Florida. (For more about him, see Chapter Forty-one.)

Among the buildings associated with a tragic

event in the town's history is the **COURTHOUSE** at 200 S. Ohio/Martin Luther King Jr. Avenue that saw the trial of a black woman, **Ruby McCollum**, for the 1952 murder of a prominent local white doctor. Florida writer **Zora Neale Hurston**, who had written the fictional *Seraph on the Suwannee* about the local turpentine industry, attended McCollum's trial and wrote about it for the *Pittsburgh Courier* newspaper, including a daily summary of the trial and a biography of the defendant. McCollum's death sentence was commuted to a prison sentence, and she spent twenty years in the state mental asylum in Chattahoochee. When she was finally released in 1974, she went to Ocala to be with her family. There she died in 1992. Don Tracy's novel, *The Hated One*, is also about a black woman who killed a popular white man in north Florida. Ruby McCollum is buried in the cemetery behind the Hopewell Baptist Church north of Live Oak.

The county courthouse in Live Oak was the scene of a famous trial that writer Zora Neale Hurston covered. *Florida State Archives*

62.

Taylor County

The Florida Legislature established this county in 1856 and named it for Zachary Taylor, commander of U.S. Army forces in Florida during part of the Second Seminole War, then twelfth President of the United States. Taylor County had a population of 19,256 in the 2000 census, 3,659 (19.0%) of whom were African Americans.

Perry

One of two sites in Taylor County on the Florida Black Heritage Trail is **JERKINS HIGH SCHOOL** at 1012 Martin Luther King Avenue. The two earliest schools for blacks in Perry were burned, one about 1919 and one about 1923. Until ground was broken for Jerkins High School in 1931, classes for Perry's African American students were held in the Masonic Hall or in various churches, for example the Springhill Missionary Baptist Church. **Henry R. Jerkins**, who arrived from Palmetto, Florida, in 1930, was the first principal, succeeded by **Homer Smith**. Mr. Jerkins served at Jerkins High School for seven years, during which time he expanded educational offerings and added more grades. The first class graduated in 1937. In 1946, the name Jerkins was officially added to the school. The Jerkins School closed when Perry schools were integrated, but it continues today as a community center, polling place, and a branch of the Boys Club and Girls Club. Ball fields and a playground on the former school grounds provide additional recreational opportunities for the youth of the area.

Directions to School: .2 miles south of the U.S. 98/U.S. 19 junction, turn right on W. Duval Street and go .2 miles (street jogs to the left) to Martin Luther King Jr. Avenue. The school is on the left.

The other county site on the Florida Black Heritage Trail is **SPRINGHILL MISSIONARY BAPTIST CHURCH** at 1095 E. Pinecrest Street. In 1853, when the area was part of Madison County, a group of free African Americans, most of whom

The Springhill Missionary Baptist Church was rebuilt in 1942.

were named **Colson**, established the church in Rosehead, which later became Perry. The present-day, wood-frame building was rebuilt in 1942 at its original location and has been continually used since that time.

Directions to church: From U.S. 19 in Perry, go east on Jefferson Street 1.5 miles, then right on E. Veterans Drive .2 miles, then left on Johnson-Stripling Road .1 mile, then right on Pinecrest Street and past Taylor County High School .3 miles to the church on the right.

The **SPRING HILL CEMETERY** is at the corner of Green Street and Ellison Road. The church was also located there, but in 1923 the Ku Klux Klan burned down the church. Many black families who lived near the church fled the area in fear of losing their lives and their property during those turbulent times. Newer sections of the cemetery still can be seen at this location, but the church was rebuilt in 1925 at the corner of Pinecrest and Myrtle Streets; the original bell was set in the belfry of the new church. Plans are underway to clear and restore the older part of the cemetery.

Florida artist George Snow Hill painted the "Cypress Logging" mural on canvas in 1938 for the Perry Post Office, erected during the Depression Era. Through the Public Works of Art Project, the federal government selected artists and subjects to embellish public buildings. The panel honors those whose labors contributed to the Taylor County lumber industry, most of them African Americans. The mural was moved to its present location in the new post office at 1600 S. Jefferson Street in 1987. The old Perry Post Office still stands at 201 E. Green Street and is now the Taylor County Administrative Annex.

Jerkins High School in Perry is on the Florida Black Heritage Trail.

63.

Union County

The Florida Legislature established this county in 1921 and named it Union County because, in the words of the sponsor of the bill, the counties "were united this time in asking for the divorce though the two parts of the [Bradford] county have never before been able to get together on this proposition." Union County had a population of 13,442 in the 2000 census, 3,065 (22.8%) of whom were African Americans.

Lake Butler

The **UNION COUNTY HISTORICAL MUSEUM** at 410 W. Main Street (S.R. 100) has articles and photographs dealing with the history of Union County, including artifacts and photographs of the black community.

Worthington Springs

One of the most popular recreational sites in Union County has been Worthington Springs, named after the Worthington family that lived there in the nineteenth century. When two boys discovered a trickle of water coming out of the ground, they informed Mr. Worthington, who had a pool dug out. After the Seminole Indian Wars, he tried to establish a store there, but the young man he hired and to whom he gave money to buy goods for the store disappeared, either absconding with the money or being kidnapped or murdered.

In disgust, Mr. Worthington stopped the flow of water at the springs, cursed the place, and left for good. Later Mr. and Mrs. William Lastinger moved to the community from Georgia and rented the place. When Mrs. Lastinger heard that there had been a spring there, she had her slaves open it up, dig out the pool, and enlarge it. Although the water emitted a strong sulphuric smell, the pool attracted more and more visitors, perhaps for its supposed health benefits. Those who enjoy the area today may be unaware of the role that slaves played in the building of the pool.

African American workers like these helped build and pave roads throughout Florida, including Union County.
Florida State Archives

64.

Volusia County

The Florida Legislature established this county in 1854 and named it for the Volusia landing on the St. Johns River. That landing took its name either from Native Americans or from a European trader named Veluché (pronounced Va-loo-SHAY), who had a trading post there, but no proof exists for either theory. Volusia County had a population of 443,343 in the 2000 census, 41,231 (9.3%) of whom were African Americans. The county is as large as Rhode Island.

Daytona Beach

Daytona Beach is now part of Volusia County, a section of Florida that used to be in Mosquito County in the days before insect control made life bearable in the state. Wealthy planters began moving to the area in the 1820s to take advantage of the cheap land, accessibility to northern markets by rivers and the ocean, and good soil for the production of sugarcane. Those planters used large numbers of slaves to clear the land, cultivate the crops, and produce sugar, molasses, and rum.

Planters like Charles and John Bulow bought slaves to work their huge plantations. When they needed more slaves, they would go to Virginia, Maryland, and Georgia or look for advertisements such as the following newspaper ad mentioned in Schene's history of Volusia County: "123 Negroes [for sale], about 80 of whom are field hands, the remainder boat hands, engineers and pilots of steamboats, bricklayers, painters, carpenters, blacksmiths, and house servants." The price of those slaves depended on their age, sex, health, and skill. A slave recently imported from Africa was worth less than one born in America, whereas skilled masons, carpenters, and mill operators brought a higher price. Healthy male slaves were worth considerably more than healthy female slaves.

One of the founders of Daytona Beach and the man after whom the city is named, Matthias Day Jr. of Mansfield, Ohio, arrived in the area in 1870, determined to operate a sawmill. According to Hebel's racial history of the area, Day found a group of freedmen who had gone there after the Civil War. To clear the land and grow crops he employed some of those former slaves who had settled north of Port Orange on present-day U.S. 1 in a settlement called Freemanville. Many of their descendants still live in Daytona Beach, a city that had an official population in 2000 of 64,112, of whom 20,994 (33%) were blacks.

Two of the sites of significance to blacks in Daytona Beach relate to **Mary McLeod Bethune** (1875–1955), one of the great educational leaders of the nation. Born in South Carolina and educated in schools in North Carolina and Illinois, she taught school in Georgia, South Carolina, and Florida before founding the Daytona Educational and Industrial Training School for Negro Girls in Daytona Beach in 1904. She also opened up a hospital on the campus for blacks, who could usually not find anywhere else to go for medical treatment. In 1923, she joined her school with Cookman Institute of Jacksonville, Florida, and formed Bethune-Cookman Institute in Daytona Beach. A year later, it affiliated with the United Methodist Church, evolved into a junior college by 1931, and became known as **BETHUNE-COOKMAN COLLEGE**, which has 123 full-time faculty and an enrollment today over 2,700 students. The school is at 640 2nd Avenue, just west of Ridgewood Avenue and north of Volusia Avenue. Phone: (386) 481-2001.

Mrs. Bethune retired in 1942, at which time **James E. Colston** became president until 1946, when Mrs. Bethune resumed the presidency for a year. **Richard V. Moore Sr.** became president in 1947, and under his tenure the school was ac-

credited by the Southern Association of Colleges and Schools in 1970 and joined the United Negro College Fund and other academic and professional organizations.

Mrs. Bethune distinguished herself in several fields. In 1924, she was elected president of the National Association of Colored Women, an organization that worked to improve the conditions of black women throughout the United States. She also established the National Council of Negro Women and worked on the Commission on Interracial Cooperation. In 1935, she received the Spingarn Award from the National Association for the Advancement of Colored People (NAACP) for her many accomplishments and was named

Mary McLeod Bethune on the steps of Bethune-Cookman College in Daytona Beach. *Florida State Archives*

one of the fifty most influential women in the country. The following year she became the first black woman to head a federal agency when she became director of the National Youth Administration's Division of Negro Affairs. The 1985 postage stamp that honored her was just one way to recognize her efforts to improve the lot of all blacks in this country.

The MARY MCLEOD BETHUNE HOUSE at 641 Pearl Street off 2nd Avenue on the campus of Bethune-Cookman College is the house where Mrs. Bethune lived from when it was built in the 1920s until her death in 1955. The two-story wood-frame house contains citations, plaques, photographs, and artifacts of Mrs. Bethune. With her philosophy of "Not for myself, but for others," she willed her home to the American people. Two years before she died, she was able to see her friend, Eleanor Roosevelt, the widow of President Franklin Roosevelt, dedicate the building as the Mary McCleod Bethune Foundation, a place that thousands of people visit each year. After Mrs. Bethune died at the age of seventy-nine, she was buried near the house. Her tombstone reads: "She has given her best that others may live a more abundant life." In 1975, officials named the House a National Historic Landmark. Open Monday-Friday. College students lead visitors on a tour of the house. Phone: (386) 481-2122, ext. 372. For more about Mrs. Bethune see the section on New Smyrna Beach below.

Several plaques on the campus of Bethune-Cookman College honor persons elected to the Great Floridians 2000 Program. One of them was Dr. **Joseph Taylor** (1929–1998). He was born in Columbia, South Carolina, earned a bachelor's degree from Howard University, served in the Korean Conflict, and earned a master's degree in history from Howard in 1959, and then in 1985 a Doctor of Arts in history from Catholic University. He served for thirty years at Bethune-Cookman College as Area Coordinator and Professor of History, Chairman of the Social Sciences Di-

vision, and Director of the Faculty Development Center. In 1983 he received Bethune-Cookman's Teacher of the Year Award and was honored in 1993 as the Faculty Member of the Year for Community Service. Taylor was chairman of the Daytona Beach Historic Preservation Board and a member of the Association for the Study of African American Life and History. His Great Floridian plaque is located on the front entrance of the Faculty Research Development Building on the campus.

Nearby at the New Mt. Zion Missionary Baptist Church, 515 Dr. Mary McLeod Bethune Boulevard is a plaque that honors **George W. Engram Sr.** (1913–1998). He was born in Montezuma, Georgia, earned a degree in electrical engineering at Tuskegee Institute (University), and moved in 1935 to Daytona Beach, where he founded Engram Electric Company. In the 1940s and 1950s he helped find investors to purchase 2.5 miles of oceanfront property south of New Smyrna Beach and became general manager and executive vice-president of a project to turn the area into a full community and resort area for African Americans, which became BETHUNE-VOLUSIA BEACH in 1945 (see page 282). Two streets in Daytona Beach were named in his honor, and he carried the torch for the 1996 Olympic Games.

In 1957, VOLUSIA COUNTY COMMUNITY COLLEGE (VCCC) was established for black students wishing to go to college, and it began offering classes the following year. The school's founder and only president was **J. Griffen Greene**, who had been principal of Lincoln Academy High School in Fort Pierce, Florida. Greene (1910–1987) was appointed president of VCCC in 1958 and remained president until the college merged with Daytona Beach Junior College (DBJC) in 1965. After the merger with DBJC, he was appointed supervisor of instructors teaching remedial courses, then was named dean of continuing education. Following his retirement in 1973, Greene taught English and education at Bethune-

Cookman College. A plaque honoring Greene is located at the J. Griffen Greene Student Resource Center, Daytona Beach Community College.

The enrollment figures for the community college, which was located close to Campbell Street High School, showed that it served many students in both the college parallel program and the vocational programs:

1958–59: 141 students
1959–60: 1,122 students
1960–61: 2,392 students
1961–62: 1,802 students
1962–63: 2,384 students
1963–64: 5,600 students
1964–65: 5,245 students

The strong academic and vocational programs of the college enabled many of its graduates to secure good-paying jobs, for example at the growing Cape Canaveral Space Center. In 1966, the school merged with Daytona Beach Community College at a time when the black school had over five thousand students, seventy-nine faculty, and eight full-time administrators. Ironically, northern visitors who had originally opposed the establishment of a separate black junior college were concerned that the merging of Volusia County Community College with the local white college would force black faculty members at Volusia to lose their jobs. The county school board solved this problem by placing the staff from Volusia in college and public school positions.

The **HOWARD THURMAN HOUSE** at 614 Whitehall Street, west of Ridgewood Avenue and south of Cedar Street, was the birthplace of Dr. **Howard Thurman** (1900–1981). The two-story, wood-frame vernacular structure, which was built around 1888 and finally recognized as a National Historic Preservation Site in 1990, was in the Waycross community, one of the oldest parts of the city and one of three areas where blacks lived in Daytona, which was later incorporated as Daytona Beach. Besides the middle-class resi-

dential neighborhood of Waycross, blacks could live in Midway (where **Mary McCleod Bethune**'s school was) and Newton (where a public school for black children was located). Blacks worked in the white communities of Daytona and, on the ocean side of the river, Sea Breeze and Daytona Beach, but they were not allowed to live in those areas or even be in them after dark.

Dr. Howard Thurman was born in Daytona Beach. *Florida State Archives*

Howard Thurman was raised by his illiterate grandmother, a former slave who recognized the importance of education. Encouraged by his grandmother, he was the first black in Florida to finish the eighth grade. He then went to Jacksonville's Florida Baptist Academy, Atlanta's Morehouse College (where he majored in economics), and the Colgate-Rochester School of Divinity, before beginning his work as a Baptist minister in 1925. He went on to become an educator, preacher, theologian, and distinguished author of twenty-two books dealing with race and religion. In 1944, in San Francisco he organized the Church for the Fellowship of All Peoples, one of the first racially integrated churches in our country. At Boston University he served as Dean of Marsh Chapel and thus became the first black to hold such a position at a predominantly white university in the U.S. In 1953, *Life* magazine named him one of the twelve outstanding preachers of the twentieth century. His Great Floridian plaque is located on the front of his birthplace at the house that honors him.

Another man who made a contribution to the black history of Daytona Beach was **Jackie Robinson** (1919–1972), the baseball player who joined the Brooklyn Dodgers in 1947 and thus became the first black baseball player in modern times to play on a major league team. He had signed with the Brooklyn Dodgers in the fall of 1945 and was sent to Daytona Beach for spring training with the Montreal Royals. When he trotted onto the city's Island Ball Park on March 17, 1946, for a spring training game, the future Hall-of-Fame second baseman was making history and breaking organized baseball's color barrier. In a game that saw the Brooklyn Dodgers beat the Montreal Royals, the Dodgers farm team, Robinson became the first black to play for a major league baseball team in the modern era.

Officials later renamed the site ·the **JACKIE ROBINSON BALLPARK** in 1988 and erected a bronze statue outside the park's gates that depicts Robinson standing with two small boys, one black and one white, both of whom represent the future. Montreal sculptor Jules LaSalle, who designed the statue after one at Montreal's Olympic Stadium, modified the Daytona Beach statue to have Robinson wearing a Montreal Royals uniform and with his feet turned further inward to resemble Robinson's pigeon-toed stance. Behind the statue is a series of curved walls of different lengths and heights that are meant to suggest the rippling effect of a pebble dropped into a pond;

Jackie Robinson Ball Park has a statue of the famous ball player.

the result reminds onlookers of the many unforeseen benefits that came from Robinson's integration of modern baseball. The ballpark is at 103 E. Orange Avenue on City Island, west of Memorial Bridge and east of Ridgewood Avenue. A plaque there honors Robinson as being part of the Great Floridians 2000 Program.

At the 1990 dedication ceremonies of the statue, **Bill White** of Lakeland, Florida, a former major league ball player and the president of the National League, noted how much Robinson had meant to him: "To me, Jackie represents perseverance. He succeeded despite a lot of obstacles, and I think that's important for any kid to learn. I know I wouldn't be where I'm at now if it hadn't been for Jackie."

When **Rachel Robinson** arrived in Daytona Beach for the 1990 dedication of the statue, she recalled how different it had been forty-four years before when she came by bus with her new husband. She and Jackie sat in the Jim Crow section of the crowded bus because bigots in New Orleans and then in Pensacola had forced them off their scheduled plane flight. Having been a star athlete at UCLA in California, Jackie was not used to Florida's segregated restrooms, the necessity to use the back doors of restaurants, separate water fountains, and racial taunting. The fact that he handled the situation so well and played baseball so skillfully reinforced Branch Rickey in his determination to integrate major league baseball. Robinson had a career batting average of .311, set a fielding record for second basemen, won the league's Most Valuable Player Award in 1949, and was elected to the Baseball Hall of Fame in 1962, his first year of eligibility.

We should mention at least one church in this city: **MOUNT BETHEL BAPTIST INSTITUTIONAL CHURCH** at 700 S. Campbell Street. This is the oldest Baptist Church in Daytona Beach, having been organized in 1885 by the late Reverend **J. B. Hankerson**. At first the church was in Silver Hill on Fremont Avenue, but a few years later was moved to Church Street (later called Marion Street).

The **MUSEUM OF ARTS AND SCIENCES** at 1040 Museum Boulevard, west of Nova Road and south of Volusia Avenue, has part of the building devoted to the African cultural history of black Floridians. The collection of African art is one of the best in the Southeast. Open 9 A.M.–4 P.M., Tuesday-Friday; 12 P.M.–5 P.M., weekends. (386) 255-0285.

One of the longtime leaders of the community, **Charles W. Cherry Sr.**, was publisher of a black newspaper, *Daytona Times*, and city commissioner. He was born in Georgia and moved to Daytona Beach around 1950; he began publishing the *Daytona Times* in the 1970s, then the *Florida Courier* for the Treasure Coast in 1992. He was the first black to seek election to the Daytona Beach City Commission in 1960, but was not elected until 1995. He also founded the Daytona Beach/Volusia County Chamber of Commerce for those small businesses not well represented by the mainstream Chamber of Commerce. Mr. Cherry died in 2004 after a long career devoted to furthering the civil rights' cause.

Finally, black author **Zora Neale Hurston** (see Chapters Forty-eight and Fifty-six for more about her) lived on two houseboats, *Wanago* and *Sun Tan*, in Daytona Beach in the 1940s. She moored them at the Howard Boat Works, 633 Ballough Road, a pleasant place where, she wrote, "all the other boat owners are very nice to me. Not a word about race." Workers recently demolished the boat works after many years of service to the area's boat owners.

DeLand

In December 1876, industrialist **Henry DeLand** founded the town that bears his last name. Settlers began moving in and setting up businesses, including a bank, restaurants, stores, sawmills, and even two stables. An 1886 fire burned up many wooden stores, but it enabled owners to rebuild with sturdier and more attractive brick. The Florida Baptists established DeLand College in 1885 and four years later changed its name to the John B. Stetson University to honor one of its donors.

At first the town relied on citrus products for its economy, but the harsh freezes of 1894–95 ruined Henry DeLand, the town, and many other settlements in the state. Determined not to give up, the town's residents rebuilt their economy, but diversified into producing naval stores, dairy products, ferns, and produce. The roads that connected DeLand to larger cities brought in tourists by car and took out by truck the goods that local residents produced. Among the black businessmen in town were **G. W. Miller**, **G. D. Taylor**, and a Mr. **Randall**.

One of the settlements in DeLand where blacks lived was called **AFRICA**, which began over a century ago to allow the workers to live in the area near where they worked. Two dozen or more houses accommodated maybe a hundred people. When the train stopped running there in the 1960s, people began moving elsewhere, and the last house was eventually torn down. Today Africa is known as PAINTERS POND PARK at the corner of Alabama and Wisconsin Avenues on downtown's north side. A bronze marker in the park mentions Africa, and a small plaque identifies the home site of two early residents: **Eddie Lee** and **Essiemae Coger**.

The YEMASSEE SETTLEMENT, which was in the area of Voorhis, Euclid, Adelle, and Clara Avenues, was an exclusive black settlement in the Progressive Era. It has some of the oldest structures associated with black residential areas of DeLand. For example, the GREATER UNION BAPTIST CHURCH at 240 S. Clara Avenue was built in 1893.

The prosperity of the town and the influx of Northerners necessitated the building of a hospital for whites, the Old DeLand Memorial Hospital, in 1920 and one for blacks, the Old DeLand Colored Hospital, in 1926, both on Stone Street.

Before construction of the OLD DELAND COLORED HOSPITAL on Stone Street in 1926, blacks had no medical facilities in the town. Those who needed care received attention in the offices of local physicians and were then cared for in the home of a midwife and practical nurse, Mrs. **Mandy Worthy**. In 1925, Dr. and Mrs. **A. J. Burgess** and others began contributing to a fund to build a hospital for blacks that would be located near the DeLand Memorial Hospital. The simple, utilitarian, masonry building that local architect Gouveneur Medwin Peek designed for what became the Old DeLand Colored Hospital contrasted sharply with its counterpart for whites. The latter building, a two-and-a-half story, Italian Renaissance–style structure, was one that local residents and visitors took great pride in.

The smaller size, lack of sophisticated medical equipment, and poorer conditions of the black hospital indicated how the races were kept separate in those days. For example, when doctors needed to perform surgery on a black patient, attendants would wheel the equipment from the white hospital across the parking lot or the doctors would use the basement emergency room of the white hospital or, at night, the main operating room, when hospital officials were away. These practices continued until the mid-1930s, at which time officials began allowing doctors to operate on blacks in the white hospital. Both buildings remained functioning until 1948, when officials transferred the medical facilities to the DeLand Naval Air Station. In 1952, a modern hospital, the Fish Memorial Hospital, opened to provide medical care for all the residents of DeLand. The original building of the DeLand Colored Hospital was torn down in 1993 after termites had infested the facility. A similar-looking building was built there and has historic exhibits from time to time, including one on black history.

A replica of the original Burgess Building, which Mr. and Mrs. Burgess had built in the 1920s to serve the medical needs of blacks, today has a display of artifacts that offer a glimpse into early life in the black community of the area. The building at 230 N. Stone Street also has the dental chair of Dr. **Poole**, an early black dentist there. Phone: (386) 740-5800. Open Wednesday through Saturday, 10 A.M.–3 P.M.

The BLACK HERITAGE EXHIBIT in Bill Dreggors Park at 230 N. Stone Street has artifacts showing life in the town's African American community, dating from the earliest settlements of freedmen along the St. Johns River. Phone: (386) 740-5800.

The J. W. WRIGHT BUILDING at 258–264 W. Voorhis Avenue, near S. Clara Avenue, was owned by **James Washington Wright** (1875–1956), a man who came to DeLand at the age of fifteen with $1.50 in his pocket. He worked for 75 cents a day, then $1 a day, until he saved up enough money to begin acquiring his own land. He

The Wright Building in DeLand was owned by important black businessmen.

bought his first five acres of citrus after the terrible 1894–95 freeze. By hard work and many late nights of working his groves by lantern, he saved enough money to buy more land and buildings, one of which is still called the Wright Building on W. Voorhis Avenue. There he and his wife, **Ethel**, operated a grocery and meat market. He also owned and operated his own shipping business on W. Minnesota Avenue, grew crops, and did much to improve the lot of other blacks.

Another building of importance to blacks is the **CHARLES P. BAILEY FUNERAL HOME** at 728 Adelle Avenue, begun by **Charles P. Bailey** of Punta Gorda, who won the Distinguished Flying Cross after flying 133 combat missions over Europe and shooting down three enemy airplanes as a fighter pilot with the all-black 99th Fighter Squadron.

BRADLEY HALL at 511 S. Clara Avenue, north of Euclid Avenue, south of both New York Avenue and Voorhis Avenue, and east of 15A, is now a private residence, but at one time the two-story, red-brick house was an orphanage for black children. Built around 1925, this building may be one of the very few black orphanages still standing, perhaps the only one. At first called Bradley Hall and then Safe Home Orphanage operated by **Eva Bradfield**, the building was converted to a private residence around 1950.

The **AFRICAN AMERICAN MUSEUM OF THE ARTS** at 325 S. Clara Avenue has exhibits and artifacts, including masks and sculptures from Africa. It has six major exhibitions a year. Open 10 A.M.–4 P.M., Wednesday through Saturday; (386) 736-4004.

The 2000 census indicated that DeLand had 4,010 African Americans or 19% of the total town population of 20,904. Although much smaller than the better-known Daytona Beach, DeLand is the county seat of Volusia.

Deltona

GARFIELD CEMETERY at Garfield Avenue and Lakeshore Drive is a long-neglected African American cemetery with unmarked graves that date back to the late nineteenth century. More research is needed to determine who is buried there.

New Smyrna Beach

This town in Volusia County on the ocean was first developed by British entrepreneur Dr. Andrew Turnbull (1720–1792), who named the Florida settlement after his Greek wife's former home of Smyrna in Asia Minor. He wanted to use indentured servants from the Mediterranean, especially the island of Minorca, to grow indigo for the making of dye, and also bought a number of black slaves to do the more onerous tasks, but the ship carrying the slaves sank in the Florida Keys, and the slaves on board died. In 1777, the Minorcans at New Smyrna Beach rebelled against Turnbull and fled to the safety of St. Augustine, where their descendants live today.

The New Smyrna area did not become settled by whites until the federal government was able to control the Indians in the 1850s. During the Civil War blockade runners brought in supplies for the Confederacy from the Bahamas. After the Civil War, settlers came by steamer up the St. Johns River; among those settlers were blacks who settled in what became known as the Westside, that part of the city west of U.S. 1. Many of them had farms and gardens and caught fish and crabs in the river. When a second railroad connection arrived in New Smyrna Beach in 1891 and the Florida East Coast Railway built a locomotive repair shop and roundhouse in 1926, many blacks found work on the railroad. A 1963 strike for higher wages put many of those men out of work and forced many black families to leave the area in search of good jobs. In 2000, only 1,335 (8%) of the city's population of 16,548 were black.

OLD SACRED HEART/ST. RITA MISSION CHURCH
at 314 Duss Street is a small wooden structure with a seating capacity of 80 people and a boxed steeple with the original bell. In 1899, workers built the church, called at that time Sacred Heart, on Faulkner Street near the downtown as a mission outpost from Saint Peter parish in DeLand to serve a small group of white Roman Catholics. When the congregation built a new parish church in 1956 on another site, they had this frame structure moved to its present location in the heart of the city's black section.

Old Sacred Heart/St. Rita Mission Church in New Smyrna Beach served the needs of Roman Catholics.

Members renamed it Saint Rita Mission and used it to replace a chapel of the same name in an old boarding house that had served the needs of black Catholics. The church was near the Madonna House, a two-story building where the Sisters of the Christian Doctrine lived; the nuns ran a daycare center and kindergarten. When integration took effect in the 1960s, church officials merged Saint Rita Mission with the new Sacred Heart Parish, and the Duss Street building was used as annex space for a child-care project. It has not been used much in the past few years. The church is just west of U.S. 1 and north of Washington Street. Today, the BLACK HERITAGE MUSEUM there has many photographs about the Catholic Sisters who ministered to African Americans, as well as many artifacts from the history of Chisholm Academy (see below). (386) 478-1934.

The CHISHOLM ACADEMY is a one-story wood frame building located in the subdivision of the Sams Estate and was the first school for black children in southeast Volusia County. The school got its start when one of the two houses where classes were being held burned; the owner of the houses, Leroy Chisholm, built and donated a two-story frame building in the 500 block of Washington Street to house the black students. The new elementary school, built in 1910 with funds raised by Chisholm and other concerned citizens, had grades one through six. Later Mrs. **Clara Wallace** raised funds to add grades seven and eight, with a ninth grade to be added later. The school was officially called "Chisholm Academy," and Chisholm became the supervisor. In 1916, the white children attending Mary Avenue Elementary were transferred to the new Faulkner Street Elementary School, and black elementary school students in grades one through four were transferred to the Mary Avenue school, which was named Kimball Elementary after its first principal. The next principal, **Fannie Walden**, remained in that position until integration took place.

S. F. Harris served as principal of Chisholm from 1930 until 1935, during which time grades ten, eleven, and twelve were added. During the 1935–42 administration of **J. B. Jones**, the school's name was changed to Chisholm High School, and the school year was increased from eight to nine months. **C. W. Harris**, who became principal in 1942, saw more changes, including the addition of music to the curriculum and the construction of an annex to house the home economics department; he was principal when the students moved to the new Chisholm High School site on Ronnoke Lane in 1954. **W. O. Berry**, who became principal in 1957, saw the building of a gymnasium, a band room, and an industrial arts complex and the addition to the curriculum of agriculture and drivers' education. **L. W. Kennedy** became principal in 1962 and had the school fully accredited by the Southern Association of Colleges and Schools. When New Smyrna Beach Senior High opened in 1969, the students from Chisholm High School were transferred there, and the elementary school students went to Faulkner and Read-Pattillo schools. Today Chisholm School at 588 Washington Street is called the ALONZO "BABE" JAMES YOUTH CENTER.

A gravesite in the town is also worth mentioning. Douglas Dummett, a white orange grower who developed Indian River citrus, had a black son, **Charles Dummett** (1844–1860), who killed himself or was accidentally killed while hunting at the age of sixteen. Author John McPhee wrote that "his death was called an accident, but some people on Merritt Island thought he had done it because of the shame he was made to feel for having Negro blood." His family buried him in part of the vast acreage they owned at the time, but eventually the city grew, more roads were built, and soon the gravesite stood in the middle of a street. Road builders have respected his final resting place and have built Canova Drive around the site; Canova Drive was named for entertainer Judy Canova's brother, who owned property there. The slab at the gravesite reads: "Sacred to the Memory of Charles Dummett, Born August 18, 1844 - Died April 23, 1860." The young man's father, Douglas, became sick in 1872 and traveled to Merritt Island to seek treatment; he died there and is buried in an unmarked grave. Charles's gravesite is in the middle of Canova Drive, which is south of Riverview Hotel.

Directions to Canova Drive: Go east across Indian River North Causeway, then onto Columbus Avenue and immediately onto Canova Drive, which is near the river to the south.

Port Orange

MOUNT MORIAH BAPTIST CHURCH is one of only two buildings remaining from FREEMANVILLE, a community founded after the Civil War by freed slaves, who worked for the Florida Land and Lumber Company. The freemen and their descendants once filled the pews of the church, which was built in 1911, but now very few attend the church services. Freemanville may have been the first and largest settlement of freedmen in the South.

A historic plaque on the east side of U.S. 1 near the Riverside Pavilion at 3431 Ridgewood Avenue describes the church, which is a few blocks away. Port Orange, which Union Army surgeon and abolitionist Dr. John Milton Hawks founded in 1867, attracted more than half the free slaves who moved to Florida after the Civil War. The U.S. Government gave them land near the Halifax River in accordance with the Southern Homestead Act of 1866. When the lumber company they worked for moved away in 1869, most of the homesteaders left, having found the soil too hard

to farm and having too few seeds to plant.

Those who remained behind established Freemanville, which attracted others seeking opportunities to work. The neighborhood thrived in the1920s, when blacks built houses on both sides of what is now U.S. 1.

Directions to Mount Moriah Baptist Church: The historic plaque is at the Riverside Pavilion Park on the east side of Ridgewood Avenue, which is about .4 miles north of Dunlawton Avenue (S.R. 421). To reach the church, which is two blocks west of Ridgewood Avenue, go south from the Riverside Pavilion Park about .1 mile. Turn right on Ocean Avenue, go two blocks to Orange Avenue, turn right on Orange Avenue, and the church is .1 mile on the left.

Six miles south of New Smyrna Beach in Volusia County over on A1A was BETHUNE-VOLUSIA BEACH (or simply BETHUNE BEACH), a 2.5-mile-long beach established for blacks in the 1940s by prominent Florida blacks, including educator **Mary McLeod Bethune**, investor **George W. Engram Sr.**, insurance executive **G. D. Rogers** of Tampa, rancher **Lawrence Silas** of Kissimmee, and other black investors who wanted a black residential resort community and recreation area. In 1943, they bought a two-and-one-half-mile stretch of beachfront property and subdivided it into lots, which they then sold to blacks who

Mount Moriah Baptist Church is one of only two buildings remaining from Freemanville, near Port Orange.

wanted to live near the ocean.

George Engram Sr. built the Welricha Motel and a bar-restaurant called the Beach Casino. When white residents with homes along A1A objected to the use of "their" road by blacks going to Bethune Beach, the whites had a separate road built from New Smyrna Beach to Bethune Beach for the blacks. The road is called Saxon Drive in honor of the commissioner who worked for its completion.

Amenities eventually included a bathhouse, picnic facilities, and a snack bar, but the project did not succeed in having blacks build houses on the beach because only a handful of wealthy landowners could afford the construction prices. By the mid-1960s, integration had opened up beaches to everyone, and the project died, especially as speculators bought up the empty lots from the black owners at low prices and resold them at high prices. Today one can see signs indicating Bethune Beach and Bethune Park, but the area is completely integrated.

65.

Wakulla County

This county was established in 1843 and has a name that comes from Native Americans although the meaning is unknown. Wakulla County had a population of 22,863 in the 2000 census, 2,629 (11.5%) of whom were African Americans.

A black cemetery still in use in the 1960s was the **RICHARDSON CEMETERY** on the northeast corner of the intersection of U.S. 98 and Spring Creek Highway, south of Wakulla Gardens. The cemetery is named after **S. B. Richardson**, who had the most slaves in the county in 1850. At that time, of the 1500 people who lived in Wakulla County 450, or about one-third, were slaves. Richardson, whose cotton plantation was near the present-day cemetery, had fifty-seven slaves. Members of the family stopped using the cemetery there years ago, but African Americans continued to use it, especially in the outer perimeter of the site.

Interestingly, some of the immigrants from New England, who had been vociferous opponents to slavery while they lived in the North, changed their minds when they moved to Wakulla County before the Civil War. For example, James W. Smith of Pawtucket, Rhode Island, had been an abolitionist while in the North, but, after moving to the Medart area of the newly formed Wakulla County around 1843 and while representing the county in the Florida Legislature in 1850, he owned a plantation with twenty-two slaves.

Port Leon

The town of Port Leon, south of Tallahassee and north of St. Marks, was the scene of a remarkable incident involving a former slave who was determined to be free. **Sandy Cornish**, a slave from Maryland who was hired out by his master, arrived in the Florida Panhandle in 1839 to begin nine years of hard work building a railroad from Tallahassee to St. Marks. He used the wages he earned in that work to buy his freedom for $3,200. The railroad line was extended to Port Leon from St. Marks, but a hurricane in 1843 destroyed the line on the south side of the St. Marks River.

Sandy Cornish claimed that a fire in the mid to late 1840s destroyed the papers that proved he was a free man. A band of six slave-catchers caught him with the intention of selling him in New Orleans, but he broke free and, before they could recapture him, in the public square of Port Leon he severely maimed himself in order to frustrate the attempts of the slave-catchers to resell him in the slave market. In a public square, accompanied by his wife, he used a knife to cut his ankle muscles, plunged the knife into one of his hip joints, and then cut off the fingers of his left hand with a hatchet. He threatened to cut the entrails out of his stomach in his determination to avoid going to New Orleans to be resold into slavery.

The white spectators refused to help him, but his black friends took him home in a wheelbarrow, and he stayed there for six months, slowly recuperating as much as possible from the disfigurement. After that, with the help of his devoted wife, he was able to use crutches to get around. No one attempted to sell him as a slave, either awestruck by his determination to be free or convinced of his intent to do himself further harm if they apprehended him.

Eventually Sandy and his wife, **Lillah Cornish**, made their way to Key West, where they helped establish the Cornish Memorial AME Zion Church. (For more about them, see Chapter Forty-Four.)

Sandy Cornish from Wakulla County eventually made his way to Key West, where he helped build the AME church there. *Florida State Archives*

66.
Walton County

The Florida Legislature established this county in 1824 and named it for Colonel George Walton, the secretary of the Territory of West Florida while Andrew Jackson was governor of the territory. Walton was the son of George Walton, the governor of Georgia and a signer of the Declaration of Independence. Colonel Walton's daughter was the one who suggested the name of Tallahassee for the new capital.

In the first half of the twentieth century, Walton County actually had a declining population because of the reduced supply of naval stores and lumbering, which in turn was caused by a cutting away of the timber. One result was a decline in the number of students attending county schools, including African American children. For example, the student population of African Americans declined from 3,178 in 1940 to 2,468 in 1947.

The county had eight elementary schools for African American children in the 1940s. The towns with those schools (with the number of teachers at each indicated in parentheses) were as follows: Bruce Creek (2), DeFuniak Springs (6), Liberia (1), Macedonia (1), Mount Zion (2), Oak Grove (2), Popular Springs (2), and St. John (1). Other than Tivoli School in DeFuniak Springs, which had six teachers, four of the county's schools for African Americans had two teachers, and three had only one teacher apiece. The one junior high school for African Americans had five teachers, and the one high school had five teachers. Tivoli School in the county seat had three schools for different-level students: an elementary, junior high, and high school. The number of African American children attending school in those days was approximately one-fifth the number of white children.

The county's chief city, DeFuniak Springs, had a population of 40,601 in the 2000 census, 2,842 (7.0%) of whom were African Americans.

Caney Creek

Gladys Milton (1924–1999) was born at Caney Creek in northern Walton County, and later became a midwife who delivered more than two thousand babies. She became nationally known in the late 1970s, when she led a legislative fight for recognition of midwives as legitimate medical practitioners. She was featured in several national magazines, and in 1992 was honored with the Sage Femme, the highest award of the Midwives Alliance of North America. Her biography is entitled *Why Not Me?* She was inducted into the Florida Women's Hall of Fame in 1994. (For more about her see Chapter Forty-six.)

Gladys Milton of Walton County became a midwife who delivered more than two thousand babies. *Florida State Archives*

67.
Washington County

The Florida Legislature established this county in 1825, the twelfth county of the state, and named it for President George Washington. Chipley is the county seat.

Washington County had a population of 20,973 in the 2000 census, 2,873 (13.7%) of whom were African Americans. Only in the last few decades has the county begun to reverse an outward migration of residents as its favorable climate and good land values have been attracting more and more people of all races.

Chipley

Chipley, the county seat, began as a railroad camp on the Pensacola and Atlantic (P&A) line and commemorates in its name a railroad official, Colonel William D. Chipley, who went to Pensacola in 1881 to be president of the P&A Railroad. The town hosted an Annexation Convention in 1889 to decide whether to try to have the Florida Panhandle try for annexation to Alabama, a movement that has surfaced every few years since the early 1800s. The 2000 census indicated that Chipley had 1,024 African Americans or 29% of the total town population of 3,592.

One of the town's schools, ROULHAC MIDDLE SCHOOL at 101 N. Pecan Street, honors an Orange Hill native, **Thomas J. Roulhac**, who became supervisor of Washington County's schools for black children in 1913. Having begun his teaching career at the age of twenty, he spent the next forty-nine years in that profession. Each of the ten children of Thomas and **Patience Roulhac** and many of the eighty Roulhac grandchildren also became educators and education advocates and showed by example how far one can advance through education. Some of those who did not go into the teaching field worked in the fields of medicine, law, business, and religion.

In 1938, Thomas J. Roulhac became principal of Chipley's first high school for black children, a school that also offered classes for elementary and junior high school students. Up until the mid-1960s Washington County, like many other counties in the United States, maintained two school systems: one for white children and one for black children. The latter schools were often much inferior to the former schools in terms of finances, teacher qualifications, and graduation rates.

In 1968–69, the schools in Washington County were integrated, and the high school students at Roulhac School were transferred to Chipley High School, the elementary school students went to Kate M. Smith School, and middle school students went to what became known as Roulhac Middle School, a name that honored Chipley's long-time black principal.

Directions: Roulhac Middle School at 101 N. Pecan Street is one block north of U.S. 90 (Jackson Avenue and S.R. 10) across the railroad tracks and Railroad Avenue North at the end of Church Avenue, which runs parallel to U.S. 90. Pecan Street is east of 7th Street and East Boulevard.

Another black, who was known only by his first name, Harry, gave his name to a swampy area near the eastern part of Orange Hill, which is just west of S.R. 273 south of Chipley. Harry's Bay is the name of a wetlands which collected runoff water during the rainy season and slowly released it during dry times. The thick foliage and dense trees made the area a perfect hiding place for Harry, a runaway slave from a nearby plantation. According to local historian E. W. Carswell in *Washington: Florida's Twelfth County*, in the mid-1800s Harry became a black Robin Hood, stealing from plantation storehouses and sharing his food with the slaves who could not escape.

Vernon

This small town was probably named after Mount Vernon, the home of President George Washington, after whom Vernon's county, Washington, was named.

MOSS HILL UNITED METHODIST CHURCH, located about three miles southeast of Vernon, is a plain, unpainted church built by Lamp Powell and slaves in 1857. Nearby is a 1.5 acre cemetery that is contemporary with the church and in use since the mid-nineteenth century. The thick growth of nearby trees, many of them covered with Spanish moss, lends a peaceful setting to the church. The forty-foot-long church on brick piers has two doors, one formerly used by women and girls, the other by men and boys. The austere inside of the church, which has remained relatively unchanged for the past 125+ years, has seven rows of pews, a pulpit, and an altar. The church, which is the oldest unaltered building in Washington County, has no electricity, plumbing, or heating devises, other than portable units located throughout the church. This building is one of the nation's best examples of what is known as frontier church architecture.

Moss Hill United Methodist Church near Vernon is a weathered structure built in a style called frontier church architecture.

Conclusion

African Americans have played a major part in the modern history of Florida, a part that has seldom received its due, partly because some white authors of that history have minimized or excluded the history of slavery and partly because the records of that contribution have often been lost. But from the time when an African slave, Estevanico the Black, came ashore with Spanish explorer Panfilo de Narváez in 1528 to the more recent times when African Americans have taken their rightful place in the halls of Congress, Africans and African Americans have helped make Florida what it is today. They were important in the economic development of the state. The back-breaking labor performed by slaves for years enriched the large plantations of Florida.

The black residents of American Beach, the Florida Keys, the "Forgotten Coast" of the Panhandle, and in the many desirable places in Florida that are close to the sea will be under increasing pressure to "sell out" to the highest bidder or will be unable to pay the increasing property taxes and will be forced to sell. From the 1970s, Florida has been attracting some six thousand new residents a week or over eight hundred a day. Many if not most of those people want their "place in the sun," which usually means proximity to water, whether ocean, gulf, lake, or river. The threat to historic communities and structures will be ceaseless. Only with a concerted effort by environmentalists and historians and archaeologists will such places be saved.

Further Reading

Chapter 1

Claudia Adrien. "Lynchings in Florida? It was a problem here, too," *Gainesville Sun*, September 3, 2005, p. 6D+; "The Newberry Six," *Gainesville Sun*, September 4, 2005; p. 1D+.

Maurine Christopher. *Black Americans in Congress*. New York: Thomas Y. Crowell Company, 1976, pp. 78–86: "Josiah T. Walls/Florida."

Algia R. Cooper. "Brown V. Board of Education and Virgil Darnell Hawkins, Twenty-Eight Years and Six Petitions to Justice." *The Journal of Negro History*, 64 (Winter 1979), pp. 1+.

Maxine D. Jones and Kevin M. McCarthy. *African Americans in Florida*. Sarasota: Pineapple Press, Inc., 1993: "Virgil D. Hawkins, 1906–1988," pp. 103–105.

Peter D. Klingman. *Josiah Walls*. Gainesville: University Presses of Florida, 1976.

Derrick Morgan. "African-Americans have rich past in Gainesville," *The Gainesville Sun*, February 27, 1994, p. 1A+.

Ben Pickard, editor. *Historic Gainesville: A Tour Guide to the Past*. Gainesville: Historic Gainesville, Inc., 1990.

Gilbert L. Porter and Leedell W. Neyland. *The History of the Florida State Teachers Association*. Washington, DC: National Education Association, 1977, p. 101+.

J. Irving E. Scott. *The Education of Black People in Florida*. Philadelphia: Dorrance & Company, 1974, p. 45.

Cheryl W. Thompson, "Recalling the days of Union Academy," *The Gainesville Sun*, February 18, 1989, p. 1A+.

Chapter 3

John Paul Jones. "Panama City, Queen City of the Gulf," *North Florida Living*, vol. 4, no. 4 (April 1984), p. 5+.

Walter L. Smith. *The Magnificent Twelve: Florida's Black Junior Colleges*. Orlando: Four-G Publishers, 1994.

Portia L. Taylor. *Community College Education for Black Students, A Case Study*. Dissertation. Gainesville: University of Florida, 1986.

Arthur O. White. *A Thirty Year History of Florida's State System of Community Colleges 1947–1977*. Dissertation. University of Florida, esp. p. 31.

Marlene Womack. *The Bay Country of Northwest Florida*. Panama City?: no publisher, 1998.

Chapter 5

Bart Bachman. "John Brothers is a proud man with a rich past." *The Times* [Melbourne], June 11, 1980.

Benjamin D. Brotemarkle. *Titusville and Mims*. Charleston, SC: Arcadia, 2004.

James C. Clark. "Death found suspects before justice could." *The Orlando Sentinel*, October 11, 1991, p. A-1+ [about the killing of Harry T. Moore].

Weona Cleveland. "Church was built on faith." *The Times* [Melbourne], October 10, 1979, p. 2B [about Macedonia Baptist Church].

Weona Cleveland. *Crossroads Towns Remembered: A Look Back at Brevard & Indian River Pioneer Communities*. Melbourne, FL: Florida Today, 1994.

Weona Cleveland. "Graveyard revitalized." *The Times* [Melbourne] November 26, 1980. Also articles by the same author in the same newspaper, September 10, 1980 and June 18, 1980.

Weona Cleveland. "Stone School history aired." *The Times* [Melbourne], February 18, 1976, p. 8A.

James A. Drake and Joseph R. Moss. *Cocoa: A Living History.* Merritt Island, FL: Creative Innovations, 1997.

Clyde A. Field and others. *Central Brevard County, Florida.* Charleston, SC: Arcadia, 1998.

Ben Green. *Before His Time: The Untold Story of Harry T. Moore, America's First Civil Rights Martyr.* Gainesville: University Press of Florida, 2005.

"Harriet Moore Buried," *Orlando Morning Sentinel,* January 9, 1952, p. 13.

David Kennedy. "Harry T. Moore: The Man, the Martyr, the Mystery," *Florida Monthly,* February 2004, pp. 28–34.

Georgiana Greene Kjerulff. *Tales of Old Brevard.* Melbourne: The Kellersberger Fund of The South Brevard Historical Society, Inc., 1972, esp. pp. 103–104: "The Black Community."

Verna G. Langlais, compiler. *Cemetery Census of Brevard County, Florida.* Titusville: no publ., 1984. This booklet lists those buried in the Line Street cemetery as well as in other local cemeteries.

John T. Manning and Robert H. Hudson. *North Brevard County.* Charleston, SC: Arcadia, 1999.

Noreda B. McKemy and Elaine Murray Stone, editors. *The Melbourne Bicentennial Book.* Melbourne: The Melbourne Bicentennial Committee, 1976.

Melbourne: A Century of Memories. Melbourne: The Melbourne Area Chamber of Commerce Centennial Committee, 1980. See esp. pp. 21, 24, 27–28, & 105.

"Moore's Funeral Held Without Trouble." *Orlando Morning Sentinel,* January 2, 1952, p. 11.

Leedell W. Neyland. *Twelve Black Floridians.* Tallahassee: Florida Agricultural and Mechanical University Foundation, 1970, pp. 85–91 [about Harry T. Moore].

Stephen Olausen. *Historic Buildings of Melbourne.* Melbourne, FL: S. Olausen?, 1991.

"Pioneer Brothers dies." *The Times,* November 25, 1981, p. 9A.

Glenn Rabac. *The City of Cocoa Beach: The First Sixty Years.* Winona, MN: Apollo Books, 1986.

Jackie Reid. "Brothers Park Ills Recounted." *The Times* [Melbourne], August 11, 1971.

Don Rider. "FBI Joins in Hunt for Killers," *Orlando Morning Sentinel,* Dec. 27, 1951, p. 1+. Also p. 13: "Mother of Slain Negro Tells of Fatal Explosion" [about the killing of Harry T. Moore].

Jerrell H. Shofner. *History of Brevard County.* Three volumes. Cocoa, FL: Brevard County Historical Commission, 1995, 1996, 2001.

Walter L. Smith. *The Magnificent Twelve: Florida's Black Junior Colleges.* Orlando: Four-G Publishers, 1994.

Elaine Murray Stone. *Brevard County: From Cape of the Canes to Space Coast.* Northridge, CA: Windsor Publications, 1988.

Portia L. Taylor. *Community College Education for Black Students, A Case Study.* Dissertation. Gainesville: University of Florida, 1986.

Arthur O. White. "The desegregation of Florida's public junior colleges, 1954–1977," *Integrated Education*, vol. 16, no. 3 (May-June 1978), pp. 31–36.

Arthur O. White. *A Thirty Year History of Florida's State System of Community Colleges 1947–1977*. Dissertation. University of Florida, esp. p. 57.

Julie Williams. "Brothers' Roots Deep in Melbourne," *Florida Today* [Melbourne], July, 1979.

Chapter 6

"Broward County is showcasing its Black achievers in extended history celebration." *The Miami Times*, February 10, 1994, p. 6D.

Peter Cary. "Fort Lauderdale's Negro Beach" in *Mostly Sunny Days: A Miami Herald Salute to South Florida's Heritage*" edited by Bob Kearney. Miami: Miami Herald Publishing Company, 1986, pp. 162–164.

Arthur S. Evans and David Lee. Pearl City, *Florida: A Black Community Remembers*. Gainesville: University Press of Florida, 1990.

Abraham D. Lavender, Adele S. News. *Black Communities in Transition: Voices from South Florida*. Lanham, MD: University Press of America, 1996.

Stuart B. McIver. *Fort Lauderdale and Broward County*. Woodland Hills, CA: Windsor Publications, Inc., 1983.

Stuart McIver. *Glimpses of South Florida History*. Miami: Florida Flair Books, 1988, p. 131: "'Doc' Sistrunk's 5,000 Babies"; and p. 159: "Galt Had His Mile and Blacks Had a Beach."

Kitty Oliver, "Early Black Doctors." Bob Kearney, editor. *Mostly Sunny Days: A Miami Herald Salute to South Florida's Heritage*. Miami: Miami Herald Publishing Company, 1986, pp. 159–161.

Joe M. Richardson. *The Negro in the Reconstruction of Florida, 1865–1877*. Tallahassee: Florida State University, 1965.

Jerrell H. Shofner. "Custom, Law, and History: The Enduring Influence of Florida's 'Black Code,'" *Florida Historical Quarterly*, vol. 55 (January 1977).

Jerrell H. Shofner. *Nor Is It Over Yet: Florida During the Era of Reconstruction, 1863–1877*. Gainesville: University of Florida Press, 1974.

Theodore Brantner Wilson. *The Black Codes of the South*. University, AL: University of Alabama Press, 1965.

Philip J. Weidling and August Burghard. *Checkered Sunshine: The Story of Fort Lauderdale, 1793–1955*. Gainesville: University of Florida Press, 1966.

Chapter 8

Martha R. Bireda. "Defying Stereotypes: Slave descendants help to shape life in early Punta Gorda," *Expressions Magazine*, July 2004, pp. 17–18.

Arch Fredric Blakey. *The Florida Phosphate Industry*. Cambridge, MA: Wertheim Committee, Harvard University, 1973.

Canter Brown Jr. *Florida's Peace River Frontier*. Orlando: University of Central Florida Press, 1991.

Fred Farris. *Once Upon a Time in Southwest Florida*. Venice, FL: Gondolier Publishing Co., 1982, pp. 103–105: "Black Teacher Became a Legend" [about Benjamin Joshua Baker].

Louise Frisbie. *Peace River Pioneers*. Miami: E. A. Seemann Publishing, Inc., 1974.

Maxine D. Jones and Kevin M. McCarthy. *African Americans in Florida*. Sarasota: Pineapple Press, Inc., 1993, pp. 37–39.

Vernon Peeples. *Punta Gorda and the Charlotte Harbor Area*. Norfolk, VA: Donning Company, 1986.

Chapter 9

Brad Bennett. "Agencies on the trail of African-American history." *Citrus Chronicle*, August 18, 1991, 1A.

Karen Dukess. "County to restore neglected cemetery." *St. Petersburg Times*. Citrus Times edition. June 2, 1988, p. 1.

Hampton Dunn. *Back Home: A History of Citrus County, Florida*. Clearwater: Citrus County Bicentennial Steering Committee, 1977?

Floral City: A Guide to Historic Architecture. Floral City: Citrus County Historical Society, Inc., 2000.

"Friends, family recall Norton's special qualities" [about Arthur Norton]. *Citrus Chronicle*, Feb. 12, 1986, p. 1+.

Lynn M. Homan and Thomas Reilly. *Citrus County*. Charleston, SC: Arcadia Publishing, 2001.

"Inverness," *North Florida Living*, June 1986, pp. 6–12.

Ken Moritsugu. "Faithful few still come to worship," [about Pleasant Hill Baptist Church] *St. Petersburg Times, Citrus Times edition*. February 24, 1992, pp. 1, 3.

Ken Moritsugu. "Silent Reminder of days gone by" [about Frasier Cemetery] *St. Petersburg Times, Citrus Times edition*. February 17, 1992, pp. 1, 2.

Tom Ritchie. *Floral City*. Floral City: Floral City Heritage Council, 2003.

Norm Swetman. "Arthur Norton Dies; Citrus' oldest at 109." *Citrus County Chronicle*. February 13, 1986, p. 1+.

Jim Twitty. "Cemetery forgotten by county," *The Tampa Tribune*. Citrus/Sumter edition. May 14, 1988, p. 1.

Chapter 10

David R. Colburn and Jane L. Landers, editors. *The African American Heritage of Florida*. Gainesville: University Press of Florida, 1995, esp. Chapter Seven: "Freedom Was as Close as the River" by Daniel L. Schafer.

Kevin Hooper. *The Early History of Clay County: A Wilderness that Could be Tamed*. Charleston, SC: History Press, 2006.

Ann Hyman. "Time to recall, lift our voices to honor Harlem Renaissance," *The Florida Times-Union*, June 23, 1991, p. C-1.

Maxine D. Jones and Kevin M. McCarthy. *African Americans in Florida*. Sarasota: Pineapple Press, Inc., 1993, pp. 66–67: "Augusta Savage, Sculptor, 1900–1962."

Randolf McCredie. "'The Parlor City,'" *North Florida Living*, September 1984, pp. 6–10.

Mary Jo McTammany. "Clay County Memoirs: Woman's passion led to extraordinary life" (about Louise Cecelia Fleming), *Jacksonville Times-Union*, February 26, 2003, M-2.

Cynthia Parks. "A 'Voice' from the past," *The Florida Times-Union*, March 25, 1990, p. G-1+.

Chapter 11

Kim Franke. "Bringing new life to Collier County" [about midwife Annie Mae Perry], *Naples Daily News*, February 7, 1993, p. 1E+.

D. D. and P. A. McGraw. *We Also Came: Black People of Collier County*. Naples, FL: Butterfly Press, Stone Enterprises, 1992.

Ray McNally. "Let's hear it from another quarter" [abut McDonald's Quarters], *Neopolitan Magazine* (September/October 1977), vol. 1, no. 3, pp. 8–12.

Charlton W. Tebeau. *Florida's Last Frontier*. Coral Gables, FL: University of Miami Press, 1966.

Chapter 12

"Florida's first Black state trooper was good role model," *The Miami Times*, February 24, 1994, p. 3D.

Gary W. McDonogh, editor. *The Florida Negro.* Jackson, MS: University Press of Mississippi, 1993 [has interviews with at least one former slave from Columbia County].

For more about an important Civil War battleground to the east of Lake City, see Chapter Two.

Chapter 13

James N. Baker with Howard Manly. "From Tragedy to Travesty." *Newsweek* 24 April 1989: 68.

Canter Brown Jr. *Florida's Peace River Frontier.* Orlando: University of Central Florida Press, 1991.

Norman Crampton. *The 100 Best Small Towns in America.* New York: Prentice Hall, 1993.

George Lane Jr. *A Pictorial History of Arcadia and DeSoto County.* St. Petersburg: Byron Kennedy, 1984?

Mark Lane. *Arcadia.* New York: Holt, 1970.

Richard Nellius. "Arcadia: Profile of a small Florida town." *Floridian* [*St. Petersburg Times*] 18 February 1968: 8–13.

"Sheriff Says He's Ready To Act On Murder Charge In Poisonings," *The Arcadian*, November 2, 1967, p. 1+. Plus subsequent editions of this newspaper from Arcadia.

Chapter 14

Stetson Kennedy. *Palmetto Country.* Tallahassee: Florida A&M University Press, 1989, reprinted from the 1942 edition.

John C. Powell. *The American Siberia or Fourteen Years Experience in a Southern Convict Camp.* 1891, reproduced in 1976: Gainesville: University of Florida Press.

Chapter 15

Abel A. Bartley. *Keeping the Faith: Race, Politics, and Social Development in Jacksonville, Florida, 1940–1970.* Westport, CT: Greenwood Press, 2000.

Charles E. Bennett. *Twelve on the River St. Johns.* Jacksonville: University of North Florida Press, 1980, pp. 89–113, 137–148.

David R. Colburn and Jane L. Landers, editors. *The African American Heritage of Florida.* Gainesville: University Press of Florida, 1995, esp. Chapter Eight: "LaVilla, Florida, 1866–1887" by Patricia Kenney.

Carita Doggett Corse. *The Key to the Golden Islands.* Chapel Hill, NC: University of North Carolina, 1931.

"EWC Inaugurates New 25th President," *The Florida Star* [Jacksonville], April 2, 1994, p. 6.

Herbert Hiller. *Highway A1A: Florida at the Edge.* Gainesville: University Press of Florida, 2005.

Jacksonville Looks At Its Negro Community. Jacksonville: Council of Social Agencies, 1946, pp. 5–6.

James Weldon Johnson. *Along This Way: The Autobiography of James Weldon Johnson.* New York: Viking Press, 1968.

Zephaniah Kingsley. *A Treatise on the Patriarchal, or Co-operative System of Society As it Exists in Some Governments, and Colonies in America, and in the United States, Under the Name of Slavery, With its Necessity and Advantages.* 1828. Reprinted Freeport, NY: Books for Libraries Press, 1970 [contains Kingsley's ideas about slavery].

Rev. Charles Sumner Long. *History of the A. M. E. Church in Florida*. Philadelphia: A. M. E. Book Concern, 1939, p. 87+.

Gary W. McDonogh, editor. *The Florida Negro*. Jackson, MS: University Press of Mississippi, 1993 [has interviews with at least one former slave from Duval County].

Leedell W. Neyland. *Twelve Black Floridians*. Tallahassee: Florida Agricultural and Mechanical University Foundation, 1970.

Edith Pope. *Colcorton*. New York: Scribner, 1944; reprinted New York: Plume, 1990 [a novel about Zephaniah Kingsley].

"Restoration of 4 Historic Black Cemeteries Underway in City," *The Florida Star* [Jacksonville], May 14, 1994, p. 1.

Barbara Ann Richardson. *A History of Blacks in Jacksonville, Florida, 1860–1895: A Socio-Economic and Political Study*. Dissertation. Carnegie-Mellon University, 1975.

Daniel L. Schafer. *Anna Madgigine Jai Kingsley: African Princess, Florida Slave, Plantation Slaveowner*. Gainesville: University Press of Florida, 2003.

J. Irving E. Scott. *The Education of Black People in Florida*. Philadelphia: Dorrance & Company, 1974, p. 49+.

Ellen Tarry. *Young Jim: The Early Years of James Weldon Johnson*. New York: Dodd, Mead, 1967.

Olav Thulesius. *Harriet Beecher Stowe in Florida, 1867 to 1884*. Jefferson, NC: McFarland & Company, 2001.

Samuel J. Tucker. *Phoenix From the Ashes: EWC's Past, Present, and Future*. Jacksonville: Convention Press, 1976 [about Edward Waters College].

Tonyaa Weathersbee. "Saving a heritage: City to help clean black cemeteries." *The Florida Times-Union* [Jacksonville], June 20, 1993, p. A-1+.

Charles Reagan Wilson and William Ferris. *Encyclopedia of Southern Culture*. Chapel Hill, NC: Univ. of North Carolina Press, 1989.

Wayne W. Wood. *Jacksonville's Architectural Heritage*. Jacksonville: University of North Florida Press, 1989.

Chapter 16

"Black Heritage Center opening at symbolic site," *News Journal* [Pensacola], February 26, 1988, p. 16A.

Earle Bowden. "Honoring our black heritage a vital part of preserving Pensacola history," *Pensacola News-Journal*, November 12, 1989, p. 19A.

Charles Boyd. "S. W. Boyd Sr., D.D.S.," [about a black dentist in Pensacola] *Pensacola History Illustrated*, vol. 1, no. 1 (summer 1983), pp. 21–22.

John W. Cole. *Pictorial History of Pensacola*. Pensacola: Fiesta of The Five Flags Association, 1952.

Frances Coleman. "Pensacola history buffs turn Julee's house into museum," *Mobile Press Register*, March 6, 1988.

Lucius and Linda Ellsworth. *Pensacola: The Deep Water City*. Tulsa, Okla.: Continental Heritage Press, Inc., 1982.

Mamie Webb Hixon. "Miss Lillie's School," in *When Black Folks Was Colored: A Collection of Memoirs and Poems by Black Americans*. Pensacola: African-American Heritage Society, Inc., 1993, pp. 35–40.

Bill Kaczor. "Legendary cottage dedicated to black history," *The Tampa Tribune*, February 11, 1991, Florida section, p. 4.

James R. McGovern. *Black Eagle: General Daniel "Chappie" James, Jr.* Tuscaloosa: University of Alabama Press, 1985.

James McGovern. *The Emergence of a City in the Modern South: Pensacola 1900–1945*. DeLeon Springs, FL: Painter, 1976.

Leedell W. Neyland. *Twelve Black Floridians.* Tallahassee: Florida Agricultural and Mechanical Foundation, 1970, pp. 7–14: "Matthew M. Lewey."

Virginia Parks. *Pensacola: Spaniards to Space Age.* Pensacola: Pensacola Historical Society, 1986.

J. Alfred Phelps. *Chappie: The Life and Times of Daniel James, Jr.* Novato, CA: Presidio Press, 1991.

Karen Smith. "For Black Businesses, The Old Days Were Good," *The Pensacola News,* January 25, 1984, p. 1+.

Walter L. Smith. *The Magnificent Twelve: Florida's Black Junior Colleges.* Orlando: Four-G Publishers, 1994.

"Story of black business unfolds," *News Journal* [Pensacola], February 28, 1988, p. 1–2D.

Leora Sutton. *Blacks and Slavery in Pensacola, 1780–1880.* Pensacola: Leora Sutton, 1992.

Portia L. Taylor. *Community College Education for Black Students, A Case Study.* Dissertation. Gainesville: University of Florida, 1986.

Robert T. Thomas. *History of The Mount Zion Baptist Church, Pensacola, Florida.* No publ. No date.

Arthur O. White. "The desegregation of Florida's public junior colleges, 1954–1977," *Integrated Education,* vol. 16, no. 3 (May-June 1978), pp. 31–36.

Arthur O. White. *A Thirty Year History of Florida's State System of Community Colleges 1947–1977.* Dissertation. University of Florida.

Chapter 17

John A. Clegg. *The History of Flagler County.* 1976.

The Pictorial History of Bunnell. Bunnell: The Pioneers of Bunnell, 1988.

Catherine P. Wickline Wilson. *A New Beginning: A Picturesque History of Flagler Beach, Florida.*

Chapter 18

Joseph Becton. "Old Hickory and the Negro Fort," *Pensacola History Illustrated,* vol. 2, no. 2 (fall 1986), pp. 25–32.

Mark F. Boyd. "Events at Prospect Bluff on the Apalachicola River, 1808–1818," *Florida Historical Quarterly,* vol. 16 (October 1937), pp. 55–96.

James W. Covington. "The Negro Fort," *Gulf Coast Historical Review,* vol. 5, no. 2 (spring 1990), pp. 78–91.

James M. Denham and Canter Brown Jr. "Black Sheriffs of Post-Civil War Florida," *The Sheriff's Star,* vol. 42, no. 5 (September/October, 1998), pp. 12–15.

Theodore Hemmingway. "Booker T. Washington in Florida, March, 1912," *Essays in Florida History.* Tampa: Florida Endowment for the Humanities, n.d., pp. 39–42.

Kevin M. McCarthy. *Apalachicola Bay.* Sarasota: Pineapple Press, Inc., 2004.

Robert B. Roberts. *Encyclopedia of Historic Forts.* New York: Macmillan, 1988, pp. 168–169.

Chapter 19

Elizabeth Roberts. "Putting the Kick Back in Quincy's Old Coke Economy." *Florida Trend* (March 1986), pp. 56–60.

"Services Saturday in Daytona Beach for former BCC president Richard Moore," *The Miami Times,* January 13, 1994, pp. 1–2A.

Julia Floyd Smith. *Slavery and Plantation Growth in Antebellum Florida, 1821–1860.* Gainesville: University of Florida Press, 1973.

Miles Kenan Womack Jr. *Gadsden: A Florida County in Word and Picture* ([Quincy]: Gadsden County Historical Commission, 1976).

Chapter 20

Kevin M. McCarthy. *The History of Gilchrist County*. Trenton: The Historical Committee of the Trenton Women's Club, 1986.

Chapter 21

Glades County, Florida History. Moore Haven, FL: Rainbow Books, 1985.

Chapter 22

Maxine D. Jones and Kevin M. McCarthy. *African Americans in Florida*. Sarasota: Pineapple Press, Inc., 1993, pp. 116–117 [about Clifford Sims].

Gene Miller. *Invitation to a Lynching*. Garden City, NY: Doubleday, 1975.

Chapter 25

Katrina Elsken. "A lynching in LaBelle," *LaBelle, Our Home*. LaBelle: LaBelle Leader, 1985.

Chapter 27

Arthur R. Ashe Jr. *A Hard Road to Glory: A History of the African-American Athlete since 1946*. New York: Warner Books, Inc., 1988.

Horace J. Fenton. *History of Avon Park, Florida, 1886–1956*. New York: Vantage Press, 1958.

Maxine D. Jones and Kevin M. McCarthy. *African Americans in Florida*. Sarasota: Pineapple Press, Inc., 1993, pp. 116–117.

Leoma Bradshaw Maxwell. *The First Hundred Years of Avon Park, Florida*. Avon Park: The Historical Society of The Old Settlers Association, Inc., 1980.

Chapter 28

Otis R. Anthony. *Black Tampa*. Tampa: City of Tampa Publications Dept., 1989.

Michael Bane and Mary Ellen Moore. *Tampa, Yesterday, Today & Tomorrow*. Tampa: Mishler and King, 1981.

Rowena Ferrell Brady and Canter Brown Jr. *Things Remembered: An Album of African Americans in Tampa*. Tampa: University of Tampa Press, 1997.

Canter Brown Jr. "The 'Sarrazota, or Runaway Negro Plantations': Tampa Bay's First Black Community, 1812–1821," *Tampa Bay History*, fall/winter 1990, vol. 12, no. 2, pp. 5–19.

Canter Brown Jr., Larry Eugene Rivers, Stephen W. Angell. *For A Great And Grand Purpose: The Beginnings Of The AMEZ Church In Florida, 1864–1905*. Gainesville: University Press of Florida, 2004.

David L. Chapman. "Documenting the Struggle for Civil Rights: The Papers of Robert and Helen Saunders," *Tampa Bay History*, fall/winter 1987, vol. 9, no. 2, pp. 47–54.

"Civil Rights Protests in Tampa: Oral Memoirs of Conflict and Accommodation." *Tampa Bay History*, spring/summer 1979, vol. 1, no. 1, pp. 37–54.

Hampton Dunn. *Yesterday's Tampa*. Miami: E.A. Seemann Publishing, Inc., 1972.

Barbara Fitzgerald and Tracie Reddick. "The Illusion of Inclusion," *The Tampa Tribune*, May 9, 1993, Nation, p. 1+; May 10, 1993, Nation, p. 1+.

Susan D. Greenbaum. "Afro-Cubans in Exile: Tampa, Florida, 1886–1984," *Tampa Bay History*, fall/winter 1985, vol. 7, no. 2, pp. 77–93.

Susan D. Greenbaum. *Afro-Cubans in Ybor City: A Centennial History*. Tampa: Tampa Printing, 1986.

Susan D. Greenbaum. *More Than Black: Afro-Cubans in Tampa*. Gainesville: University Press of Florida, 2002.

Leland Hawes. "Award salutes loyalty to Cuba" [about Paulina Pedroso], *The Tampa Tribune*, December 12, 1993, BayLife 1, 4. Also "Marti park linked to Pedroso," p. 4.

Leland Hawes. "Hospital for blacks suffered from neglect" and "Black hospital began in nurse's home," *The Tampa Tribune*, February 26, 1989, 6-I+.

Leland Hawes. "More on Walker," *The Tampa Tribune*, May 16, 1993, BayLife, p. 4. [About Tampa's first black city council member, Joseph A. Walker, who served in 1887–1888.]

Leland Hawes. "One official's untold story," *The Tampa Tribune*, February 13, 1994, BayLife, p. 4. [About Joseph N. Clinton, a black who served almost fifteen years as head of the Tampa office of the U.S. Internal Revenue office.]

Leland Hawes. "Scenes from a family album," *The Tampa Tribune*, March 6, 1994, BayLife, p. 4. [About a teacher, Rowena Brady, and her book about Tampa's blacks.]

Leland Hawes. "Secret plan included martial law," *The Tampa Tribune*, February 27, 1994, BayLife, p. 1, 4. Also "Tampa had share of clashes" [about racial flare-ups in World War II], p. 4.

Leland Hawes. "Tampa had share of clashes," *The Tampa Tribune*, February 27, 1994, BayLife 4.

Walter Howard. "'A Blot on Tampa's History': The 1934 Lynching of Robert Johnson," *Tampa Bay History*, fall/winter 1984, vol. 6, no. 2, pp. 5–18.

Robert P. Ingalls. *Urban Vigilantes in the New South: Tampa, 1882–1936*. Knoxville: University of Tennessee Press, 1988.

Elizabeth Jacoway and David R. Colburn, editors. *Southern Businessmen and Desegregation*. Baton Rouge: Louisiana State University Press, 1982, pp.257–281: Steven F. Lawson, "From Sit-in to Race Riot."

Maxine D. Jones and Kevin M. McCarthy. *African Americans in Florida*. Sarasota: Pineapple Press, Inc., 1993.

Rev. Charles Sumner Long. *History of The A. M. E. Church in Florida*. Philadelphia: A. M. E. Book Concern, 1939, p. 77.

Karen Haymon Long. "Black Baptist church celebrates 100-year anniversary," *The Tampa Tribune*, November 21, 1993, pp. 1–2 (about Greater Bethel Missionary Baptist).

Tony Marrero. "The Birth of Bealsville," *The Courier*, Oct. 17, 2002, pp.1, 24.

Benjamin E. Mays. *Born to Rebel*. Athens: University of Georgia Press, 1971. This is the autobiography of a man who went to Tampa in 1926 to become executive secretary of the Urban League.

Gary R. Mormino and Anthony P. Pizzo. *Tampa, The Treasure City*. Tulsa, Okla.: Continental Heritage Press, 1983.

Mary Ellen Murphy. "School's alumni hope to resurrect their alma mater," *The Tampa Tribune*, September 19, 1991, p. 1+.

Anthony P. Pizzo. *Tampa Town, 1824–1886: The Cracker Village With a Latin Accent*. Miami: Hurricane House Publishers, 1968.

Arthur Franklin Raper. *A Study of Negro Life in Tampa*. Tampa: no publ., 1927 [this report is commonly known as the Raper Report for one of its authors].

Larry Eugene Rivers and Canter Brown Jr. *Laborers in the Vineyard of the Lord*. Gainesville: University Press of Florida, 2001.

Robert Snyder and Jack B. Moore. *Pioneer Commercial Photography: The Burgert Brothers, Tampa, Florida*. Gainesville: University Press of Florida, 1992.

Kelli Tharrington. "The Historic District Stretches Further Than You May Think" [about the Bing Rooming House in Plant City], *Focus: Plant City Edition*, Dec. 15-Jan. 15, 2003, p. 18.

Chapter 29

Elba Wilson Carswell. *Holmes Valley: A West Florida Cradle of Christianity*. Bonifay, FL: Central Press, 1969.

E. W. Carswell. *Holmesteading: The History of Holmes County, Florida*. Chipley, FL: E. W. Carswell, 1986.

Chapter 30

Adam Chrzan. "Woman Claims Church," *Vero Beach Press Journal* January 9, 1994, p. 4 [about the Old Macedonia Colored Church]

A Guide to Historic Sebastian and Roseland. Sebastian: Sebastian Area Historical Society, Inc., 2002.

Leon Hayes. *Strength of Our Ancestors*. Wabasso, FL: no publisher, 1992.

Walter R. Hellier. *Indian River, Florida's Treasure Coast*. Coconut Grove: Hurricane House Publishers, 1965.

Charlotte Lockwood. *Florida's Historic Indian River County*. Vero Beach: MediaTronics, 1975.

Jeremy Milarsky. "Black History Comes Alive With Church Dedication," *Vero Beach Press-Journal*, February 8, 1998, p. 4A [about the Old Macedonia Colored Church].

More Tales of Sebastian. Sebastian: Sebastian River Area Historical Society, 1992.

Anna Pearl Leonard Newman, compiler. *Stories of Early Life Along Beautiful Indian River*. Stuart: Printed by Stuart Daily News, 1953.

Treasure Coast Black Heritage: A Pictorial History. Virginia Beach, VA: Donning Publishers, 1996 [about Indian River County, Martin County, and St. Lucie County].

Arline Westfahl. "Our Black Residents," in *Tales of Sebastian*. Sebastian: Sebastian River Area Historical Society, 1990, pp. 111–118.

Chapter 31

Gene Burnett. "T. T. Fortune: Florida's Black Militant," in *Florida's Past: People and Events that Shaped the State*. Sarasota: Pineapple Press, 1986. Vol. I, pp. 50–53.

David R. Colburn and Jane L. Landers, editors. *The African American Heritage of Florida*. Gainesville: University Press of Florida, 1995.

Rita Dickens. *Marse Ned: The Story of an Old Southern Family*. New York: Exposition Press, 1959. This is the story of a slave plantation near Marianna in the nineteenth century.

Gilmore Academy-Jackson County Training School Alumni Association, Inc. *Jackson County Florida. Black America Series.* Charleston: Arcadia Publishing, 2000.

Jacquelyn Dowd Hall. *Revolt Against Chivalry: Jessie Daniel Ames and the Woman's Campaign Against Lynching*. New York: Columbia University Press, 1979.

John Paul Jones. "Florida's Cavern City," *Florida Living* (July 1986), pp. 6–13.

Steve Liner, editor. *A Brief History of Marianna*. Marianna: City of Marianna, 1979.

James R. McGovern. *Anatomy of a Lynching*. Baton Rouge: Louisiana State University Press, 1982 [about the Claude Neal execution].

Kevin Metz. "Looking for justice," *The Tampa Tribune*, February 20, 1994, pp. 1, 18.

Arthur F. Raper. *The Tragedy of Lynching*. Chapel Hill, NC: University of North Carolina Press, 1933.

Jerrell H. Shofner. *Jackson County, Florida: A History*. Marianna: Jackson County Heritage Association, 1985.

Julia Floyd Smith. *Slavery and Plantation Growth in Antebellum Florida, 1821–1860*. Gainesville: University of Florida Press, 1973.

Walter L. Smith. *The Magnificent Twelve: Florida's Black Junior Colleges*. Orlando: Four-G Publishers, 1994.

J. Randall Stanley. *History of Jackson County*. Marianna: Jackson County Historical Society, 1950.

Portia L. Taylor. *Community College Education for Black Students, A Case Study*. Dissertation. Gainesville: University of Florida, 1986.

Emma Lou Thornbrough. *T. Thomas Fortune, Militant Journalist.* Chicago: University of Chicago Press, 1972.

Walter White. *Rope and Faggot: A Biography of Judge Lynch.* New York: Knopf, 1929.

Chapter 32

Gary W. McDonogh, editor. *The Florida Negro.* Jackson, Miss.: University Press of Mississippi, 1993 [has interviews with at least one former slave from Jefferson County].

Jerrell H. Shofner. *History of Jefferson County.* Tallahassee: Sentry Press, 1976.

Chapter 34

David R. Colburn and Jane L. Landers, editors. *The African American Heritage of Florida.* Gainesville: University Press of Florida, 1995, esp. Chapter Twelve: "Groveland: Florida's Little Scottsboro."

Walter L. Smith. *The Magnificent Twelve: Florida's Black Junior Colleges.* Orlando: Four-G Publishers, 1994.

Portia L. Taylor. *Community College Education for Black Students, A Case Study.* Dissertation. Gainesville: University of Florida, 1986.

Arthur O. White. "The desegregation of Florida's public junior colleges, 1954–1977," *Integrated Education*, vol. 16, no. 3 (May-June 1978), pp. 31–36.

Arthur O. White *A Thirty Year History of Florida's State System of Community Colleges 1947–1977.* Dissertation. University of Florida, esp. p. 49.

Chapter 35

Prudy Taylor Board. "Thoroughly modern Ella," *Fort Myers News-Press*, June 10, 1984, p. 1E+. [about Ella Piper] Also see November 26, 1989, p. 13A.

Prudy Taylor Board. *Remembering Fort Myers: The City of Palms.* Charleston, SC: History Press, 2006.

Prudy Taylor Board and Patricia Pope Bartlett. *Lee County: A Pictorial History.* Norfolk, VA: The Donning Company, 1985.

Prudy Taylor Board and Esther B. Colcord. *Historic Fort Myers.* Virginia Beach, VA: The Donning Company, 1992.

Prudy Taylor Board and Esther B. Colcord. *Pages From the Past: A Pictorial Retrospective of Lee County, Florida.* Norfolk, VA: The Donning Company, 1990.

Miller Davis. "Pioneer Club honors first black family in Fort Myers," *Fort Myers News-Press*, April 27, 1980, p. 2B. [about Nelson Tillis] Also see September 16, 1985, p. 1B+.

Elinore Mayer Dormer. *The Sea Shell Islands: A History of Sanibel and Captiva.* Tallahassee: Rose Printing Company, 1979.

Linda Firestone & Whit Morse. *Sanibel & Captiva: A Visitor's Guide to Florida's Enchanting Islands.* Richmond, VA: Good Life Publications, 1976.

Florence Fritz. *The Unknown Story of Sanibel and Captiva (Ybel y Cautivo).* Parsons, WV: no publ., 1974.

Marian Godown & Alberta Rawchuck. *Yesterday's Fort Myers.* Miami: E. A. Seamann Publishing, Inc., 1975.

Karl H. Grismer. *The Story of Fort Myers.* St. Petersburg: St. Petersburg Printing Company, 1949.

Mary Ann Husty. "Saving Sanibel's sights," *News-Press* [Fort Myers], South Lee Sun edition, July 24, 1991, pp. 1–2.

Suzanne Jeffries and Lee Melsek. "Far from the Dream," *Fort Myers News-Press*, February 26, 1989, p. 1A+. Also see September 24, 1989, p. 1A+; February 21, 1993, 1F+.

"McCullum Hall was full of fun, entertainment," *Fort Myers News-Press*, February 1, 1993, p. 3D.

Lee Melsek. "ECC teacher named newest regent," *Fort Myers News-Press*, November 10, 1993, p. 1A+. [about Audrea Anderson]

Jessie Bennett Sams. *White Mother.* New York: McGraw-Hill, 1957.

Mark Stephens. "Harlem Heights," *Fort Myers News-Press*, November 14, 1982, p. 1A, 13A. Other articles on this section are in subsequent issues of the newspaper: November 15, 1982, p. 1A, 9A; November 16, 1982, p. 1A, 9A. Also February 27, 1994, p. 1G+.

Donald O. Stone and Beth W. Carter. *The First 100 Years: Lee County Public Schools, 1887–1987*. Fort Myers: School Board of Lee County, 1988.

Ray Weiss. "One man considers his island paradise," *Fort Myers News Press*, December 2, 1980. [About the Gavin family, the first black family on Sanibel.]

Chapter 36

Kathryn T. Abbey. "The Union Bank of Tallahassee," *The Florida Historical Quarterly*, vol. 15, no. 4 (April 1937), pp. 207–231.

Fenton Garnett Davis Avant. *My Tallahassee*. Edited by David A. Avant Jr. Tallahassee: L'Avant Studios, 1983.

Althemese Barnes and Ann Roberts. *Tallahassee, Florida* - Black America Series. Charleston, SC: Arcadia Publishing, 2000.

Wyatt Blassingame. *Jake Gaither: Winning Coach*. Champaign, IL: Garrard Publishing Co., 1969 [a biography of one of FAMU's famous football coaches].

Hampton Dunn. *Yesterday's Tallahassee*. Miami: E. A. Seemann, 1974.

Mary Louise Ellis and William Warren Rogers. *Favored Land: Tallahassee. A History of Tallahassee and Leon County*. Norfolk, Va.: Donning, 1988.

Mary Louise Ellis and William Warren Rogers. *Tallahassee & Leon County: A History and Bibliography*. Tallahassee: Historic Tallahassee Preservation Board, Florida Dept. of State, 1986.

Bertram H. Groene. *Ante-Bellum Tallahassee*. Tallahassee: Florida Heritage Foundation, 1971.

William Guzmán and Tameka Bradley Hobbs. *Landmarks & Legacies: A Guide to Tallahassee's African American Heritage, 1865–1970*. Tallahassee: John G. Riley Center and Museum of African American History and Culture, Inc., 2000.

Robert L. Hall. "Tallahassee's Black Churches, 1865–1885," *Florida Historical Quarterly*, vol. 58. no. 2 (October 1979), pp. 185–196.

Debra Herman and Althemese Barnes. *A History of African-American Education in Leon County, Florida: Emancipation Through Desegregation, 1863–1968*. Tallahassee: Riley House? 1997.

Bea L. Hines. "Gilbert Porter: 'Tom' or Pioneer?" *The Miami Herald*, December 3, 1978, p. 11G.

David H. Jackson Jr. and Canter Brown Jr., editors. *Go Sound the Trumpet: Selections in Florida's African American History*. Tampa: University of Tampa Press, 2005.

Maxine D. Jones and Kevin M. McCarthy. *African Americans in Florida*. Sarasota: Pineapple Press, Inc., 1993.

Gary W. McDonogh, editor. *The Florida Negro*. Jackson, MS.: University Press of Mississippi, 1993 [has interviews with at least one former slave from Leon County].

R. C. Morgan-Wilde. "They gathered together," *Tallahassee Democrat*, August 11, 1985, Local/State section, p. 1 [about the family reunion of the Jiles family at the former shoe store].

Joan Perry Morris and Lee H. Warner, editors. *The Photographs of Alvan S. Harper, Tallahassee, 1885–1910*. Tallahassee: University Presses of Florida, 1983.

Leedell W. Neyland and John W. Riley. *The History of Florida Agricultural and Mechanical University*. Gainesville: University of Florida Press, 1963.

Gregory B. Padgett. "C.K. Steele and the Tallahassee Bus Boycott," M.A. Thesis, The Florida State University, 1977.

Glenda A. Rabby. "Out of the Past: The Civil Rights Movement in Tallahassee, Florida," Ph.D. dissertation, The Florida State University, 1984.

Glenda Alice Rabby. *The Pain and the Promise: The Struggle for Civil Rights in Tallahassee, Florida.* Athens: University of Georgia Press. 1999.

Joe M. Richardson. "Jonathan C. Gibbs: Florida's Only Negro Cabinet Member," *Florida Historical Quarterly*, vol. 42, no. 4 (April 1964), pp. 363–368.

Charles U. Smith. *The Civil Rights Movement in Florida and the United States.* Tallahassee: Father and Son Publishing, 1989.

Charles U. Smith and Lewis M. Killian. *The Tallahassee Bus Protest.* New York: Anti-Defamation League of B'nai B'rith, 1958.

Chapter 37

Carolyn Cohens. *Levy County, Florida.* Charleston, SC: Arcadia Publishing Co., 2005 [in the Black America series].

David Colburn. "Rosewood," *The Gainesville Sun*, January 14, 1994, p. 15A.

Michael D'Orso. *Like Judgment Day: The Ruin and Redemption of a Town Called Rosewood.* New York: G. P. Putnam's Sons, 1996.

Lizzie P. Robinson Jenkins. *The Real Rosewood.* Gainesville, FL: BookEnds Press, 2003.

Maxine D. Jones and Kevin M. McCarthy. *African Americans in Florida.* Sarasota: Pineapple Press, Inc., 1993, pp. 83–84: "The Rosewood Massacre, January 1923."

Maxine D. Jones and others. *A Documented History of the Incident Which Occurred at Rosewood, Florida, in January 1923.* Tallahassee: Board of Regents, 1993.

Gary Moore, "Rosewood," *The Floridian*," July 25, 1982, pp. 6–19.

"Nothing left but to fight to be heard," *The Florida Times-Union* [Jacksonville], January 3, 1993, p. A-1+. Also the article on p. A-6: "Survivor recalls terror of day Rosewood died."

Karen Voyles. "Survivors dredge up painful memories," *The Gainesville Sun*, February 26, 1994, p. 1B+.

Chapter 39

James M. Denham and Canter Brown Jr. "Black Sheriffs of Post-Civil War Florida," *The Sheriff's Star*, vol. 42, no. 5 (September/October, 1998), pp. 12–15.

Gary W. McDonogh, editor. *The Florida Negro.* Jackson, Miss.: University Press of Mississippi, 1993 [has interviews with at least one former slave from Madison County].

Walter L. Smith. *The Magnificent Twelve: Florida's Black Junior Colleges.* Orlando: Four-G Publishers, 1994.

Chapter 40

"Digging for Tampa Bay's Slave Past" [about the settlement of Angola on the Manatee River], *Flavour: Black Florida Life & Style*, vol. 5, no. 4 (winter 2004/05), pp. 17–18.

Rosalyn Howard. *Black Seminoles in the Bahamas.* Gainesville: University Press of Florida, 2002.

Maxine D. Jones and Kevin M. McCarthy. *African Americans in Florida.* Sarasota: Pineapple Press, Inc., 1993, pp. 9–10: "Estevanico the Black, 1528."

Arthur C. Schofield. *Yesterday's Bradenton, Including Manatee County.* Miami: E.A. Seemann Publishing, Inc., 1975.

Elizabeth H. Sims. *A History of Madison County, Florida.* Madison: Madison County Historical Society, 1986.

"Storied Black Seminole History Ebbing Away" [about the escaped blacks who went to Andros Island], *Flavour: Black Florida Life & Style*, vol. 6, no. 2 (summer 2005), p. 16+.

Portia L. Taylor. *Community College Education for Black Students, A Case Study*. Dissertation. Gainesville: University of Florida, 1986.

John Upton Terrell. *Estevanico the Black*. Los Angeles: Westernlore Press, 1968.

William Zinsser. *Spring Training*. New York: Harper & Row, 1989 [about the Pittsburgh Pirates' 1988 spring-training camp in Bradenton].

Chapter 41

Arch Fredric Blakey. *The Florida Phosphate Industry*. Cambridge, Mass.: Wertheim Committee, Harvard University, 1973.

Gene Burnett. "Phosphate Lured the Greedy, the Untamed." *Florida Trend* January 1976: pp. 111–114.

James Cramer. "FAMU grad gains seat on Cabinet," *Tallahassee Democrat*, July 20, 1978, p. 1+.

J. Lester Dinkins. *Dunnellon: Boomtown of the 1890's*. St. Petersburg: Great Outdoors Publishing Company, 1969.

Hampton Dunn. *Back Home: A History of Citrus County, Florida*. Clearwater: Citrus County Bicentennial Steering Committee, 1977?

Judy Hill. "Successfully challenged," [about Fessenden Academy] *The Tampa Tribune*, August 2, 1991, Baylife 1–2.

John Paul Jones. "Dunnellon." *Florida Living* July 1989: pp. 57–59.

Maxine D. Jones and Kevin M. McCarthy. *African Americans in Florida*. Sarasota: Pineapple Press, Inc., 1993, pp. 130–131.

John McDermott. "First Black Since Reconstruction Is Named to the Florida Cabinet," *The Miami Herald*, July 20, 1978, p. 1A+.

Ken Moritsugu. "A century's place of worship." *St. Petersburg Times. Citrus Times Edition*. February 10, 1992, pp. 1, 7.

Mount Zion African Methodist Episcopal Church. 1984 [a pamphlet from the church].

Eloise Robinson Ott and Louis Hickman Chazal. *Ocali Country: Kingdom of the Sun, A History of Marion County, Florida*. Oklawaha, FL: Marion Publishers, 1966.

Larry Eugene Rivers and Canter Brown Jr. *Laborers in the Vineyard of the Lord: The Beginnings of the AME Church in Florida, 1865–1895*. Gainesville: University Press of Florida, 2001.

J. Irving E. Scott. *The Education of Black People in Florida*. Philadelphia: Dorrance & Company, 1974, p. 43+.

Walter L. Smith. *The Magnificent Twelve: Florida's Black Junior Colleges*. Orlando: Four-G Publishers, 1994.

The Struggle for Survival: A Partial History of the Negroes of Marion County, 1865 to 1976. Ocala: Black Historical Organization of Marion County, 1977.

Portia L. Taylor. *Community College Education for Black Students, A Case Study*. Dissertation. Gainesville: University of Florida, 1986, esp. pp. 78–109: "A History of Hampton Junior College, 1958–1966."

Chapter 42

Annie Kate Jackson, Audria V. Moore, Dr. A. Ronald Hudson, and Susan Cohen. *Treasure Coast Black Heritage: A Pictorial History*. Virginia Beach, VA: Donning Publishers, 1996 [about Indian River County, Martin County, and St. Lucie County].

Chapter 43

Kathryne Ashley. *George E. Merrick and Coral Gables, Florida*. Coral Gables: Crystal Bay Publishers, 1985.

Gene Burnett. "The Peacock Inn Was the Center of Coconut Grove." *Florida Trend*, June 1978: pp. 71–74.

"Carrie Meek Remembers: Florida's Grand Dame . . . For the People," *Flavour: Black Florida Life & Style*, vol. 6, no. 2 (summer 2005), p. 24+.

Peter Cary. "Fort Lauderdale's Negro Beach." Bob Kearney, editor. *Mostly Sunny Days: A Miami Herald Salute to South Florida's Heritage.* Miami: Miami Herald Publishing Company, 1986, pp. 162–164.

Arthur M. Cohen. "The Process of Desegregation: A Case Study," *The Journal of Negro Education*, vol. 35 (fall 1966), pp. 445–451.

Arthur M. Cohen. "Racial Integration in a Southern Junior College," *Junior College Journal*, vol. 35 (March 1965), pp. 8–11.

David R. Colburn. Jane L. Landers. *The African American Heritage of Florida.* Gainesville: University Press of Florida, 1995, esp. Chapter Thirteen: "The Pattern of Race Relations in Miami Since the 1920s" by Raymond A. Mohl.

Tananarive Due and Patricia Due. *Freedom in the Family: A Mother-Daughter Memoir of the Fight for Civil Rights.* New York: Ballantine, 2003.

"Coconut Grove Marks Black History." *Florida Heritage.* Summer 1993: p. 6.

Alma J. Crawford. "Old-style procession marks tribute to Miami pioneers," *The Miami Times*, April 14, 1994, p. 1A.

Derek T. Davis. "Annie M. Coleman led way for library, hiring of Black officers," *The Miami Times*, February 18, 1993, p. 4D.

Derek T. Davis. "Georgette Tea Room is example of Black identity in Miami," *The Miami Times*, April 8, 1993, Lifestyle, p. 1.

Love Dean. "Pirates and Legends," *Florida Keys Magazine* (1st quarter, 1981), pp. 10–14.

Beth Dunlop. "Opa-Locka Was Araby In Mrs. Higgins' Day," *The Miami Herald*, May 4, 1977, p. 1D.

Marvin Dunn. *Black Miami in the Twentieth Century.* Gainesville: University Press of Florida, 1997.

Anthony Faiola. "Black activists seek to preserve school," *The Miami Herald, Neighbors* Magazine, July 28, 1991, p. 2.

Dorothy Fields. "Black Entertainment, 1908–1919," *Update*, December 1974, p. 11.

Dorothy Jenkins Fields. "Reflections on Black History: Cocoanut Grove, 1880–1903, A Selected Chronology." *Update* [Historical Association of Southern Florida], December 1975, pp. 3, 12.

Dorothy Jenkins Fields. "Reflections on Black History: Miami's First Newspaper" — about *The Industrial Reporter, Update* February 1976, p. 10.

Dorothy Jenkins Fields. "Reflections on Black History: Miami's Incorporation," *Update* [Historical Association of Southern Florida], August 1976, p. 10. This article lists all the blacks who were present at the incorporation of Miami.

Dorothy J. Fields. "Reflections on Black History: Stevedores," *Update*, June 1975, p. 9.

Dorothy Jenkins Fields. "Reflections on Black History," *Update*, October 1975, p. 8.

Frank S. FitzGerald-Bush. *A Dream of Araby: Glenn H. Curtiss and the Founding of Opa-locka.* Opa-Locka: South Florida Archaeological Museum, 1976.

Thomas F. Fleischmann. "Black Miamians in *The Miami Metropolis*, 1896–1900," *Tequesta*, vol. 52 (1992), pp. 21–38.

From Wilderness to Metropolis: The History and Architecture of Dade County, Florida, 1825–1940. Miami: Metropolitan Dade County, 1982.

Dorothy Gaiter. "26 Grove Townhouses Dedicated to Builder," *The Miami Herald*, May 1, 1976, p. 2B.

Paul S. George. "Colored Town: Miami's Black Community, 1896–1930," *Florida Historical Quarterly*, vol. 56 (April 1978), pp. 432–447.

Paul S. George. *A Journey Through Time: A Pictorial History of South Dade.* Virginia Beach, VA: Donning Company, 1995.

Charisse L. Grant. "Restoring pioneer home skyrockets to $800,000." *The Miami Herald*, September 12, 1991, p. 1B+.

Bea Hines. "Overtown: Good Times, Bad Times." Bob Kearney, editor. *Mostly Sunny Days: A Miami Herald Salute to South Florida's Heritage*. Miami: Miami Herald Publishing Company, 1986, pp. 96–98.

"The Industrial Reporter," *Update*, August 1976, p. 4.

Lisa Jacques. "John Johnson rose from humble origins to become pioneering judge," *The Miami Times*, February 18, 1993, p. 3D.

Erick Johnson. "Kids get preview of restored Chapman House for opening." *The Miami Times*, April 15, 1993, p. 4C.

Dr. S. H. Johnson as told to Dorothy Jenkins Fields. "Reflections on Black History: Fun and Games Overtown," *Update*, August 1977, p. 8+ [about Virginia Key Beach].

Howard Kleinberg, editor. Miami: The Way We Were. Tampa: Surfside Publishing, 1989, pp. 12–13: "Black Caesar"; pp. 54–55: "Black church in Grove as early as 1894."

Abraham D. Lavender and Adele S. News. *Black Communities in Transition: Voices from South Florida*. Lanham, MD: University Press of America, 1996.

Robert Liss. "Coconut Grove: 105-Year Effort to Preserve an Idea," *The Miami Herald*, March 11, 1978, p. 1A+.

"Mariah Brown House to be restored in Coconut Grove as tribute to Bahamians," *The Miami Times*, May 19, 1994, p. 3A.

Kevin M. McCarthy. *Florida Lighthouses*. Gainesville: University of Florida Press, 1990, pp. 41–44.

Kevin M. McCarthy. *Twenty Florida Pirates*. Sarasota: Pineapple Press, 1994, pp. 38–41 [about Black Caesar].

Raymond A. Mohl, Matilda Graff, and Shirley M. Zoloth. *South of the South: Jewish Activists and the Civil Rights Movement in Miami, 1945–1960*. Gainesville: University Press of Florida, 2004.

Harry A. Ploski and James Williams, compilers and editors. *The Negro Almanac: A Reference Work on the African American*. Detroit: Gale Research Inc., 1989, p. 250.

Kim A. O'Connell. "The Keepers of the Keys" [about Porgy Key], *National Parks*, vol. 77, no. 5–6 (May/June 2003), pp. 30–33.

Arva Moore Parks. "Yesterday." *Coconut Grove U.S.A. Centennial, 1873–1973*. Coconut Grove: no publ., 1974, pp. 6–10.

Shelia Payton. "'Everybody Cared in The Grove,'" *The Miami Herald*, May 30, 1976, pp. 1B-2B.

Shelia Payton. "Looking Back at Being Black," *The Miami Herald*, February 1, 1976, p. 1G+.

Eve Reed. "Funky Nights in Overtown," *South Florida History Magazine*, spring/summer 1993, pp. 8–14. This article includes a list of performers who appeared in Overtown in the 1940s, 1950s, and 1960s.

Schools For the Miami Area. Tallahassee: State Department of Education, 1940.

J. Irving E. Scott. *The Education of Black People in Florida*. Philadelphia: Dorrance & Company, 1974, pp. 53–54.

John Sewell. *Miami Memoirs: A New Pictorial Edition of John Sewell's Own Story* by Arva Moore Parks. Miami: Arva Parks & Co., 1987.

Melanie Shell-Weiss. "Coming North to the South: Migration, Labor and City-Building in Twentieth-Century Miami," *Florida Historical Quarterly*, vol. 84, no. 1 (summer 2005), pp. 79–99.

Jean C. Taylor. "South Dade's Black Pioneers," *Update*, June 1976, pp. 10–12.

Jean Taylor. *Villages of South Dade*. St. Petersburg: Byron Kennedy and Company, 1985?

Albert Payson Terhune. *Black Caesar's Clan*. New York: George H. Doran Company, 1922.

David O. True. "Pirates and Treasure Trove of South Florida," *Tequesta: The Journal of the Historical Association of Southern Florida* (1947), pp. 3–13.

Eugene C. Thomas. "Episcopal Church was born of struggle for dignity of Blacks, *The Miami Times*, February 10, 1994, p. 4D.

Marjorie Valbrun. "Cleanup is just a start for all-black cemetery." *The Miami Herald*. March 15, 1992, p. 2B.

Arthur O. White. "The desegregation of Florida's public junior colleges, 1954–1977," *Integrated Education*, vol. 16, no. 3 (May-June 1978), pp. 31–36.

Arthur O. White. *A Thirty Year History of Florida's State System of Community Colleges 1947–1977*. Dissertation. University of Florida, esp. pp. 38–40.

Jim Woodman. *The Book of Key Biscayne*. Miami: Miami Post, 1961.

Chapter 44

Anthony Atwood. "Five Blacks in Navy Blue: A Report on Civil War Sailors Buried in Key West Cemetery," *Florida Keys Sea Heritage Journal*, vol. 15, no. 1 (fall 2004), pp. 3–7.

Rodman Bethel. *Flagler's Folly: The Railroad That Went to Sea and Was Blown Away*. Key West: Bethel, 1987.

Rodman Bethel. *A Slumbering Giant of the Past: Fort Jefferson, U.S.A. in the Dry Tortugas*. Key West? R. Bethel, 1979.

George Walter Born. *Preserving Paradise: The Architectural Heritage and History of the Florida Keys*. Charleston, SC: History Press, 2006.

J. Wills Burke. *The Streets of Key West: A History Through Street Names*. Sarasota: Pineapple Press, 2004.

Gene Burnett. "The 'Gibraltar' Gripped by an Ancient Curse," *Florida Trend*, vol. 17 (February 1975), pp. 54–55 [about Fort Jefferson].

David R. Colburn and Jane L. Landers. *The African American Heritage of Florida*. Gainesville: University Press of Florida, 1995, esp. Chapter Seven: "Freedom Was as Close as the River" by Daniel L. Schafer.

Christopher Cox. *A Key West Companion*. New York: St. Martin's Press, 1983, especially pp. 73–78: "Whitelaw Reid Visits Sandy Cornish" and "Cornish Memorial AME ZION Church."

James M. Denham and Canter Brown Jr. "Black Sheriffs of Post-Civil War Florida," *The Sheriff's Star*, vol. 42, no. 5 (September/October, 1998), pp. 12–15.

George Hall. *Key West*. London: Osprey, 1991.

Maxine D. Jones and Kevin M. McCarthy. *African Americans in Florida*. Sarasota: Pineapple Press, 1993, pp. 25–26.

Herbert S. Klein. *The Middle Passage: Comparative Studies in the Atlantic Slave Trade*. Princeton: Princeton University Press, 1978.

Joan & Wright Langley. *Key West: Images of the Past*. Key West: C. C. Belland & E. O. Swift, 1982.

Daniel P. Mannix. *Black Cargoes: A History of the Atlantic Slave Trade, 1518–1865*. New York: Viking, 1962.

Kevin M. McCarthy. *Thirty Florida Shipwrecks*. Sarasota: Pineapple Press, 1992, pp. 29–31 [about the *Henrietta Marie*].

Stuart McIver. *Glimpses of South Florida History*. Miami: Florida Flair Books, 1988, p. 49: "Working on the Overseas Railroad."

Maureen Ogle. *Key West: History of an Island of Dreams*. Gainesville: University Press of Florida, 2003.

Pat Parks. *The Railroad That Died at Sea*. Brattleboro, Vermont: Stephen Greene Press, 1968.

Shelia Payton. "Looking Back at Being Black," *The Miami Herald*, February 1, 1976, p. 8G.

Jerry and June Powell. *Marathon: Heart of the Florida Keys*. Marathon: Seagrape Publications, 1980.

Larry E. Rivers and Canter Brown Jr. "African Americans in South Florida: A Home and a Haven for Reconstruction-era Leaders," *Tequesta*, no. 56 (1996), pp. 5–23.

Lewis G. Schmidt. "From Slavery to Freedom and Success: Sandy Cornish and Lillah Cornish," *Florida Keys Sea Heritage Journal*, vol. 4, no. 3 (spring 1994), p. 1+.

Larry Thompson. "'The Rock': Marathon's historic black area changes." *The Key West Citizen*, September 27, 1993: p. 5A.

Dinizulu Gene Tinnie. "Divers honor Ancestors at site of wreck of slave ship," *The Miami Times*, May 20, 1993, p. 9A 31 [about the *Henrietta Marie*].

Jonathan Walker. *Trial and Imprisonment of Jonathan Walker, at Pensacola, Florida, for Aiding Slaves to Escape from Bondage.* 1845. Reprinted Gainesville: University Presses of Florida, 1974.

Sharon Wells. *Forgotten Legacy: Blacks in Nineteenth Century Key West.* Key West: Historic Key West Preservation Board, 1982.

Joy Williams. *The Florida Keys: A History & Guide.* New York: Random House, 1987.

Writers' Program. *History of the Fort Jefferson National Monument.* No place or date.

Chapter 45

Michelle Genz. "Pride and Prejudice," *Tropic* September 30, 1990.

Pat Keck. "Burney Park dedication held at American Beach," *News-Leader* [Fernandina Beach, Florida], October 24, 1990, p. 7A.

Thomas L. Johnson and Phillip C. Dunn, editors. *A True Likeness: The Black South of Richard Samuel Roberts, 1920–1936.* Columbia, SC: Bruccoli Clark, 1986.

Leedell W. Neyland. *Twelve Black Floridians.* Tallahassee: Florida Agricultural and Mechanical University Foundation, 1970, pp. 53–59.

Marsha Dean Phelts. *An American Beach for African Americans.* Gainesville: University Press of Florida, 1997.

Marsha Dean Phelts. "The Beginnings of an American Beach for African Americans on Amelia Island," *The Florida Star* [Jacksonville], February 5, 1994, p. 14; February 12, 1994, p. 13; February 19, 1994, p. 13; February 26, 1994, pp. 12–13.

Russ Rymer. *American Beach: A Saga of Race, Wealth, and Memory.* New York: HarperCollins, 1998.

Chapter 46

Wendy L. Bovard. *Why Not Me?: The Story of Gladys Milton, Midwife.* TN: Book Publishing Company, 1993.

Edwin R. Embree and Julia Waxman. *Investment in People: The Story of the Julius Rosenwald Fund.* New York: Harper & Brothers Publishers, 1949.

Nancy M. Kenaston. *From Cabin to Campus: A History of the Okaloosa County School System.* Crestview: Okaloosa County School Board, 1977.

J. Irving E. Scott. *The Education of Black People in Florida.* Philadelphia: Dorrance & Company, 1974, p. 27+ - about the Rosenwald Fund.

Debra Anne Susie. *In the Way of Our Grandmothers: A Cultural View of Twentieth-Century Midwifery in Florida.* Athens: University of Georgia Press, 1988.

Chapter 47

Kyle S. VanLandingham and Alma Hetherington. *History of Okeechobee County.* Fort Pierce, FL: Kyle S. Van Landingham, 1978.

Chapter 48

Eve Bacon. *Orlando: A Centennial History.* Chuluota, FL.: The Mickler House, 1977. Vol. 2, pp. 145–46.

Allen G. Breed. "80 years later, man finds he cannot go home." *Gainesville Sun*, Feb. 11, 2001, p. 11B [about the Ocoee massacre].

Lester Dabbs. "A Report of the Circumstances and Events of the Race Riot on November 2, 1920, in Ocoee Florida," M.A. Thesis, Stetson University, 1969.

Joy Wallace Dickinson. *Remembering Orlando: Tales from Elvis to Disney. A History.* Charleston, SC: History Press, 2006.

Steve Glassman and Kathryn Lee Seidel, editors. *Zora in Florida.* Orlando: University of Central Florida Press, 1991: Anna Lillios, "Excursions into Zora Neale Hurston's Eatonville," pp. 13–27.

Robert E. Hemenway. *Zora Neale Hurston: A Literary Biography.* Urbana, IL: University of Illinois Press, 1977.

Zora Neale Hurston. *Dust Tracks on a Road.* Philadelphia: Lippincott, 1942.

Baynard Kendrick. *Orlando, A Century Plus.* Orlando: Sentinel Star Company, 1976.

N.Y. Nathiri, editor. *Zora! Zora Neale Hurston: A Woman and Her Community.* Orlando: Sentinel Communications Company, 1991.

Orlando: History in Architecture. Orlando: Orlando Historic Preservation Board, 1984.

Frank M. Otey. *Eatonville, Florida: A Brief History of One of America's First Freedmen's Towns.* Winter Park, FL: Four-G Publishers, 1989.

J. Irving E. Scott. *The Education of Black People in Florida.* Philadelphia: Dorrance & Company, 1974, p. 44.

Jerrell H. Shofner. *Orlando: The City Beautiful.* Tulsa: Continental Heritage Press, 1984.

Geraldine Fortenberry Thompson. *Orlando, Florida.* Charleston, SC: Arcadia Publishing, 2003.

Janelle Yates. *Zora Neale Hurston: A Storyteller's Life.* Staten Island: Ward Hill Press, 1991.

Chapter 49

Al and Bob Cody. "The Past Hundred Years . . . Contributions of the Black Community." Kissimmee: First Florida Bank, 1987.

Zora Neale Hurston. "Lawrence of the River," *Saturday Evening Post,* September 5, 1942, pp. 18, 55–57. The same article was condensed in *Negro Digest,* 1 (March 1943), pp. 47–49.

Betty Metzger, editor. *The History of Kissimmee.* St. Petersburg: Byron Kennedy & Company, 1983?

Minnie Moore Willson. *History of Osceola County, Florida Frontier Life.* Orlando: Inland Press, 1935.

Chapter 50

Jacqueline Ashton. *Boca Raton: From Pioneer Days to the Fabulous Twenties.* Boca Raton: Dedication Press, 1979, esp. pp. 85–93.

Brent Cantrell. "Black Daily Life in Northwestern Palm Beach County: Glimpses from a Half-Century Ago," *South Florida History Magazine,* Spring/Summer 1993, pp. 20–27.

Everee Jimerson Clarke. *Pleasant City, West Palm Beach.* Charleston, SC: Arcadia Publishing Co., 2005.

Donald W. Curl. *Palm Beach County: An Illustrated History.* Northridge, CA: Windsor Publications, Inc., 1986.

Julie Eagle. "Alice's place," *News/Sun-Sentinel,* Sept. 16, 1984, p. 1B+.

Arthur S. Evans Jr., and David Lee. *Pearl City, Florida: A Black Community Remembers.* Boca Raton: Florida Atlantic University Press, 1990.

H.D. Gates. *Pioneer Days at Boca Raton.* Boca Raton: Gates, 1948?

"Harma Miller: from migrant to mayor." *Essence* (July 1991), p. 33.

Robert E. Hemenway. *Zora Neale Hurston: A Literary Biography.* Urbana, IL: University of Illinois Press, 1977.

Zora Neale Hurston. *Their Eyes Were Watching God.* Philadelphia: Lippincott, 1937.

Amy Huttunen, "Architect's Home Part of Dream," *The Post* [Palm Beach], June 20, 1982, North County edition, p. B1 [about the Hazel Augustus Home].

Maxine D. Jones and Kevin M. McCarthy. *African Americans in Florida.* Sarasota: Pineapple Press, Inc., 1993, pp. 120–121 [about Gwen Cherry].

"Junior College Integrated By Negro Girl's Enrolling," *The Palm Beach Post,* September 12, 1961, pp. 1, 5.

Eliot Kleinberg. *Black Cloud: The Great Florida Hurricane of 1928.* New York: Carroll & Graf Publishers, 2003.

Eliot Kleinberg. *Palm Beach Past: The Best of "Post Time."* Charleston, SC: The History Press, 2006.

James R. Knott. *Palm Beach Revisited: Historical Vignettes of Palm Beach County.* Palm Beach: J. R. Knott, 1987.

Bill McGoun. "Dr. Thomas Leroy Jefferson," *The Palm Beach Post,* June 20, 1977, pp. B1–2.

Stuart McIver. "Cooks to Catchers, Bellhops to Batters," *Sunshine* [*News/Sun-Sentinel,* Fort Lauderdale], August 22, 1993, p.23+.

Stuart McIver. *Yesterday's Palm Beach, Including Palm Beach County.* Miami: E. A. Seemann, 1976.

James McJunkins and Brenda Lane. "Up From the Styx = the black experience." *The Palm Beach Post-Times,* September 9, 1973, C1+. Continued September 10, 1973, p. A7+; September 11, 1973, p. A7+; September 12, 1973, p. B1+; September 13, 1973, p. B1+; September 14, 1973, p. B1+; September 15, 1973, p. A4+.

Dan Moffett. "Charred History: Styx' Burning Was the End of Palm Beach's Black Community." *The Post* [Palm Beach] June 13, 1982, p. B1, 3.

Theodore Pratt. *That Was Palm Beach.* St. Petersburg: Great Outdoors, 1968.

Vivian Reissland Rouson-Gossett, editor. *Like a Mighty Banyan: Contributions of Black People to the History of Palm Beach County.* Palm Beach County: Palm Beach Junior College, 1982.

Walter L. Smith. *The Magnificent Twelve: Florida's Black Junior Colleges.* Orlando: Four-G Publishers, 1994.

Wilma Bell Spencer. *Palm Beach: A Century of Heritage.* Washington, DC: Mount Vernon Publishing Co., 1975.

Portia L. Taylor. *Community College Education for Black Students, A Case Study.* Dissertation. Gainesville: University of Florida, 1986.

Arthur O. White. "The desegregation of Florida's public junior colleges, 1954–1977," *Integrated Education,* vol. 16, no. 3 (May-June 1978), pp. 31–36.

Arthur O. White. *A Thirty Year History of Florida's State System of Community Colleges 1947–1977.* Dissertation. University of Florida, esp. pp. 29–30.

Alec Wilkinson. *Big Sugar: Seasons in the Cane Fields of Florida.* New York: Knopf, 1989.

Lawrence E. Will. *Swamp to Sugar Bowl: Pioneer Days in Belle Glade.* St. Petersburg: Great Outdoors Publishing, 1968.

Chapter 51

James J. Horgan. *The Historic Places of Pasco County.* Pasco County: Pasco County Historical Preservation Committee, 1992.

Carol Jeffares. *Pasco Heritage.* Tampa: Tribune Company, 1987, esp. pp. 21–22: "The quest for equality" [about J.D. Moore and the school for black children].

Chapter 52

Raymond Arsenault. *St. Petersburg and the Florida Dream, 1888–1950.* Norfolk, Va.: Donning Company, 1988.

Roy Cadwell. *Clearwater, "A Sparkling City."* Minneapolis, MN: T.S. Denison & Company, Inc., 1977.

Hampton Dunn. *Yesterday's Clearwater.* Miami: Seemann Publishing Co., 1973.

Hampton Dunn. *Yesterday's St. Petersburg.* Miami: E. A. Seemann, 1973.

Barbara Fitzgerald and Tracie Reddick. "The Illusion of Inclusion," *The Tampa Tribune*, May 9, 1993, Nation, p. 1+; May 10, 1993, Nation, p. 1+.

Samuel D. Fitzsimmons. *Economic and Social Structure of St. Petersburg and Connotation on Clearwater.*

Karl H. Grismer. *The Story of St. Petersburg.* St. Petersburg: P. K. Smith, 1948.

Scott Taylor Hartzell. *Remembering St. Petersburg, Florida: Sunshine City Stories.* Charleston, SC: History Press, 2006.

Scott Taylor Hartzell. *Remembering St. Petersburg, Florida: Volume 2, More Sunshine City Stories.* Charleston, SC: History Press, 2006.

Maxine D. Jones and Kevin M. McCarthy. *African Americans in Florida.* Sarasota: Pineapple Press, Inc., 1993: pp. 124–125 [about Judge Hackett] and pp. 132–134 [about Harry Singletary Jr.].

Susan Lykes. "Hatchett offers 'real understanding,'" *Tallahassee Democrat*, October 24, 1975, p. 11.

Del Marth. *St. Petersburg: Once Upon a Time.* St. Petersburg: The City of St. Petersburg Bicentennial Committee, 1976.

Leedell W. Neyland. *Twelve Black Floridians.* Tallahassee: Florida Agricultural and Mechanical University Foundation, 1970, pp. 1–5.

Darryl Paulson. "Stay Out, The Water's Fine: Desegregating Municipal Swimming Facilities in St. Petersburg, Florida," *Tampa Bay History*, vol. 4, no. 2 (fall/winter 1982), pp. 6–19.

Darryl Paulson and Milly St. Julien. "Desegregating Public Schools in Manatee and Pinellas Counties, 1954–71," *Tampa Bay History*, vol. 7, no. 1 (spring/summer 1985), pp. 30–41.

Joe M. Richardson. "Jonathan C. Gibbs: Florida's Only Negro Cabinet Member," *Florida Historical Quarterly*, vol. 42, no. 4 (April 1964), pp. 363–368.

Sandra W. Rooks. *St. Petersburg, Florida.* Black America Series. Charleston, SC: Arcadia Publishing, 2003.

Sandra W. Rooks and Carol Mountain. *Tarpon Springs, Florida.* Black America Series. Charleston, SC: Arcadia Publishing, 2003.

Sandra W. Rooks and Randolph Lightfoot. *Clearwater Florida.* Black America Series. Charleston, SC: Arcadia Publishing, 2002.

Michael Sanders. *Clearwater.* Norfolk, VA: Donning, 1983.

Mark S. Schantz. "Historic status, volunteers, sought for withering Rose Cemetery," *The Suncoast News*, August 19, 2000.

James A. Schnur. "Desegregation of Public Schools in Pinellas County, Florida," *Tampa Bay History*, vol. 13, no. 1 (spring/summer 1991), pp. 26–43.

Walter L. Smith, *The Magnificent Twelve: Florida's Black Junior Colleges.* Orlando: Four-G Publishers, 1994.

Gertrude K. Stoughton. *Tarpon Springs Florida: The Early Years.* Tarpon Springs: Tarpon Springs Area Historical Society, Inc., 1975.

Portia L. Taylor. *Community College Education for Black Students, A Case Study.* Dissertation. Gainesville: University of Florida, 1986.

Diane Tunick. "Clearwater: Still Sparkling," *Florida Trend*, May 1981, pp. 60–67.

John Van Gieson. "Hatchett becomes Florida's first black justice," *Tallahassee Democrat*, September 2, 1975, p. 1.

Arthur O. White. "The desegregation of Florida's public junior colleges, 1954–1977," *Integrated Education*, vol. 16, no. 3 (May-June 1978), pp. 31–36.

Arthur O. White. *A Thirty Year History of Florida's State System of Community Colleges 1947–1977*. Dissertation. University of Florida, esp. p. 28.

Jon L. Wilson. "Days of Fear: A Lynching in St. Petersburg," *Tampa Bay History*, vol. 5, no. 2 (fall/winter 1983), pp. 4–26.

Jon Wilson and Rosalie Peck. *St. Petersburg's Historic 22nd Street South*. Charleston, SC: History Press, 2006.

June Hurley Young. *Pinellas Peninsula*. St. Petersburg, FL: Byron Kennedy & Co., 1984.

William Zinsser. *Willie and Dwike*. New York: Harper & Row, 1984.

Chapter 53

Bernice More Barber. *From Beginnings to Boom*. Haines City: Barber, 1975, pp. 187–190: "Haines City's Black Community (1907–1926)."

Bartow, Florida. Bartow: Greater Bartow Cham. of Com., 1965.

Canter Brown Jr. *Florida's Peace River Frontier*. Orlando: University of Central Florida Press, 1991.

Louise Frisbie. *Peace River Pioneers*. Miami: Seemann Publishing, Inc., 1974.

"New Tombstone A Memorial To America's Oldest Man" *Jet* August 2, 1982, p. 16 [about Charlie Smith].

Chapter 54

Jervis Anderson. *A. Philip Randolph: A Biographical Portrait*. New York: Harcourt Brace Jovanovich, 1973.

June D. Bell. "A Wealth of History," *The Florida Times-Union* [Jacksonville], March 15, 1994, p. A-1+ [about a black dentist, Napoleon Ben Hester, who lived in Palatka from 1914 until the 1970s].

David R. Colburn and Jane L. Landers. *The African American Heritage of Florida*. Gainesville: University Press of Florida, 1995, esp. Chapter Seven: "Freedom Was as Close as the River" by Daniel L. Schafer.

Susan Clark. *A Historic Tour Guide of Palatka and Putnam County, Florida*. Palatka: Putnam County Historical Society, 1992.

John Holway, editor. *Black Diamonds: Life in the Negro Leagues from the Men Who Lived It*. Westport, CT.: Meckler, 1989.

John B. Holway. *Blackball Stars: Negro League Pioneers*. Westport, Conn.: Meckler, 1988.

Maxine D. Jones and Kevin M. McCarthy. *African Americans in Florida*. Sarasota: Pineapple Press, Inc., 1993, pp. 116–117: "Two African American War Heroes, 1968–1969" [about Robert H. Jenkins Jr.].

Rayford W. Logan and Michael R. Winston, editors. *Dictionary of American Negro Biography*. New York: Norton, 1982, p. 397+.

Brian E. Michaels. *The River Flows North: A History of Putnam County*. Palatka, FL: The Putnam County Archives and History Commission, 1976, pp. 195–207.

Robert Peterson. *Only the Ball Was White: A History of Legendary Black Players and All-black Professional Teams*. New York: McGraw-Hill, 1984.

Paula F. Pfeffer. *A. Philip Randolph, Pioneer of the Civil Rights Movement*. Baton Rouge: Louisiana State University Press, 1990.

David L. Porter, editor. *Biographical Dictionary of American Sports: Baseball*. Westport, Conn.: Greenwood Press, 1987, p. 333+.

Walter L. Smith. *The Magnificent Twelve: Florida's Black Junior Colleges*. Orlando: Four-G Publishers, 1994.

Portia L. Taylor. *Community College Education for Black Students, A Case Study*. Dissertation. Gainesville: University of Florida, 1986.

Arthur O. White. "The desegregation of Florida's public junior colleges, 1954–1977," *Integrated Education*, vol. 16, no. 3 (May-June 1978), pp. 31–36.

Chapter 55

R. Michael Anderson. "Old college campus may shine anew if plans pan out," *The Florida Times-Union* [Jacksonville], September 14, 1987, p. B3 [about Florida Memorial College].

Kim Bradley. "City's civil rights struggle recalled." *The St. Augustine Record*, March 29, 1992, p. 4A. That page also contains a list of those who were honored for participating in the city's civil rights movement of the 1960s.

Ray Charles and David Ritz. *Brother Ray, Ray Charles' Own Story*. New York: Dial, 1978.

David R. Colburn. *Racial Change and Community Crisis: St. Augustine, Florida, 1877–1980*. Gainesville: University of Florida Press, 1991.

David R. Colburn and Jane L. Landers. *The African American Heritage of Florida*. Gainesville: University Press of Florida, 1995, esp. Chapter Two: "Traditions of African American Freedom and Community in Spanish Colonial Florida."

Kathleen A. Deagan. "Fort Mose: America's First Free Black Community," in *Spanish Pathways in Florida* edited by Ann L. Henderson and Gary Mormino. Sarasota: Pineapple Press, 1991.

Kathleen A. Deagan and Darcie A. MacMahon. *Fort Mose: Colonial America's Black Fortress of Freedom*. Gainesville: University Press of Florida, 1995.

David J. Garrow. *Bearing the Cross*. New York: William Morrow and Company, 1986, esp. pp. 316–341.

David J. Garrow, editor. *St. Augustine, Florida, 1963–1964: Mass Protest and Racial Violence*. Brooklyn, NY: Carlson, 1989.

Deric A. Gilliard. *Living in the Shadows of a Legend: Unsung Heroes and "Sheroes" Who Marched With Dr. Martin Luther King, Jr.* Decatur, GA: Gilliard Communications, 2003.

Paul Good. *Once to Every Man*. New York: Putnam, 1970 [a novel about the demonstrations].

Paul Good. *The Trouble I've Seen*. Washington, DC: Howard University Press, 1975.

Patricia C. Griffin and Diana S. Edwards. "Results and Future Directions" [about the black community photographed by Twine], *The East-Florida Gazette* [newspaper of the St. Augustine Historical Society], February 1990. The same issue has articles about Richard Twine, his photographs, and Lincolnville.

Karen Harvey. *Legends and Tales: Anecdotal Histories of St. Augustine, Florida*. Charleston, SC: History Press, 2005.

Karen Harvey. *Legends and Tales, Volume II: Remembering St. Augustine*. Charleston, SC: History Press, 2006.

Ann Hyman. "Photos of Lincolnville at Edward Waters," *The Florida Times-Union* [Jacksonville], October 28, 1990, p. D-6.

Maxine D. Jones and Kevin M. McCarthy. *African Americans in Florida*. Sarasota: Pineapple Press, Inc., 1993, pp. 1–14.

William Kunstler. *Deep in My Heart*. New York: Morrow, 1966.

Jane Landers. "Blacks in Spanish Florida," *F.E.H. Forum*, vol. 12, no. 1 (spring 1989), pp. 9–12.

Jane Landers. *Black Society in Spanish Florida*. Urbana: University of Illinois Press, 1999.

Jane Landers. *Fort Mose*. St. Augustine: St. Augustine Historical Society, 1992. This is a reprint of an article that appeared in *The American Historical Review*, vol. 95, no. 1.

Jane Landers. "Jorge Biassou, Black Chieftain," in *Clash Between Cultures*, edited by Jacqueline K. Fretwell and Susan R. Parker. St. Augustine: St. Augustine Historical Society, 1988.

"Lincolnville Festival All-Day Fun July 5," *The Independent Traveler*, June 18–24, 1980, p. 15.

Gary W. McDonogh, editor. *The Florida Negro*. Jackson, MS: University Press of Mississippi, 1993 [has interviews with at least one former slave from St. Johns County].

Michael A. W. Ottey. "Exploring a Heritage" [about Fort Mose], *The Miami-Herald*, Feb. 2, 2003, p. 3BH+.

Idella Parker with Mark Keating. *Idella: Marjorie Rawlings' "Perfect Maid."* Gainesville, University Press of Florida, 1992.

Idella Parker with Bud and Liz Crussell. *From Reddick to Cross Creek*. Gainesville: University Press of Florida, 1999.

Randolph Pendleton. "A racial wrinkle for the Oldest City," *The Florida Times-Union*, January 20, 1991, p. C-1+.

Kenneth W. Porter. *The Negro on the American Frontier*. New York: Arno Press, 1971.

James Salzer. "Civil rights fight shattered 'quaint' town," *The Florida Times-Union*, January 18, 1988, p. B-3.

Daniel L. Schafer. "Freedom Was as Close as the River: The Blacks of Northeast Florida and the Civil War," *El Escribano*, vol. 23 (1986), pp. 91–116.

"'Spot-Shot' Galimore," *Ebony*, vol. 14, no. 3 (January 1959), pp. 72–76.

Time. August 7, 1964, p. 88 [Galimore's obituary].

Dana Treen. "Lincolnville fighting to regain heritage," *The Florida Times-Union* [Jacksonville], December 1, 1991, p. B-1+.

Barbara Walch. *Frank B. Butler: Lincolnville Businessman and Founder of St. Augustine, Florida's Historic Black Beach*. St. Augustine: Rudolph B. Hadley Sr., 1992.

Lee Warner. *Free Men in an Age of Servitude*. Lexington, KY: University Press of Kentucky, 1992.

Joseph White. "Lincolnville: The Historic St. Augustine Visitors May Never See," *Folio Weekly*, Sept. 15, 1992, pp. 16–23.

Chapter 56

Walter R. Hellier. *Indian River - Florida's Treasure Coast*. Coconut Grove, FL: Hurricane House, 1965.

Walter R. Hellier. *Palmetto Rambler*. New York: Vantage Press, 1973.

Robert E. Hemenway. *Zora Neale Hurston: A Literary Biography*. Urbana, IL: University of Illinois Press, 1977.

Annie Kate Jackson, Audria V. Moore, Dr. A. Ronald Hudson, and Susan Cohen. *Treasure Coast Black Heritage: A Pictorial History*. Virginia Beach, VA: Donning Publishers, 1996 [about St. Lucie County, Martin County, and Indian River County].

James Lyons. "Famous Negro Author Working As Maid Here Just 'To Live a Little." *The Miami Herald*. March 27, 1950, p. 1-B [about Zora Neale Hurston].

Gary Monroe. *The Highwaymen: Florida's African-American Landscape Painters*. Gainesville: University Press of Florida, 2001.

Gordon Patterson. "Zora Neale Hurston as English Teacher: A Lost Chapter Found," *The Marjorie Kinnan Rawlings Journal of Florida Literature*, vol. 5 (1993), pp. 51–60.

Lucille Rights. *A Historical View of Fort Pierce and the Indian River Environmental Community.* Fort Pierce, FL: St. Lucie County Schools, 1979.

Walter L. Smith. *The Magnificent Twelve: Florida's Black Junior Colleges.* Orlando: Four-G Publishers, 1994.

Portia L. Taylor. *Community College Education for Black Students, A Case Study.* Dissertation. Gainesville: University of Florida, 1986.

Kyle S. Van Landingham. *Pictorial History of Saint Lucie County, 1565–1910.* Fort Pierce, FL: St. Lucie Historical Society, 1976.

Alice Walker. *In Search of Our Mothers' Gardens.* San Diego: Harcourt Brace Jovanovich, 1983.

Chapter 57

Jacqueline Cochran. *The Stars at Noon.* Boston: Little, Brown and Company, 1954.

M. Luther King. *History of Santa Rosa County: A King's Country.* Milton, FL: no publ., 1972.

Brian Rucker. *Blackwater and Yellow Pine: The Development of Santa Rosa County.* Tallahassee: Florida State University, 1990.

Brian Rucker. "A Bagdad Christmas." Milton, FL: Patagonia Press, 1990.

Raymonde Slack-White. "The Grand Old House on School Street," in *When Black Folks Was Colored: A Collection of Memoirs and Poems by Black Americans.* Pensacola: African-American Heritage Society, Inc., 1993, pp. 64–65 [a description of what Bagdad life was like for blacks in the 1950s, including school, church, and home life].

Chapter 58

Bernice Brooks Bergen. *Sarasota Times Past.* Miami: Valiant Press, 1993, esp. p. 24 [about the AME Payne Chapel on the corner of Fifth and Central Avenue] and 29 [about turpentine camps].

Karl H. Grismer. *The Story of Sarasota.* Sarasota: M. E. Russell, 1946.

Jeff LaHurd. *Gulf Coast Chronicles: Remembering Sarasota's Past.* Charleston, SC: History Press, 2005.

Jeff LaHurd. *Quintessential Sarasota: Stories and Pictures from the 1920s to the 1950s.* Charleston, SC: History Press, 2006.

Jeff LaHurd. *Sarasota: A History.* Charleston, SC: History Press, 2006.

Del Marth. *Yesterday's Sarasota, Including Sarasota County.* Miami: E. A. Seemann, 1973.

Janet Snyder Matthews. *Edge of Wilderness: A Settlement History of Manatee River and Sarasota Bay, 1528–1885.* Tulsa, Okla.: Caprine Press, 1983.

Annie M. McElroy. *But Your World and My World: The Struggle For Survival: A Partial History of Blacks in Sarasota County, 1884–1986.* Sarasota: Black South Press, 1986.

Gilbert L. Porter and Leedell W. Neyland. *The History of the Florida State Teachers Association.* Washington: National Education Association, 1977.

Chapter 59

Arthur R. Ashe Jr. *A Hard Road to Glory: A History of the African-American Athlete Since 1946.* New York: Warner Books, Inc., 1988.

Altermese Smith Bentley. *Georgetown: The History of a Black Neighborhood.* Sanford?: Altermese Smith Bentley, 1989.

Victoria Brown-Smith. *Midway-the Midpoint: My Precious Memories of Times Gone By.* Sanford?: Luthers Publishing, 2002.

Charlie Carlson with Charlie Morgan. *Bookertown: A Journey to the Past.* Sanford?: Black Heritage of Seminole County, Florida, 2003.

Margaret Sprout Green. *Lake Mary's Beginnings and the Roaring Twenties in Lake Mary and Sanford, Florida.* Chuluota, FL.: Mickler House Publishers, 1986.

John Paul Jones. "City on the St. Johns: Why they all love Sanford," *North Florida Living,* May 1986, pp. 6–13.

Peter Schaal. *Sanford As I Knew It, 1912–1935.* Orlando?, 1970.

Albery A. Whitman. *The Rape of Florida.* St. Louis: Nixon-Jones Printing Co., 1884.

Chapter 60

Alcione M. Amos. *The Life of Luis Fatio Pacheco: Last Survivor of Dade's Battle.* Dade City, FL: Seminole Wars Historic Foundation, 2006.

Piers Anthony. *Tatham Mound.* New York: Morrow, 1991 [a novel about an Indian mound near the Withlacoochee River].

Mark F. Boyd. "The Seminole War: Its Background and Onset." *Florida Historical Quarterly* vol. 30. July 1951: 3–115.

David R. Colburn and Jane L. Landers. *The African American Heritage of Florida.* Gainesville: University Press of Florida, 1995, esp. Chapter Six: "Blacks and the Seminole Removal Debate, 1821–1835" by George Klos.

George Klos. "Blacks and Seminoles," *South Florida History Magazine.* Spring 1991, pp. 12–15.

Frank Laumer. *Massacre!* Gainesville, FL: University of Florida Press, 1968.

Daniel F. Littlefield Jr. *Africans and Seminoles.* Westport, CT: Greenwood Press, 1977.

Kenneth W. Porter. "The Early Life of Luis Pacheco Né Fatio." *The Negro History Bulletin.* Vol. 7, No. 3 (December 1943), pp. 52+.

Kenneth Wiggins Porter. *The Negro on the American Frontier.* New York: Arno Press and the *New York Times,* 1971, esp. pp. 182–358.

"Scholar with a Shovel" [about Terrance Weik and his archaeological work at Pilaklikaha] *Flavour: Black Florida Life & Style,* vol. 6, no. 2 (summer 2005), pp. 20–23.

Scott Thybony. "Against All Odds, Black Seminoles Won Their Freedom." *Smithsonian* (August 1991), pp. 90–101.

Brent Richards Weisman. *Like Beads on a String: A Culture History of the Seminole Indians in Northern Peninsular Florida.* Tuscaloosa, AL: University of Alabama Press, 1989.

Chapter 61

Timothy Evans. *The Silencing of Ruby McCollum: Race, Class, and Gender in the South.* Gainesville: University Press of Florida, 2006.

"Focus on Live Oak Centennial, 1878–1978." Live Oak: Suwannee Democrat, 1978.

Steve Glassman and Kathryn Lee Seidel, editors. *Zora in Florida.* Orlando: University of Central Florida Press, 1991: "Three Legal Entanglements of Zora Neale Hurston," pp. 174–182.

E. Arthur Ellis Jr. and Leslie E. Ellis. *The Trial of Ruby McCollum.* Bloomington, Indiana: 1st Books Library, 2003.

Robert L. Hall. "Tallahassee's Black Churches, 1865–1885," *Florida Historical Quarterly,* vol. 58. no. 2 (October 1979), pp. 185–196 [about Brown Theological Institute in Live Oak].

William Bradford Huie. *Ruby McCollum: Woman in the Suwannee Jail.* New York: Dutton, 1956.

William Bradford Huie. "The Strange Case of Ruby McCollum." *Ebony,* November 1954, p. 16.

Zora Neale Hurston. "The Life Story of Mrs. Ruby J. McCollum!" *Pittsburgh Courier,* May 2, 1953, p. 2, 26.

John Paul Jones. "Suwannee County—Florida's New Frontier," *Guide to North Florida Living* (May-June, 1982), pp. 25–33.

John Paul Jones. "Live Oak: 'Belle' of the Suwannee," *Florida Living* (November 1989), p. 10+.

Don Tracy. *The Hated One.* New York: Simon and Schuster, 1963.

Chapter 63

Lake Butler Women's Club. *History: Union County, Florida, 1921–1971. Celebrating 50th Anniversary of Union County, Florida.* Lake Butler: no publ., 1971.

Chapter 64

Ella Kaiser Carruth. *She Wanted To Read.* New York: Abingdon Press, 1966.

John Carter. "Rachel Robinson: 'I love the statue,'" *The News-Journal* [Daytona Beach] September 15, 1990, D1.

Susan Daker. "State marker honors a heritage of freedom" [about Freemanville and Mount Moriah Baptist Church in Port Orange], *Orlando Sentinel*, February 11, 2003, p. B1+.

Jesse Walter Dees. *The College Built on Prayer.* Daytona Beach: Bethune-Cookman College, 1953.

"Florida's First Negro Resort," *Ebony*, vol. 3, no. 4 (February 1948), pp. 24–26.

Arthur E. Francke Jr., Alyce Hockaday Gillingham, and Maxine Carey Turner. *Volusia: The West Side.* DeLand: West Volusia Historical Society, 1986.

Pleasant D. Gold. *History of Volusia County, Florida.* DeLand: Painter Printing Co., 1927.

Patricia C. Griffin. *Mullet on the Beach: The Minorcans of Florida, 1768–1788.* Jacksonville: University of North Florida Press, 1991.

Malu Halasa. *Mary McLeod Bethune: Educator.* New York: Chelsea House Publishers, 1989.

Ianthe B. Hebel. *Centennial History of Volusia County, Florida.* Daytona Beach: College Publishing Co., 1955.

Ianthe Bond Hebel. *Daytona Beach, Florida's Racial History.* Daytona Beach: no publ., 1966.

Rackham Holt. *Mary McLeod Bethune.* Garden City, NY: Doubleday, 1964.

"Howard Thurman Home Now National Historic Preservation Site," *The Miami Times*, August 23, 1990, p. 6A.

Lois Kaplan. "Dr. Thurman's Legacy." *Daytona Beach Morning Journal*, July 1, 1985: 1.

Gary Luther, editor. *History of New Smyrna, East Florida.* New Smyrna Beach: G. Luther, 1987, p. 15: "Mt. Pleasant and a Grave in the Street."

Patricia C. McKissack. *Mary McLeod Bethune.* Chicago: Children's Press, 1985.

John McPhee. *Oranges.* New York: Farrar, Straus and Giroux, 1967.

Milton Meltzer. *Mary McLeod Bethune.* New York: Viking Kestrel, 1987.

Steve Moore. "Robinson: A hero honored." *The News-Journal* [Daytona Beach] September 16, 1990, p. C-1+.

Catherine Owens Peare. *Mary McLeod Bethune.* New York: Vanguard, 1951.

E.P. Panagopoulos. *New Smyrna: An Eighteenth Century Greek Odyssey.* Gainesville: University of Florida Press, 1966.

A Pictorial History of New Smyrna's Westside. New Smyrna Beach: Senior Ushers, 1991.

Jane Quinn. *Minorcans in Florida: Their History and Heritage.* St. Augustine: Mission Press, 1975.

Philip D. Rasico. *The Minorcans of Florida: Their History, Language, and Culture.* New Smyrna Beach: Luthers, 1990.

Reflections: West Volusia County, 100 Years of Progress. DeLand: Bicentennial Commission, 1976, pp. 66–67: "James Washington Wright."

Jackie Robinson as told to Alfred Duckett. *I Never Had It Made.* New York: Putnam, 1972.

Carl Rowan with Jackie Robinson. *Wait Till Next Year.* New York: Random House, 1960.

Michael G. Schene. *Hopes, Dreams, and Promises: A History of Volusia County, Florida.* Daytona Beach: News-Journal Corporation, 1976, esp. pp. 37–38 [about the working conditions, housing, clothing, and food of the slaves].

J. Irving E. Scott. *The Education of Black People in Florida.* Philadelphia: Dorrance & Company, 1974, p. 55+.

Barb Shepherd. "A landmark of black heritage" [about Bradley Hall], *The Orlando Sentinel*, March 15, 1992, p. K-1+.

Walter L. Smith. *The Magnificent Twelve: Florida's Black Junior Colleges*. Orlando: Four-G Publishers, 1994.

Emma Gelders Sterne. *Mary McLeod Bethune*. New York: Knopf, 1957.

Zelia Wilson Sweett. "New Smyrna Beach and Neighboring Communities," in *Centennial History of Volusia County, Florida, 1854–1954*, edited by Ianthe Bond Hebel. Daytona Beach: College Publishing Company, 1955, p. 83+.

Zelia Wilson Sweett and J. C. Marsden. *New Smyrna, Florida: Its History and Antiquities*. DeLand: Painter, 1925

Portia L. Taylor. *Community College Education for Black Students, A Case Study*. Dissertation. Gainesville: University of Florida, 1986.

Howard Thurman. *With Head and Heart: The Autobiography of Howard Thurman*. New York: Harcourt Brace Jovanovich, 1979.

Jules Tygiel. *Baseball's Great Experiment: Jackie Robinson and His Legacy*. New York: Oxford University Press, 1983.

Arthur O. White. "The desegregation of Florida's public junior colleges, 1954–1977," *Integrated Education*, vol. 16, no. 3 (May-June 1978), pp. 31–36.

Arthur O. White. *A Thirty Year History of Florida's State System of Community Colleges 1947–1977*. Dissertation. University of Florida, esp. p. 30.

Ronald Williamson. "DeLand's Africans - 'There's just a few of us left'" [about the Africa community in DeLand], *News-Journal* (Daytona Beach), July 31, 1999, p. 1C.

Elizabeth Yates. *Howard Thurman: Portrait of a Practical Dreamer*. New York: John Day Co., 1964.

Chapter 65

Lewis G. Schmidt, "From Slavery To Freedom and Success: Sandy Cornish and Lillah Cornish," *Florida Keys Sea Heritage Journal*, vol. 4, no. 3 (spring 1994), p. 1+.

"Wakulla County Slave Census in 1850," *Magnolia Monthly*, vol. III, no. 8 (October 1965), pp. *Magnolia Monthly* was a journal that covered Wakulla County.

Chapter 66

Wendy L. Bovard. *Why Not Me?: The Story of Gladys Milton, Midwife*. Tenn.: Book Publishing Company, 1993.

Doris Gosdin Glenn. *A Study of the Qualifications of the Teaching Personnel, White and Colored, in Walton County, Florida*. University of Florida thesis; Gainesville, FL: University of Florida, 1948.

Chapter 67

Elba Wilson Carswell. *Holmes Valley: A West Florida Cradle of Christianity*. Bonifay, FL: Central Press, 1969.

E. W. Carswell. *Tempestuous Triangle: The History of Washington County, Florida*. Chipley: Washington County School Board, 1974.

E. W. Carswell. *Washington: Florida's Twelfth County*. Chipley, FL: E. W. Carswell, 1991.

Index

Note: Illustrations are indicated by boldface type.

If you enjoyed reading this book, here are some other titles from Pineapple Press. To request a catalog or to place an order, write to Pineapple Press, P.O. Box 3889, Sarasota, Florida 34230, or call 1-800-PINEAPL (746-3275). Or visit our website at www.pineapplepress.com.

African Americans in Florida by Maxine Jones and Kevin McCarthy. This book examines the lives and contributions of more than 50 notable African Americans during four centuries of Florida history. 80 black and white photos. (hb & pb)

Historical Traveler's Guide to Florida, 2nd Edition by Eliot Kleinberg. Visit Henry Plant's Tampa hotel, the wreck of the *San Pedro,* and Ernest Hemingway's Key West home. Here are 74 travel destinations in Florida of historical significance—17 are new to this edition and the rest have been completely updated. (pb)

Legends of the Seminoles by Betty Mae Jumper. This collection of rich spoken tales—written down for the first time—impart valuable lessons about living in harmony with nature and about why the world is the way it is. Each story is illustrated with an original painting by Guy LaBree. (hb & pb)

Native Americans in Florida by Kevin M. McCarthy. Teaches about the many diverse Indian tribes in Florida from prehistoric times to the present. Also includes information about archaeology, an extensive glossary, and legends that teach moral lessons. (hb & pb)

Solomon by Marilyn Bishop Shaw. Young adult fiction. Young Solomon Freeman and his parents, Moses and Lela, survive the Civil War, gain their freedom, and gamble their dreams, risking their very existence on a homestead in the remote environs of north central Florida. (hb)